Purposive Behavior in Animals and Men

PURPOSIVE BEHAVIOR IN ANIMALS AND MEN

By

EDWARD CHACE TOLMAN

PROFESSOR OF PSYCHOLOGY, UNIVERSITY OF CALIFORNIA

UNIVERSITY OF CALIFORNIA PRESS

BERKELEY AND LOS ANGELES

1951

UNIVERSITY OF CALIFORNIA PRESS
BERKELEY AND LOS ANGELES
CALIFORNIA

◇

CAMBRIDGE UNIVERSITY PRESS
LONDON, ENGLAND

PRINTED BY OFFSET IN THE UNITED STATES OF AMERICA
BY THE GEORGE BANTA PUBLISHING COMPANY

To

M. N. A.

EDITOR'S INTRODUCTION

We are nearing the close of the second decade since an explicit behaviorism was first set forth. Even the most severe and stand-offish historian, or rather chronicler, of developments in psychology in some degree allied with the behavioristic movement in America could not fail to record that there have been twenty years of achievement and growth. However, there are not a few persons who still think of behaviorism proper (or improper) as but an *enfant terrible* among its sober elders, and no psychologist today hesitates to stigmatize some of its phases as puerile, cocksure, *simpliste*, strident, precipitate, or bootless.

Furthermore, the widespread tendency to call all psychology behavioristic which is not patently something else should be challenged. Even without the leadership of the band whose prophet was Watson, psychology twenty years ago was ripe for a try at the problems of everyday life where experimental fact-finding could never be more than methodologically behavioristic, and in fact was most often only accidentally so. Psychology ploughed up fields from which it extracted entirely adventitious nourishment for the original behavioristic doctrines, simply because in those fields any besides commonsense methods of cultivation, i.e. research, would have been so out of place that it could never occur to anyone to propose their use.

Of behavioristic system-making there has been little. Perhaps this can be counted for gain, hitherto. The skeleton of a system is certain to be sketched before there is a sufficient body of facts to make it impressive. It can not be an accident that persons of practical and dogmatic temperament are drawn to behaviorism and that they are poor theorizers. At any rate, for whatever reason, the roster of system-making behaviorists is a short one.

Watson, fighting for a physiological and reflex psychology, led the assault against orthodoxy, and has ever since laid about him intrepidly with such weapons as the conditioned reflex and his theory of implicit language reactions. Meyer formulated laws of behavioral mechanics derived from a largely hypothetical nervous system. Weiss was eager to prove that the materials of psychological science were assimilable to a space-time frame of reference and that any opposed view could be traced to insufficient understanding of social communication. Lashley, emerging briefly from the experimental laboratory, showed that the supposedly unique and private data of introspective psychology could be identified with the data of physical science. Holt, after long silence, is now brilliantly elaborating the implications of circular reflexes, conditioned reflexes, and "specific response." Other names might be cited, but for the most part they are either of those who have been willing to be "behavioristic" rather than behaviorists or of those who have not sponsored a sustained and influential formulation of first principles.

In the present volume Professor Tolman has done a unique thing. He has given us not only a complete psychology but a behaviorism which is neither physiological nor metaphysical. It is a thoroughly intrabehavioral system, dependent on nothing outside itself except experimental observations of animal and human behavior. Its basis is in the facts and laws of learning. Behavior is shown by citation of experiments, and therefore in no obscurantist sense, to be inherently purposive. Many of these experiments are recent and many are from Professor Tolman's own laboratory. Their findings, pooled for interpretation, become excitingly significant.

Behavior is also shown to possess the totalizing or field characters attributed to it by *Gestalt* psychology when freed of mysticism and anti-analytical bias. It is made clear that the events which occur on this earth because it is tenanted by animals and men can happen as they do only by virtue of certain "immanent and objective" characteristics of behavior. Among the hitherto most neglected of these are the behavior-producing factors intermediate between stimuli and responses for which Woodworth employed the term *reaction tendency*. The dogged ingenuity (the adjective is chosen advisedly) of Professor Tolman at running to earth these characters, and at worrying out their elusive and sometimes intricate details, sets a new standard in behavioristic theory. Throughout his exposition a wholesome combination of fact-mindedness and informality stifles every trace of pedantry.

Professor Tolman's argument may be ignored in some quarters;

it will certainly be amplified by himself and others as new and crucial research data come to light; it will not, I think, be radically revised, that is "disproved"; and it will never be discredited, that is, shown to be either fictitious or unnecessary. Behaviorism of this sort has come of age.

R. M. E.

PREFACE

This book has grown out of an experimental interest in animal learning grafted upon an arm-chair urge towards speculation. And the result, as might have been expected, is neither a complete and unbiased account of all the experimental work on animal learning nor a brief and concise presentation of a system of psychology. I should like to apologize, therefore, in two particulars. First, I would ask forgiveness in that, as a presentation of a system, this book is not shorter and more to the point. No mere system is worth so many pages nor deserves so laborious and minute a treatment. And, secondly, I would ask the reader's indulgence—especially if he be himself an animal psychologist—in that my citations of the experiments on animal learning have certain large lacunæ. Very obviously, I have reported only those experiments with which I personally happened to be most familiar. But this does not mean that they were necessarily better or more important, even for my own argument, than would have been other experiments with which I happened to be less well acquainted.

Further, I would like to be pardoned for having introduced so many new terms and misused so many old ones, although, to be sure, I have sought to lessen somewhat the resulting task for the reader by the inclusion of a glossary. Such a glossary will, I hope, be found useful for refreshing the reader's memory in later portions of the book as to the definitions of terms provided in earlier portions. Or, again, in a few cases it may be helpful for finding the definitions of certain terms introduced early which, however, are not defined by the text itself until later. Or, finally, the perusal of this glossary as a whole may even serve as a convenient way of reviewing and summarizing the entire doctrine.

I wish now, once and for all, to put myself on record as feeling a distaste for most of the terms and neologisms I have introduced. I especially dislike the terms *purpose* and *cognition* and the title *Purposive Behavior*. I have, I believe, a strong anti-theological and anti-introspectionistic bias; and yet here my words and my title seem to be lending support to some sort of an ultimately teleological and ultimately mentalistic interpretation of animal and human behavior. Actually, I have used these terms *purpose* and *cognition,* and the various derivates and synonyms I have coined, in a purely neutral and objective sense. Yet I know that, in spite of this fact, most readers will persist in believing that I mean by *purposes* and *cognitions* entities ultimately subjective in character and metaphysically teleological in import. I can but hope that all such readers will read and reread the glossary.

My indebtedness to the many students whose ideas have stimulated me (which ideas I have no doubt often quite shamelessly appropriated as if they were my own) can never adequately be stated. If it had not been for these students, this book could not have been written. From Professor Warner Brown and my other colleagues in the psychology department of the University of California I have received indulgence, forbearance, and encouragement. To Miss Esther W. Robinson I give thanks for constant help and assistance in the ordering and correlation of manuscript, cuts, and proof.

To Dr. Willis D. Ellis and to Dr. Katherine A. Williams, who have read, criticized, and advised at many different stages, I owe more than I can attempt to thank them for. If the argument has any semblance of form and order or of sense, it is due to them. To Professor Richard M. Elliott, the editor of this series, I also owe much sound criticism, which I have taken to heart and sought to meet, as best I might, in a final rewriting.

Lastly, in inscribing this book to M. N. A. (*Mus norvegicus albinus*) I have sought to indicate where perhaps, most of all, the final credit or discredit belongs.

E. C. T.

Berkeley, California,
April 14, 1931.

CONTENTS

PART I

BEHAVIORISM—WHEREFORE AND WHAT SORT

The motives which lead to the assertion of a behaviorism are simple. All that can ever actually be observed in fellow human beings and in the lower animals is behavior. Another organism's private mind, if he have any, can never be got at. And even the supposed ease and obviousness of "looking within" and observing one's own mental processes, directly and at first hand, have proved, when subjected to laboratory control, in large part chimerical; the dictates of "introspection" have been shown over and over again to be artifacts of the particular laboratory in which they were obtained.

The behaviorism here to be presented will contend that mental processes are most usefully to be conceived as but dynamic aspects, or determinants, of behavior. They are functional variables which intermediate in the causal equation between environmental stimuli and initiating physiological states or excitements, on the one side, and final overt behavior, on the other.

Further, it is to be pointed out that although behaviorism exerts an emotional appeal because it appears radical, modern and simple, actually we shall find it recondite, difficult, but, we may hope, scientific.

Chapter I

BEHAVIOR, A MOLAR PHENOMENON [1]

1. Mentalism vs. Behaviorism

THE mentalist is one who assumes that "minds" are essentially streams of "inner happenings." Human beings, he says, "look within" and observe such "inner happenings." And although sub-human organisms cannot thus "look within," or at any rate cannot report the results of any such lookings within, the mentalist supposes that they also have "inner happenings." The task of the animal psychologist is conceived by the mentalist as that of inferring such "inner happenings" from outer behavior; animal psychology is reduced by him to a series of arguments by analogy.

Contrast, now, the thesis of behaviorism. For the behaviorist, "mental processes" are to be identified and defined in terms of the behaviors to which they lead. "Mental processes" are, for the behaviorist, naught but inferred determinants of behavior, which ultimately are deducible from behavior. Behavior and these inferred determinants are both objectively defined types of entity. There is about them, the behaviorist would declare, nothing private or "inside." Organisms, human and sub-human, are biological entities immersed in environments. To these environments they must, by virtue of their physiological needs, adjust. Their "mental processes" are functionally defined aspects determining their adjustments. For the behaviorist all things are open and above-board; for him, animal psychology plays into the hands of human psychology.[2]

[1] Much of the argument of the present chapter has already appeared in the following articles:

E. C. Tolman, A new formula for behaviorism, *Psychol. Rev.*, 1922, **29**, 44-53.

———, Behaviorism and purpose, *J. Phil.*, 1925, **22**, 36-41.

———, A behavioristic theory of ideas, *Psychol. Rev.*, 1926, **5**, 352-369.

[2] It is obvious that we have oversimplified the views of both "mentalist" and "behaviorist." One ought no doubt to eschew any attempt to envisage

2. Behaviorisms and Behaviorisms

The general position adopted in this essay will be that of behaviorism, but it will be a behaviorism of a rather special variety, for there are behaviorisms and behaviorisms. Watson, the arch-behaviorist, proposed one brand. But others, particularly Holt, Perry, Singer, de Laguna, Hunter, Weiss, Lashley, and Frost, have since all offered other rather different varieties.[3] No complete analysis and comparison of all these can be attempted. We shall here present merely certain distinctive features as a way of introducing what is to be our own variety.

3. Watson: The Molecular Definition

Watson, in most places, seems to describe behavior in terms of simple stimulus-response connections. And these stimuli and these responses he also seems to conceive in relatively immediate physical and physiological terms. Thus, in the first complete statement of his doctrine, he wrote:

"We use the term *stimulus* in psychology as it is used in physiology. Only in psychology we have to extend somewhat the usage of the term. In the psychological laboratory, when we are dealing with relatively simple factors, such as the effect of ether waves of different lengths, the effect of sound waves, etc., and are attempting to isolate their effects upon the adjustment of men, we speak of stimuli. On the other hand, when factors leading to reactions are more complex, as, for example, in the social world,

progress as a too simple contest between "movements" (cf. E. G. Boring, Psychology for Eclectics, *Psychologies of 1930* [Worcester, Mass., Clark Univ. Press, 1930], pp. 115-127). But the temptation is too great.

[3] W. McDougall (Men or Robots, *Psychologies of 1925* [Worcester, Mass., Clark Univ. Press, 1926], p. 277) declares that he was the first to define psychology as the study of behavior. He says: "As long ago as 1905 I began my attempt to remedy this state of affairs [i.e., the inadequacies of an "Idea" psychology] by proposing to define psychology as the positive science of conduct, using the word 'positive' to distinguish it from ethics, the normative science of conduct." Cf. also, his *Psychology, the Study of Behavior* (New York, Henry Holt and Company, 1912), p. 19, "We may then define psychology as the positive science of the behavior of living things." But the credit or discredit for the raising of this definition of psychology to an *ism* must certainly be given to Watson (Psychology as a behaviorist views it, *Psychol. Rev.*, 1913, 20, 158-177; Image and affection in behavior, *J. Philos. Psychol. Sci. Meth.*, 1913, 10, 421-428). For the best analysis and bibliography of the different varieties of behaviorism extant to 1923, see A. A. Roback, *Behaviorism and Psychology* (Cambridge, Mass., Sci.-Art, 1923), pp. 231-242.

we speak of *situations*. A situation is, of course, upon final analysis, resolvable into a complex group of stimuli. As examples of stimuli we may name such things as rays of light of different wave lengths; sound waves differing in amplitude, length, phase, and combination; gaseous particles given off in such small diameters that they affect the membrane of the nose; solutions which contain particles of matter of such size that the taste buds are thrown into action; solid objects which affect the skin and mucous membrane; radiant stimuli which call out temperature response; noxious stimuli, such as cutting, pricking, and those injuring tissue generally. Finally, movements of the muscles and activity in the glands themselves serve as stimuli by acting upon the afferent nerve endings in the moving muscles. . . .

"In a similar way we employ in psychology the physiological term 'response,' but again we must slightly extend its use. The movements which result from a tap on the patellar tendon, or from stroking the soles of the feet are 'simple' responses which are studied both in physiology and in medicine. In psychology our study, too, is sometimes concerned with simple responses of these types, but more often with several complex responses taking place simultaneously." [4]

It must be noted, however, that along with this definition of behavior in terms of the strict physical and physiological *muscletwitches* which make it up, Watson was apt to slip in a different and somewhat conflicting notion. Thus, for example, at the end of the quotation just cited he went on to say:

"In the latter case [that is, when in psychology our study is with several complex responses taking place simultaneously] we sometimes use the popular term 'act' or adjustment, meaning by that that the whole group of responses is integrated in such a way (instinct or habit) that the individual does something which we have a name for, that is, 'takes food,' 'builds a house,' 'swims,' 'writes a letter,' 'talks.'" [5]

Now these "integrated responses" have, perhaps, qualities different from those of the physiological elements which make them up. Indeed, Watson himself seems to suggest such a possibility when he remarks in a footnote to his chapter on "Emotions":

"It is perfectly possible for a student of behavior entirely ignorant of the sympathetic nervous system and of the glands

[4] J. B. Watson, *Psychology from the Standpoint of a Behaviorist* (Philadelphia, J. B. Lippincott Company, 1919), pp. 10 ff. (References same for 1929 edition.)

[5] *Op. cit.*, pp. 11 f.

and smooth muscles, or even of the central nervous system as a whole, to write a thoroughly comprehensive and accurate study of the emotions—the types, their interrelations with habits, their rôle, etc." [6]

This last statement seems, however, rather to contradict the preceding ones. For, if, as he in those preceding citations contended, the study of behavior concerns nothing "but stimuli as the physicist defines them," and "muscle contraction and gland secretion as the physiologist describes them," it certainly would *not* be possible for a "student of behavior entirely ignorant of the sympathetic nervous system and of the glands and smooth muscles, or even of the central nervous system as a whole, to write a thoroughly comprehensive and accurate study of the emotions."

Again, in his most recent pronouncement,[7] we find Watson making statements such as the following:

"Some psychologists seem to have the notion that the behaviorist is interested only in the recording of minute muscular responses. Nothing could be further from the truth. Let me emphasize again that the behaviorist is primarily interested in the behavior of the whole man. From morning to night he watches him perform his daily round of duties. If it is brick-laying, he would like to measure the number of bricks he can lay under different conditions, how long he can go without dropping from fatigue, how long it takes him to learn his trade, whether we can improve his efficiency or get him to do the same amount of work in a less period of time. In other words, the response the behaviorist is interested in is the commonsense answer to the question 'what is he doing and why is he doing it?' Surely with this as a general statement, no one can distort the behaviorist's platform to such an extent that it can be claimed that the behaviorist is merely a muscle physiologist." [8]

These statements emphasize the whole response as contrasted with the physiological elements of such whole responses. In short, our conclusion must be that Watson has in reality dallied with two different notions of behavior, though he himself has not clearly seen how different they are. On the one hand, he has de-

---

[6] *Op. cit.,* p. 195. (Reference for 1929 ed., p. 225.)

[7] J. B. Watson, *Behaviorism* (New York, W. W. Norton and Company, rev. ed., 1930).

[8] *Op. cit.,* p. 15.

fined behavior in terms of its strict underlying physical and physiological details, i.e., in terms of receptor-process, conductor-process, and effector-process per se. We shall designate this as the *molecular* definition of behavior. And, on the other hand, he has come to recognize, albeit perhaps but dimly, that behavior, as such, is more than and different from the sum of its physiological parts. Behavior, as such, is an "emergent" phenomenon that has descriptive and defining properties of its own.[9] And we shall designate this latter as the *molar* definition of behavior.[10]

4. The Molar Definition

It is this second, or molar, conception of behavior that is to be defended in the present treatise. It will be contended by us (if not by Watson) that "behavior-acts," though no doubt in complete one-to-one correspondence with the underlying molecular facts of physics and physiology, have, as "molar" wholes, certain emergent properties of their own. And it is these, the molar properties of behavior-acts, which are of prime interest to us as psychologists. Further, these molar properties of behavior-acts cannot in the present state of our knowledge, i.e., prior to the working-out of many empirical correlations between behavior and its physiological correlates, be known even inferentially from a mere knowledge of the underlying, molecular, facts of physics and

[9] For a very clear summary of the various different notions of "emergence" which are now becoming so popular among philosophers see W. McDougall, *Modern Materialism and Emergent Evolution* (New York, D. Van Nostrand Company, Inc., 1929). It should be emphasized, however, that in here designating behavior as having "emergent" properties we are using the term in a descriptive sense only. We are not here aligning ourselves with any philosophical interpretation as to the ultimate philosophical status of such emergents. "Emergent" behavior phenomena are correlated with physiological phenomena of muscle and gland and sense organ. But descriptively they are different from the latter. Whether they are or are not ultimately in some metaphysical sense completely reducible to the latter we are not here attempting to say.

[10] The distinction of molar and molecular behaviorism originates with C. D. Broad (*The Mind and Its Place in Nature* [New York, Harcourt, Brace and Company, 2nd impression, 1929], pp. 616 f.), and was suggested to us by Dr. D. C. Williams (A metaphysical interpretation of behaviorism, Harvard Ph.D. thesis, 1928). Broad intends primarily to distinguish behaviorism which appeals only to *some* gross observable activity, from behaviorism which must appeal to hypothetical processes among the molecules of the brain and nervous system.

physiology. For, just as the properties of a beaker of water are not, prior to experience, in any way envisageable from the properties of individual water molecules, so neither are the properties of a "behavior-act" deducible directly from the properties of the underlying physical and physiological processes which make it up. Behavior as such cannot, at any rate at present, be deduced from a mere enumeration of the muscle twitches, the mere motions *qua* motions, which make it up. It must as yet be studied first hand and for its own sake.

An act *qua* "behavior" has distinctive properties all its own. These are to be identified and described irrespective of whatever muscular, glandular, or neural processes underlie them. These new properties, thus distinctive of molar behavior, are presumably strictly correlated with, and, if you will, dependent upon, physiological motions. But descriptively and per se they are other than those motions.

A rat running a maze; a cat getting out of a puzzle box; a man driving home to dinner; a child hiding from a stranger; a woman doing her washing or gossiping over the telephone; a pupil marking a mental-test sheet; a psychologist reciting a list of nonsense syllables; my friend and I telling one another our thoughts and feelings—*these are behaviors* (qua *molar*). And it must be noted that in mentioning no one of them have we referred to, or, we blush to confess it, for the most part even known, what were the exact muscles and glands, sensory nerves, and motor nerves involved. For these responses somehow had other sufficiently identifying properties of their own.

5.   Other Proponents of a Molar Definition

It must be noted now further that this molar notion of behavior —this notion that behavior presents characterizable and defining properties of its own, which are other than the properties of the underlying physics and physiology—has been defended by other theorists than ourselves. In particular, acknowledgment must be made to Holt, de Laguna, Weiss, and Kantor.

Holt:

"The often too materialistically-minded biologist is so fearful of meeting a certain bogy, the 'psyche,' that he hastens to analyse every case of behavior into its component reflexes without venturing first to observe it as a whole." [11]

"The phenomena evinced by the integrated organism are no longer merely the excitation of nerve or the twitching of muscle, nor yet the play merely of reflexes touched off by stimuli. These are all present and essential to the phenomena in question, but they are merely components now, for they have been integrated. And this integration of reflex arcs, with all that they involve, into a state of systematic interdependence has produced something that is not merely reflex action. The biological sciences have long recognized this new and further thing, and called it 'behavior.' " [12]

De Laguna:

"The total response initiated by the distance receptor and reinforced by the contact stimulus (e.g., reaching out toward, pecking at, and swallowing) forms a functional unit. The act is a *whole* and is stimulated or inhibited as a whole . . . Where behavior is more complex, we still find a similar relationship." [13]

"The functioning of the group [of sensory cells] as a whole, since it is a *functioning,* and not merely a 'chemical discharge' is not in any sense a resultant of the functioning of the separate cells which compose it." [14]

Weiss:

"The investigation of the internal neural conditions form part of the behaviorist's programme, of course, but the inability to trace the ramifications of any given nervous excitation through the nervous system is no more a restriction on the study of effective stimuli and reactions in the educational, industrial or social phases of life, than is the physicist's inability to determine just what is going on in the electrolyte of a battery while a current is passing, a limitation that makes research in electricity impossible." [15]

[11] E. B. Holt, *The Freudian Wish* (New York, Henry Holt and Company, 1915), p. 78.

[12] *Op. cit.,* p. 155. The present chapter, as well as most of the subsequent ones, was written before the appearance of Holt's most recent book (*Animal Drive and the Learning Process* [New York, Henry Holt and Company, 1931]).

[13] Grace A. de Laguna, *Speech, Its Function and Development* (New Haven, Yale Univ. Press, 1927), pp. 169 f.

[14] Grace A. de Laguna, Sensation and perception, *J. Philos. Psychol. Sci. Meth.,* 1916, **13**, 617-630, p. 630.

[15] A. P. Weiss, The relation between physiological psychology and behavior psychology, *J. Philos. Psychol. Sci. Meth.,* 1919, **16**, 626-634, p. 634. Cf. also *A Theoretical Basis of Human Behavior* (Columbus, Ohio, R. G. Adams Company, 1925), esp. chapter VI.

Kantor:

"Psychologists are attempting to express facts more and more in terms of the complete organism rather than in specific parts (brain, etc.) or isolated functions (neural)." [16]

"Briefly, psychological organisms, as differentiated from biological organisms, may be considered as a sum of reactions plus their various integrations." [17]

6. The Descriptive Properties of Behavior as Molar

Granting, then, that behavior *qua* behavior has descriptive properties of its own, we must next ask just what, in more detail, these identifying properties are.

The first item in answer to this question is to be found in the fact that behavior, which is behavior in our sense, always seems to have the character of getting-to or getting-from a specific goal-object, or goal-situation.[18] The complete identification of any single behavior-act requires, that is, a reference first to some particular goal-object or objects which that act is getting to, or, it may be, getting from, or both. Thus, for example, the rat's behavior of "running the maze" has as its first and perhaps most important identifying feature the fact that it is a getting to food. Similarly, the behavior of Thorndike's kitten in opening the puzzle box would have as its first identifying feature the fact that it is a getting away from the confinement of the box, or, if you will, a getting to the freedom outside. Or, again, the behavior of the psychologist reciting nonsense syllables in the laboratory has as its first descriptive feature the fact that it is a getting to (shall we say) "an offer from another university." Or, finally, the gossiping remarks of my friend and myself have as their first identifying feature a set of gettings to such and such mutual readinesses for further behaviors.

As the second descriptive feature of a behavior-act we note

[16] J. R. Kantor, The evolution of psychological textbooks since 1912, *Psychol. Bull.*, 1922, 19, 429-442, p. 429.

[17] J. R. Kantor, *Principles of Psychology* (New York, Alfred A. Knopf, 1924) I, p. 3.

[18] For convenience we shall throughout use the terms *goal* and *end* to cover situations being got away from, as well as for situations being arrived at, i.e., for *termini a quo* as well as for *termini ad quem*.

the further fact that such a getting to or from is characterized not only by the character of the goal-object and this persistence to or from it, but also by the fact that it always involves a specific pattern of commerce-, intercourse-, engagement-, communion-with such and such intervening means-objects, as the way to get thus to or from.[19]

For example, the rat's running is a getting to food which expresses itself in terms of a specific pattern of running, and of running in some alleys rather than in others. Similarly the behavior of Thorndike's kitten is not merely a getting from the confinement of the box but it is also the exhibition of a specific pattern of biting, chewing, and clawing such and such features of the box. Or, again, the man's behavior is not merely that of getting from his office to his be-wife-ed and be-pantry-ed home; it is also the doing so by means of such and such a specific pattern of commerce with the means-objects—automobile, roads, etc. Or, finally, the psychologist's behavior is not merely that of getting to an offer from another university; but also it is characterized in that it expresses itself as a specific pattern of means-activities or means-object commerces, viz., those of reading aloud and reciting nonsense syllables; of recording the results of these, and a lot of other bosh besides, in a *Protokoll*, and later in a typed manuscript, etc.

As the third descriptive feature of behavior-acts we find that, in the service of such gettings to and from specific goal-objects by means of commerces with such and such means-objects, behavior-acts are to be characterized, also, in terms of a *selectively greater readiness* for *short* (i.e., easy) means activities as against *long* ones. Thus, for example, if a rat is presented with two alternative spatial means-object routes to a given goal-object, one longer and one shorter, he will within limits select the shorter. And so in similar fashion for temporally and gravitationally shorter means-object routes. And what thus holds for rats will hold, no doubt, in similar and even more distinctive fashion for still higher animals and for man. But this is equivalent to saying that this selectiveness towards means-objects and means-routes

---

[19] These terms, *commerce-, intercourse-, engagement-, communion-with,* are attempts at describing a peculiar sort of mutual interchange between a behavior-act and the environment which we here have in mind. But for convenience we shall hereafter use for the most part the single term *commerce-with.*

is relative to the means-end "direction" and "distance" of the goal-object. The animal when presented with alternatives always comes sooner or later to select those only which finally get him to, or from, the given demanded, or to-be-avoided, goal-object or situation and which get him there by the shorter commerce-with routes.

To sum up, the complete descriptive identification of any behavior-act per se requires descriptive statements relative to (a) the goal-object or objects, being got to or from; (b) the specific pattern of commerces with means-objects involved in this getting to or from; and (c) the facts exhibited relative to the selective identification of routes and means-objects as involving short (easy) commerces with means-objects for thus getting to or from.

7. Purposive and Cognitive Determinants

But surely any "tough-minded" reader will by now be up in arms. For it is clear that thus to identify behaviors in terms of goal-objects, and patterns of commerces with means-objects as selected short ways to get to or from the goal-objects, is to imply something perilously like purposes and cognitions. And this surely will be offensive to any hard-headed, well-brought-up psychologist of the present day.

And yet, there seems to be no other way out. Behavior as behavior, that is, as molar, *is* purposive and *is* cognitive. These purposes and cognitions are of its immediate descriptive warp and woof. It, no doubt, is strictly and completely dependent upon an underlying manifold of physics and chemistry, but initially and as a matter of first identification, behavior as behavior reeks of purpose and of cognition. And such purposes and such cognitions are just as evident, as we shall see later, if this behavior be that of a rat as if it be that of a human being.[20]

Finally, however, it must nonetheless be emphasized that pur-

[20] McDougall, in his lecture entitled "Men or Robots" (*Psychologies of 1925* [Worcester, Mass., Clark Univ. Press, 1926]), divided all behaviorists into "Strict Behaviorists," "Near Behaviorists," and "Purposive Behaviorists." He classed the present writer and Professor R. B. Perry in the last group. It is then to Professor McDougall that we owe the title "Purposive Behavior," while it is primarily to Professor Perry (see below) that we are indebted for

poses and cognitions which are thus immediately, immanently,[21] in behavior are wholly objective as to definition. They are defined by characters and relationships which we observe out there in the behavior. We, the observers, watch the behavior of the rat, the cat, or the man, and note its character as a getting to such and such by means of such and such a selected pattern of commerces-with. It is we, the independent neutral observers, who note these perfectly objective characters as immanent in the behavior and have happened to choose the terms *purpose* and *cognition* as generic names for such characters.

8. The Objective Definition of Behavior Purposes

Let us consider these immediate dynamic characters which we call purpose and cognition in more detail; we begin with purpose. By way of illustration, take the case of Thorndike's cat. The cat's purpose of getting to the outside, by bursting through the confinement of the box, is simply our name for a quite objective character of his behavior. It is our name for a determinant of the cat's behavior which, it will now appear, is defined in the last analysis by certain facts of learning. Thorndike's description of the actual behavior reads:

"When put into the box the cat would show evident signs of discomfort and of an impulse to escape from confinement. It tries to squeeze through any opening; it claws and bites at the bars of wire; it thrusts its paws out through any opening and claws at everything it reaches; it continues its efforts when it strikes anything loose and shaky; it may claw at things within the box . . . The vigor with which it struggles is extraordinary.

the original notions both of the immediate purposiveness and of the immediate cognitiveness of behavior.

Finally, it is to be noted that purposiveness and cognitiveness seem to go together, so that if we conceive behavior as purposive we *pari passu* conceive it also as cognitive. This complementary character of purpose and cognition has likewise been emphasized by McDougall (*Modern Materialism and Emergent Evolution* [New York, D. Van Nostrand Company, Inc., 1929], Chapter III); and by Perry, who also points out in some detail that "there is no purpose without cognition" (The cognitive interest and its refinements, *J. Philos.*, 1921, **18**, 365-375). And that "all forms of purposive behavior depend on beliefs for the issue" (The independent variability of purpose and belief, *J. Philos.*, 1921, **18**, 169-180). See also R. B. Perry, The appeal to reason, *Philos. Rev.*, 1921, **30**, 131-169.

21 The term *immanent* is used by us in a purely colorless sense to mean merely directly in behavior. (See Glossary.)

For eight or ten minutes it will claw and bite and squeeze incessantly. . . . And gradually all the other non-successful impulses will be stamped out and the particular impulse leading to the successful act will be stamped in by the resulting pleasure, until, after many trials, the cat will, when put in the box, immediately claw the button or loop in a definite way." [22]

We note two significant features in this description: (a) the fact of the behaving organism's readiness to persist through trial and error, and (b) the fact of his tendency on successive occasions to select sooner and sooner the act which gets him out easily and quickly—i.e., the fact of *docility*.[23] And it is these two correlative features which, we shall now declare, define that immediate character which we call the cat's purpose to get to the freedom outside. The doctrine we here contend for is, in short, that wherever a response shows docility relative to some end—wherever a response is ready (a) to break out into trial and error and (b) to select gradually, or suddenly, the more efficient of such trials and errors with respect to getting to that end—such a response expresses and defines something which, for convenience, we name as a purpose. Wherever such a set of facts appears (and where save in the simplest and most rigid tropisms and reflexes does it not?), there we have objectively manifested and defined that which is conveniently called a purpose.

The first clear recognition and pronouncement of this fact that the docility of behavior is an objective definition of something appropriately to be called its purposiveness, we owe to Perry. In an article published in 1918 he wrote:

"If the kitten should be excited to effort by the mere appearance of a button in a vertical position; if these efforts should continue until a way was hit upon to turn it horizontally; and if the random efforts should then be replaced by a stable propensity to perform the successful act, then we could say that the kitten was *trying to turn the button*. . . ." [i.e., purposing the turning of the button] "In order that an organism may be said to act in a certain way because of [by virtue of purposing] a certain result, it is necessary that acts, proving

[22] E. L. Thorndike, *Animal Intelligence* (New York, The Macmillan Company, 1911), p. 35 f.

[23] Webster defines *docility* as (a) teachableness, docileness; (b) willingness to be taught or trained; submissiveness, tractableness. We use it throughout in the sense of "teachableness." (See Glossary.)

themselves to have a certain result, should derive a tendency to occur from this fact; and that other acts, proving not to have the result, should derive from that fact a tendency to be excluded. It is necessary that acts of the eligible type and of the ineligible type should occur *tentatively*, and then take on a stable or dispositional character according to the result." [24]

Finally, it must be noted that McDougall has also sponsored a seemingly similar doctrine. For he, like Perry (and ourselves), finds that behavior, as such, has distinctive properties of its own, and these distinctive properties he cites as six:

(1) "a certain spontaneity of movement"; (2) "the persistence of activity independently of the continuance of the impression which may have initiated it"; (3) "variation of direction of persistent movements"; (4) [the] "coming to an end of the animal's movements as soon as they have brought about a particular kind of change in its situation"; (5) "preparation for the new situation toward the production of which the action contributes"; (6) "some degree of improvement in the effectiveness of behavior, when it is repeated by the animal under similar circumstances." [25]

And the first five of these, he says, indicate purpose. McDougall's doctrine also seems, therefore, at least superficially, very similar to ours.

It must be noted, however, that he does not particularly emphasize the sixth character, "some degree of improvement" —i.e., the "docility" of behavior which, as we see it, following Perry, is the crown and significance of the other five.[26]

[24] R. B. Perry, Docility and purposiveness, *Psychol. Rev.*, 1918, **25**, 1-20, p. 13 f. This emphasis upon the docility of behavior as the definition of its purposiveness (and also of its cognitiveness) has been expanded by Perry in other places, to wit: Purpose as systematic unity, *Monist*, 1917, **27**, 352-375; and Purpose as tendency and adaptation, *Philos. Rev.*, 1917, **26**, 477-495; A behavioristic view of purpose, *J. Philos.*, 1921, **18**, 85-105; The independent variability of purpose and belief, *J. Philos.*, 1921, **18**, 169-180; The cognitive interest and its refinements, *J. Philos.*, 1921, **18**, 365-375; The appeal to reason, *Philos. Rev.* 1921, **30**, 131-169; and *General Theory of Value* (New York, Longmans, Green & Co., 1926), pp. 288 f.

[25] W. McDougall, *Outline of Psychology* (New York, Charles Scribner's Sons, 1923), Chapter II, pp. 44-46; see also his Purposive or mechanical psychology, *Psychol. Rev.*, 1923, **30**, 273-288.

[26] In this connection it may be remarked parenthetically that we formerly tended to side with McDougall (E. C. Tolman, Instinct and purpose, *Psychol. Rev.*, 1920, **27**, 217-233; also Behaviorism and purpose, *J. Philos.*, 1925, **22**, 36-41). That is, we then tended to hold that purpose might be said to inhere

And one further difference must also be emphasized. For whereas, for Professor Perry and for us, purpose is a purely objectively defined variable, which is defined by the facts of trial and error and of resultant docility; for Professor Mc-Dougall, purpose seems to be an introspectively defined subjective 'somewhat,' which is a something other, and more than, the manner in which it appears in behavior; it is a "psychic," "mentalistic" somewhat, behind such objective appearances, and to be known in the last analysis through introspection only. This difference between our point of view and McDougall's is fundamental and implies a *bouleversement complet*.[27]

9. The Objective Definition of Behavior Cognitions

Consider, now, the fact of cognition. The docility feature of behavior also objectively defines, we shall declare, certain immediate, immanent characters for which the generic name *cognitions* or *cognition-processes* is appropriate. More specifically, our contention will be that the characteristic patterns of preferred routes and of commerces-with which identify any given behavior-

in mere trial and error and in mere persistence-until, irrespective of whether or not these tended to produce resultant learning. This seems to us now, however, an error. We have come to accept Professor Perry's *dictum* as to the need of *docility* for a true definition of purpose. It is only because there is implied in the category of trial and error and of persistence-until the further category of a resultant docility that trial and error and persistence-until have the meaning they do. Mere variability of response which involved no resultant selection among the "tries" would not be one's ordinary notion of "trial and error." Nor would mere keeping-on-ness seem a real "persistence-until." It is only when such variations and such persistences have implicit within them the further character of a resultant selection of the more efficient of the tries (i.e., *docility*) that they have their usual significance and are to be said to define purpose.

It should be noted that Singer also seems to hold much the same notion as that presented here of behavior as such and of purpose as one of its most fundamental characters. He says, to cite at random: "The history of my body's behavior reveals a purpose running through its various acts, a purpose quite like that which characterizes my neighbor, my dog, the moth which flutters by me." E. A. Singer, "Mind as behavior," *Studies in Empirical Idealism* (Columbus, Ohio, R. G. Adams Company, 1924), p. 59. See also E. A. Singer, On the conscious mind, *J. Philos.*, 1929, **26**, 561-575.

[27] This was written before the appearance of McDougall's chapter entitled "The Hormic Psychology" in *Psychologies of 1930* (Worcester, Mass., Clark Univ. Press, 1930). In this latter place McDougall seems to deny any necessary connection between his doctrine of purpose and an animism.

act can be shown to be docile relative to, and may *pari passu* be said cognitively to assert: (a) the character of a goal-object, (b) this goal-object's initial "position" (i.e., direction and distance) relative to actual and possible means-objects, and (c) the characters of the specifically presented means-object as capable of supporting such and such commerces-with. For, if any one of these environmental entities does not prove to be so and so, the given behavior-act will break down and show disruption. It will be followed by subsequent alteration. It is, then, such contingencies in the continuance of any given behavior-act upon environmental characters actually proving to be so and so, which define that act's cognitive aspects.

The fact of these cognitive aspects is readily illustrated in the case of a rat's behavior in the maze. After a rat has once learned a given maze his behavior is a very specific dashing through it. But the continued release upon successive occasions of this same very specific dashing can easily be shown, experimentally, to be contingent upon the environmental facts *actually proving to be so and so*. It is contingent upon the food at the goal-box actually proving to have such and such a character. It is also contingent upon such and such alleys actually proving to be the best and shortest way to that food. And, finally, this dashing is contingent upon these alleys actually being shaped the way they are. For, if any of these environmental facts be unexpectedly changed, i.e., no longer prove to be so and so, this given behavior, this given dashing, will break down. It will exhibit disruption. Its continuing to go off as it does constitutes, then, the objective expression of a set of immediate contingencies. Its continuing to go off as it does asserts that the environmental features have those characters for which such behavior does not break down. And it is such contingencies (assertions) for which the generic name cognitions seems appropriate.

10. The Organism as a Whole

The above doctrine that behavior is docile and, as thus docile, purposive and cognitive, also means, it should now be pointed out, that behavior is always an affair of the organism as a whole and not of individual sensory and motor segments going off *in situ*, exclusively and by themselves. For such docilities, as we have illustrated, mean shifts and selections and substitutions among motor responses and among sensory activities often widely distributed throughout the parts of the organism. The readiness to persist can involve wide shifts from one sensory and motor segment to another. Behavior as a type of commerce with the environment can take place only in a whole organism. It does not take place in specific sensory and motor segments, which are insulated and each by itself.

Indeed, this fact that behavior is an adjustment of the whole organism and not a response of isolated sensory and motor segments, going off, each in lonely isolation, can readily be demonstrated for organisms even lower in the scale than rats. Thus, for example, the behavior of crayfish in a simple T-maze led Gilhousen to conclude:

"No definite evidence was found to substantiate *any* doctrine of learning that would conceive it, even in the case of these relatively low animals, as primarily a reënforcement or inhibition of a particular reaction to a given stimulus. As has been illustrated . . . in the analysis of runs, the learning was characterized by continuously *differing* reactions to the maze situation. Intact crayfish which performed in a superior manner did so, *not by reacting invariably to the same specific cues with some invariable reaction*, but, as far as could be observed, by *reacting in properly modified ways to different cues on different trials*." [28]

In this connection, it must be noted that certain behaviorists have tended to take this fact that behavior is of the whole organism as *the* fundamentally distinctive feature of behavior, as molar. For example, Perry, to whom we owe the original emphasis upon the docility of behavior, often tends to emphasize as the one distinctive thing about behavior the fact that it is of the *whole* organism. He writes:

"Psychology [i.e., behaviorism] deals with the grosser facts of organic behavior, and particularly with those external and internal adjustments by which the organism acts as a unit, while physiology deals with the more elementary constituent processes, such as metabolism or the nervous impulse. But in so far as psychology divides the organism it approaches physiology, and in so far as physiology integrates the organism it approaches psychology." [29]

[28] H. C. Gilhousen, The use of vision and of the antennæ in the learning of crayfish, *Univ. Calif. Publ. Physiol.*, 1929, **7**, 73-89. Final italics ours.

[29] R. B. Perry, A behavioristic view of purpose, *J. Philos.*, 1921, **18**, 85-105, p. 85.

He says further:

"The central feature of this conception of human behavior is that general state of the organism which has been termed a determining tendency. The organism as a whole is for a time preoccupied with a certain task which absorbs its energy and appropriates its mechanisms." [30]

And again:

"In proportion as the organism is unified and functions as a whole its behavior is incapable of being translated into simple reactions correlated severally with external events." [31]

Weiss and de Laguna also emphasize this same point.[32]

It may be noted finally, however, that from the point of view here presented the fact that behavior is of the whole organism seems to be derivative rather than primary. It is a mere corollary of the more fundamental fact that behavior *qua* behavior, as molar, is docile and that successful docility requires mutual interconnections between all the parts of an organism.

11. The Initiating Causes and the Three Varieties of Behavior Determinant

We have sought to show that immanent in any behavior there are certain immediate "in-lying" purposes and cognitions. These are functionally defined variables which are the last step in the causal equation determining behavior. They are to be discovered and defined by appropriate experimental devices. They are objective and it is we, the outside observers, who discover—or, if you will, infer or invent—them as immanent in, and determining, behavior. They are the last and most immediate causes of behavior. We call them, therefore, the "immanent determinants."

But these immanent determinants, it must now briefly be pointed out, are, in their turn, caused by environmental stimuli and initiating physiological states. Such environmental stimuli and

[30] R. B. Perry, A behavioristic view of purpose, *J. Philos.*, 1921, **18**, 85-105, p. 97.
[31] *Op. cit.*, p. 102.
[32] A. P. Weiss, *A Theoretical Basis of Human Behavior* (Columbus, Ohio, R. G. Adams Company, 1925), p. 346. G. A. de Laguna, *Speech, Its Function and Development* (New Haven, Yale Univ. Press, 1927), esp. Chapter VI.

such organic states we designate as the ultimate or "initiating causes" of behavior. The immanent determinants intermediate in the causal equation between the initiating causes and the final resultant behavior.

Further, however, it must now also be made clear that beside the intermediating immanent determinants there are really two other classes of behavior-determinants intervening between stimuli (and the initiating physiological states) and behavior. They are to be designated as "capacities" and "behavior-adjustments." Such capacities and behavior-adjustments will be discussed at length in various later portions of the book. For the present it must suffice to draw attention to the fact of them and to suggest a few preliminary characterizations.

First, as to capacities. It is fairly evident in these days of mental tests and the insistence upon individual and genetic differences that the nature of the finally aroused immanent determinants will themselves on any given occasion be dependent not only upon the characters of the initiating causes—stimuli and physiological states—occurring on that occasion, but also upon the capacities of the individual organism or species of organism in question. Stimuli and initiating states work through capacities to produce the immanent purposive and cognitive determinants and thus the final resulting behavior.

Second, as to behavior-adjustments. It must also be noted that in certain special types of situation it will appear that the immanent purposes and cognitions eventually allowed to function may depend for their characters upon a preliminary arousal in the organism of something to be called behavior-adjustments. Behavior-adjustments constitute our behavioristic substitute for, or definition of, what the mentalists would call conscious awareness and ideas. (See Chapters XIII and XIV.) They are unique organic events which may on certain occasions occur in an organism as a substitute, or surrogate, for actual behavior. And they function to produce some sort of modifications or improvements in what were the organism's initially aroused immanent determinants, such that his final behavior, corresponding to these new modified immanent determinants, is different from what it otherwise would have been.

To sum up. The first initiating causes of behavior are environmental stimuli and initiating physiological states. These operate on or through the behavior-determinants. The behavior-determinants are, it appears further, subdivisible into three classes: (a) immediately "in-lying" objectively defined purposes and cognitions—i.e., the "immanent determinants"; (b) the purposive and cognitive "capacities" of the given individual or species, which mediate the specific immanent determinants as a result of the given stimuli and the given initiating states; (c) "behavior-adjustments," which, under certain special conditions, are produced by the immanent determinants in place of actual overt behavior and which serve to act back upon such immanent determinants, to remould and "correct" the latter and thus finally to produce a new and different overt behavior from that which would otherwise have occurred.

12. Recapitulation

Behavior, as such, is a molar phenomenon as contrasted with the molecular phenomena which constitute its underlying physiology. And, as a molar phenomenon, behavior's immediate descriptive properties appear to be those of: getting to or from goal-objects by selecting certain means-object-routes as against others and by exhibiting specific patterns of commerces with these selected means-objects. But these descriptions in terms of gettings to or from, selections of routes and patterns of commerces-with imply and define immediate, immanent purpose and cognition aspects in the behavior. These two aspects of behavior are, however, but objectively and functionally defined entities. They are implicit in the facts of behavior docility. They are defined neither in the last analysis, nor in the first instance, by introspection. They are envisaged as readily in the behavior-acts of the cat and of the rat as in the more refined speech reactions of man. Such purposes and cognitions, such docility, are, obviously, functions of the organism as a whole.[33] Lastly, it has also been pointed out that there are two other classes of behavior-determinants in addition to the immanent determinants, viz., capacities and behavior-adjustments. These also intervene in the

[33] It should be noted that both Koffka (*The Growth of the Mind*, 2d ed. rev. [New York, Harcourt, Brace and Company, 1928]) and Mead (A behavioristic account of the significant symbol, *J. Philos.*, 1922, **19**, 157-163) have suggested the term *conduct* for much the same thing, it would seem, that we here designate as behavior *qua* behavior, that is, behavior as a molar phenomenon.

equation between stimuli and initiating physiological states on the one side and behavior on the other.

REFERENCES

Boring, E. G., Psychology for Eclectics. *Psychologies of 1930* (Worcester, Mass., Clark Univ. Press, 1930), 115-127.
Broad, C. D., *The Mind and Its Place in Nature* (New York, Harcourt, Brace and Company, 2d impression, 1929).
Gilhousen, H. C., The use of vision and of the antennæ in the learning of crayfish. *Univ. Calif. Publ. Physiol.*, 1929, 7, 73-89.
Holt, E. B., *The Freudian Wish* (New York, Henry Holt and Company, 1915).
—————, *Animal Drive and the Learning Process* (New York, Henry Holt and Company, 1931).
Kantor, J. R., The evolution of psychological textbooks since 1912. *Psychol. Bull.*, 1922, 19, 429-442.
—————, *Principles of Psychology* (New York, Alfred A. Knopf, 1924), Vol. 1.
Koffka, K., *The Growth of the Mind*, 2d ed. rev. (New York, Harcourt, Brace and Company, 1928).
Laguna, Grace A. de, Sensation and perception. *J. Philos., Psychol. Sci. Meth.*, 1916, 13, 533-547; 617-630.
—————, *Speech, its Function and Development* (New Haven, Yale Univ. Press, 1927).
McDougall, W., *Psychology, the Study of Behavior* (New York, Henry Holt and Company, 1912).
—————, *Outline of Psychology* (New York, Charles Scribner's Sons, 1923).
—————, Purposive or mechanical psychology. *Psychol. Rev.*, 1923, 30, 273-288.
—————, Men or robots? I and II, *Psychologies of 1925* (Worcester, Mass., Clark Univ. Press, 1926), 273-305.
—————, *Modern Materialism and Emergent Evolution* (New York, D. Van Nostrand Company, Inc., 1929).
—————, The hormic psychology, *Psychologies of 1930* (Worcester, Mass., Clark Univ. Press, 1930), 3-36.
Mead, G. H., A behavioristic account of the significant symbol. *J. Philos.*, 1922, 19, 157-163.
Perry, R. B., Purpose as systematic unity. *Monist*, 1917, 27, 352-375.
—————, Purpose as tendency and adaptation. *Philos. Rev.*, 1917, 26, 477-495.
—————, Docility and purposiveness. *Psychol. Rev.*, 1918, 25, 1-21.
—————, A behavioristic view of purpose. *J. Philos.*, 1921, 18, 85-105.

Perry, R. B., The independent variability of purpose and belief. *J. Philos.*, 1921, **18**, 169-180.

——————, The cognitive interest and its refinements. *J. Philos.*, 1921, **18**, 365-375.

——————, The appeal to reason. *Philos. Rev.*, 1921, **30**, 131-169.

——————, *General Theory of Value* (New York, Longmans Green & Co., 1926).

Roback, A. A., *Behaviorism and Psychology* (Cambridge, Mass., Sci-art, 1923).

Singer, E. A., *Mind as Behavior and Studies in Empirical Idealism* (Columbus, O., R. G. Adams Company, 1924).

——————, On the conscious mind. *J. Philos.*, 1929, **26**, 561-575.

Thorndike, E. L., *Animal Intelligence* (New York, The Macmillan Company, 1911).

Tolman, E. C., Instinct and purpose. *Psychol. Rev.*, 1920, **27**, 217-233.

——————, A new formula for behaviorism. *Psychol. Rev.*, 1922, **29**, 44-53.

——————, Behaviorism and purpose. *J. Philos.*, 1925, **22**, 35-41.

——————, A behavioristic theory of ideas. *Psychol. Rev.*, 1926, **33**, 352-369.

Watson, J. B., Psychology as a behaviorist views it. *Psychol. Rev.*, 1913, **20**, 158-177.

——————, Image and affection in behavior. *J. Philos., Psychol. Sci. Meth.*, 1913, **10**, 421-428.

——————, *Psychology from the Standpoint of a Behaviorist* (Philadelphia, Lippincott, 1919. Rev. ed. 1929).

——————, *Behaviorism*, rev. ed. (New York, W. W. Norton and Company, 1930).

Weiss, A. P., The relation between physiological psychology and behavior psychology. *J. Philos., Psychol. Sci. Meth.*, 1919, **16**, 626-634.

——————, *A Theoretical basis of Human Behavior* (Columbus, O., R. G. Adams Company, 1925).

Williams, D. C., A metaphysical interpretation of behaviorism. Harvard Ph.D. Thesis, 1928.

PART II
THE RAT IN THE MAZE

The general principles which have been indicated in Chapter I will be applied now to the specific case of rats learning mazes. Behavior, as a molar phenomenon, i.e., *qua* docile, is both purposive and cognitive. But we must attempt now to indicate this specifically and in detail for so lowly and so non-introspecting an organism as the rat.

The white rats that, throughout all the psychological laboratories of this country, are so nobly devoting large portions of their daily existences to the running of mazes are, in so doing, exhibiting sets of precisely definable purposive and cognitive behavior aspects or determinants. They are exhibiting objectively definable purposes and cognitions with respect to goal-objects and with respect to means-objects and with respect to the means-end-relations of the former to the latter. It shall be our task now to uncover and to define these immanent determinants *rodentium*.

Chapter II

DEMANDS AND MEANS-END-READINESSES [1]

1. The Rat

IT has been contended in the preceding chapter that, in so far as behavior exhibits persistent, docile gettings-to or gettings-from, it is to be described as containing immanent purposes. It has also been contended that, in so far as it exhibits also, and *pari passu,* docile contingencies upon the environmental features proving so and so, it contains immanent cognitions.

We wish now to elaborate these two concepts of immanent purposes and cognitions. And to this end we begin with the rat. For, as is well known, the white rat, probably because of his resistance to disease and cheapness in maintenance, has become the favorite laboratory animal for psychologists as well as for biologists. And, furthermore, "rat-psychologists" have of late [2] presented us with manifold maze-learning, discrimination-box and other experiments which, as we shall see, are capable of providing concrete definitions of such immanent behavior-purposes and behavior-cognitions.

2. Physiological Quiescences and Disturbances

The ultimate purpose of a rat in a maze, discrimination-box or other problem-box situation is in the last analysis, it would

[1] Many of the concepts elaborated in Chapters II to XI inclusive have already been presented in more tentative forms in the following articles:

E. C. Tolman, Purpose and cognition: the determiners of animal learning, *Psychol. Rev.,* 1925, **32,** 285-297.

——————— Habit formation and higher mental processes in animals, *Psychol. Bull.,* 1927, **24,** 1-35; 1928, **25,** 24-53.

——————— Purposive behavior, *Psychol. Rev.,* 1928, **35,** 524-530.

——————— Maze performance a function of motivation and of reward as well as of knowledge of the maze paths, *J. Gen. Psychol.,* 1930, **4,** 338-343.

[2] The use of rats as laboratory animals seems to have begun about 1895 and their use in mazes in about 1898. Cf. W. R. Miles, On the history of research with rats and mazes—a collection of notes, *J. Gen. Psychol.,* 1930, **3,** 324-336.

seem, one of getting *to* a final physiological quiescence or *from* a final physiological disturbance, or both. The rat is getting to hunger-satiation, or it may be to thirst-satiation, or he is getting from physiological injury, or from an electric shock, or the like. That is, rat experiments are, in fact, always so arranged as to arouse in the animal one or more of what may be called the first-order drives—i.e., the appetites and aversions. These first-order drives, appetites and aversions, are to be conceived as due to initiating physiological excitements, as their primary "initiating causes" which, once they are aroused, keep the animal in a condition of "demand for" the final presence of some physiological quiescence, e.g., hunger-satiation, thirst-satiation, sex-satiation, etc., or in one of "demand against" the final presence of some physiological disturbance, e.g., injury, physiological blocking, etc.

These first-order drives are, that is, demands for the presence of specific physiological quiescences (appetites) or against the presence of specific physiological disturbances (aversions) which result from initiating organic excitements. A more detailed discussion of such appetites and aversions will have to be reserved for a later chapter.[3] For the present it suffices to assert their ubiquity. It is such demanded physiological states of quiescence and disturbance which constitute the final goal-objects which the rat, and all other animals, are to be conceived as persisting to or from.

3. Superordinate and Subordinate Goals

The next point to be noted is that subordinate to such "demands" for or against final physiological goals there also function, or come to function, various more proximate and environmentally directed demands—demands for and against such environmental entities as foods, blind-alley-terminations, electric grills, openings-which-lead-on, and the like. In short, as we shall attempt to show more concretely in the succeeding chapters, it appears that the rat accepts or rejects and persists to or from food, blind-alleys, true path sections, electric grills, etc., only in so far as these latter function for him as subordinate goals (i.e., means-objects) for the getting to or from the more ultimate physiological qui-

[3] See below, Chapter XVIII.

escences and disturbances. But it is to be emphasized that these subordinate objects remain ends only in so far as they prove, in the long run, to be appropriate routes for getting to or from those more ultimate goals.[4] A hungry rat demands hunger-satiation; more secondarily he demands food as the route to hunger-satiation; and still more secondarily he demands open, leading-on alleys as the route to food.

4. Means-End-Readinesses

It will be asserted next that the subordination of such secondary demands to the superordinate ones is due to the interconnection of what we shall designate as means-end-readinesses. The rat, who because hungry and satiation-demanding therefore demands food, exhibits, we should assert, an interconnecting means-end-readiness, viz., the readiness for commerce with that type of food as a means to satiation. Similarly, the rat who, because food-demanding, is therefore peculiarly ready for explorable objects, exhibits another more subordinate means-end-readiness, viz., the readiness for commerce with such and such explorable objects as the means to food.

Further, we are contending that such means-end-readinesses are "judgmental" in character in that they tend to be docile relative to the actual relationships. If the given type of food does not prove, in the long run, to lead on to satiation, then sooner or later that type of food will, we believe, no longer tend to be included in the list of subordinate means-objects for which the satiation-demanding rat will as such continue to be ready. And, if such be the case, such a means-end-readiness is, we are saying, equivalent to a *judgment* that the given type of food has proved in the past, and will continue to prove in the future, a "good" type of means-object route for getting on to satiation. Similarly, if a given type of explorable object (shape of alley, type of crevice, or what not) proves in the long run not to lead on to food, this type of explorable object will, we believe, no longer tend to be included in the list of those types of explorable object for which the food-demanding rat will as such be ready. And,

[4] For a very pretty demonstration that a specific goal-box at the end of a maze is sought by the hungry rat only so long as it seems to be a route to food, see the experiment by K. A. Williams described below, Chapter X, p. 148 f.

in so far, readinesses for such explorable objects are to be said to be judgmental.

5. The Docility of Means-End-Readinesses (Foods)

A certain amount of evidence as to this judgmental character seems to be on hand for human babies. When hungry, the human infant, as is well known, is peculiarly ready to suck anything which at all conforms in sensory and motor make-up to a nipple, e.g., fingers, corner of a blanket, or the like. And this readiness is, we would now point out, docile. For the hungry infant comes to be ready finally to suck certain of such nipple-like entities only. And the ones, which he thus comes to limit himself to, seem to be the ones which have led to satiation in his individual past. The evidence seems to be that the infant gets "attached" specifically to bottle or breast according to his own individual past experience as to what has brought satiation. (And it may take a lot of proving to him that he is now wrong.)

In the case of rats, certain further evidences as to such judgmental characters are to be found perhaps in some observations of Yoshioka's.[5] The latter discovered that both wild grey rats and tame albino rats, when presented with equal numbers of "large" and "small" sunflower seeds, tended in any given time to eat a greater number of large seeds than of small ones. Further, he demonstrated that in the case of the tame albino rats, with whom he tried additional control tests, this preferential selection of large seeds was dependent upon vision. For when the seeds were presented in the dark no average difference was found between the numbers of large and small seeds selected. And still further, he found that this preferential selection of large seeds was also dependent on hunger, since it disappeared when the rats were not hungry. Such observations seem to demonstrate, that is, an innately provided means-end-readiness (judgment) to the effect that the goal, satiation, lies more by way of large seeds than by way of small ones.

It is to be noted further that this judgmental readiness was

[5] J. G. Yoshioka, Size preference of wild rats, *J. Genet. Psychol.*, 1930, 37, 159-162.
————— Size preference of albino rats, *J. Genet. Psychol.*, 1930, 37, 427-430.

in this case innate and not a result of previous learning. This appears from the fact that, as Yoshioka further demonstrated, it was a mistaken readiness (judgment). The large-appearing seeds did not actually contain any larger meats than did the small ones. Furthermore, the large seeds took more time to crack and eat. Hence it is evident that this preferential choice could not have been a product of previous experience, for sufficient experience would have shown that in reality the large seeds are a poorer subordinate goal than are the small ones.

It must be pointed out finally, however, that unless the rats would show a tendency, on further training, finally to be docile to this fact that the larger seeds are really no better and, if anything, worse than the smaller seeds, then the above described subordinate readiness for the larger seeds would after all be not truly judgmental. In this latter case it would have to be conceived, rather, as of the nature of what we might call a means-end-*fixation*.[6]

Finally, as the last and only true evidence of the judgmental character of such readinesses for specific foods (as means to satiation) we would suggest operative physiological experiments. We would suggest experiments in which the animal's esophagus was divided and brought to the outside so that all food chewed and swallowed would fall outside. Only such pieces, or types, of food as the experimenter desired could then be reintroduced into the stomach through a gastric fistula and allowed to produce satiation. The experimenter could thus prescribe which types of food should produce satiation and which not. And he could therefore discover whether actually the animal's preferences for, and readiness to eat, specific types of food are, or are not, docile relative to the final achievement of such satiation. Only, if they did thus prove docile, would our assumption that the subordinate means-end-readiness for types of food is judgmental be finally justified.[7]

[6] See below, Chapter X, p. 152, for a further discussion of this concept of "fixation." (Also see Glossary.)

[7] The operation in question has actually been performed successfully by Pavlov in the case of dogs. He discovered that "sham feeding," in which the food dropped out and was not reintroduced into the stomach, would continue to cause secretion of the digestive juices for a number of hours. But the further experiment (as far as we have been able to determine) was apparently not carried out of discovering if the "likings" and "dislikings" relative to

6.   The Docility of Means-End-Readinesses
(Types of Exploration)

Richter [8] has shown that general exploratory activity of the rat occurs in cycles corresponding to the cycles in the contractive activity of the stomach. And, further, if there be attached to the rat's main living cage a small cage in which there is food, he found that it is at the height of each activity cycle that the rat passes into the food-cage and eats, after which the animal returns to

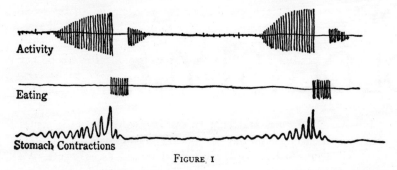

FIGURE. I

the living cage, cleans himself and then subsides. Richter therefore represents the relationship between the stomach contractions, the animal's activity in his main living cage and in the smaller attached eating cage, by the above schematic diagram (FIGURE I).[9]

To quote:

"Thus we see that the small contractions give rise to the diffuse activity in the large cage. The animal seems at first simply to be annoyed and becomes more and more restless as the con-

(the demands for and demands against) specific foods could be controlled by consistently reintroducing certain foods and not others. See:

I. P. Pavlov, *The Work of the Digestive Glands*, 2d. Eng. ed. (London, Charles Griffin & Company, 1910), pp. 53 ff.

A. J. Carlson, *The Control of Hunger in Health and Disease* (Chicago, Univ. Chicago Press, 1916).

W. B. Cannon, *Bodily Changes in Pain, Hunger, Fear and Rage*, 2d ed. (New York, D. Appleton and Company, 1929), especially Chapter I.

[8] C. P. Richter, Behavioristic study of the activity of the rat, *Comp. Psychol. Monog.*, 1922, **1**, No. 2.

———— Animal behavior and internal drives, *Quart. Rev. Biol.*, 1927, **2**, 307-343.

[9] "Animal behavior and internal drives," p. 312.

tractions grow larger, until the 'main' contractions set in and the general discomfort becomes centralized in the hunger sensation. This stimulus dominates the behavior of the organism and it enters the food-box to eat. When its appetite has been satisfied, it passes into a period of quiescence which lasts until the stomach has become empty and the contractions have started up again." [10]

It appears, in short, that it is the hungry, or satiation-demanding, rat who is the exploration-demanding rat. And further it also appears that at the height of hunger, the exploratoriness is specifically directed towards food. [11]

The further point we now wish to make is that such exploratoriness will prove docile relative to the actual finding of food. We want to show that an animal's exploratoriness embodies a means-end-readiness, judgmental in character, to the effect that certain types of exploration (exploratory object) are more likely to lead to food than are others. And, in fact, general evidence of this is to be seen, at once, in certain general findings as regards maze-adaptation. A "naïve" rat, when first run in a maze, is quite as likely to try to push through impossible crevices or to run upside down on the wire cover as he is to run in the alleys proper. A "maze-wise" rat, on the other hand, has become ready for alley-explorations only, i.e., for those general types of exploration which he has actually found tend to lead to food.

Or again it is to be observed that if a rat has learned in a given simple maze always to take, say, a right-turn at a T, he will tend to prefer such a right-turn when transferred to a second maze which presents another T under somewhat, but by no means exactly, similar conditions to those of the first maze. A rat will "abstract" the goodness of right-turning from his first maze. This has recently been demonstrated specifically and very prettily by Gengerelli,[12] who reports that the group of rats who most clearly carried over the "generalized habit," or what we are call-

---

[10] Op. cit., p. 313.

[11] See also in this general connection: T. Wada, An experimental study of hunger in its relation to activity, *Arch. Psychol.*, 1922, **8**, No. 57; and G. H. Wang, The relation between "spontaneous" activity and oestrous cycle in the white rat, *Comp. Psychol. Monog.*, 1923, **2**, No. 6; and E. Wolf, Die Aktivität der Japanischen Tanzmaus und ihre rhythmische Verteilung, *Zsch. f. vergl. Physiol.*, 1930, **11**, 321-344.

[12] J. A. Gengerelli, Studies in abstraction with the white rat, *J. Genet. Psychol.*, 1930, **38**, 171-202.

ing the means-end-readiness, from the one situation to the other were not acting in any reflex fashion. He describes one of the most striking cases of such "transfer" as follows:

"The rats by this time did not run the maze as if it were a stereotyped habit. The continual changing of maze patterns from day to day had caused them to adopt a more circumspect poise in their running. By this time there was very little, if any, bumping of noses at bifurcations and elbows. The animals had become more exploratory in their running attitude. They invariably slowed up or paused as they approached anything that looked like a turn in the maze.

"Practically all of the animals, therefore, approached the bifurcation in the maze pattern used in this experiment slowly and deliberately. There was, accordingly, some hesitation at the cross-roads, and a great deal of looking from side to side before the choice was made.[13]

And yet they carried the right (or the left) turning-readiness over from the previous training.

Indeed it is obvious that according to us all so-called "transfer" experiments would be evidence of the formation and carrying over of specific (judgmental) means-end-readinesses. Thus Vincent's demonstrations of the formation and transfer of the choice of white alleys rather than black from discrimination box to "white-black" maze and *vice versa*[14] would similarly be a demonstration of an acquired and truly docile means-end-readiness to the effect that white alleys are better than black for leading on to food.[15]

7.   Innate Endowment and Previous Learning

From what has gone before, it is obvious that, according to us, means-end-readinesses are of the nature of innate generalized

[13] *Op. cit.*, p. 191.
Cf. also for somewhat related findings as regards the transfer of a propensity towards specific types of turns. R. Hamill, Sequence of turns versus distances as essential pattern-elements in the maze problem, *J. Comp. Psychol.*, 1931, **2**, 367-382.
[14] S. B. Vincent, The white rat and the maze problem, I. The introduction of a visual control, *J. Animal Behav.*, 1915, **5**, 1-24.
[15] Cf. also on the general problem of transfer from one type of maze to another, L. W. Webb, Transfer of training and retroaction, *Psychol. Monog.*, 1917, **24**, No. 104, and R. T. Wiltbank, Transfer of training in white rats upon various series of mazes, *Behav. Monog.*, 1914, **4**, No. 1.
See below, Chapter X, pp. 151 f.

sets, resulting from previous learning, or provided vaguely by innate endowment. There is nothing recondite about them. They are matters of common observation. The rat, it appears, is innately "ready," when hungry, with some sort of generalized demands for eatable objects and, when thus demanding eatable objects, he is also innately "ready" to demand explorable objects. But when he has had actual experiences with particular types of eatables and particular types of explorable objects he may correct such innate readinesses in the light of these experiences. He will become more ready for, and demanding of, those specific types of food and those specific types of explorable object which have proved actually, in his particular past, to be the more successful. He is provided innately with certain relatively vague means-end-readinesses (judgments). And these become refined and specified through experience.

8.   Responsiveness to Stimuli

Finally, we must now note a situation as regards both rats and other organisms which "stimulus-response" psychologies, as well as "behaviorisms" proper, seem largely to have overlooked.[16] It is a situation which orthodox mentalisms were well aware of. The latter sought to care for it by their doctrines of attention and apperception. It is the fact that rats and men have hundreds, not to say thousands, of stimuli impinging upon them every instant of their waking lives; and yet to by far the majority of these stimuli they do not, at the given moment, respond. But in order now, in our system, to explain this choosiness as to stimuli, we have merely to refer to these facts of superordinate and subordinate demands and means-end-readinesses as just outlined.

Consider the case of food-stimuli. It is the hungry rat only who is responsive to food-stimuli. The satiated rat "pays no attention" to food. He even lies down and goes to sleep in its presence and so, also, does the satiated human being. The reason the hungry rat is responsive is, we would assert, (a) because he is demanding hunger-satiation, and (b) because he is provided with a means-end-readiness (innate or acquired, "judgmental" or "fixated"), to the effect that commerce with the type of food, presented by the given stimuli, will lead on to satiation.

16 Thurstone is the one outstanding exception. Cf. L. L. Thurstone, *The Nature of Intelligence* (New York, Harcourt, Brace and Company, 1927).

Similarly as regards the rat's responsiveness to concrete maze stimuli. It is only the food (or consummatory object) seeking rat that is responsive to the maze stimuli. And, as such a rat becomes more and more "maze-wise," because of many experiences of the same or different mazes, he becomes more and more selective in this subordinate responsiveness to types of maze-stimuli. An inexperienced rat responds to all the stimuli provided by a maze—those coming from the wire covers over the alleys, those coming from slight cracks at the corners (because of poor carpentry), those coming from extraneous noises in the surrounding room, etc. The "maze-wise" rat, on the other hand—i.e., the rat whose means-end-judgment has become more specific through many experiences—becomes responsive only to such stimuli as come from maze-alleys proper. The demand for food plus a means-end-readiness to the effect that explorable objects are the means-objects for getting to food initially sensitizes the rat to all maze-stimuli. But this means-end-readiness becomes refined through experience, his responsiveness tends to become more and more limited to the stimuli from only such types of maze-feature as are usually true types of leading-on objects.

9. Summary

In this chapter we have sought to show in a general way: (a) that the rat's behavior expresses certain superordinate and subordinate demands for and against; and (b) that it also expresses certain means-end-readinesses which serve to align the specific subordinate demands under the specific superordinate ones and to make the animal responsive to the stimuli which seem to present instances of the thus, superordinately or subordinately, demanded goals.

The ultimate goal-objects for the rat, or other animal, are certain finally-to-be-sought, or to-be-avoided, physiological states of quiescence and disturbance due to initiating physiological states or conditions. Subordinate to the demand for or against these there are various types of environmental presence, e.g., food, electric grill, etc., demanded for or against as the last steps in reaching such quiescences or in avoiding such disturbances. And subordinate to these latter there may be still other types of still more subordinate environmental presences also to be sought and avoided. The environment takes on for the physiologically aroused organism, by dint of his innate endowment and past ·experience, the character of a hierarchy of to-be-sought and to-be-avoided superordinate and subordinate objects. Environmental presences possess or acquire what have been picturesquely designated by Lewin as positive and negative "invitation-characters" or "valencies." [17] The ultimate appetites and aversions plus the depending means-end-readinesses, make of the environment a field of superordinately and subordinately "demanded" and hence "to-be-responded-to" types of objects.

The next chapter will present in some detail the experimental evidence indicating the reality and objective definition of the rat's "demands for" specific types of goal-object, when in a maze.

[17] *Aufforderungscharaktere.* Cf. K. Lewin, Untersuchungen zur Handlungs- und Affektpsychologie. Esp. I. Vorbemerküngen über die seelischen Kräfte und Energien und über die Struktur des Seelischen, *Psychol. Forsch.*, 1926, **7**, 294-329. II. Vorsatz, Wille und Bedürfnis, *Psychol. Forsch.*, 1926, **7**, 330-385.

In general, it is to be said that a great deal of the doctrine to be outlined in the present treatise seems to bear a close relationship to the doctrine of Lewin, as the latter is to be gleaned from his writings and from those of his students.

REFERENCES

Carlson, A. J., *The Control of Hunger in Health and Disease* (Chicago, Univ. Chicago Press, 1916).

Cannon, W. B., *Bodily Changes in Pain, Hunger, Fear and Rage.* 2d ed. (New York, D. Appleton and Company, 1929).

Gengerelli, J. A., Studies in abstraction with the white rat. *J. Genet. Psychol.*, 1930, **38**, 171-202.

Hamill, R., Sequence of turns versus distances as essential pattern elements in the maze problem. *J. Comp. Psychol.*, 1931, **11**, 367-382.

Lewin, K., Untersuchungen zur Handlungs- und Affektpsychologie. I. Vorbemerkungen über die seelischen Kräfte und Energien und über die Struktur des Seelischen. *Psychol. Forsch.*, 1926, **7**, 294-329. II. Vorsatz, Wille und Bedürfnis. *Psychol. Forsch.*, 1926, **7**, 330-385.

Miles, W. R., On the history of research with rats and mazes— a collection of notes. *J. Gen. Psychol.*, 1930, **3**, 324-337.

Pavlov, I. P., *The Work of the Digestive Glands.* 2d Eng. ed. (London, Charles Griffin and Company, 1910).

Richter, C. P., Behavioristic study of the activity of the rat. *Comp. Psychol. Monog.*, 1922, **1**, No. 2.

——————, Animal behavior and internal drives. *Quart. Rev. Biol.*, 1927, **2**, 307-343.

Thurstone, L. L., *The Nature of Intelligence* (New York, Harcourt, Brace and Company, 1927).

Tolman, E. C., Purpose and cognition: the determiners of animal learning. *Psychol. Rev.*, 1925, **32**, 285-297.

―――――, Habit formation and higher mental processes in animals. *Psychol. Bull.*, 1927, **24**, 1-35; 1928, **25**, 24-53.

―――――, Purposive behavior. *Psychol. Rev.*, 1928, **35**, 524-530.

―――――, Maze performance a function of motivation and of reward as well as of knowledge of the maze paths. *J. Gen. Psychol.*, 1930, **4**, 338-343.

Vincent, S. B., The white rat and the maze problem. I. The introduction of a visual control. *J. Anim. Behav.*, 1915, **5**, 1-24.

Wada, T., An experimental study of hunger in its relation to activity. *Arch. Psychol.*, 1922, **8**, No. 57.

Wang, G. H., The relation between "spontaneous" activity and oestrous cycle in the white rat. *Comp. Psychol. Monog.*, 1923, **2**, No. 6.

Webb, L. W., Transfer of training and retroaction. *Psychol. Monog.*, 1917, **24**, No. 104.

Wiltbank, R. J., Transfer of training in white rats upon various series of mazes. *Behav. Monog.*, 1914, **4**, No. 1.

Wolf, E., Die Aktivität der Japonischen Tanzmaus und ihre rhythmische Verteilung. *Zsch. f. vergl. Physiol.*, 1930, **11**, 321-344.

Yoshioka, J. G., Size preference of wild rats. *J. Genet. Psychol.*, 1930, **37**, 159-162.

―――――, Size preference of albino rats. *J. Genet. Psychol.*, 1930, **37**, 427-430.

Chapter III

DEMANDS FOR GOAL-OBJECTS

1. Maze Performance and Demand for Goal-Object

IN every typical maze experiment, the rat is provided by the experimenter with some sort of a reward at the exit from the maze. He is given food, water, sex-satisfaction, and the like. Or, at the very least, he is taken out and returned to his home cage. The present chapter will survey some of the experiments which have sought to analyze the effects of such goal-objects or rewards upon the maze behavior. These experiments indicate the need for the concept of the "demand for" a given type of maze goal-object or goal-situation.[1]

2. Some Goal-Objects Demanded More than Others

First we shall review some experiments which, while keeping the physiological drive—hunger, thirst, sex-drive—the same, compare, with different groups, the effects of different goal-objects or goal-situations. These experiments indicate that, for one and the same drive, some goal-objects cause learning to appear more rapidly than do others.

Simmons ran different groups of hungry rats, with respectively different rewards in mazes similar to that shown in FIGURE 2.[2]

---

[1] This concept of "demand for" is closely related to what M. H. Elliott has called "reward-value." See, Some determining factors in maze performance, *Amer. J. Psychol.*, 1930, **42**, 315-317. It is also similar to what K. Lewin has designated as the fact that certain objects *locken* (i.e., "entice"). Cf. Die Auswirkung von Umweltkräfter, *Proc. Ninth Internat. Cong. Psychol.* (Princeton, Psychol. Rev. Co., 1930), 286-288.

[2] R. Simmons, The relative effectiveness of certain incentives in animal learning, *Comp. Psychol. Monog.*, 1924, **2**, No. 7.

In the diagram as shown the animals start from the center, F (foodbox), and return to it as indicated by the arrows. In Simmons' mazes, which were otherwise very similar, the food-box instead of being in the center was in one corner.

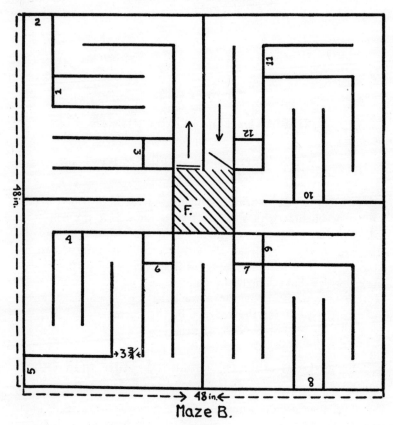

Maze B.

Figure 2

We quote the description of her general technique.

"As to the method of procedure, each rat was given one trial on the first day and afterwards two trials per day until nine out of ten successive runs were without error . . . Records were kept of the number of trials necessary to meet this criterion, the time required for each trial, and the number of errors made. A retracing or an entrance into a blind alley either in the forward or backward direction, i.e., any change in orientation disadvantageous to reaching the food-box, was regarded as an error." [3]

All her groups obtained their main day's ration some hour and a half after the day's training in special feeding cages. The groups were differentiated from one another, however, as follows:

[3] *Op. cit.,* p. 16.

Bread and milk plus return home. This group received a nibble of bread and milk in the food-box of the maze at the end of each of the two daily runs. They were then returned to their home cages until some hour and a half later when they were taken out again and fed in the special feeding cages.

Bread and milk. This group likewise received a nibble of bread and milk in the food-box after each of the two daily runs. They were then, however, transferred to the special feeding cages, rather than to their home cages, where they stayed without food until the feeding time an hour and a half later.

Sunflower seed. This group was treated like the bread and milk group, save that at the end of each run in the maze they received in the food-box of the maze a sunflower seed rather than a nibble of bread and milk.

Return home. This group received no food of whatever sort at the end of the maze. They, however, waited the interval of an hour and a half before feeding in their home cages rather than in the feeding cages.

Escape. This group also received no food at the end of the maze. They spent the hour and a half interval until feeding time not in the home cages but in the special feeding cages.

Turning now to the results, it appears that the groups may be arranged in the order of the goodness of their performances. The bread-and-milk-plus-return-home group ranks first, the bread-and-milk group next, the sunflower seed group next, the return home group next, and the escape group last. It appears, in short, that with one and the same drive, degree of hunger specified in terms of times and characters of the preceding feedings, certain goal-objects or situations produce better total maze performance than do others. And this introduces us to the conception that certain goal-objects are, given one and the same drive, demanded more than are others. If a goal-object be supplied which is of the type strongly demanded, given the specific drive, it causes faster learning and a better final performance than a goal-object of a type less strongly demanded. The strength of the demand for the type of goal-object provided is thus one of the immediate immanent aspects inherent in, and defining itself through, maze performances.

The next experiment we would report is one by Hamilton.[4] She

---

[4] E. L. Hamilton, The effect of delayed incentive on the hunger drive in the white rat, *Genet. Psychol. Monog.*, 1929, 5, No. 2.

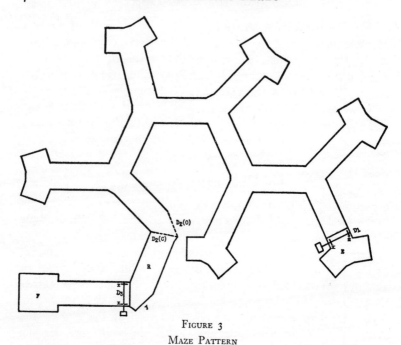

FIGURE 3

MAZE PATTERN

E, entrance compartment; F, food-box; R, restraining compartment; D_1, door separating entrance compartment from maze; D_2, door separating restraining compartment from maze; (O) and (C) represent door (D_2) in open and closed positions, respectively; D_3, door separating restraining compartment from food-box.[5]

[5] *Op. cit.*, p. 169.

This maze is an improvement over that used by Simmons—in that every blind counts. The animal has to make a positive choice between the blind and the true path at each successive point. It was developed on the general plan of that used by C. J. Warden and L. H. Warner (cf. The development of a standardized animal maze, *Arch. Psychol.*, 1927, **14**, No. 92) and shares with the Blodgett-Stone type of maze (see FIGURE 4) and the Tryon maze the credit for being both logically and empirically the best maze for obtaining reliable and consistent results. See articles by Tolman and Nyswander (E. C. Tolman and D. B. Nyswander, The reliability and validity of maze-measures for rats, *J. Comp. Psychol.*, 1927, **7**, 425-460), Stone and Nyswander (C. P. Stone and D. B. Nyswander, Reliability of rat learning scores from the multiple-T maze as determined by four different methods, *J. Genet. Psychol.*, 1927, **34**, 497-524), and Tryon (R. C. Tryon, Studies in individual differences in maze ability, I. The measurement of the reliability of individual differences, *J. Comp. Psychol.*, 1930, **11**, 145-170; II. The determination of individual differences by age, weight, sex and pigmentation, *J. Comp. Psychol.*, 1931, **12**, 1-22; III. The community of function between two maze abilities, *J. Comp. Psychol.*, 1931, **12**, 95-116).

used a maze such as that shown in FIGURE 3. And she compared the results for a group of rats that were fed immediately upon reaching the goal-box (delay = o) with those for groups that were fed only after delays of one, three, five and seven minutes.

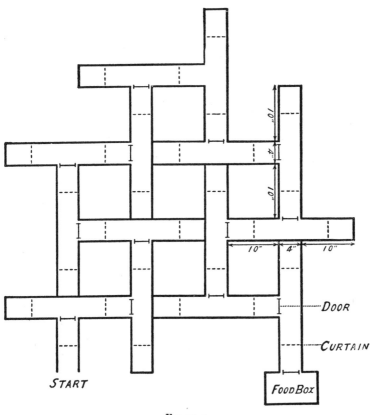

FIGURE 4

She found that the group that was fed immediately learned more rapidly than did any of the delayed groups.

Again, it appears that the one goal-situation, that of immediate food, corresponded to a stronger demand than did the others, those of delayed food. And this difference in demands again is illustrated by, and may be assumed to be causative of, the final differences in performance.

Still a third set of results falling under this same head are

Elliott's.[6] Using a maze such as that shown in FIGURE 4, he compared the learning of two equally hungry groups, one fed bran mash at the end of the maze, and the other fed sunflower seed at the end of the maze. The rest of their daily rations were equalized and were fed to them later in the day in their living

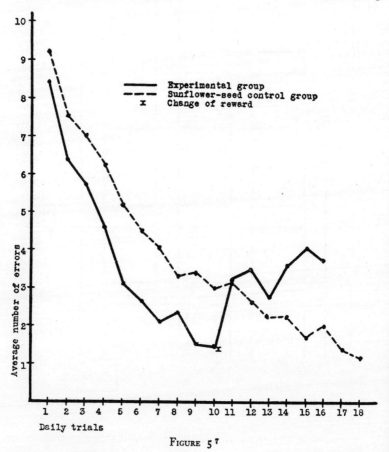

FIGURE 5 [7]

[6] M. H. Elliott, The effect of change of reward on the maze performance of rats, *Univ. Calif. Publ. Psychol.*, 1928, 4, 19-30, p. 20.

[7] *Op. cit.*, p. 26.

For the purposes of the present argument, we are considering trials one to ten only. On the tenth trial a new condition was introduced which need not concern us here. The unbroken lines represent the learning curves for the animals fed on *bran mash* and the broken curves those for the animals fed *sunflower seed,*

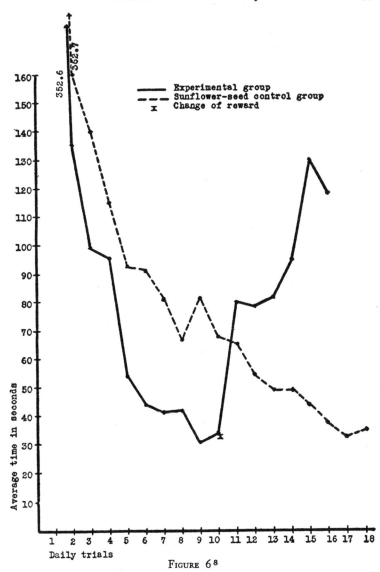

FIGURE 6[8]

cages.[9] He found (as seen in FIGURES 5 and 6) that the animals fed the bran mash in the maze had a somewhat better learning

[8] *Op. cit.*, p. 27.

[9] Both Simmons and Elliott sought to keep general nutrition conditions the same for the different groups by equalizing diets in the home cages.

curve in terms of both errors and time than those fed the sunflower seed. In other words, the bran mash corresponded to a somewhat stronger demand than did the sunflower seed when hunger conditions were as far as possible alike. This difference in demands was an aspect of behavior appearing in both error and time curves.

To sum up: the three experiments just cited all indicate that, given one and the same hunger condition, different groups of rats, provided with different types of food or food-situation at the goal-box, will exhibit different apparent rates of learning and different degrees of final performance. And this, we say, defines an immanent determinant of maze performance which we may designate as the demand for certain types of goal-object (given a particular physiological drive).[10]

It is now to be emphasized, however, that such differences in demands cannot be completely defined by any single such experiment taken by itself. The final identification and definition of a difference in demand would always require the addition of other parallel experiments. It would require, that is, the using of the same contrasted pair of goal-objects in many other types

[10] It should be noted that the above three experiments are but samples cited from a longer list of experiments, all of which have compared in somewhat similar fashion the relative effectiveness of different food-situations as goal-objects, for learning by animals with one average degree of drive (See Glossary). Such a longer list would include at least all of the following and perhaps others as well:

J. S. Szymanski, Versuche über die Wirkung der Faktoren, die als Antrieb zum Erlernen einer Handlung dienen können, *Pflüg. Arch. f. d. ges. Physiol.*, 1918, **171**, 374-385.

J. B. Watson, The effect of delayed feeding upon learning, *Psychobiol.*, 1917, **1**, 51-60.

R. Simmons, The relative effectiveness of certain incentives in animal learning, *Comp. Psychol. Monog.*, 1924, **2**, No. 7.

C. J. Warden and E. L. Haas, The effect of short intervals of delay in feeding upon speed of maze learning, *J. Comp. Psychol.*, 1927, **7**, 107-116.

M. H. Elliott, The effect of change of reward on the maze performance of rats, *Univ. Calif. Publ. Psychol.*, 1928, **4**, 19-30.

E. L. Hamilton, The effect of delayed incentive on the hunger drive in the white rat, *Genet. Psychol. Monog.*, 1929, **5**, No. 2.

G. C. Grindley, Experiments on the influence of the amount of reward on learning in young chickens, *Brit. J. Psychol.*, Gen. Sect., 1929, **20**, 173-180.

M. E. McGillivray and C. P. Stone, The incentive value of food and escape from water for albino rats forming the light discrimination habit, *J. Comp. Psychol.*, 1931, **11**, 319-324.

E. C. Tolman and C. H. Honzik, Degrees of hunger; reward and non-reward; and maze-learning in rats, *Univ. Calif. Publ. Psychol.*, 1930, **4**, 241-256.

of situation, e.g., in other mazes, choice boxes, obstruction boxes, and the like, to see if the same rankings in degree of pulling power would manifest themselves in these other situations also. In concluding, therefore, that the results of the above experiments defined such differences in demands, we were assuming implicitly, if not explicitly, that such other experiments with various other types of apparatus would actually indicate the same rankings of goal-objects.

Finally, in this connection it must be noted that Warden has carried out, and instigated others to carry out, a long series of experiments comparing the effects of different goal-objects (also different physiological drives) in causing animals to cross an electric grill. And, in general, it seems to have been found by these workers that the same rank orders of demand hold for inducing frequent crossings of the grill as for causing rapid maze learning.[11]

[11] The first use of this obstruction-box method was by Moss.

F. A. Moss, A study of animal drives, *J. Exp. Psychol.*, 1924, **7**, 165-185.

Since then the following experiments have been carried out under Warden's direction:

T. N. Jenkins, L. H. Warner, and C. J. Warden, Standard apparatus for the study of animal motivation, *J. Comp. Psychol.*, 1926, **6**, 361-382.

F. Holden, A study of the effect of starvation upon behavior by means of the obstruction method, *Comp. Psychol. Monog.*, 1926, **3**, No. 17.

L. H. Warner, A study of sex behavior in the white rat by means of the obstruction method, *Comp. Psychol. Monog.*, 1927, **4**, No. 22.

M. Jenkins, The effect of segregation on the sex behavior of the white rat as measured by the obstruction method, *Genet. Psychol. Monog.*, 1928, **3**, No. 6.

C. H. Warden and H. W. Nissen, An experimental analysis of the obstruction method of measuring animal drives, *J. Comp. Psychol.*, 1928, **8**, 325-342.

L. H. Warner, A study of hunger behavior in the white rat by means of the obstruction method, *J. Comp. Psychol.*, 1928, **8**, 273-299.

———— A study of thirst behavior in the white rat by means of the obstruction method. *J. Genet. Psychol.*, 1928, **35**, 178-192.

E. L. Hamilton, The effect of delayed incentive on the hunger drive in the white rat, *Genet. Psychol. Monog.*, 1929, **5**, 137-207.

H. W. Nissen, The effects of gonadectomy, vasectomy, and injections of placental and orchic extracts on the sex behavior of the white rat, *Genet. Psychol. Monog.*, 1929, **5**, 451-550.

———— A study of exploratory behavior in the white rat by means of the obstruction method, *J. Genet. Psychol.*, 1930, **37**, 361-376.

———— A study of maternal behavior in the white rat by means of the obstruction method, *J. Genet. Psychol.*, 1930, **37**, 377-393.

These experiments and others have just been brought together by Warden in a single book. Cf. C. J. Warden, *Animal Motivation—Experimental Studies on the Albino Rat* (New York, Columbia Univ. Press, 1931).

3. Substitution of a More Demanded Goal-Object

In the further specification of this notion of demands for types of goal-object, we would cite next some experiments in which the goal-object was changed during the course of learning. The first sub-group of these experiments indicates that when a goal-object which is more demanded is substituted for one which is less demanded, maze errors and times suddenly decrease.

The first experiment to be cited in this sub-group is that of Blodgett.[12] Blodgett used the maze shown in FIGURE 7.

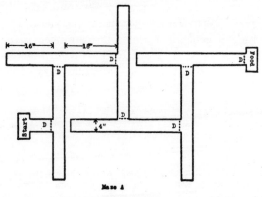

FIGURE 7 [13]

In this maze he ran three groups of hungry rats. Each group had one trial per day. The *control group* (Group I) was allowed to eat in the usual manner for three minutes in the food-box at the end of the maze. They were then immediately fed the remainder of their day's ration in another cage (not the home cage). The *first experimental group* (Group II) ran the maze for the first six days, without immediate reward. That is, at the end of the maze they were confined in the exit-box without food for two minutes and obtained their day's ration only one hour, or more, afterwards in another cage (not the home cage). After six

---

[12] H. C. Blodgett, The effect of the introduction of reward upon the maze performance of rats, *Univ. Calif. Publ. Psychol.*, 1929, 4, 113-134. Experiments of a similar sort, but with fewer animals and less controlled conditions, were earlier performed by Simmons, *op. cit.*, and by Szymanski, *op. cit.*

[13] Blodgett, *op. cit.*, p. 117.
This maze is similar to that shown in FIGURE 4, save that it consists of six T-units instead of fourteen such units, and it has no curtains.

days of such running, this group, on the seventh day, suddenly found food in the exit-box, and continued so to find it on all subsequent days. A *second experimental group* (Group III) ran the maze without food at the exit-box for two days. For these two days they, like Group II, obtained their day's ration only one hour or more afterwards in another cage. On the third day, however, food was given them in the exit-box and they continued to find it there on all subsequent days.

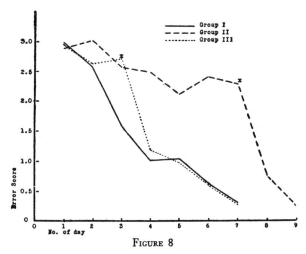

FIGURE 8

The results for the three groups as to blind-entrances (errors) are shown in FIGURE 8.

It appears that, during the periods in which they were receiving no reward in the food-box, Groups II and III made little appreciable decrease in their numbers of blind-entrances. But on the first day after food was found they both made tremendous improvements. They cut their errors nearly in half. And on the next day after that, they had decreased their errors to the corresponding levels of the control group, which had received food in the maze from the very beginning. In other words, the change from a goal-situation which was less demanded (i.e., no food) to one which was more demanded (i.e., food[14]) caused

---

[14] It is to be noted that again we are assuming that the one goal-situation, the presence of food which can be eaten, would prove generally (i.e., in all sorts of learning and immediate choice situations) to be more demanded than the other goal-situation, being shut up without food.

very decided drops in errors. Similar results were obtained by Blodgett for time.

The second experiment to be cited in the present group is one by Elliott.[15] In the same maze shown in FIGURE 4, he ran

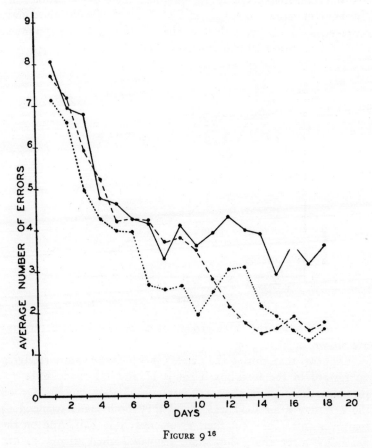

FIGURE 9 [16]

......Group E (very hungry, very thirsty)
————Group F (very hungry, slightly thirsty)
--------Group G (slightly hungry, very thirsty)

All groups rewarded with food for nine days and then changed to water reward.

[15] M. H. Elliott, The effect of appropriateness of reward and of complex incentives on maze performance, *Univ. Calif. Publ. Psychol*, 1929, **4**, 91-98.
[16] Elliott, *op. cit.*, p. 93.

three groups of rats: one very hungry and very thirsty throughout; one very hungry and slightly thirsty throughout; and one
slightly hungry and very thirsty throughout. FIGURES 9 and 10
present the results as to errors and times for all three groups.
For the purposes of the present argument we shall consider at
this moment, however, *only those for the last group* (i.e., Group
G, FIGURES 9 and 10).

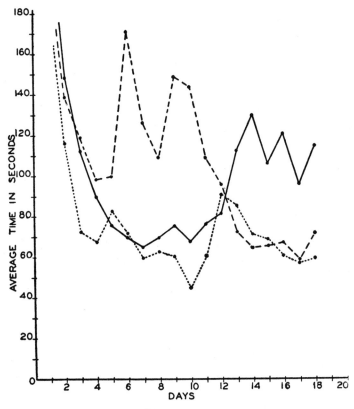

FIGURE 10 [17]

......Group E (very hungry, very thirsty)
————Group F (very hungry, slightly thirsty)
--------Group G (slightly hungry, very thirsty)

All groups were rewarded with food for nine days and then changed to water
reward.

[17] Elliott, *op. cit.*, p. 95.

The rats had one trial a day, and during the first nine days were provided with food—bran mash only—at the end-box. Their main daily rations of both food and water were provided one hour later in their living cages. On the tenth day, however, they suddenly found water instead of food at the end box. As appears, particularly in Figure 10, the rats of Group G, i.e., these slightly hungry but very thirsty animals, did somewhat poorly while they were receiving merely food in the end-box. But on the very first day after they had received water they showed a decided spurt downwards in both errors and times. The results for this group are thus similar to those obtained by Blodgett.

Or, in other words, again it appears that when a goal-object which is more demanded is substituted for one which is less demanded, a decided sudden improvement in performance appears.

Finally, as a third experiment demonstrating the same point, we may cite a group run by Tolman and Honzik.[18] This group of rats ran a fourteen-unit T-maze, such as is shown in Figure 4, for ten days without food at the exit-box. They were fed only some two hours later in their living cages. On the eleventh day food was introduced. On the twelfth day they exhibited an enormous drop in both errors and times, as is shown in Figures 11 and 12. This group is labeled HNR-R (hungry, non-reward—reward) in both figures. The other two curves HNR and HR are for two control groups taken from another experiment [19] but run in the same maze under the same general conditions. Of these the HNR (hungry, non-reward) is a group that received no food in the exit-box throughout the entire experimental period but were always fed some two hours later in their living cages. And the HR (hungry, reward) group is one that received food in the exit-box from the very beginning of the experiment. It will be observed that the experimental, HNR-R, group started out like the non-reward group but that on the day after food was introduced they dropped in both errors and times to the level of (or even below the level of) the HR group.

[18] E. C. Tolman and C. H. Honzik, Introduction and removal of reward, and maze performance in rats, *Univ. Calif. Publ. Psychol.*, 1930, **4**, 257-275.

[19] E. C. Tolman and C. H. Honzik, Degrees of hunger, reward and non-reward, and maze learning in rats, *Univ. Calif. Publ. Psychol.*, 1930, **4**, 241-256.

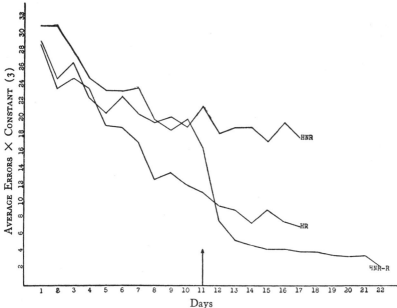

Error Curves for HR, HNR, and HNR-R

FIGURE 11 [20]

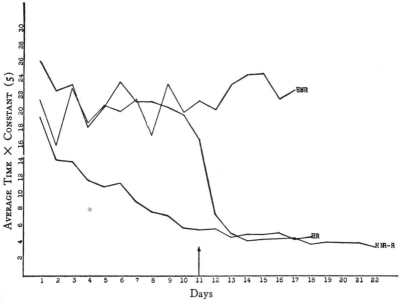

Time Curves for HR, HNR, and HNR-R

FIGURE 12 [21]

[20] "Introduction and Removal of Reward," p. 267.
[21] *Ibid.*, p. 267.

4. Substitution of a Less Demanded Goal-Object

We turn, now, to the reverse sort of phenomenon; viz., the fact that maze-performance degenerates when a goal-object which had great pulling power is removed and a goal-object or goal-situation with less pulling power is substituted. As a first bit of evidence on this point we may call attention to a second ex-

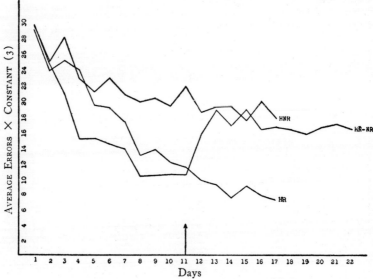

ERROR CURVES FOR HR, HNR, AND HR-NR

FIGURE 13 [22]

perimental group also run in the experiment of Tolman and Honzik, just cited. This group began the learning of the maze with food each time in the exit-box but on the eleventh day the food was removed and thereafter they were fed only in their living cages some two hours later. The results as to errors and times are shown in FIGURES 13 and 14. The two control groups HNR and HR are the same as in the two preceding figures. It is evident, at once, that the experimental HR-NR (hungry, reward—non-reward) group, on the day after the removal of the reward, degenerated in performance. They never became quite so slow as

[22] "Introduction and Removal of Reward," p. 262.

the control HNR group, who were non-rewarded throughout, but they did come to make almost as many errors.

As further evidence of this same sort we may now also call attention to the result for Elliott's Group F (see above FIGURES 9 and 10). These animals, who were very hungry but only slightly thirsty throughout, did very much more poorly, it will be observed, when they were changed from the more demanded food to the less demanded water.

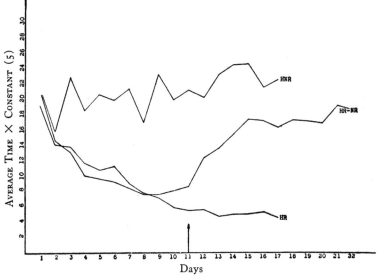

TIME CURVES FOR HR, HNR, AND HR-NR

FIGURE 14 [23]

Next we may cite an experiment by Bruce.[24] He used the very simple maze, presenting one long path and one short path, shown in FIGURE 15. And he found that the removal of the goal-object, on trial 11, i.e., after the maze had been practically learned, caused a sudden jump-up in excess wanderings up and down alleys, and in time, as appears in FIGURES 16 and 17.

Further, it should be noted that on the twenty-third day the animals of the experimental group were not fed. This was to

[23] "Introduction and Removal of Reward," p. 263.
[24] R. H. Bruce, The effect of removal of reward on the maze performance of rats, *Univ. Calif. Publ. Psychol.*, 1930, **4,** 203-214.

increase their hunger from that due to a twenty-four hour period without food to that due to a forty-eight hour period without food. And it will be observed that, as a result, on the twenty-fourth day their times and their excess runnings again went up. This seems to indicate that the "non-demandedness" of the goal box without food in it becomes greater the greater the degree of hunger.

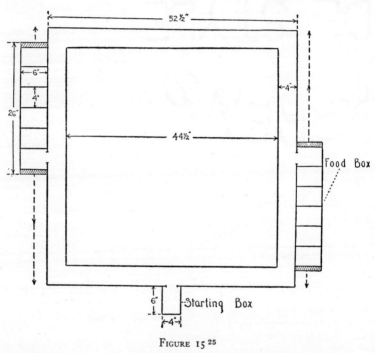

FIGURE 15 [25]

Finally, we may consider again a previously cited experiment of Elliott's. In this experiment (see above, FIGURES 5 and 6) for the first nine days the experimental group received bran mash at the end of the maze. On the tenth day, they were shifted to sunflower seed. A control group received sunflower seed throughout. Sunflower seed was, as such, somewhat less demanded than bran mash. And when the shift was made from bran mash to sunflower seed, there was a very decided jump-up in both errors and times.

[25] *Op. cit.*, p. 206.

To sum up: it appears from each of these experiments that whenever, at a point somewhat advanced in learning, a change is made from a goal-object or situation which, given the specific physiological drive, is more demanded to one which is

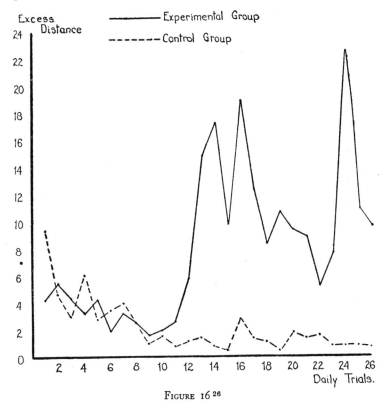

FIGURE 16 [26]

less demanded, there is exhibited a decided degeneration in performance. Jump-ups in both errors and times occur.[27]

[26] *Op. cit.*, p. 208.

[27] Reference should also be made to two other experiments of a similar nature:

W. L. Sharp, Disintegrative effects of continuous running and removal of the food incentive upon a maze habit of albino rats, *J. Comp. Psychol.*, 1929, 9, 405-423.

K. A. Williams, The reward value of a conditioned stimulus, *Univ. Calif. Publ. Psychol.*, 1929, 4, 31-55.

(This last experiment is described in some detail in Chapter X, p. 148.)

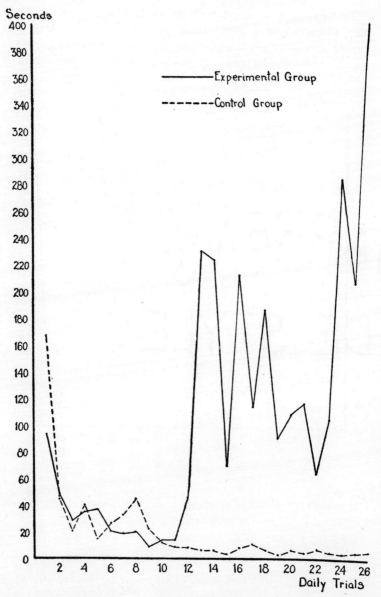

FIGURE 17 [28]

[28] *Op. cit.*, p. 209.

5. Alternative Goal-Objects—One More Demanded Than the Other

We shall now cite an experiment which indicates that also, if the animal be presented simultaneously with two alternative goal-objects, one of which is more demanded than the other, he will learn to choose the path which leads to the more demanded goal-object. The experiment we have in mind is that of Tsai.[29] Tsai presented his animals with a simple two-way maze shown in FIGURE 18 with food on one side and with a female in heat as goal-object on the other side. That is, the animals could reach

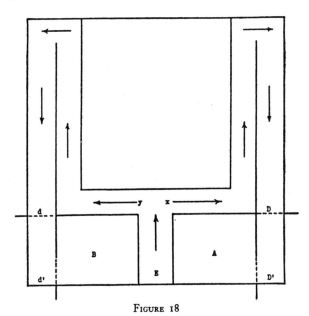

FIGURE 18

"The pattern of the apparatus . . . consists of two stimulus boxes, A and B, on each side of the entrance alley, E, which is bifurcated into x and y alleys. From x the path is led to box A and from y to box B. The walls of the stimulus boxes facing the alleys x and y are made of wire mesh, so that the animals tested may easily sense the stimuli in each box. Doors D and D[1] were provided to prevent the animals from turning back and doors d and d^1 to keep the female used as incentive from running out of the stimulus box." [30]

[29] C. Tsai, The relative strength of sex and hunger motives in the albino rat, *J. Comp. Psychol.*, 1925, 5, 407-415.

[30] *Op. cit.*, p. 409.

food by turning to one side, and by turning to the other they could reach a female in heat. And he found that there was a bigger percentage of turns towards food (77%) than towards the female (23%).[31]

It is very evident that further experiments of an analogous nature should be carried out—for example, experiments in which one goal-box is provided with a strongly demanded food, and the other alternative goal-box provided with a second less demanded food, and the like.

6. Physiological Drive and Strength of Demand

The strength of the demand for a given goal-object of course goes back in the last analysis to the character of the physiological drive which is then and there in force. And we wish now to describe some further experiments which specifically indicate this. The first of these experiments which we shall present is that of Tolman and Honzik.[32] They ran two groups of very hungry rats, and two groups of less hungry rats, in the 14-unit multiple T-maze of the pattern shown in FIGURE 4. The very hungry rats were kept on short rations as compared with the less hungry rats. That is, the former *lost* in weight from five to twenty-six grams each, during the course of the experiment, while the latter *gained* from five to thirty-eight grams each.

Of the two groups of hungry rats, one group was fed at the end of the maze-run. (These were designated as the Hungry Reward Rats, HR.) But the other group was not fed until some two hours later in the living cages. (These were designated as the Hungry Non-Reward Rats, HNR.) Similarly, for the two less hungry groups: the Less Hungry Reward Group, LHR, was rewarded at the end of the maze, and the other, the Less Hungry Non-Reward Group, LHNR, was not rewarded in the maze, but fed only some two hours later in the living cages. The results in errors and times for all four groups are shown in FIGURES 19

---

[31] This agrees with the general finding of Warden and his co-workers that the hunger drive is stronger than the sex drive when these are measured independently of the maze situation by the obstruction-box method. See above p. 47, note 11.

[32] E. C. Tolman and C. H. Honzik, Degrees of hunger, reward and non-reward, and maze learning in rats, *Univ. Calif. Publ. Psychol.*, 1930, **4**, 241-256.

and 20. Compare first the results for the two rewarded groups, i.e., the Hungry Reward and the Less Hungry Reward. It appears at once that the goal-object consisting in reward at the end of the maze was much more demanded, given the physiological drive of hunger, than it was, given that of less hunger. Compare, now, secondly, the results for the two non-rewarded groups, the HNR and the LHNR groups. These groups were not fed at the end of the maze, but were merely returned to their

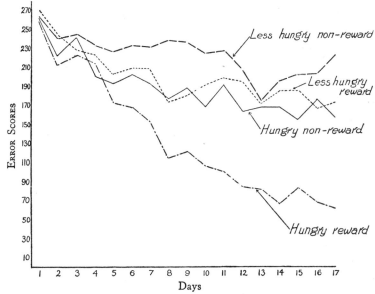

ERROR CURVES FOR FOUR GROUPS, 36 RATS

FIGURE 19 [33]

living cages where they were fed some two hours later. It appears, however, that even this goal-situation, that of merely getting through the maze and being returned to the living cage, is more demanded, when the physiological drive of hunger exists, than it is when that of less hunger exists.

The next experiment to be cited under this same head is that of Washburn.[34] She used white mice in a Watson circular maze,

[33] *Op. cit.*, p. 246.

[34] M. F. Washburn, Hunger and speed of running as factors in maze learning in mice, *J. Comp. Psychol.*, 1926, **6**, 181-187.

such as is shown in FIGURE 21, and she measured both the length of time during which each individual actually ate, i.e., lapped the milk provided as food, when he reached the food-box, and his actual average speed of running per unit distance. And on a basis of these figures, she divided her animals into a hunger-driven group, and an activity-driven group. That is, for one group she assumed that the food (milk) in the goal-box was

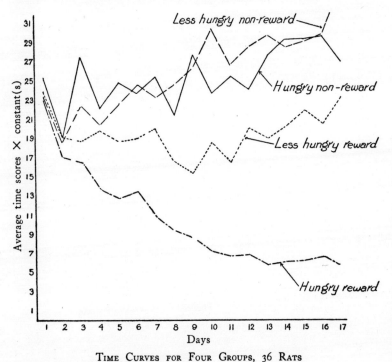

TIME CURVES FOR FOUR GROUPS, 36 RATS

FIGURE 20 [35]

relatively strongly demanded; while for the other group to cover distance (i.e., to explore) was more strongly demanded. And when she compared the results for these two groups of animals, she found that the former eliminated blinds more readily, i.e., went more directly to the food-box than did the latter. In other words, since the food was more demanded for the hunger-driven rats than it was for the activity-driven rats, the former group

[35] *Op. cit.*, p. 247.

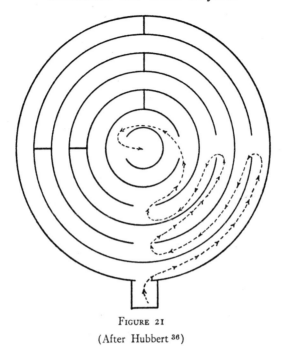

FIGURE 21

(After Hubbert [36])

made a better performance in terms of getting to the food-box, i.e., in eliminating blinds, than did the latter group.

Another experiment to be cited under this same head is that of Tolman, Honzik and Robinson.[37] They ran hungry rats and less hungry rats, under reward conditions, in the special mazes, shown in FIGURES 22 and 23. The conditions of hunger and less hunger were controlled in the same manner as that described above, p. 60, for the experiment of Tolman and Honzik. These special mazes each presented a long blind contrasted with a short one. And the experimenters found, as did Tolman and Honzik for the multiple T-maze, that counting both types of blind together the very hungry rats learn sooner than the less hungry rats. They also found a significant further point. It appeared that the hungry rats tended to eliminate the long blinds before, or at least as soon

[36] H. B. Hubbert, Time versus distance in learning, *J. Anim. Behav.*, 1914, **4**, 62. The dotted line shows the correct path.

[37] E. C. Tolman, C. H. Honzik, and E. W. Robinson, The effect of degrees of hunger upon the order of elimination of long and short blinds, *Univ. Calif. Publ. Psychol.*, 1930, **4**, 189-202.

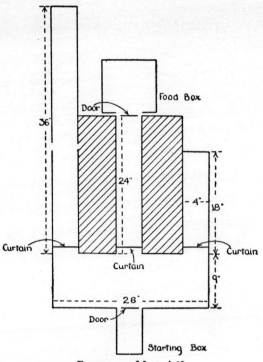

FIGURE 22   MAZE A [38]

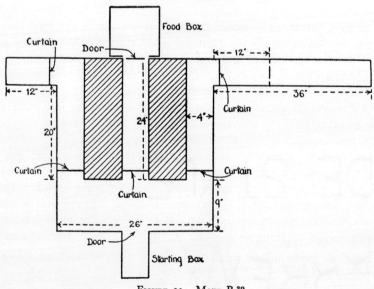

FIGURE 23   MAZE B [39]

[38] *Op. cit.*, p. 190.   [39] *Op. cit.*, p. 196.

as, they did the short ones; whereas with the less hungry rats
a reverse tendency held; these latter tended to eliminate the short
blinds before they did the long blinds. The results are shown by
the curves of Figures 24 and 25. And this outcome suggests the
further conclusion that when the food at the exit-box is less
demanded (as a result of less hunger), then *long* blinds become
peculiarly attractive. They become in and of themselves de-

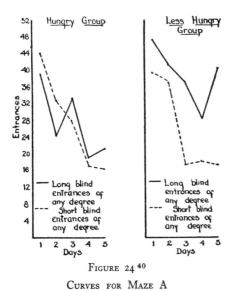

FIGURE 24 [40]

CURVES FOR MAZE A

manded, given a motive which is now probably more nearly that
of mere explorativeness.

That mere explorativeness per se is a drive and that a maze
structure which is conducive to exploration can be really demanded is suggested by the experiments of Dashiell and of Nissen. Dashiell provided his rats with a checkerboard sort of maze
such as is shown below in Figure 26. Even "just fed" rats had
a considerable tendency to explore it. If our above hypothesis
be correct, and if the alleys had had some legs longer than others,
such "fed" rats should have gone particularly into the longer
legs; whereas hungry rats would soon have eliminated these
longer legs.

[40] *Op. cit.*, p. 194.

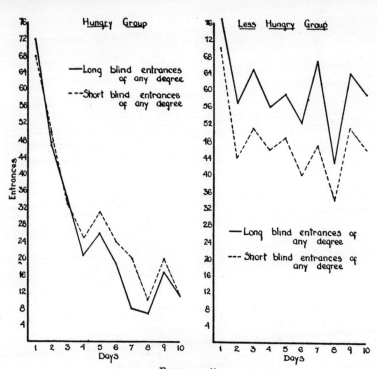

FIGURE 25 [41]

CURVES FOR MAZE B

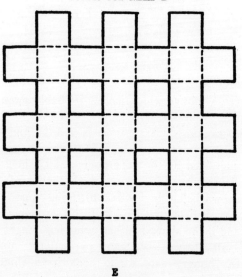

E

FIGURE 26 [42]

(After Dashiell [43])

[41] *Op. cit.*, p. 199.   [42] *Op. cit.*, p. 206.
[43] J. F. Dashiell, A quantitative demonstration of animal drive, *J. Comp. Psychol.*, 1925, **5**, 205-208.

66

Nissen [44] used the opportunity to explore this Dashiell checkerboard as the reward for crossing the electric grill in the obstruction box (see above, p. 47, note 11), and found that non-hungry, non-thirsty and non-sexually-excited males will cross such a grill to reach such an exploration opportunity with greater readiness than they will to reach a small empty box.

7. Goal-Object Constant but Physiological Drive Changed

The experiment we here have in mind is that of Szymanski.[45] Using a very simple maze, he trained a single female to go through the maze in order to reach her litter. And he discovered that, when her young became too old for nursing, her speed and accuracy of threading the maze became decidedly less. From about the fortieth day on, the performance curves rose again. In other words, here is an experiment in which the animal was provided always with one and the same goal-object (litter in exit-box) but in which the degree of physiological drive (need to nurse young) changed. With relatively strong nursing-need the litter was strongly demanded; with a relatively slight nursing-need it was but slightly demanded. And corresponding to these differences in the demand the maze performance improved and degenerated.

8. Summary as to Demand

We may now briefly summarize all the foregoing.

(1) It appears that, given one and the same physiological drive, certain goal-objects, when provided at the end of the maze, produce more efficient maze-performance than do others. And this leads us to the assumption of a variable to be designated *the demand for the goal-object*. More specifically, the facts which lead to this concept of demand are: (a) If different groups of animals, but with the same physiological drive, are run with different goal-objects, the groups run with certain goal-objects

---

[44] H. W. Nissen, A study of exploratory behavior in the white rat by means of the obstruction method, *J. Genet. Psychol.*, 1930, **37**, 361-376.

[45] J. S. Szymanski, Versuche über die Wirkung der Faktoren, die als Antrieb zum Erlernen einer Handlung dienen können, *Pflüg. Arch. f. d. ges. Physiol.*, 1918, **171**, 374-385.

learn faster than the others. (b) If a relatively "good" goal-object be substituted during the course of learning for a relatively "poor" goal-object, the rat's performance shows a sudden improvement. (c) Conversely, if a "bad" goal-object be substituted during the course of learning for a "good" one, the animal's performance shows a sudden degeneration. (d) If an animal be presented with alternative routes to two different goal-objects, one "better" than the other, he will select more frequently the path leading to the "better" goal-object. It is all such facts which, combined together, lead to our assumption of an immanent determinant to be called the demand for the specific goal-object.

(2) It appears further, however, that once having assumed such differences in demand, it turns out that these differences are dependent not upon the characters of the goal-objects per se but rather upon their characters with reference to conditions of physiological drive. The further facts which bring out this additional feature are: (a) If different groups of animals are run with the same goal-object but with different degrees or types of physiological drive, the performance improves faster for one degree or type of drive than for another. (b) And some ordinarily merely auxiliary goal-objects, such as the mere chance for exploration, may under certain drive conditions become relatively strongly demanded in and of themselves. (c) Finally, if during the course of the experiment the drive be changed from strong to weak, the demand for the given goal-object will change from strong to weak and the performance correspondingly will degenerate.

REFERENCES

Blodgett, H. C., The effect of the introduction of reward upon the maze performance of rats. *Univ. Calif. Publ. Psychol.*, 1929, **4**, 113-134.

Bruce, R. H., The effect of removal of reward on the maze performance of rats. *Univ. Calif. Publ. Psychol.*, 1930, **4**, 203-214.

Dashiell, J. F., A quantitative demonstration of animal drive. *J. Comp. Psychol.*, 1925, **5**, 205-208.

Elliott, M. H., The effect of change of reward on the maze performance of rats. *Univ. Calif. Publ. Psychol.*, 1928, **4**, 19-30.

——————, The effect of appropriateness of reward and of complex incentives on maze performance. *Univ. Calif. Publ. Psychol.*, 1929, **4**, 91-98.

Elliott, M. H., Some determining factors in maze performance. *Amer. J. Psychol.*, 1930, **42**, 315-317.

Grindley, G. C., Experiments on the influence of the amount of reward on learning in young chickens. *Brit. J. Psychol.*, Gen. Sect., 1929, **20**, 173-180.

Hamilton, E. L., The effect of delayed incentive on the hunger drive in the white rat. *Genet. Psychol. Monog.*, 1929, **5**, No. 2.

Holden, F., A study of the effect of starvation upon behavior by means of the obstruction method. *Comp. Psychol. Monog.*, 1926, **3**, No. 17.

Hubbert, H. B., Time versus distance in learning. *J. Anim. Behav.*, 1914, **4**, 60-69.

Jenkins, M., The effect of segregation on the sex behavior of the white rat as measured by the obstruction method. *Genet. Psychol. Monog.*, 1928, **3**, No. 6.

Jenkins, T. N., Warner, L. H., and Warden, C. J., Standard apparatus for the study of animal motivation. *J. Comp. Psychol.*, 1926, **6**, 361-382.

Lewin, K., Die Auswirkung von Umweltkräfter. *Proc. Ninth Internat. Cong. Psychol.* (Princeton, Psychol. Rev. Co., 1930), 286-288.

McGillivray, M. E., and Stone, C. P., The incentive value of food and escape from water for albino rats forming the light discrimination habit. *J. Comp. Psychol.*, 1931, **11**, 319-324.

Moss, F. A., A study of animal drives. *J. Exper. Psychol.*, 1924, **7**, 165-185.

Nissen, H. W., The effects of gonadectomy, vasectomy, and injections of placental and orchic extracts on the sex behavior of the white rat. *Genet. Psychol. Monog.*, 1929, **5**, No. 6.

—————, A study of exploratory behavior in the white rat by means of the obstruction method. *J. Genet. Psychol.*, 1930, **37**, 361-376.

—————, A study of maternal behavior in the white rat by means of the obstruction method. *J. Genet. Psychol.*, 1930, **37**, 377-393.

Sharp, W. L., Disintegrative effects of continuous running and removal of the food incentive upon a maze habit of albino rats. *J. Comp. Psychol.*, 1929, **9**, 405-423.

Simmons, R., The relative effectiveness of certain incentives in animal learning. *Comp. Psychol. Monog.*, 1924, **2**, No. 7.

Stone, C. P., and Nyswander, D. B., Reliability of rat learning scores from the multiple-T maze as determined by four different methods. *J. Genet. Psychol.*, 1927, **34**, 497-524.

Szymanski, J. S., Versuche über die Wirkung der Factoren, die als Antrieb zum Erlernen einer Handlung dienen können. *Pflüg. Arch. f. d. ges. Physiol.*, 1918, **171**, 374-385.

Tolman, E. C., and Nyswander, D. B., The reliability and validity of maze-measures for rats. *J. Comp. Psychol.*, 1927, **7**, 425-460.

Tolman, E. C., Honzik, C. H., and Robinson, E. W., The effect of degrees of hunger upon the order of elimination of long and short blinds. *Univ. Calif. Publ. Psychol.*, 1930, **4**, 189-202.

Tolman, E. C., and Honzik, C. H., Degrees of hunger, reward and non-reward, and maze-learning in rats. *Univ. Calif. Publ. Psychol.*, 1930, **4**, 241-256.

————— and —————, Introduction and removal of reward, and maze performance in rats. *Univ. Calif. Publ. Psychol.*, 1930, **4**, 257-275.

Tryon, R. C., Studies of individual differences in maze ability. I. The measurement of the reliability of individual differences. *J. Comp. Psychol.*, 1930, **11**, 145-170.

—————, Individual differences in maze ability. II. The determination of individual differences by age, weight, sex and pigmentation. *J. Comp. Psychol.*, 1931, **12**, 1-22.

—————, Individual differences in maze ability. III. The community of function between two maze abilities. *J. Comp. Psychol.*, 1931, **12**, 95-116.

Tsai, L. S., The relative strength of sex and hunger motives in the albino rat. *J. Comp. Psychol.*, 1925, **5**, 407-415.

Warden, C. J., *Animal Motivation, Experimental Studies on the Albino Rat* (New York, Columbia Univ. Press, 1931).

Warden, C. J., and Haas, E. L., The effect of short intervals of delay in feeding upon speed of maze-learning. *J. Comp. Psychol.*, 1927, **7**, 107-116.

Warden, C. J., and Nissen, H. W., An experimental analysis of the obstruction method of measuring animal drives. *J. Comp. Psychol.*, 1928, **8**, 325-342.

Warden, C. J., and Warner, L. H., The development of a standardized animal maze. *Arch. Psychol.*, 1927, **14**, No. 92.

Warner, L. H., A study of sex behavior in the white rat by means of the obstruction method. *Comp. Psychol. Monog.*, 1927, **4**, No. 22.

—————, A study of hunger behavior in the white rat by means of the obstruction method: a comparison of sex and hunger behavior. *J. Comp. Psychol.*, 1928, **8**, 273-299.

—————, A study of thirst behavior in the white rat by means of the obstruction method. *J. Genet. Psychol.*, 1928, **35**, 178-192.

Washburn, M. F., Hunger and speed of running as factors in maze learning in mice. *J. Comp. Psychol.*, 1926, **6**, 181-187.

Watson, J. B., The effect of delayed feeding upon learning. *Psychobiol.*, 1917, **1**, 51-60.

Williams, K. A., The reward value of a conditioned stimulus. *Univ. Calif. Publ. Psychol.*, 1929, **4**, 31-55.

Chapter IV

EXPECTATIONS OF GOAL-OBJECTS AND MEANS-OBJECTS

1. Cognitive Expectation of Goal-Object

IT has been shown that different types of goal-object, given one and the same physiological drive, are demanded with different strengths. But it must now also be pointed out that such differences in demand can, to use the vernacular, 'get in their licks' only by virtue of some sort of accompanying "cognitive expectations" as to the character of such coming goal-objects. Thus if (as in the experiments cited in the last chapter) a change be made from a "good" reward to a "poor" one, or *vice versa*, it seems obvious that this change can induce a corresponding change in behavior only after the new reward has had a chance to be experienced one or more times—only after, that is, it has had a chance to induce a new cognitive expectation. The rats must have experienced the new "better" or "worse" reward for one or more times, before their behavior can change so as to become appropriate to it. They must have had a chance to build up a "cognitive expectation" for this new reward with its greater or less satisfactoriness for the given demand.

Let us turn now to the specific experiments which justify this concept of an immediate, immanent, cognitive expectation as to the coming goal.

2. Change in Drive with Corresponding Change in Goal-Object

We cite first another experiment of Elliott's.[1] In this experiment a group of rats ran for the first nine days (one trial a day) under the drive of thirst, with water as the goal-object provided

[1] M. H. Elliott, The effect of change of "drive" on maze performance, *Univ. Calif. Publ. in Psychol.*, 1929, **4**, 185-188.

in the exit-box. On the tenth day, their drive was changed from thirst to hunger and simultaneously the provided goal-object was changed from water to food.[2] On the tenth day, i.e., the day of the change, when they were for the *first* time hungry and before they had as yet found food, their error and time curves went up. (See "Experimental Groups," FIGURES 27 and 28.) (The

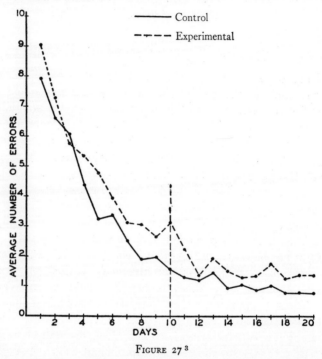

FIGURE 27 [3]

control groups were kept thirsty and received water throughout the whole of training.) On the next day, however, their curves dropped again to the previous level, and continued from then on as if nothing had happened.

In other words, on the first day of the change, when the animals were for the first time hungry, and before they had as yet experienced food in the maze, though they had experienced water, their behavior was apparently directed, to some extent, by something to be designated as the "old" cognitive expectation of water.

[2] The same 14-unit multiple T-maze shown in FIGURE 4 was used.
[3] *Op. cit.*, p. 186.

But water is not so satisfactory, so demanded a goal, given hunger, as was the old goal of food. Hence there appeared on this day some disruption in the performance. Upon getting to the goal-box at the end of this day, however, the rats actually found not water, as they had expected, but food. And *one* experience of this new goal-object was, it seems, enough to change their ex-

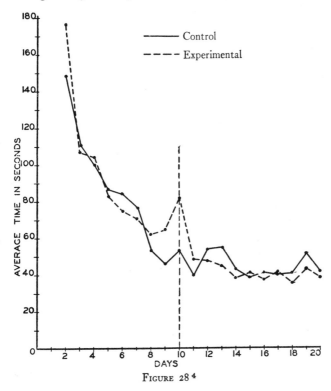

FIGURE 28 [4]

pectation to the new one of food. For, on the next subsequent day, their behavior dropped to the normal level. That is, the rats again now expected a goal satisfactory to their new drive.

3. Drive Constant but Goal-Object Changed to One Less Demanded

It is to be noted now that all the experiments cited in Chapter III, in which there was a change from a goal with a greater demand to one with a less demand also gave evidences of such carryings-over of preceding expectations.

For example, consider again Elliott's experiment (see above, pp. 44, 45, 56) in which, after the rats had practically learned the maze, they were changed from bran mash as goal to sunflower seed as goal. On the trials immediately after this change, Elliott observed a disrupted, searching sort of behavior. He writes:

"The change in performance appears to be more than a mere temporary disturbance, since it increases rather than decreases during the course of six days. On the day of the change of reward, the tenth day, the animals *did not eat steadily while in the food-box but divided their time between eating and random searching.*" [5]

The point we would make is that such "searching," i.e., disruption, is to be taken as the empirical evidence for, and definition of, an immanent expectation of the previously obtained bran mash. The justification for taking it as such evidence and definition lies, we would assert, in two further empirical features of the situation undoubtedly to be discovered. It would, that is, undoubtedly be discovered further: (a) that there was a definite range of goal-object qualities, i.e., those of bran mash, or of foods so closely similar to such mash that the rat could not distinguish them from the latter, which would lead to no such disruption as long as they were found at the exit-box. And it would undoubtedly also be found (b) that, even when the new goal was at first distinguishable and did at first cause disruption, such a disruption would after enough experiences disappear. That is, it would undoubtedly be found that the behavior was *docile* with respect to the new goal-object. The rats would never, perhaps, run as well for the new goal, if it were less desirable, as they did for the old, but the disruption in their behavior, *qua* disruption, would disappear.

4. Experiments with Monkeys

It may be noted, now, that this disruption phenomenon (which thus seems to have been demonstrated with fair certainty in the rat) was earlier shown by Tinklepaugh with overpowering con-

[5] M. H. Elliott, The effect of change of reward on the maze performance of rats, *Univ. Calif. Publ. Psychol.*, 1928, **4**, 23. (Italics ours.)

vincingness in the monkey.[6] In some experiments to test the "delayed reaction" capacities of monkeys, Tinklepaugh used the so-called "direct" method of testing for the animal's ability to choose correctly after delay.[7] That is, while the monkey was looking, the experimenter placed food under one of two containers. After a certain predetermined delay, the monkey was allowed to come forward and choose, if he could, the container under which he had "seen" the food placed. But the feature which is the one of interest to us here consisted in Tinklepaugh's further "substitution" procedure. In this procedure, introduced only occasionally, he would substitute behind a screen (which during the delay was always put up between the monkey and the containers, whether a substitution was to be made or not) a different food from the one the animal had originally seen hidden. In such cases, when the substitution had been made from a more demanded type to a less demanded type of food, for example from banana to lettuce, the monkey upon finding the unexpected less demanded food exhibited a "surprised hunting behavior." We quote Tinklepaugh's description of a typical instance:

"With the same setting as before, the experimenter displays a piece of banana, lowers the board and places the banana under one of the cups. The board is then raised, and working behind it, with his hands hidden from the view of the monkey, *the experimenter takes the banana out and deposits a piece of lettuce in its place.* After the delay, the monkey is told to 'come get the food.' She jumps down from the chair, rushes to the proper container and picks it up. She extends her hand to seize the food. But her hand drops to the floor without touching it. She looks at the lettuce but (unless very hungry) does not touch it. She looks around the cup and behind the board. She stands up and looks under and around her. She picks the cup up and examines it thoroughly inside and out. She has on occasion turned toward observers present in the room and shrieked at them in apparent anger. After several seconds spent searching, she gives a glance toward the other cup, which she has been taught not to look into, and then walks off to a nearby window. The lettuce is left untouched on the floor."[8]

[6] O. L. Tinklepaugh, An experimental study of representative factors in monkeys, *J. Comp. Psychol.*, 1928, **8**, 197-236. Indeed the experiment of changing from bran mash to sunflower seed was perhaps first suggested to Elliott by these experiments of Tinklepaugh's.

[7] For a further discussion of what is tested by the "delayed reaction" experiment, see below, Chapter X, pp. 154 ff.

[8] O. L. Tinklepaugh, *ibid.*, p. 224. Striking reproductions from moving pictures of this behavior are also presented in the article.

Or, in other words, the monkey, upon finding the unexpected, less demanded food, showed "disruption" as did the rat—only in the case of the monkey, this behavior exhibited lineaments more amusingly human.

5. Disruption Not Yet Demonstrated for Changes in Reverse Direction

A further point must, however, be emphasized. Both for the monkeys and for the rats, such disruptions have, *as yet,* been observed *only when the change was from a more demanded to a less demanded goal-object*. No overt disruptions have, that is, been observed in either species when there was a change *from a less demanded to a more demanded goal*. Neither Elliott nor Tinklepaugh detected any evidences of overt "surprise" when a more desirable goal was substituted for a less desirable. In all such cases, the animals simply ate the new food immediately and without ado. It seems quite possible, however, that with more refined methods for observing, e.g., by the use of a moving-picture camera, or the like, some sort of a "surprise" response such, perhaps, as a startled speeding-up in the behavior, might be detected even in these latter cases. And, in fact, we shall assume that such would indeed be the case. We shall suppose, in general, that in behavior there is always immanent the expectation of some more or less specific type of goal-object. If such type of goal-object be not found, whether it be because a better, a worse, or merely a different, goal-object has been substituted for it, then the animal's behavior will show some sort of disruption such as hunting, startled speeding-up, or what not. The appearance of such disruption will define the fact of an immanent expectation of the previous type of goal-object, i.e., the type of goal-object which, as long as it is present, does not cause disruption.

6. "Perceptual" vs. "Memorial" Expectations

In the experiments described above, such immanent expectations are to be characterized further as *"memories"* (or, more technically, mnemonizations. [See Glossary.]) That is, the conditions which led to the immanent expectations were preceding experiences with a given type of goal-object. They were all cases in which the given goal-object had, as such, already been experienced. In the case of the rat experiments, this preceding experience was in a preceding trial or trials. In the case of the monkey experiments, it was at the time of the just preceding pantomime of "hiding the food" which had been enacted by the experimenter.

It seems reasonable to suppose, however, that "perceptual" expectations (as well as "memorial" ones) are possible. Suppose, for example, that a maze is arranged with wire sides, or in the form of an elevated track with no sides at all, so that the stimuli coming from the goal can reach the rat directly during the course of running itself. In such a case, these continuously and concurrently present goal-stimuli should also evoke an immanent expectation; [9] and, in such a case, this immanent expectation would be defined as a "perception." A definite proof of the presence and operation of such a perceptual expectation would appear in experiments which by some legerdemain caused the goal-object actually to be changed unknown to the animal during the course of a given trial, so that upon reaching the goal-box he would, in spite of all the preceding stimuli, find a goal different from one normally corresponding to such stimuli. If, in such legerdemain experiments, he, similarly, showed "disruption" and "hunting," on reaching the goal-box, this would be evidence, we would say, of a "perceptual" expectation which had led him to expect the goal-object, normally corresponding to the preceding stimuli. Particularly would this be so, if such disruption proved docile and disappeared as a result of repeated experiences of the new relation between the actual goal-object and the initial stimuli.

7.   Memorial Expectations of Immediate Maze Characters

Thus far, only such experiments have been considered as testify to the presence and character of immediate cognitive expectations relative to goal-objects. Now we wish to consider some

[9] A maze of the elevated track variety has recently been worked out and standardized by Miles.

See W. R. Miles, The narrow-path elevated maze for studying rats, *Proc. Soc. Exper. Biol. and Med.*, 1927, **24**, 454-456.

Also W. R. Miles, The comparative learning of rats on elevated and alley mazes of the same pattern, *J. Comp. Psychol.*, 1930, **10**, 237-261

experiments which seem to testify to the presence as well of immanent cognitive expectations as to means-objects, i.e., as to the more immediate alley-features themselves.

Carr and Watson. The first to be cited are the classical experiments of Carr and Watson.[10] Carr and Watson taught rats a Hampton Court maze. After the animals were running this with considerable speed and accuracy, the experimenter shortened a given alley between trials. And then, on the trial after this change, they found that several of their rats ran "kerplunk" into the end of the new shortened alley. The animals behaved, that is, as if the original length of the alley were still present. And, in the immediately succeeding trials, their behavior also showed a "disruption" similar to that exhibited in the experiments cited above in which the goal-object was changed.

In other cases, the experimenters lengthened an alley between trials, and several rats, upon the first trial after the change, tried to turn at the old place. And, again, in the succeeding trials, their behavior showed "disruption," followed by subsequent learning.

We conclude then that the going-off of the original manner of running, i.e., speed, pattern of turning, etc., involved immanent expectations that the coming alleys were of such and such lengths and had such and such patterns of turning.

It appears, again, however, that the exact definition of that which was thus expected ("remembered") in any such case would finally be statable only by means of a long series of experiments. It would have to be discovered just what changes in all the various alley-characters—their lengths, their widths, etc.— could be made without causing upsets, and just what changes could not so be made. And the final definition of that which was expected would then be expressible in terms of whatever was common to all such actual lengths, widths, etc., as could thus be indifferently substituted without causing disruption, as contrasted with all those others which could not thus be substituted.

Elliott. A second set of experiments to be reported are some as yet unpublished experiments of M. H. Elliott's.[11] In these

[10] H. Carr and J. B. Watson, Orientation in the white rat, *J. Comp. Neurol. & Psychol.*, 1908, **18**, 27-44.

[11] These were some preliminary experiments performed at the University of California during the years 1926-1927. The experiments were never completely finished but the results here reported were indicated. I am indebted to Dr. Elliott for permission to cite them now.

he examined in a simple two-way maze similar to that used by Bruce (see FIGURE 15 above, Chapter III, p. 56) the effect of changing, between trials, certain of the purely sensory features of the paths. At points around the corner from the choice point, he introduced new types of maze-wall, leaving all the actual dimensions unchanged, or he put in unusual odors. And he found that the animals were much upset upon first reaching these new sensory conditions—and this in spite of the fact that the actual dimensions remained unchanged. The behavior of the rats in the subsequent trials showed disruption and extra "exploring," but finally they readjusted.

Again, it is obvious that an exact definition of the immanent expectations, thus demonstrated, could be achieved only by a whole series of experiments, in which many such sensory changes were made, and it was discovered just which ones would cause disruption and which ones would not.

Macfarlane. The last experiment to be cited, as similarly indicating and defining immanent expectations of immediate maze-features, is one by Macfarlane.[12] Macfarlane taught his rats to swim a maze of the design shown in FIGURE 29 [13] and then by introducing a submerged bottom an inch below the surface caused them to wade the maze instead. Similarly, a second group were taught first to wade the maze and then suddenly were made to swim it. (The alleys as far as Y—see FIGURE 29—were always the same. That is, they had no false bottom, and always had to be swum whichever the set-up for the rest of the maze.) In general, the behavior of the rats showed an upset (disruption) when they first met the new condition. Particularly was this evident for the animals changed from swimming to wading. Macfarlane writes:

"When the animal begins the test run and finds himself, at the end of alley 5, with a floor to stand on, he stands on it. This

---

[12] D. A. Macfarlane, The rôle of kinesthesis in maze learning, *Univ. Calif. Publ. Psychol.*, 1930, **4**, 277-305.

[13] This type of maze is probably not so good for giving consistent and reliable results as either the Warden Y-maze or the Stone-Blodgett T-maze. (See above, Chapter III.) It has, however, the practical convenience of greater compactness. This was important in the Macfarlane experiment in that the whole maze had to be set in a tank of water.

For a general historical discussion on mazes of various shapes and types, see C. H. Warden and L. H. Warner, The development of a standardized animal maze, *Arch. Psychol.*, 1927, **15**, No. 92.

gives him an opportunity to inspect the features of the new situation, an opportunity of which all the animals availed themselves. They halted, sniffed, stood upright, tested the strength of the

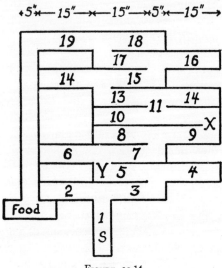

FIGURE 29 [14]

wire mesh above them and *then*—travelled down the correct alley. The entire run, for the most part, was made in this hesitant manner." [15]

Such hesitations and slight tendencies to make errors disappeared, however, in the very next trial. Again, it appears that the change in the maze-features caused a disruption, but that this disruption disappeared upon further experiences. This experiment testifies, therefore, to an immanent (memorial) expectation of the preceding type of "alley-filling," i.e., either open water or submerged floor.[16]

[14] *Op. cit.*, p. 281.
[15] *Op. cit.*, p. 285 f.
[16] It may be noted, incidentally, that the results of this experiment were, on other counts, such as to prove surprising to anyone convinced of the old kinesthetic doctrine of maze learning. (See, for example, Watson, *Behavior, An Introduction to Comparative Psychology* [New York, Henry Holt and Company, 1914], Ch. VII). The kinesthetic impulses received as a result of wading must have been quite different in quality, and very different in quantity, from those received from swimming and *vice versa*, and yet the change from the one condition to the other, although it caused evident disruption, surprise, etc., did not cause any considerable increase in the error scores, per se. The rats still

8. Perceptual Expectations of Means-Objects

Earlier in the chapter, it was suggested that, in order to demonstrate perceptual expectations of goal-objects, a maze might be used which had wire sides or no sides at all, so that the animal could "see" or, perhaps, "smell" the goal-object *throughout* the entire course of the maze. With such an arrangement, the stimuli coming from the goal-object would, during the given trial itself, evoke an expectation as to the character of this goal-object. That is, the fact of such a perceptual expectation would be demonstrated, if during the course of the given trial the actual goal-object could by some legerdemain be made other than that "normally" indicated, and if the rat, upon reaching this new goal-object, showed disruption in his behavior. We suggest, now, that similar experiments could be carried out to demonstrate perceptual expectations of *means-objects*. That is, such perceptual expectations would be demonstrated if conjuror's tricks were introduced whereby the relations between the stimuli and their immediate "normal" "implications" were changed and, if, further, the behavior of the rats upon reaching these new "unexpected" maze-features, showed upset and disruption.

The only actual experiments of such a sort of which we are aware are the classical experiments on the space-perceptions of human beings by Stratton [17] and their recent verification and amplification by Ewert.[18] Unfortunately, however, for our barbarian point of view, both of these researches were carried out not with rats but with human beings, so we cannot be absolutely sure that the same findings would have held for the rodents. It appears reasonable, however, to suppose that in principle the

---

"knew" where to go, although at first their behavior was obviously upset (disrupted) at finding free water instead of submerged bottom, or *vice versa*.

See also in connection with the present argument an investigation similar to that by Carr and Watson, which has appeared since the above was written: R. Hamill, Sequence of turns versus distances as essential pattern-elements in the maze problem, *J. Comp. Psychol.*, 1931, **2**, 367-382.

[17] G. M. Stratton, Some preliminary experiments on vision without inversion of the retinal image, *Psychol. Rev.*, 1896, **3**, 611-617; Upright vision and the retinal image, *ibid.*, 1897, **4**, 182-187; Vision without inversion of the retinal image, *ibid.*, 1897, **4**, 341-360, 463-481.

[18] P. H. Ewert, A study of the effect of inverted retinal stimulation upon spatially coördinated behavior, *Genet. Psychol. Monog.*, 1930, **7**, Nos. 3 & 4; cf. his bibliography, pp. 358 ff.

outcomes would have been similar. Stratton tried the effect of wearing during his waking hours, for a period of eight days, specially designed prismatic glasses which inverted his visual field in the vertical plane. This at first caused complete "disruption." Most of his normal motor responses were tremendously interfered with. With the passage of time, however, this interference became less and less. And eventually at the end of the eight days, he was performing, as far as his motor responses went, quite normally. The original disruption and the subsequent readjustment testified, that is, to the fact of initial immanent expectations as to the up-and-downness of immediate means-objects. And these initial expectations had to give way to new ones. Ewert's experiments have, from the present point of view, merely amplified and extended this technique and its results.

Turning now to rats, our assumption is that for them also every little act, such as a group of steps this way rather than that, a set of whisker explorations, an investigatory rising upon the hind legs, a twisting of the body to the right, contains immanent within itself *perceptual* expectations to such effect as: "here is an open space to step into"; "there is a wall to run the whiskers along"; "yonder is a crevice to be nosed into"; and "here is a corner to turn around in." And the empirical demonstration of such immediate perceptual expectations would be found by means of conjuror's tricks—e.g., by the substituting of false bottoms, distorting mirrors, and the like (e.g., Stratton's prisms) which would provide the animal with abnormal relations between the stimuli and these results. The rats would, that is, we suppose, then run "amuck"—or at any rate, show disruption and "surprise"—but would later readjust, i.e., show docility relative to the new implications. And this double outcome would again demonstrate and define the fact of corresponding initial, immanent (and in this case perceptual) expectations.

REFERENCES

Carr, H., and Watson, J. B., Orientation in the white rat. *J. Comp. Neur. & Psychol.*, 1908, **18**, 27-44.
Elliott, M. H., The effect of change of reward on the maze performance of rats. *Univ. Calif. Publ. Psychol.*, 1928, **4**, 19-30.
————, The effect of change of "drive" on maze performance. *Univ. Calif. Publ. Psychol.*, 1929, **4**, 185-188.

Ewert, P. H., A study of the effect of inverted retinal stimulation upon spatially co-ordinated behavior. *Genet. Psychol. Monog.*, 1930, **7**, Nos. 3 & 4.

Hamill, R., Sequence of turns versus distances as essential pattern-elements in the maze problem. *J. Comp. Psychol.*, 1931, **11**, 367-382.

Macfarlane, D. A., The rôle of kinesthesis in maze learning. *Univ. Calif. Publ. Psychol.*, 1930, **4**, 277-305.

Miles, W. R., The narrow-path elevated maze for studying rats. *Proc. Soc. Exper. Biol. & Med.*, 1927, **24**, 454-456.

——————, The comparative learning of rats on elevated and alley mazes of the same pattern. *J. Comp. Psychol.*, 1930, **10**, 237-261.

Stratton, G. M., Some preliminary experiments on vision without inversion of the retinal image. *Psychol. Rev.* 1896, **3**, 611-617.

——————, Upright vision and the retinal image. *Psychol. Rev.*, 1897, **4**, 182-187.

——————, Vision without inversion of the retinal image. *Psychol. Rev.*, 1897, **4**, 341-360; 463-481.

Tinklepaugh, O. L., An experimental study of representative factors in monkeys. *J. Comp. Psychol.*, 1928, **8**, 197-236.

Warden, C. H. and Warner, L. H., The development of a standardized animal maze. *Arch. Psychol.*, 1927, **15**, No. 92.

Watson, J. B., *Behavior, an Introduction to Comparative Psychology* (New York, Henry Holt and Company, 1914).

Chapter V

DISCRIMINANDA AND MANIPULANDA

1. Expectations Are Forward-pointing

IT is time now to make explicit a feature merely implicit in the preceding discussion. Expectations, those of means-objects as well as those of goal-objects, those to be called perceptions as well as those to be called memories, are always forward-pointing. This fact of their forward-pointingness is relatively obvious for expectations of goal-objects. For here the stimuli and the resultant expectations which they release quite evidently precede the later goal-object encounters, which verify or fail to verify such expectations. The expectations in such cases very evidently point forward to the later moments of goal-object encounter and verification. But a similar situation really likewise obtains for expectations of immediate means-objects. In these latter cases also, the perception or memory, as an expectation, is a prior "setting" of the behavior for such subsequent encounter as: "here an opening"; "there a wall"; "here a smellable crevice"; and the like. Again, the actual encounter which verifies or fails to verify that "this is an opening, a wall, or a crevice," is a temporally separate and later event. It is an event which occurs after the stimuli and the immanent expectations which these stimuli release. The moment of stimulation, and its accompanying release of an expectation, and the later moment of environmental encounter of or commerce with the given means-object which verifies or fails to verify this expectation, are always, both temporally and qualitatively, *two*. A moment of stimulation is prior in time to, and qualitatively other than, a direct encounter or commerce-with. That which "sets" a cognitive expectation is a complex of stimuli; that which verifies or fails to verify it is a resulting commerce with such and such immediate environmental presences or supports.

84

2. Behavior Supports

This statement of the duality of stimulation and verification is but another way of saying that any behavior-act requires not only stimuli to release it, but also, later, more substantial environmental actualities such as *fulcra, media* and *planes*, to *support* it (i.e., verify it, make it possible). Stimuli by themselves are not enough; *supports* also are needed. Behavior cannot go-off *in vacuo*. It requires a complementary "supporting" or "holding-up." The organism, as a result of stimuli, expects that such and such "behavior-supports" are going to be in the environment. A rat cannot "run down an alley" without an actual floor to push his feet against, actual walls to steer between, actual free space ahead to catapult into. And in a discrimination-box, he cannot "choose" the white side from the black without actual whites and blacks continuously to support and verify such a choice. Behavior-acts and their immanent expectations are released by stimuli; but they demand and are sustained by later coming *behavior-supports*.

In parenthesis it may be remarked that this fact that supports, and not merely stimuli, are needed for the actual going-off of any act and are expected by such an act, is a feature about behavior which orthodox psychologies, both stimulus-response psychologies and mentalisms, seem hitherto to have overlooked.

3. Discriminanda and Manipulanda

It is to be noted next that there are at least two sub-classes among "supports." [1] These two sub-classes may be broadly distinguished as "sensory" supports, on the one hand, and "motor" supports, on the other. Thus Elliott's experiments quoted in the previous chapter (pp. 78-79) illustrated primarily expectations of "sensory" supports; whereas those of Carr and Watson and of Macfarlane illustrated expectations of "motor" supports. Elliott's experiments were designed to demonstrate that the rat is set for certain to-come sensory possibilities—e.g., possibilities as to color-discrimination, smell-discrimination, and the like. The Carr and Watson and the Macfarlane experiments were designed, on the other hand, to demonstrate that the rat is set also for

[1] We shall see later that there is also a third sub-class. See next chapter.

certain to-come motor or manipulation possibilities—e.g., possibilities as to distance of running, points and manner of turning, wading *versus* swimming, swimming *versus* wading, and the like.

We propose now the terms *discriminanda* and *manipulanda* for these two varieties of support.[2] In so far as the support features, which are demonstrated as expected and set-for, are the consistent possibilities of such and such sensory affections (discriminations), we shall designate such supports, discriminanda. In so far, on the other hand, as these expected support-features are the possibilities of such and such patterns of motor activity (manipulations), we shall designate them manipulanda.

Actually, of course, in any given case, a rat will be set for, i.e., expect, both discriminanda and manipulanda. Thus in Elliott's experiments the rat obviously was actually set for, not only the immediate maze-parts to "look" and "smell" and "feel" so and so, i.e., discriminanda, but also for them to "be" so and so for the purposes of running, turning, swimming, i.e., manipulanda. And, conversely, in Carr and Watson's and in Macfarlane's experiments, the rat was, of course, actually set for not only the maze-alleys to "be" so and so for running, swimming, and the like, but also for them to "look" and "feel" and "smell" so and so. The one sort of "set" (expectation) can never actually function without the other.

Again, it is important to emphasize, as regards both types of expectation, those for discriminanda as well as those for manipulanda, that stimuli release them. For this means, further, that it is especially necessary in the case of discriminanda not to confuse the immediate momentary *stimuli*, which do the releasing, with the relatively permanent *discriminanda* which function as *supports*.

4. The Definition of Discriminanda

The final definitions of expected discriminanda can, it must now be noted, be determined in the last analysis only by a whole series of experiments. Suppose, for example, we discover that a given behavior seems to be "expecting" the presence of a certain specific color. This behavior, it is found, will, under the given

---

[2] These words are obviously formed on the analogy of the Latin gerundive, to denote things-to-be-discriminated and to-be-manipulated, respectively.

conditions, continue to go off only so long as this specific color proves actually to be there. If on any occasion this specific color fails to be present, the given behavior will, that is, by hypothesis, show disruption; it will give way to some other behavior on the immediately subsequent occasions. To define exactly, however, the expected discriminandum in such a case, we must discover (a) just what other light waves can be interchanged for the original one without causing such disruption, and (b) just what range of other waves cannot be thus substituted.

But these are only the first two steps. For a final and complete definition, we must discover also (c) just in how far, for the given organism, light wave-lengths are generally differentiable one from another. We must discover what Prall [3] has called the "intrinsic orders" of sensory discriminations. We must know what these intrinsic orders are for the specific case of color and for the specific species of animal. We must know, that is, the sort of information which we already know for the average human being, and which is summed up by the familiar color-pyramid.[4]

The color-pyramid is indeed simply a schematic way of representing the whole system of interdifferentiabilities of colors for a normal human being. It indicates that for this average, or normal, human being all light-wave stimulations range themselves into the three main similarity-difference dimensions of hue, chroma (saturation), and tint (lightness or darkness). It also indicates that, within the one dimension of hue, there are the four similarity-difference sub-dimensions of red-to-yellow, yellow-to-green, green-to-blue, and blue-to-red.

Finally, (d), having worked out the nature of the color-pyramid, or it may be some other shape of polyhedron which obtains for the species in question, the last step in the definition will consist in locating the acceptable range of mutually substitutable wave-lengths, as defined by points (a) and (b) upon this polyhedron. The final definition of the expected discriminandum will thus be this range of mutually interchangeable wave-lengths, any one of which may be substituted in the given situation—this range to be characterized further by virtue of its relations of

---

[3] D. W. Prall, Æsthetic Judgment (New York, Thomas Y. Crowell Company, 1929), especially Chapters V to IX.
[4] For a comprehensive description of the color-pyramid see E. B. Titchener, A Textbook of Psychology (New York, The Macmillan Company, 1911), p. 59 f.

similarity and difference as indicated by its position on the total color scheme (polyhedron).

To sum up then, in more general terms, an expected discriminandum is to be defined by the range of sense-characters, any one of which may be substituted in the given situation and support the discrimination behavior in question equally well. But, further, this empirically determined range of such satisfactory or supporting environmental characters must in its turn be defined not in simple physical terms, but rather in terms of that whole system or *intrinsic order* of differentiabilities, which is found to obtain relative to this class of sensory characters for this type of organism. In other words, by means of purely objective discrimination experiments, there is to be worked out for every type of organism sense-polyhedrons (analogous to the color-pyramid for human beings) in each sense mode of the given organism. And an expected discriminandum is always to be defined, in the last analysis, with reference to such a polyhedron or "intrinsic order" of differentiabilities.[5]

5. The Definition of Manipulanda

Turn now to the definition of manipulanda. The release of a behavior-act expects, as we have seen, not only certain present and immediately-to-come sensory supports, discriminanda, but also certain immediately-to-come motor supports, manipulanda. In order to stand, to walk, to climb, to run, to swim, to make noises, an organism expects, and must have, motor supports such as a solid surface to walk on, an actual physical height to climb over, an unobstructed stretch to run through, a liquid to swim in, a gaseous medium to vocalize with.

For the precise definition of such expected manipulanda, the total procedure is, however, relatively arduous. It is similar to that involved in the definition of expected discriminanda. (a) One must discover just what other physical characters besides the given one could be substituted and cause no disruption in the given behavior; (b) one must discover just what others could not thus be substituted; and (c) one must work out a system of correlation between types of physical character and resultant manipulation-possibilities, analogous to that which the sense-

[5] For a further elaboration of this same doctrine, see below Chapter XVI.

polyhedrons summarize as between types of stimulus characters and discrimination-possibilities. One must know, for example, that while a thing of the size and shape and weight, etc., of a chair will, for a man, present manipulation-possibilities such as "to-sit-upon," "to-pick-up-and-use-as-a-weapon," etc., for a rat it will present quite a different set of manipulation-possibilities, those, say, of "to-build-a-nest-in," "to-hide-behind," etc. One must know just what slight changes in physically defined characters will, for the given organism, lead to differences in such manipulation-possibilities. One must work out the whole system of manipulation-possibilities for each type of organism in some sort of a summarizing table or figure. Finally (d) one must interpret and define the acceptable range of mutually substitutable and acceptable manipulanda, which are found in the given case, in terms of their positions in this total table or figure of manipulanda-physical-character correlations—as worked out for the given type of organism.

6. Primary vs. Secondary Qualities

Further, there is to be noted an important interrelationship between discriminanda and manipulanda—an interrelationship which seems historically to have led to considerable philosophical dispute. For it appears that certain types of discriminanda tend to be relatively consistently correlated with certain manipulanda, whereas other types of discriminanda do not tend to be so correlated.

For instance, I am now (in a somewhat erratic fashion) pounding upon my typewriter. And this series of finger movements, behavior-acts, seems to require for its support that it be met by a certain specific complementary stream of tactual and kinesthetic discriminanda. Further, it requires along with these tactual and kinesthetic discriminanda, certain intimately correlated manipulanda, i.e., such and such "resistances" and "distributions" and "locations" of the individual keys. It appears, that is, in this case that the tactual and kinesthetic discriminanda are closely correlated to the accompanying manipulanda. It must be noted further, however, that my typewriter also presents to me, at the same time, certain other discriminanda, e.g., its color, its temperature, and the like. But it appears that these latter, on the

other hand, have no such intimate correlation with the manipulanda of the resistances, distributions and locations of the keys.
The color and temperature may vary and yet, as something for
me to pound, i.e., as such and such a set of manipulanda, the
typewriter can and will remain unchanged. Tactual and kinesthetic discriminanda tend to be closely correlated with manipulanda; color and temperature and odor do not.

But here we descry, do we not, the classical philosophical
distinction between the so-called "primary" and the so-called
"secondary" qualities. The former are, in our terms, discriminanda which tend to be relatively consistently correlated with
specific manipulanda; the latter are discriminanda which do
not tend to be thus correlated. It is to be noted, however, that
the difference is probably one of degree only. The orthodox list
of primary qualities contains those discriminanda whose associations with specific manipulanda are relatively fixed and constant;
while the orthodox list of secondary qualities contains those whose
associations with specific manipulanda are relatively less consistent. Visual and tactual size and shape and number and pressure are pretty uniformly indicative of specific sizes and shapes
and weights as supports for motor-possibilities, i.e., as manipulanda. Colors and temperatures and odors, on the other hand,
are not so uniformly indicative.

But the so-called secondary qualities do often have definite
manipulation indicative-values—at least in specific situations.
Thus, for example, the color is probably the significant cue for
a housewife who needs the manipulanda which define an apple,
and who dives rapidly into box or basket or cooler shelf, half
filled, as it usually is, with a medley of oranges, lemons, apples,
and tissue paper wrappings. In such a case, it very probably is
the distinctive color of the apple which indicates to her quickly
the whereabouts of an apple's manipulanda.

And there is also the opposite fact. The so-called primary qualities themselves do not always have absolutely fixed and invariable
implications—witness our old friend, the "bent stick" half in
water and half out. The difference between primary qualities and
secondary qualities is, therefore, one of degree rather than of
kind. It was easier for God (or the Devil) to arrange it so that
colors and temperatures and tastes could be more easily smeared
on and off surfaces of things than could visual and tactual shapes

and sizes and resistances. But that is the only difference. Discriminanda, whether primary or secondary, always remain discriminanda. Visual and tactual shape and size and resistance, as such, i.e., as pure discriminanda, are no more at one with their associated manipulanda than are color, taste, temperature, and smell. Both sets are merely more or less uniformly associated with their correlates of "sit-on-able-nesses," "pick-up-able-nesses," "step-between-able-nesses," "cut-up-able-nesses," and the like.

7. Discriminanda and Manipulanda Capacities

Finally, in concluding this chapter we must point out that such processes of expectation for discriminanda and manipulanda obviously involve certain capacities on the part of the organism. Discriminanda and manipulanda are behavior-supports which, as we have seen, the organism first expects and then enjoys. And his ability thus to expect and subsequently to enjoy depends, it is obvious, upon certain capacities. First, he must be able to differentiate the given discriminanda and manipulanda in the moments in which the behavior is actually supported by them, i.e., in the moments of their actual enjoyment. It is this sort of capacity which is indicated in the case of the discriminanda by the color-pyramid, and other sense-polyhedrons which obtain for the given organism or species of organism, and in the case of manipulanda by the manipulanda diagrams or tables, when these shall have been worked out. These are the sorts of capacities which are testified to by "threshold" experiments. Many such thresholds have been worked out for human beings in the case of discriminanda. Fewer such discriminanda thresholds, however, have been worked out for the lower animals.[6] And no manipulanda thresholds have been worked for either human beings or for the lower animals.

Secondly, however, the organism must also have the capacity for being endowed with, or for acquiring, the correct expectational relationships (perceptual or memorial) between the given

---

[6] See, however, for the best and most recent work as to visual thresholds in the case of the rat:

K. S. Lashley, The mechanism of vision: I, A method for rapid analysis of pattern-vision in the rat, *J. Genet. Psychol.*, 1930, **37**, 453-460.

———————— The mechanism of vision: II, The influence of cerebral lesions

sets of immediately presented stimuli and the to-be-expected discriminanda and manipulanda. The fact of these capacities in reference to particular types of material have hardly been studied at all. In the case of memory we speak roughly of retentivities. But in the case of perception the problem has hardly been analyzed. We want to know, for example, not only how well an animal can see under normal, standard conditions—i.e., the facts concerning his discriminanda-capacities—but also how well he can *expect* the true color, size, or what not, from given stimuli when the distorting factors of perspective, and the like, enter in.

To sum up, discrimination- and manipulation-capacities involve two sub-features: (a) differentiation- or threshold-capacities and (b) expectational-capacities (perceptive and memorial). And the fact that these two sub-elements are really involved in what we shall hereafter, for convenience, designate merely as discriminanda-capacity and manipulanda-capacity, should be kept in mind in later discussions.

upon the threshold of discrimination for brightness in the rat, *J. Genet. Psychol.*, 1930, **37**, 461-480.

K. S. Lashley, The mechanism of vision: III, The comparative visual acuity of pigmented and albino rats, *J. Genet. Psychol.*, 1930, **37**, 481-484.

See also,

N. L. Munn, Concerning visual form discrimination in the white rat, *J. Genet. Psychol.*, 1929, **36**, 291-300.

——————— Visual pattern discrimination in the white rat, *J. Comp. Psychol.*, 1930, **10**, 145-166.

P. E. Fields, Form discrimination in the white rat, *J. Comp. Psychol.*, 1928, **8**, 143-158.

——————— The white rat's use of visual stimuli in the discrimination of geometrical figures, *J. Comp. Psychol.*, 1929, **9**, 107-122.

——————— Contributions to visual figure discrimination in the white rat, Part I, *J. Comp. Psychol.*, 1931, **11**, 327-348.

——————— Contributions to visual figure discrimination in the white rat, Part II, *J. Comp. Psychol.*, 1931, **11**, 349-366.

REFERENCES

Fields, P. E., Form discrimination in the white rat. *J. Comp. Psychol.*, 1928, 8, 143-158.

——————————, The white rat's use of visual stimuli in the discrimination of geometric figures. *J. Comp. Psychol.*, 1929, 9, 107-122.

——————————, Contributions to visual figure discrimination in the white rat. Part I. *J. Comp. Psychol.*, 1931, 11, 327-348.

Fields, P. E., Contributions to visual figure discrimination in the white rat. Part II. *J. Comp. Psychol.*, 1931, **11**, 349-366.

Lashley, K. S., The mechanism of vision: I. A method for rapid analysis of pattern-vision in the rat. *J. Genet. Psychol.*, 1930, **37**, 453-460.

————, The mechanism of vision: II. The influence of cerebral lesions upon the threshold of discrimination for brightness in the rat. *J. Genet. Psychol.*, 1930, **37**, 461-480.

————, The mechanism of vision: III. The comparative visual acuity of pigmented and albino rats. *J. Genet. Psychol.*, 1930, **37**, 481-484.

Munn, N. L., Concerning visual form discrimination in the white rat. *J. Genet. Psychol.*, 1929, **36**, 291-300.

————, Visual pattern discrimination in the white rat. *J. Comp. Psychol.*, 1930, **10**, 145-166.

Prall, D. W., Æsthetic Judgment (New York, Thomas Y. Crowell Company, 1929).

Titchener, E. B., *A Textbook of Psychology* (New York, The Macmillan Company, 1911).

Chapter VI

EXPECTATIONS OF MEANS-END-RELATIONS

1. Means-End-Readinesses and Means-End-Expectations

IT was pointed out in Chapter II that subordinate demands depend from superordinate ones by virtue of interconnecting means-end-readinesses. Because of such readinesses the organism, when demanding given superordinate goal-objects, is ready to be responsive to, to try to have commerce with, and to demand such and such subordinate goals or means-objects. Such means-end-readinesses arise out of innate endowment and previous experience. By virtue of innate endowment a rat, when subject to the organic excitement of hunger, exhibits the "readiness" to be a satiation-demanding rat. Further, as such a satiation-demanding animal he exhibits also the readiness to be a food-demanding one. And, finally, as a food-demanding one he exhibits also the readiness to be an exploration-demanding one. But, again due to specific past experiences, his general food-demandingness will have become limited and specified and so also will have his general exploration-demandingness. He will have become more ready to eat such types of foods as have been found by him in the past to lead to satiation; and he will also have become more ready for such types of explorable object, e.g., white alleys, right-turning alleys, etc., which in his particular past have led to food. In short, his means-end-readinesses are docile relative to the degree to which the given types of subordinate means-objects have or have not tended, in the long run, to lead to the given demanded superordinate objects. And as thus docile these means-end-readinesses are, we said, cognitive or judgmental. They are of the nature of preliminary "hunches" which the rat brings with him to any new problem. They are means-end "judgments," resulting from innate endowment and previous experience, which he carries around with him as a silent partner wherever he goes.

94

It is to be noted, however, that not only do rats thus come to a specific problem with certain innate and acquired means-end-readinesses—but also, and this is the further feature now to be brought out, they immediately experience qualifications and specifications of these readinesses as a result of the specific concrete concatenations of stimuli which are actually presented. And we suggest that these specifications which thus result from particular stimuli (whether such stimuli be presented all simultaneously as in perception or whether they be presented partly in the past as in memory) are to be designated as specific means-end-expectations. The rat upon being presented with concrete stimuli releases specific and particular means-end-expectations within the frame of the generalized means-end-readinesses which he brings with him.

2. Selectivity—the Evidence of Means-End-Expectations

The hungry and maze-wise rat, when put in a new maze or problem-box will perceive, or after one or more complete runs, remember (i.e., will have an expectation as to) which of the immediately presented features of this specific maze or problem-box are most likely to lead on to the given expected food and which are most likely to lead to it by the shorter routes. And such perceptions, or memories, as to the specific routes, thus called out by the maze-features in hand, we are designating as means-end-expectations. They are expectations that such and such of the immediately presented means-objects (discriminanda and manipulanda complexes) are going to be better or worse for reaching (or avoiding) the given goal-object (discriminanda and manipulanda complex). The experimental definition and evidence of a means-end-expectation is to be found, in other words, in the fact of an animal's selectivity among some array of actually presented means-objects. Such selectivities arise out of the sort of means-end-readinesses which the rat brings with him plus the specific concatenations of presented stimuli and his resulting perceptual and mnemonic expectations of specific means-objects and goal-objects. The selectivities define an expectation as to means-end-relations —an expectation which falls within the frame of the general means-end-readinesses which he has brought with him.

3. Distance and Direction

But let us consider such means-end-expectations in more detail. Two, more specifically defining, characters appear. On the one hand, there is (a) the expectation of what we would call the "distances" presented by the alternative means-objects, and, on the other hand, there is (b) the expectation or assertion of the correlated "directions" of these same means-objects. For in selecting the one instance, or type, of means-object rather than another— in selecting, for example, alleys rather than interstices in the wire covers, or the right-turning alley at a specific point in a maze rather than the left-turning one, or a white alley in a discrimination-box rather than a black alley—the rat seems to be expecting both (a) that the given instance of selected alley will prove relatively "short" as to "distance" and (b) that its character, or more generally what we are calling its "direction," is of a sort to indicate such relative "shortness."

It should be observed that we are here using the terms *distance* and *direction* in a special, somewhat arbitrary sense. By distance we are covering the general situation whereby a given object affords (or does not afford) a relatively "short" way of getting to the demanded goal. And by direction we are meaning not merely differences of spatial pointing, such as right-turning-ness as against left-turning-ness and the like, but also differences in the general characters or qualities of the object, as, for example, its whiteness vs. its blackness, its alley-like character vs. its crevice-like character, and the like. By distance we are going to mean all kinds of "goodness" or "badness" for getting-on—spatial, temporal, gravitational, physiological, rhetorical, social, or what not. And by direction we are going to mean all kinds of qualitative characterization of the given to-be-selected means-object, irrespective of whether this characterization really be one of spatial direction, or one, rather, of color, size, weight, type of muscular activity, type of verbal phrase, type of social performance, or what not.

4. Perception, Mnemonization, Inference

Further, it is to be noted that there are three possible *moods* to such means-end (i.e., direction-distance) expectations: (a) A rat, or other organism, may *perceive* that the given direction of means-object leads on by some relative degree of shortness to the given demanded goal-object, before he has tried it out and simply as a result of the concatenation of immediately presented stimuli. (b) Or he may *remember* it (mnemonize it, see below, page 134 f.) as a result of actually trying out the various alternatives a number of times and discovering which direction of means-object it was which thus led on to the goal-object by the relatively short route. (c) Or, finally, he may *infer* it, not as a result of stimuli all given then and there or as a result of actually having tried out this specific direction of means-object on previous trials, but rather as a result of having tried out some of the other means-objects.[1] Rats and higher organisms are immersed in means-end fields or manifolds, and they are capable, in varying degrees, not merely of perceiving and mnemonizing certain of the specific individual direction-distance correlations presented by such fields, but also of inferring other direction-distance correlations before they have as yet perceived them or had a chance to build up a memory (mnemonization) of them.

5. Means-End-Hierarchies

Finally, it may be well here to emphasize once again the fact of hierarchies or successions of superordinate and subordinate goal-objects. To some extent, rats, and to a large extent the higher animals, seem capable of expecting not merely simple, and single, direction-distance correlations but also successions or hierarchies of such correlations. They can postulate that this type or direction of means-object leads by a short distance to such and such a sub-goal-object, and that this latter leads by such and such a further relatively short distance to such and such a further more superordinate goal-object; and so on.

Every organism, given his fundamental appetites and aversions, plus his innate or acquired accompanying means-end-readinesses, is to be conceived as immersed at any moment in a more or less

---

[1] It will appear, in the subsequent chapters, that *inferences* in the above sense, at least within narrow limits and for primarily spatial material, are possible for even so lowly an animal as the rat. That is, the rat, and of course in much higher degree the higher animals, are capable of responding to relatively difficult combinations of direction and distance in the sense that from the actual perceptual or memorial experience of certain of them they may *infer* others.

enduring hierarchy, or sequential order, of means-end possibilities. Types of object present themselves to the envisagement of such an organism as falling into certain successions or hierarchies of means-end possibilities—i.e., direction-distance correlations. And, if the organism is to be successful in achieving his final ultimately desired physiological state, his hierarchy of means-end-readinesses and resultant means-end-expectations must be correct. The organism must be "ready" for and finally expect the appropriate final consummatory objects as the last step in reaching the ultimately desired physiological state; and he must also be "ready" for and finally expect the appropriate subordinate means-object as providing appropriate subordinate routes to such consummatory objects.

One is, of course, indebted primarily to Woodworth for the concepts and terms *consummatory* and *preparatory,* or as we have called them superordinate and subordinate, and also for his concept of reaction tendency, which latter seems closely related to our concept of means-end-readiness.[2]

6. Types of Hierarchy: Chain Successions vs. Lever (Tool) Successions

In considering this concept of sequential orders or hierarchies, it must be noted finally, however, that there appear to be two types of such means-end successions (i.e., direction-distance correlations). On the one hand, there are what may be called chain successions, and, on the other, there are what may be called lever (or tool) successions.

In a chain succession, the two members of any pair of successive means-objects lie with respect to each other as successive links in a chain. Commerce with one leads to the presence of the next. And commerce with this next leads to the presence of the still next; and so on. An example of such a chain means-end succession is presented by a spatial field, such as that offered to a rat in a maze. The rat runs through one part of the maze to get to the presence of the next; and through this to get to the presence of a still further part; and so on.

In the lever, or tool, type of means-end succession (direction-

---

[2] R. S. Woodworth, *Dynamic Psychology* (New York, Columbia Univ. Press, 1918). Also, *Psychology, A Study of Mental Life* (New York, Henry Holt and Company, 1921).

distance correlation), on the other hand, the two members of any pair of successive means-objects lie relative to one another as the two ends of a lever, or other tool. And, just as a movement of the one end of a lever causes some correlated movement of the other end to be described simultaneously, so, in what we are here calling the lever, or tool, type of means-end succession, commerce with the one means-object achieves directly and simultaneously a correlated commerce with the next. Examples of such lever, or tool, combinations are to be found for the most part only among animals relatively higher in the scale than rats.[3] For, in the last analysis, such "lever" types of combination are cases of "tool-using." The organism has commerce with the one "end" of the tool in order to achieve thereby such and such commerces with the other end of the tool. One of the simplest of such tools is, of course, the "lever" itself, which we may here take as the *exemplar* of all tools. Adams [4] has demonstrated very prettily the ability in *cats* to learn to push the one end of a lever projecting out from a puzzle box in order thereby to bring the other end loaded with food inside the box and within reach. Köhler's apes gave many instances of the ability to use tools, beginning with simple strings tied to food, and passing on up to the using of sticks and the piling of boxes.[5] And it goes without saying that in the case of human beings the kinds and complexities of tool-using are legion.

Finally, however, it is of course obvious that any extended means-end hierarchy will often involve both chain and lever

[3] Some evidence of tool-using, even in the case of rats, seems to have been demonstrated by W. McDougall and K. D. McDougall, Notes on instinct and intelligence in rats and cats, *J. Comp. Psychol.*, 1927, **7**, 145-176, who found that rats would pull up food on the end of a string and learn to manipulate a series of levers in order to open a food-box. See also M. F. Fritz, A note on the use of tools by the white rat, *J. Genet. Psychol.*, 1930, **37**, 330-331.

The use of tools by such higher organisms as birds, monkeys, and apes, has of recent years been overwhelmingly demonstrated.

Cf. M. Hertz, Beobachtungen an gefangenen Rabenvögeln, *Psychol. Forsch.*, 1926, **8**, 336-397.

H. Nellmann and W. Trendelenburg, Ein Beitrag zur Intelligenzprüfungen niederer Affen., *Ztsch. f. vergl. Physiol.*, 1926, **4**, 142-201.

R. M. Yerkes and A. W. Yerkes, *The Great Apes* (New Haven, Yale University Press, 1929).

[4] D. K. Adams, Experimental studies of adaptive behavior in cats, *Comp. Psychol. Mon.*, 1929, **6**, No. 27.

[5] W. Köhler, *Intelligenzprüfungen an Menschenaffen* (1917); Eng. tr., *The Mentality of Apes*, by Ella Winter (New York, Harcourt, Brace and Company, 1925).

relations. Thus, for example, in the case of a man driving his automobile home to dinner, the automobile is a tool, the one "end" of which, the steering wheel, he manipulates in order that the other "end," the running wheels, shall pass through a succession of chain means-end commerces extending from office to home.

7. Experimental Evidence of Means-End-Expectations

The next two chapters will present experimental evidence, in the case of the rat, for expectations, perceptual and mnemonic, of direction and distance correlations and of successions or hierarchies of such correlations. But Chapter VII will be devoted more to the problems of distance and Chapter VIII more to those of direction and hierarchies. A discussion of inferential expectations of means-end-relations (direction and distance correlations) will be postponed until Chapter XI.

REFERENCES

Adams, D. K., Experimental studies of adaptive behavior in cats. *Comp. Psychol. Monog.*, 1929, **6**, No. 27.
Fritz, M. F., A note on the use of tools by the white rat. *J. Genet. Psychol.*, 1930, **37**, 330-331.
Hertz, M., Beobachtung an gefangengen Rabenvögeln. *Psychol. Forsch.*, 1926, **8**, 336-397.
Köhler, W., *The Mentality of Apes* (New York, Harcourt, Brace and Company, 1925).
McDougall, W. and McDougall, K. D., Notes on instinct and intelligence in rats and cats. *J. Comp. Psychol.*, 1927, 7, 145-176.
Nellmann, H. and Trendelenburg, W., Ein Beitrag zur Intelligenzprüfungen niederer Affen. *Ztsch. f. vergl. Physiol.*, 1926, **4**, 142-201.
Woodworth, R. S., *Dynamic Psychology* (New York, Columbia Univ. Press, 1918).
—————, *Psychology*, rev. ed. (New York, Henry Holt and Company, 1929).
Yerkes, R. M. and Yerkes, A. W., *The Great Apes* (New Haven, Yale Univ. Press, 1929).

Chapter VII

MEANS-END-DISTANCES

1. Expectations of Distance

IN this chapter we are to present the results of various experiments which indicate the ability and tendency of the rat to differentiate and to prefer various kinds of "short" paths as constrasted with the corresponding "long" paths, and *pari passu* to expect these short paths to be correlated with such and such types or "direction" of alley-entrance. That is, the rat both differentiates certain differences of "distance" in the moments of passing through those distances, and comes later to release a means-end-expectation as to which of these distances are correlated with which "direction" of means-object.

2. Spatial Distances

The first, and pioneer, experiment to be reported is that of De Camp.[1] For it was De Camp who first clearly envisaged the significance of the two-way (i.e., a long-path—short-path) spatial maze. The final form which he used is shown in FIGURE 30. At the beginning of the experiment, the food was at F_1 (F_2 was blocked off), and the two paths, one longer and one shorter, both led to F_1; but the left hand one was the shorter. With this arrangement, the rats soon learned to go by the shorter path. After, however, this preference had been acquired, the food was shifted to F_2, and F_1 was blocked. What happened? On the next few trials, rats went to the left as before. But, upon finding F_1 blocked, they continued to explore; and either by continuing around to the left or by retracing back to S and then going down to the right, they eventually reached the food at F_2. Sooner or later, however, they all changed to going directly to the right,

---

[1] J. E. De Camp, Relative distance as a factor in the white rat's selection of a path, *Psychobiol.*, 1920, **2**, 245-253.

rather than either going the long way round, via F_1, or first
going towards F_1 and then backing out again. The original going
down to the left was, that is, contingent upon this continuing
to be the shorter route to food. Similarly, the later going to the
right, rather than to the left, was contingent upon the change in
the position of the food such that the right was now the shorter

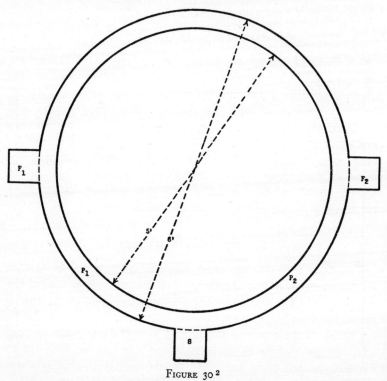

FIGURE 30 [2]

route. We have to thank De Camp for first bringing clearly to
light this fact of the preference of the rat for the spatially shorter
of two alternative routes.[3]

[2] *Op. cit.*, p. 247.

[3] De Camp was not, of course, the first to *use* a maze which involved alternative routes of different spatial lengths. The original Hampton Court maze used
by W. S. Small and L. W. Kline at Clark in 1900 (*vide* H. A. Carr and
J. B. Watson, Orientation in the white rat, *J. Comp. Neurol. & Psychol.*, 1908,
18, 27-44) had some alleys involving this principle. But the methodological
and theoretical significance of the principle does not seem to have been
realized, previous to De Camp.

3.   Further Examples

We must present, next, some experiments of Gengerelli's.[4] The general procedure in these experiments was to present the rats with many possible, and relatively undefined, paths between entrance and food-box, in order to discover in how far the animals would come to select the more direct, i.e., the spatially (and temporally) shorter routes.

FIGURE 31 [5]

[4] J. A. Gengerelli, The principle of maxima and minima in animal learning, *J. Comp. Psychol.*, 1930, 11, 193-236.
[5] *Op. cit.*, p. 208.

In many of the experiments this intervening area between entrance and food-box consisted of a large enclosed square, which was in most cases broken up by means of short baffles arranged, for example, as shown in FIGURE 31. Both normal and blind animals were usually tried.

The results with the seeing rats were that in the first trials the animals wandered all about between entrance and exit, but with subsequent practice they came more and more to take, as nearly as the baffles would permit, a direct diagonal route from entrance to exit. With the blind animals, who in general tended to bump themselves on the baffles, the finally selected route tended, at least in such a set-up as that indicated in the figure, to hug two of the outer walls of the square.

In a second set of experiments the problem box arrangement shown in FIGURE 32 was used.

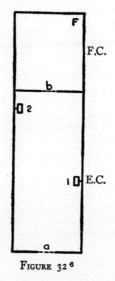

FIGURE 32 [6]

The two small squares represent platforms which the rat had to depress, in either order, before the door into the food-compartment would open.

It was found that the rat, in the early trials, tended to hit platform 2 first. This was because in his strugglings back and forth in front of b, the door into the food-compartment, he was

[6] *Op. cit.*, p. 220.

very likely to hit 2 by accident. And he tended to hit 1 only after a longer delay. Finally, however, after the path to 2 and then back again to 1, had become relatively smooth and errorless, it gave way to the still more efficient path, 1 followed by 2. We quote the experimenter's notes on the behavior of an individual animal:

"At the end of the 20th trial: The animal dashes through the experimental compartment and scratches vigorously at the door leading to the F.C. (food compartment). This is repeated run after run. The reason why plate 2 is pressed so often *first* lies in the fact that the rat, in scratching and walking back and forth across the entrance to the F.C., steps on it accidentally. The animal also tries to clamber up over the partition occasionally."

"At the end of the 30th trial: Shows unmistakable signs of associating the pressing of plate 1 with the opening of the door. This has taken place because the order of pressing on the plates is usually 2-1, and therefore 1 is the plate touched when the door opens. On the 28th and 29th runs he pressed on it first and since the door did not open, he pressed on it *two or three times in succession* before going to No. 2. Did this repeatedly in the next ten runs, even going so far as ignoring 2 altogether and dashing back and forth from the door to No. 1."

"Up to the 360th run, the path of the animal is, in regard to his 2-1 runs, as follows: Once within the E.C. (experimental compartment), the rat dashed straight down to the closed entrance to the food compartment, turned without hesitation, pressed on No. 2, ran up to and pressed No. 1, then ran back down to the food-box. (The animal had ceased scratching at the door by the 30th trial.) Shortly after the 360th trial, a gradual change was observed in the behavior. The rat, in running headlong from the entrance to the E.C. to the entrance of the F.C., instead of advancing clear up to the door before pressing on 2, as he had done, now paused within a few inches of the door, turned, pressed on 2, then ran up to No. 1, pressed it, and came back to the F.C. Eventually, the animal did not run *past* No. 2 at all, but pressed on that corner which was *nearest to him* as he approached it."

"The runs having the 1-2 sequence have greatly increased by the time the 450th trial is given. By far the greatest majority of the 1-2 runs are of the following type: The rat runs five or six inches past plate 1, turns, presses on that plate, turns, runs down and presses on plate 2, and enters the F.C. With each successive set of trials, however, the distance which the animal runs past No. 1 before turning to press it *gradually diminishes*. It is almost unbelievable."

"At the 600th trial: The rat by this time has ceased to run past plate 1 altogether. He stops beside the platform, turns to one side (the right), presses it, and goes on to plate 2 and to the F.C. The animal has thus arrived at the 'optimum' solution." [7]

Summing up the results of both sets of experiments, we must conclude that there is a very strong tendency for rats eventually to differentiate and select the spatially shortest route from a set of alternative, relatively undefined possibilities.

Whereas De Camp's experiment indicated that if the rats are limited to two alternative and restricted paths, one longer than the other, they will, finally, select the spatially shorter; these experiments of Gengerelli's indicate that where the possible routes are very numerous and relatively undefined, the animals also will tend, eventually, to achieve the spatially shortest of all the alternatives (save in the case of blind rats, who may achieve a compromise between spatial shortness and safety from injury). [8]

Finally, before passing on to the next section, it is to be noted that in all such experiments on spatial shortnesses there is inevitably also involved the correlated fact of temporal shortnesses. A rat in differentiating, preferring and taking a spatially shorter path is *pari passu* necessarily differentiating, preferring and taking the temporally shorter path also. And this raises the question: To what extent may the results obtained in such experiments be a measure of temporal differentiations rather than of spatial ones? In order to answer, experiments must be devised in which temporal distances are varied while spatial ones are held constant. Such an experiment is presented in the next section.

4. Temporal Distances

Sams and Tolman (in, to be sure, only a preliminary sort of way) have demonstrated that, other things being equal, rats will take the temporally shorter of two routes to food, even though

[7] *Op. cit.*, pp. 223-224.

[8] There should also be mentioned in connection with this propensity of the rat to take the spatially shorter of two alternative routes to food, an experiment by Higginson in which he found that his rats, when given an opportunity, immediately short-circuited a blind which previously they had entered on every one of many preceding trials. Cf. G. D. Higginson, Visual perception in the white rat, *J. Exper. Psychol.*, 1926, **9**, 337-347. It should be noted, further, however, in this connection that Valentine repeated Higginson's experiment (with slightly different conditions) and obtained no such immediate short-circuiting. Cf. W. L. Valentine, "Visual perception in the white rat." *J. Comp. Psychol.*, 1928, **8**, 369-375.

the spatial length of the two paths is the same.[9] They used a
simple, spatially symmetrical maze, such as is shown in FIGURE
33. It presents two alternative paths to food, each of which has

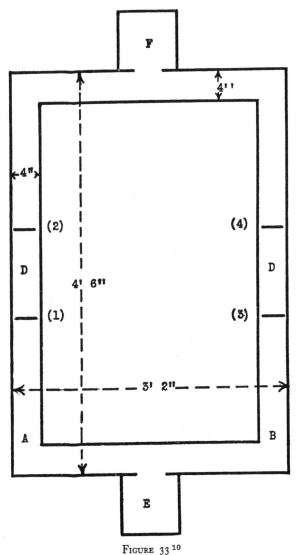

FIGURE 33 [10]

[9] E. C. Tolman and C. F. Sams, Time discrimination in white rats, *J. Comp.
Psychol.*, 1925, **5**, 255-263.
[10] *Op. cit.*, p. 255.

in the middle of its course a detention chamber, i.e., 1 to 2, on the left, and 3 to 4, on the right. With this arrangement, they found that, if the rat was detained, say, four minutes on the right and only one minute on the left, or for still larger differences between the two sides, he would sooner or later come to take the left side only. In other words, they found that, within certain very gross limits of differentiation, rats can learn to take the shorter of two alternative routes which differ in temporal lengths only.

The point to be stressed now, however, is that although this fact of pure temporal differentiation and preference was thus demonstrated, it was very gross—not nearly refined enough to explain the results for the spatial differences reported above. The differences in time involved in spatially differentiated paths such as those considered above would have been a matter of mere seconds—whereas the time differences discriminated in the experiment just cited were a matter of minutes.

We turn now, finally, to force-resisting distances.

5.   Force-resisting Distances

Unfortunately no actual experiment has, so far as we know, been carried out to demonstrate the reality or non-reality of such force-resisting preferences. It is our belief, however, that if a rat were given a choice between two alternative paths to food, both of the same spatial and temporal length, but one involving more "work," more overcoming of gravitational or other force than the other, he would come, sooner or later, and within certain limits, to prefer, and to differentiate, that involving the less force-resistance, i.e., the less physical work.

Imagine, for example, a simple, two-way maze, such as that shown in FIGURE 34, where from opposite sides of a starting box S, two paths of equal length, P_1 and P_2, lead to two similar food-chambers, F_1 and F_2, but where one of these paths, P_1, is horizontal and the other, P_2, is inclined. In such a case, we should expect the rats to come eventually to take P_1 rather than P_2. Suppose, again, that P_2 were inclined downward rather than upward. In this second situation also, we should expect that in all probability the rats would likewise come eventually to prefer P_1 to P_2. For, again, the horizontal path would probably involve iess overcoming of force on the part of the rat than would the walking or running "with brakes on" which would be required in descending a decline.

Undoubtedly the whole situation might prove more complicated than the above simple account suggests. It is known, for example, that rats and mice (at any rate, young ones) have very definite geotropisms. They tend to crawl *up* inclined planes.[11] And this

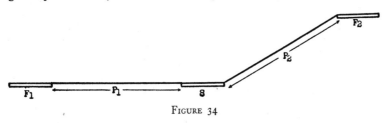

FIGURE 34

might completely upset, or at any rate, complicate the picture. We believe, however, that it would not overthrow our fundamental principles. It is our belief that rats, when given a choice between more force-resisting and less force-resisting ways of getting to the same types of further goal, will eventually come to

[11] See in this connection the extremely interesting and important series of studies by Crozier and his students. W. J. Crozier, Tropisms, *J. Gen. Psychol.*, 1928, **1**, 213-238.

W. J. Crozier and T. T. Oxnard, Geotropic orientation of young mice, *J. Gen. Physiol*, 1927-28, **11**, 141-146.

W. J. Crozier and G. Pincus, Tropisms of mammals, *Proc. Nat. Acad. Sci.*, 1926, **12**, 612-616.

——————— and ———————, The geotropic conduct of young rats, *J. Gen. Physiol.*, 1926-1927, **10**, 257-269.

——————— and ———————, On the equilibration of geotropic and phototropic excitations in the rat, *J. Gen. Physiol.*, 1926-1927, **10**, 419-424.

——————— and ———————, On the geotropic orientation of young mammals, *J. Gen. Physiol.*, 1927-1928, **11**, 789-802.

——————— and ———————, Analysis of the geotropic orientation of young rats, I. *J. Gen. Physiol.*, 1929-1930, **13**, 57-80. II. *J. Gen. Physiol.*, 1929-1930, **13**, 81-120.

C. E. Keeler, The geotropic reaction of rodless mice in light and in darkness, *J. Gen. Physiol.*, 1927-28, **11**, 361-368.

G. Pincus, Geotropic creeping of young rats, *J. Gen. Physiol.*, 1926-1927, **10**, 525-532.

G. Pincus and W. J. Crozier, On the geotropic response in young rats, *Proc. Nat. Acad. Sci.*, 1929, **15**, 581-586.

See also

W. S. Hunter, The behavior of white rats on inclined planes, *J. Genet. Psychol.*, 1927, **34**, 299-332.

take the less force-resisting of such alternative ways, except as this may be complicated by "up-desires" or "down-desires" per se.

But undoubtedly the whole problem is one which will need more investigation. These statements concerning force-resistance as a type of distance preference have been introduced more in the hope that they may suggest further experimentation than in the belief that the assumptions implied in them are necessarily correct.

6. Least Effort

We have seen that rats prefer spatially shorter and temporally shorter routes; and we have suggested that probably they also can differentiate and prefer gravitationally (i.e., force-resistingly) shorter routes. The possibility now suggests itself, however, that perhaps all three of these preferences may, in the last analysis, be reducible to a single, more fundamental, one—to be called the preference for "Least Effort." It appears possible, in other words, that further experiments, in which spatial and temporal and force-resisting delays were paired in all possible permutations and combinations, one against another, would uncover the fact of a single dimension of "Least Effort" running through them all.

That there is such a single, more fundamental, principle of "Least Effort" has in fact already been suggested by a number of writers.[12] And it certainly seems *prima facie* a most reasonable hypothesis. It must be pointed out, however, that, even if there be such a single physiological principle at the basis of all means-

[12] Cf. H. Helson, Insight in the white rat, *J. Exper. Psychol.*, 1927, **10**, 378-396.

J. A. Gengerelli, Preliminary experiments on the causal factors in animal learning, *J. Comp. Psychol.*, 1928, **8**, 435-458.

Cf. also J. A. Gengerelli, The effect of rotating the maze on the performance of the hooded rat, *J. Comp. Psychol.*, 1928, **8**, 377-384.

This principle has been emphasized also by Wheeler who designates it as the Law of Least Action.

Cf. R. H. Wheeler, *The Science of Psychology* (New York, Thomas Y. Crowell Company, 1929), esp. p. 79 f. Synonyms suggested by Wheeler are: "The law of least constraint, of least energy, of greatest economy, of least resistance," p. 80 n.

Cf. also W. R. B. Gibson, The principle of least action as a psychological principle, *Mind*, N. S., 1900, **9**, 469-495.

Finally, something like this principle has also been suggested by Borovski. Cf. W. M. Borovski, Über adaptive Ökonomie und ihre Bedeutung für den Lernprozess, *Biol. Zentralblatt*, 1930, **50**, 4-60.

end shortness-preferences, a knowledge of this fact is per se relatively barren. For, given the present parlous state of our physiological knowledge, it appears that the mere fact of such a principle
allows us to predict nothing beforehand and prior to concrete
behavior experiments. We cannot, that is, predict how in concrete types of means-end dimension, this Principle of Least Effort
is going to express itself. In each instance, what actually has
to be done is to discover separately, for each type of organism,
and for each type of permutation and combination of dimensional extents—spatial, temporal, force-resisting, and the like—in
how far differences between or within such dimensions will or
will not give rise to preferences. There may be, and probably is,
some single underlying Principle of Least Effort, but even so,
many concrete experiments will be needed to discover the specific
forms in which this single principle will clothe itself.

7.   Measurements of Distance Thresholds

We emphasize, now, a further aspect of the situation. For it
must be noted that the sort of experiments cited demonstrate
only roughly the refinements of shortness differentiations. They
demonstrate that the rat prefers the spatially shorter, temporally
shorter, or force-resisting shorter, route, and also that he can
roughly differentiate, and come to expect, the direction of the
spatially shorter, the temporally shorter, etc., routes. But they
do not measure the precise degrees in which he can differentiate
such shorternesses. Indeed, only one attempt at a precise measurement of such a differentiation has, as far as we know, as yet
been made. It is an experiment of Yoshioka's on the threshold
of spatial-distance differentiations and expectations in the rat.[13]

In this experiment, Yoshioka used two mazes exactly similar
in pattern, save that the alleys in one were just twice as long as
the corresponding alleys in the other. Figure 35 presents the
ground plan of the smaller of these two mazes. In the other
maze, all the dimensions were doubled (save the widths of the
alleys and the width of the doorway).

This maze, it will be observed, was essentially a two-alley
discrimination box in the shape of a toadstool. The animal en-

---

[13] J. G. Yoshioka, Weber's law in the discrimination of maze distance by
the white rat, *Univ. Calif. Publ. Psychol.*, 1929, **4**, 155-184.

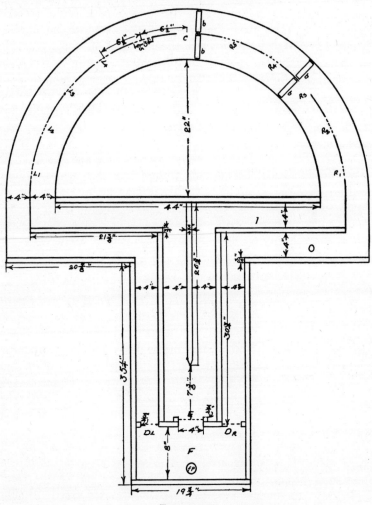

FIGURE 35 [14]

E, pulley door at entrance; I, inner alley; O, outer alley; C, central door (always open); R_1, R_2, R_3, R_4, R_5, L_5, L_4, L_3, L_2, L_1, adjustable doors (R_3 open); b, block; D_R, D_L, pulley doors; F, food-box, f_p, food-pan.

tering at E could choose either the right hand, or the left hand, inner path. Of the "adjustable" doors, R_1, R_2, R_3, R_4, R_5, and L_1, L_2, L_3, L_4, L_5, leading from the inner path to the outer path and hence back to f_p, the food-pan, only one was left open in

[14] Op. cit., p. 159.

any given set-up. This might be on the left-hand side or on the right-hand side. In the set-up depicted in the figure, it was R_3 on the right-hand side which was thus open. In addition, the central door, C, was always open; in the set-up illustrated, this central door was to be reached on the left-hand side. The animal entering the discrimination chamber at E always had to choose between a path leading through one of the adjustable doors R_1, R_2, R_3, R_4, R_5 or L_1, L_2, L_3, L_4, L_5 on the one side, and the central door C to be reached by the opposite side. Blocks b, b, b, b, were inserted in the manner indicated in the figure to prevent excess running beyond the doors.

The path passing through the central door constituted a "standard" long path, which was the same for all set-ups. The adjustable doors, R_1, R_2, R_3, R_4, R_5, L_1, L_2, L_3, L_4, L_5, constituted different "compared" short paths, one of which was paired in each set-up as the alternative to the standard long path.

A group of ten rats was trained on each set-up and the results for the group trained with central door to the left and a compared door to the right, were combined with those for the homologous group trained with central door to the right and the corresponding, to be compared, door to the left. This gave results for five "situations," each "situation" having one ratio of compared short path to standard long path.

The results for the five "situations" for the two mazes are shown by FIGURE 36. The P scores are the average numbers of "perfect" scores, i.e., choices of the short path made in thirty trials, six trials per day for five days.[15]

It will be observed that the results obtained for the two mazes were alike. In other words, Weber's Law (i.e., that relative distances rather than absolute distances determined the ease of differentiation) was found to hold. And it is to be noted that these spatial distances were experienced by the rat only in the act of running over them. When the ratio of long path to short path was 1.14 (Situation IV, see legend) the rats in Maze I were beginning to take the short path more than eleven times out of

---

[15] It is to be noted, however, that only seventy-three per cent or approximately twenty-two of these thirty trials were counted as truly discriminative, i.e., as involving a direct choice of either the short path or the long path. The other trials seemed to be haphazard retracings and were discarded. This means that any P score above eleven suggests a true discrimination of the short path.

the twenty-two. And when the ratio was 1.23 (Situation III) the rats in both mazes were very decidedly taking the short path more than eleven times out of the twenty-two. In other words, the threshold of differentiability for short path seems to lie between the ratios of 1.07 and 1.14 of long path to short path.

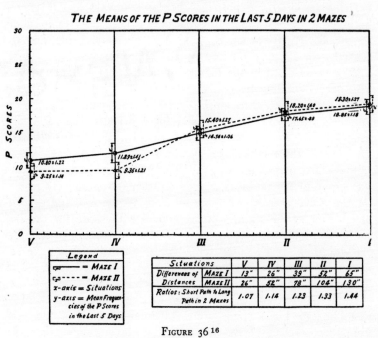

FIGURE 36 [16]

So much for an experiment illustrating a precise measurement of distance differentiations and resultant expectations in the dimension of space.

8. Interrelations between the Three Dimensions

Finally, it is obvious that experiments in the other two dimensions (time and force-resistance), and in comparing one such dimension with another, will have to be carried out before any final statement of the exact nature of distance-expectations in the case of the rat will be possible. We shall need to have experiments analogous to this of Yoshioka, for the temporal and

[16] *Op. cit.*, p. 176.

force-resisting dimensions. And we shall need to have experiments in which distance displacements in one dimension are paired against those in each of the other dimensions. Only by working out all such interrelations, both within and between the dimensions, can we finally build up a complete understanding of distance relations as preferred by the rat (or any other species of animal).

9. Other Dimensions

In the above experiments we have considered only the three most obvious types, or dimensions of distance—viz., distances in space, distances in time, and distances in force-resistance. It must be noted now, however, that mayhap the rat and certainly higher organisms can also differentiate, prefer, and expect the "shorter" of two alternative distances within still other types of dimension than those of space, time and force-resistance. Thus, to take the highest organism of all, it is obvious that man comes to differentiate, prefer, and predict the shorter routes within, say, social and rhetorical dimensions, as well as within the simpler ones of space, time, and gravitation. Wherever, in short, an organism is capable of building up and reacting to some characteristic type of means-end succession, he develops differentiations and expectations relative to the characteristic "medium" of those successions. He comes to react not only to the laws of space and time and gravitation but also to those of society and language, and physiology, and the rest. This matter of types and kinds of distance (dimension) is, however, obviously a complicated affair. It needs much further analyzing and consideration. In the present treatise, we merely suggest that there are these other dimensions —perhaps they are in some way dependent upon, or are built out of, the simpler ones of space and time and force-resistance— but we restrict ourselves here primarily to the consideration of the latter three.

REFERENCES

Borovski, W. M., Über adaptive Ökonomie und ihre Bedeutung für den Lernprozess. *Biol. Zentralblatt*, 1930, **50**, 4-60.
Carr, H. A. and Watson, J. B., Orientation in the white rat. *J. Comp. Neurol. & Psychol.*, 1908, **18**, 27-44.
Crozier, W. J., Tropisms. *J. Gen. Psychol.*, 1928, **1**, 213-238.
Crozier, W. J. and Oxnard, T. T., Geotropic orientation of young mice. *J. Gen. Physiol.*, 1927-28, **11**, 141-146.

Crozier, W. J. and Pincus, G., The geotropic conduct of young rats. *J. Gen. Physiol.*, 1926-1927, 10, 257-269.

——— and ———, On the equilibration of geotropic and phototropic excitations in the rat. *J. Gen. Physiol.*, 1926-1927, 10, 419-424.

——— and ———, Tropisms of mammals. *Proc. Nat. Acad. Sci.*, 1926, 12, 612-616.

——— and ———, On the geotropic orientation of young mammals. *J. Gen. Physiol.*, 1927-1928, 11, 789-802.

——— and ———, Analysis of the geotropic orientation of young rats, I. *J. Gen. Physiol.*, 1929-1930, 13, 57-80. II. *J. Gen. Physiol.*, 1929-1930, 13, 81-120.

De Camp, J. E., Relative distance as a factor in the white rat's selection of a path. *Psychobiol.*, 1920, 2, 245-253.

Gengerelli, J. A., The effect of rotating the maze on the performance of the hooded rat. *J. Comp. Psychol.*, 1928, 8, 377-384.

———, Preliminary experiments on the causal factors in animal learning. *J. Comp. Psychol.*, 1928, 8, 435-458; 377-384.

———, The principle of maxima and minima in animal learning. *J. Comp. Psychol.*, 1930, 11, 193-236.

Gibson, W. R. B., The principle of least action as a psychological principle. *Mind*, N. S., 1900, 9, 469-495.

Helson, H., Insight in the white rat. *J. Exper. Psychol.*, 1927, 10, 378-396.

Higginson, G. D., Visual perception in the white rat. *J. Exper. Psychol.*, 1926, 9, 337-347.

Hunter, W. S., The behavior of white rats on inclined planes. *J. Genet. Psychol.*, 1927, 34, 299-332.

Keeler, C. E., The geotropic reaction of rodless mice in light and in darkness. *J. Gen. Physiol.*, 1927-28, 11, 361-368.

Pincus, G., Geotropic creeping of young rats. *J. Gen. Physiol.*, 1927, 10, 525-532.

Tolman, E. C. and Sams, C. F., Time discrimination in white rats. *J. Comp. Psychol.*, 1925, 5, 255-263.

Valentine, W. L., "Visual perception in the white rat." *J. Comp. Psychol.*, 1928, 8, 369-375.

Wheeler, R. H., *The Science of Psychology* (New York, Thomas Y. Crowell Company, 1929).

Yoshioka, J. G., Weber's law in the discrimination of maze distance by the white rat. *Univ. Calif. Publ. Psychol.*, 1929, 4, 155-184.

Chapter VIII

SPATIAL DIRECTION AND SPATIAL HIERARCHIES

1. Perceptual Expectation of Spatial Direction of Goal-Object

CONSIDER, first, an experiment illustrating a rat's propensity, before learning and on a basis of immediate stimuli (i.e., perceptually), to select certain spatially directed paths. Whenever a rat is placed within sight or smell of food, it appears quite obvious, and therefore it tends to remain unremarked, that his selectivities as to surrounding means-objects are thereby affected.

Suppose that food be placed inside a wire container and the rat outside. The rat's strugglings most certainly will tend to be more on the side of the container which is nearer the food. And, if the food be moved to a new spot in the container, the array and direction of these strugglings will also move. In any such set-up the array of released strugglings will be selective relative to the actual spatial direction of the goal. And this selection, in such a case, is shown to depend upon stimuli then and there present, i.e., stimuli that come from the means-object (in this case the means-object in question, the wire container, is a "negative" or "obstruction" means-object), from the goal-object and from the concrete spatial relations of goal-object to means-object. Hence it is a *perceptual* expectation. And, as we have said, it is so obvious a phenomenon that the fact of it usually tends to be overlooked. The fact of it would, however, immediately become less obvious and more striking if, by some sleight of hand, the food could be made to prove to be, not there where his strugglings had been directed, but somewhere else. The rat's behavior would then exhibit disruption and "surprise." This would show that his strugglings had been informed by a true means-end-expectation which by some magic had now been made non-consonant with the facts.

2.   Mnemonic Expectation of Spatial Direction of Goal-Object

We turn now to experiments illustrating the rat's propensity, after learning, to select certain types of spatially directed or arranged paths more readily than others. For convenience, we may subdivide these experiments into the following four groups:

(i) Experiments using a maze which allows a wide variety of equally long alternative routes to one and the same goal; (ii) experiments using ordinary T-mazes in which certain blinds point toward the food-box and others do not; (iii) experiments presenting the rat with two alternative routes of equal length to the goal-box, but of which one points back toward the goal sooner than the other; (iv) an experiment in which the position of the goal-object was varied with respect to the direction of the maze-paths.

Let us consider these one at a time.

(i) *Experiments allowing a wide variety of alternative routes.* The experiments we here have in mind are some very important ones reported by Dashiell.[1] In his main experiments [2] (to which we shall restrict ourselves here) he used a maze such as that shown in FIGURE 37.

This maze offered, it will be seen, a great number of alternative and equal-length pathways from the entrance to the food-box exit. There are in fact twenty such different pathways, all equally correct in that none of them includes entrances into the pockets on the sides or retracings toward the two sides of the maze adjacent to the entrance. And the results were that:

"Each animal learned soon to adjust to the situation not by fixating some particular pathway but by running in the general direction of the exit now by one succession of turns and now by

[1] J. F. Dashiell, Direction orientation in maze running by the white rat, *Comp. Psychol. Monog.,* 1930, **7,** No. 32. Also, J. F. Dashiell and A. G. Bayroff, A forward-going tendency in maze running, *J. Comp. Psychol.,* 1931, **12,** 77-94. And for a brief abstract of this experiment cf. J. F. Dashiell, Spatial orientation in maze-learning as a species of animal *Gestaltung, Proc. Ninth Internat. Cong. Psychol.* (Princeton, Psychol. Rev. Co., 1930), pp. 139-140.

[2] In some preliminary experiments he used a T-maze and obtained results showing more entrances into food-pointing blinds similar to those obtained by Tolman and Honzik to be reported below. He also used another type of blind maze which also indicated that blinds pointing towards the food were entered more than those pointing away from the food.

another, so that in a series of trials it followed a variety of different courses from entrance to exit. Each course was followed without error and each without any previous practice therein." [3]

In other words, a rat, after learning, continued to take a variety of different paths all equally long and involving successions of right-angle turns, but all correct—in that they involved

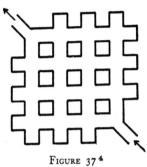

FIGURE 37 [4]

no entering of blinds and no excess distances. Now an animal's ability to do this indicates, it would seem, that the animal was possessed (to quote Dashiell again)

"of some more *general orientation* function. This general function enabled it to pursue new pathways while remaining successfully oriented toward the objective." [5]

Or, in our terms, it would indicate that the rats had acquired means-end-expectations as to the general spatial direction of the goal-box. [6]

(ii) *Experiments using T-mazes indicating that the food-pointing blinds are entered more frequently than the non-food-pointing blinds.* We wish to report here again the two experiments by Tolman and Honzik previously presented but in another connection (see above, Chapter III). [7]

[3] *Proc. Ninth International Cong. Psychol.* (Princeton, Psychol. Rev. Co., 1930). p. 139.

[4] *Comp. Psychol. Monog.*, 1930, **7**, p. 15.

[5] *Proc. Ninth Internat. Cong. Psychol.*, p. 139.

[6] This brief summary does not do justice to the extent and range of Dashiell's experiments. See, also, the important bibliography at the end of his monograph.

[7] E. C. Tolman and C. H. Honzik, Degrees of hunger, reward and non-reward, and maze learning in rats, *Univ. Calif. Publ. Psychol.*, 1930, **4**, 241-256. And

E. C. Tolman and C. H. Honzik, Introduction and removal of reward and maze performance in rats, *Univ. Calif. Publ. Psychol.*, 1930, **4**, 257-275.

In the first of these, four groups of rats were run in a fourteen-unit T-maze: a hungry reward group, a hungry non-reward group, a less hungry reward group, and a less hungry non-reward group. In general, it was found that the hungry and rewarded groups learned faster as regards the elimination of both times and errors than did the less hungry and the non-rewarded groups. (See above, Chapter III, p. 61 f.) The further point, now to be made, is that if the blind-alleys be considered in two groups: (a) blinds pointing away from the start or to the left (see above, Chapter III, Figure 4), i.e., the non-exit-pointing blinds; and (b) blinds pointing back towards the start and to the right, i.e., the exit-pointing blinds, it appears that all groups enter the exit-pointing blinds much more frequently than they do the non-

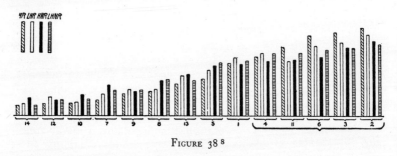

FIGURE 38 [8]

exit-pointing blinds. And also it appears that this greater tendency to enter the exit-pointing blinds at the expense of the non-exit-pointing ones was, generally speaking, decidedly more pronounced for the hungry reward group than for any of the others. These facts are shown by the bar diagram illustrated in FIGURE 38.

The blinds are arranged from left to right in order of total number of entrances. The heights of the bars for any group represent the percentage distributions for that group of its total errors into the various blinds. The five blinds at the right of the diagram, i.e., numbers 4, 11, 6, 3 and 2, are the five exit-pointing blinds. It is obvious that for all four groups of animals these exit-pointing blinds have the bigger percentages of errors. It appears further, however, comparing the different groups among themselves, that in these five exit-pointing blinds the hungry

8 "Degrees of hunger, reward and non-reward, and maze learning in rats," p. 250.

reward group (HR) tends to have bigger percentages of errors than do the other groups, whereas in the nine non-exit-pointing blinds this hungry reward group tends to have smaller percentages of errors than do any of the other groups.

These results we take as evidencing: (a) that all groups built up an expectation as to the general direction of the exit-box (all groups tend to make more errors in the blinds pointing toward the exit than in those pointing in the two opposite directions); and (b) that this expectation was in general more active if a group were hungry and if it were rewarded (i.e., the propensity to enter the exit-pointing blinds at the expense of the non-exit-point-

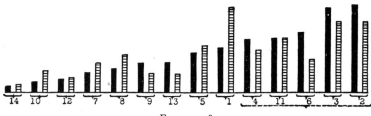

| 14 | 10 | 12 | 7 | 8 | 9 | 13 | 5 | 1 | 4 | 11 | 6 | 3 | 2 |

FIGURE 39 [9]

SOLID BARS BEFORE THE CHANGE. CROSS-HATCHED BARS AFTER THE CHANGE.

ing blinds was strongest for groups which were hungry and which found food).

We turn now to the other experiment (see above, Chapter III, pp. 53-55). In this there were two experimental groups: a hungry group run first for eleven days under normal conditions and then run for eleven days under non-reward conditions; and a hungry group run first for eleven days under non-reward conditions and then run for eleven days under reward conditions. The percentage distributions of errors in the different blinds, under reward and non-reward conditions, respectively, for these two groups, are shown in the bar diagrams in FIGURES 39 and 40.

In the case of the group changed from reward to non-reward, FIGURE 39, it will be seen that in the nine non-exit-pointing blinds the percentages of errors tended to be bigger after the removal of the reward; whereas the errors into the five exit-pointing blinds tended to be smaller after this removal of the reward.

In the case of the group which began with non-reward and

[9] "Introduction and removal of reward and maze performance in rats," p. 269.

changed to reward, FIGURE 40, the results are not quite so clear: that is, the order of difficulty of the exit-pointing and the non-exit-pointing blinds is more mixed up. But, in general, it can be said for this group that, *after* the introduction of reward, there tended to be relatively fewer entrances into the non-exit-pointing blinds and a very great increase in one at least of the exit-pointing blinds, viz., number 3.

These results as a whole suggest, again, that both groups were governed by expectations of the general spatial direction of the

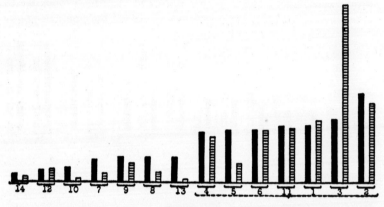

FIGURE 40 [10]

SOLID BARS BEFORE THE CHANGE. CROSS-HATCHED BARS AFTER THE CHANGE.

exit and that finding reward at the exit-box increased the strength of these expectations.[11]

(iii) *Experiments with two equally long alternative routes, one of which points back towards the goal sooner than the other.*

[10] *Op. cit.*, p. 270.

[11] Finally, however, it must now be noted that although we have labeled this section a demonstration of mnemonic expectations of the position of the goal-box, it seems possible that in reality the results of both the experiments just cited may have demonstrated, in part, perceptual expectations rather than mnemonic ones. It seems possible, in short, that the rats may have smelled the position of the food directly. The latest and most careful work now suggests that rats in learning ordinary mazes are to some slight extent aided by odors. At any rate anosmic animals do not do quite so well as do normal animals. (See S. B. Lindley, The maze-learning ability of anosmic and blind anosmic rats, *J. Genet. Psychol.*, 1930, **37**, 245-267.) But, on the other hand, it is to be argued against such a possibility that the non-reward group who found no food at the exit still tended to enter the exit-pointing blinds far more frequently than the non-exit-pointing ones.

The experiments we have in mind here are some by Yoshioka.[12] He first ran a group of rats in the maze shown in FIGURE 41.

It will be observed that the animals were offered a choice between a circumscribed triangle and an inscribed pentagon of the same length. During a preliminary training period they were forced down both paths an equal number of times by shifting

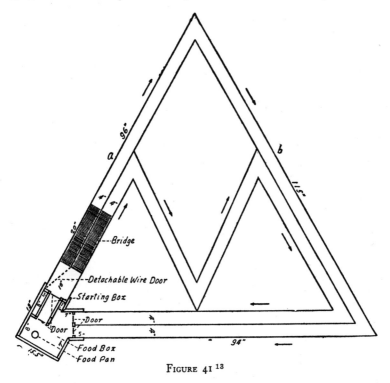

FIGURE 41 [13]

the "detachable wire door" (see FIGURE) from one side to the other. (The cross hatched section labeled "bridge" was a rise in the floor of both alleys which hid the further features of these alleys from the choice point.) During the discrimination runs, proper, the wire door was removed and the rats chose freely either path.

The outcome in the final discrimination trials for each of

[12] J. G. Yoshioka, A preliminary study in discrimination of maze patterns by the rat, *Univ. Calif. Publ. Psychol.*, 1928, **4**, 1-18.

[13] *Op. cit.*, p. 4.

two groups of rats (each group consisted of thirty rats and each rat was given six trials a day for ten days) was a significantly bigger percentage of choices of the inscribed pentagon than of the circumscribed triangle.

This result we interpret as due to the fact that the pentagon turns back toward the goal sooner than the triangle. We assume, in short, that the rats soon came to expect the general direction of the goal and that, given this expectation of the goal's direction, the pentagon seems to them better—to offer a more direct route to the goal than did the triangle. This interpretation seems to us further justified by the results of a series of additional experiments.[14] In these added experiments Yoshioka compared, in like fashion, various other pairs of circumscribed and inscribed paths. FIGURE 42 gives schematic drawings of the mazes he used in these additional experiments.

In each maze a group of 30 rats, after preliminary training,[15] was given six discrimination trials a day for ten days, i.e., a total of sixty trials. And the following table shows the average number of trials, out of the sixty, for which each group selected the inscribed path.

No. of maze figure	Patterns offered for choice	Mean of the choice of the inscribed pattern	Critical ratio of the difference between this mean and 30
Fig. 1	3 vs 3 sides	29.13	0.19
Fig. 2	3 vs 5 "	36.37	1.41
Fig. 3	3 vs 9 "	37.67	1.64
Fig. 4	5 vs 9 "	30.33	0.68
Fig. 5	3 vs 17 "	34.40	0.97
Fig. 6	5 vs 17 "	32.13	0.46
Fig. 7	3 vs 5 No. 2	35.13	1.09

Comparing these results with the diagrams we note:

(a) In Figure 1, where both paths are practically the same, there appeared what, on our hypothesis, would be the expected and obvious result—viz., no greater percentage of choice for the inscribed path.

[14] J. G. Yoshioka, A further study in discrimination of maze patterns, *Univ. Calif. Publ. Psychol.*, 1929, 4, 135-153.

[15] In these experiments the rats, in addition to the preliminary training, were also given one forced run down each of the two alternative paths at the beginning of the day's experiment to refresh their "minds" as to the two possibilities.

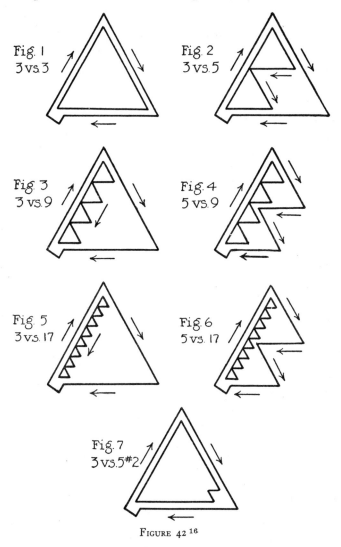

FIGURE 42 [16]

(b) In Figures 2 and 3, where the inscribed path was a pentagon in the one case and a nonagon in the other, and where both pentagon and nonagon turned back at about the same place and decidedly before the triangle, we observe from the table very definite preferences for the pentagon and for the nonagon

[16] *Op. cit.*, p. 137.

as against the triangle. And this also would fit in with the hypothesis.

(c) In Figure 4, where nonagon is compared with pentagon, no greater preference was found for the nonagon. This was to be expected since pentagon and nonagon both turned back at practically the same point.

(d) In Figure 5, where a heptadecagon is compared with the triangle, a considerable preference was obtained for the heptadecagon. This, however, was not so great a preference as that shown for the pentagon and for the nonagon, when compared with the triangle. But on our hypothesis it would seem that a still greater preference should have been obtained for the heptadecagon. This contradiction with the hypothesis is to be explained, however, we believe by the fact that the turns in the heptadecagon were so short that the rats experienced considerable difficulty and bumping in going through this path rapidly. This probably counteracted its otherwise greater preferentiability.

(e) In Figure 6, where a heptadecagon is compared with the pentagon, the rats seemed to show a slight preference for the former. It is to be stated, however, that this difference was probably not a statistically significant one. Both pentagon and heptadecagon (as indicated above) are better than a triangle. But the heptadecagon (because it turns back sooner) one would expect to be preferred to the pentagon. And it was so, although the obtained difference was only slight, and, under the conditions, not statistically valid. But this meagerness in the outcome we believe to be explained by the fact that, as said above, the heptadecagon, because of the shortness of its turns, also possessed a certain degree of inherent to-be-avoidedness.

(f) Finally, in Figure 7, where a pentagon formed by cutting only a slight notch out of the far corner was compared with the triangle, some preference was shown for this pentagon (though it should be noted that this preference was not so great, nor so reliable statistically, as the preferences shown for the bigger pentagon and for the nonagon). We believe that this preference once more testifies to the fact that the animals first built up an expectation as to the general direction of the food, and that the reason they showed a preference for this notch-formed pentagon was because it turned back sooner towards that goal-direction.

(iv) *Experiment in which rats hugged that wall of an open space which was nearer the goal-object.* This experiment also was one performed by Yoshioka.[17]

A group of rats was made to run a straight path which expanded in the middle into a diamond formed of an inner and outer square. The diamond offered two detour paths, right and left of equal length. The maze was placed on the east-west line. The food-box and the start were interchanged at each trial, so that the rats running east on the first trial headed west on the second trial, east on the third, and so on. The food-box was placed on the end of an arm, so that it could be shifted out of the main east-west line. Five different positions of the food-box were tried:—$0°$, $22\frac{1}{2}°$, $45°$, $67\frac{1}{2}°$, and $90°$ north, respectively, with reference to the east-west line. For none of these positions of the food-box was the north side of the diamond taken with any greater frequency than the south side.

Finally, however, in the last situation with the food-box $90°$ north, the inner square was removed. And under these conditions the rats hugged the north wall—a statistically significantly greater number of times than they did the south wall. When the food-box was brought back to $0°$ the choice of the north wall dropped considerably.

We conclude, therefore, that this experiment also indicated, under certain conditions (though not under others), a behavior which indicated a mnemonic expectation as to the general spatial direction of the goal-object.[18]

[17] Cf. J. G. Yoshioka, A study of orientation in a maze. Abstract in *Psychol. Bull.*, 1929, **26**, 591-592. Also ————— Direction as a factor in maze education in rats, *J. Genet. Psychol.*, 1930, **38**, 307-318.

[18] There have also been, from time to time, various other incidental observations gathered by other experimenters all pointing towards this same general outcome that rats seem to acquire a set for the general spatial direction of the goal. Most of these have been splendidly summarized by Dashiell in the monograph referred to. (Cf. J. F. Dashiell, Direction orientation in maze running by the white rat, *Comp. Psychol. Monog.*, 1930, **7**, Serial No. 32.)

Lashley and Hubbert as early as 1917 discovered that in the Watson circular maze (See above Chapter III, Figure 21) the rats ran with their heads close to the inner partitions (the food was in the center) and tried to climb over these inner partitions only, never the outer one. (Cf. K. S. Lashley and H. B. Hubbert, Retroactive association and the elimination of errors in the maze, *J. Anim. Behav.*, 1917, **7**, 130-138.)

And again Lashley more recently reports the significant case of two rats who after some training climbed out over the top of a maze and took a direct

3. Perceptual Expectation of Spatial Direction of Sub-Goal-Object

We turn now, finally, to an experiment which indicates the ability of the rat to respond to a hierarchy of subordinate and superordinate goals. This is an experiment by Robinson and Wever.[19] It indicated that the rat can choose a given means-object by virtue of whether or not it leads to a given *subordinate* goal-object (in this case, to be sure, a negative, or avoidance, subordinate goal-object).

The maze which they used was the simple one shown in FIGURE 43.

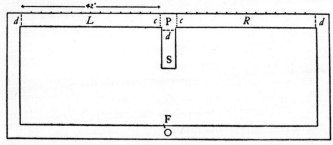

FIGURE 43 [20]

"Two paths, *R* and *L*, led from the entrance to the food, but doors of the vertical sliding type, and of the same material and color as the walls of the maze, were provided at *d, d* to permit the closing of either path, as desired. Along the top of the paths a row of electric lights gave even illumination. At the choice point, *P,* the right and left alleys were obscured from view by two black flannel curtains, *c, c,* making it necessary for the rat to enter the blind in order to see whether the path was open.

"For about every third trial both paths were left open and

course back towards the food-box. This is a sort of performance which no doubt has often been verified by other observers. (Cf. K. S. Lashley, *Brain Mechanisms and Intelligence* [Chicago Univ. Press, 1929], pp. 137-138.)

A similar observation to this last has also been made by Helson. (Cf. H. Helson, Insight in the white rat, *J. Exper. Psychol.,* 1927, **10,** 378-396.) He observed two rats who, when shocked upon entering the wrong compartment of a discrimination box, made their exit, not by returning out through the door and thus over a live grid, but by climbing directly over a high middle partition into the food compartment.

[19] E. W. Robinson and E. G. Wever, Visual distance perception in the rat, *Univ. Calif. Publ. Psychol.,* 1930, **4,** 233-239.

[20] *Op. cit.,* p. 235.

the rat made his way unimpeded to the food. But for the remaining trials both doors were closed until the rat had passed into one alley, had turned around and started back; then the door of the unentered alley was quietly opened by means of a cord in the hands of the experimenter and the animal thus permitted to pass along that way." [21]

The tasks for the animals which we are here interested in were (a) that of mnemonizing that the closed door on either side meant the non-availability of that side as a route to food, and (b) that of perceiving, as soon as possible, after passing under the curtain, the presence or absence of the sub-goal-object (in this case a negative or avoidance goal-object), the closed door. The results indicate that on the first few days the rats ran way up to the door before rejecting a given side and turning back. It appears, further, that they then learned to turn back sooner and sooner until, finally, each animal reached a relatively constant level of performance of turning back at some characteristic distance from the door.

Figures 44 and 45 represent, that is, typical records for seven albino rats (A_1 to A_7) and for eight rats with pigmented eyes (P_8 to P_{13}; and G_{14} and G_{15}).

The solid curves, marked N, represent the average number of inches from the door for seven trials per day at which the animal turned back (the door being closed). The broken line curves, marked R, show the animal's performance later, when the illumination was reduced a step at a time each day until supposedly complete darkness was reached. The little curves at the extreme right represent the previous performance of the same animals, when tested in complete darkness in a 14-unit T-maze, such as is shown in Chapter III, Figure 4.

It is evident that whereas at first, under normal illumination, the animals had to go practically all the way to the door before they had learned the task and before they had perceived the door, they eventually were ready to turn back as soon as they could perceive the presence or absence of the door. And it is an interesting point that the rats with pigmented eyes (P_8 to G_{15}, Figure 45) were able to achieve this perception at a greater distance from the door than were the albino animals with non-pigmented eyes (A_1 to A_7, Figure 44).

21 *Op. cit.*, p. 234.

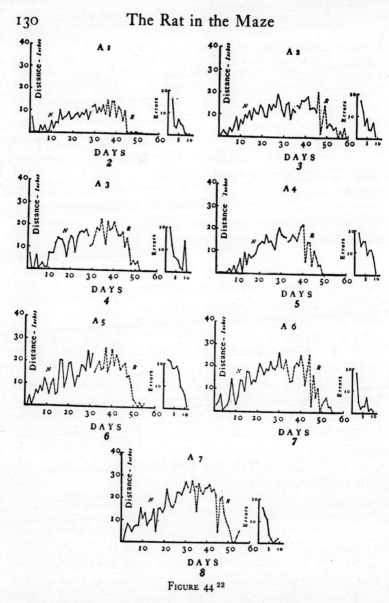

FIGURE 44 [22]

Interpretation. We suggest, now, that the first rises in the N curves represent the acquisition of *mnemonic* expectations of the direction of the superordinate goal-object, food—i.e., expectations to the effect that the food does not lie in the direction of

[22] *Op. cit.*, p. 237.

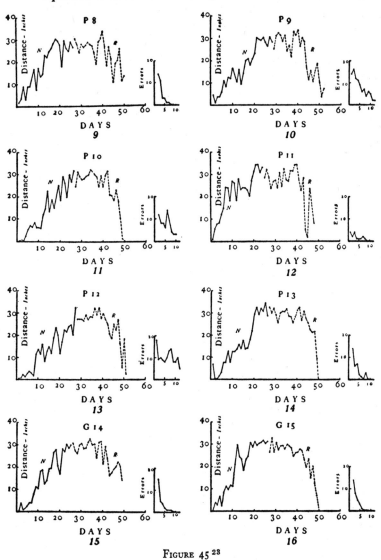

FIGURE 45 [23]

such a means-object as the door; while the final plateaus of the
N curves demonstrate subsequent *perceptual* expectations of the
direction of this means-object, i.e., negative sub-goal-object, door.

The expectation of the direction of the final goal-object, food,

[23] *Op. cit.*, p. 238

as not lying on the side of the door is to be conceived as a *mnemonic* expectation and for two reasons: (a) It had to be built up by successive experiences (the rats, at first, went up to the doors and examined them in detail). (b) There were no stimuli coming from this food at the moment of choice, i.e., at the moment of the operation of this expectation. Such a mnemonic expectation of the direction of the goal-object relative to a subordinate goal-object was, in short, one which had to be learned —one which operated in the absence of any direct stimuli from the final goal-object in question.

The expectation of the direction of the sub-goal-object, the door, on the other hand, which evinced itself in the turning back at some given distance when the door was there, and not turning back in the "check" trials (of which three were given every day) when the door was not there, was a *perceptual* expectation, because there were stimuli directly present from this sub-avoidance object at the moment of its functioning.[24]

4. Summary

In the present chapter it has been shown that rats, more or less quickly, come to show evidence of what we may call a spatial-direction-of-the-goal-expectation in that they show a greater readiness for taking paths which point spatially in that general direction than for taking paths which do not point in that general direction. Furthermore, rats will learn to avoid a path which they "perceive" as leading in the direction of a subordinate avoidance-object such as a door.

[24] Another experiment indicating the building of a hierarchical expectation of a means-object relative to a goal-object seems to be that of Roberts. Cf. W. H. Roberts, The effect of delayed feeding of white rats in a problem cage, *J. Genet. Psychol.*, 1930, **37**, 35-58.

See also, for still another experiment contributing somewhat to this same problem, W. M. Borovski, Experimentelle Untersuchungen über den Lernprozess Nr. 4 (Über Labilität der Gewohnheiten), *Zsch. f. vergl. Physiol.*, 1930, **11**, 549-564.

Finally, examine also K. A. Williams, The reward value of a conditioned stimulus, *Univ. Calif. Publ. Psychol.*, 1929, **4**, 31-55. This experiment is described in detail, see below Chapter X, pp. 148 ff.

REFERENCES

Borovski, W. M., Experimentelle Untersuchungen über den Lernprozess Nr. 4. (Über Labilität der Gewohnheiten.), *Zsch. f. vergl. Physiol.*, 1930, **11**, 549-564.

Dashiell, J. F., Direction orientation in maze running by the white rat. *Comp. Psychol. Monog.*, 1930, 7, No. 32.

——————, Spatial orientation in maze-learning as a species of animal *Gestaltung. Proc. Ninth Internat. Cong. Psychol.* (Princeton, Psychol. Rev. Co., 1930), pp. 139-140.

Helson, H., Insight in the white rat. *J. Exper. Psychol.*, 1927, 10, 378-396.

Lashley, K. S., *Brain Mechanisms and Intelligence* (Chicago, Chicago Univ. Press, 1929).

Lashley, K. S. and Hubbert, H. B., Retroactive association and the elimination of errors in the maze. *J. Anim. Behav.*, 1917, 7, 130-138.

Lindley, S. B., The maze-learning ability of anosmic and blind anosmic rats. *J. Genet. Psychol.*, 1930, 37, 245-267.

Roberts, W. H., The effect of delayed feeding of white rats in a problem cage. *J. Genet. Psychol.*, 1930, 37, 35-58.

Robinson, E. W. and Wever, E. G., Visual distance perception in the rat. *Univ. Calif. Publ. Psychol.*, 1930, 4, 233-239.

Tolman, E. C. and Honzik, C. H., Degrees of hunger, reward and non-reward, and maze learning in rats. *Univ. Calif. Publ. Psychol.*, 1930, 4, 241-256.

—————— and ——————, Introduction and removal of reward and maze performance in rats. *Univ. Calif. Publ. Psychol.*, 1930, 4, 257-275.

Williams, K. A., The reward value of a conditioned stimulus, *Univ. Calif. Publ. Psychol.*, 1929, 4, 31-55.

Yoshioka, J. G., A preliminary study in discrimination of maze patterns by the rat. *Univ. Calif. Publ. Psychol.*, 1928, 4, 1-18.

——————, A further study in discrimination of maze patterns by the rat. *Univ. Calif. Publ. Psychol.*, 1929, 4, 135-153.

——————, A study of orientation in a maze. *Psychol. Bull.*, 1929, 26, 591-592.

——————, Direction as a factor in maze solution in rats. *J. Genet. Psychol.*, 1930, 38, 307-318.

Chapter IX

MNEMONIZATION, PERCEPTION, INFERENCE—SIGN-GESTALT-EXPECTATIONS

1. Mnemonization vs. Perception

IN the present chapter we shall begin by considering in more detail the difference between mnemonizations and perceptions in the case of means-end-expectations. A mnemonization, i.e., a memory in the most general sense,[1] we shall define as a means-end-expectation in which the expectation of the specific character of the more distant object, e.g., food, the terminal parts of the maze, etc., arise in part out of past stimuli no longer sensorially present at the moment in question. A perception, on the other hand, we shall define as a means-end-expectation in which the expectation of the character of the more distant object obviously depends primarily upon present stimuli, i.e., stimuli coming then and there from this more distant object. But such a distinction needs further analysis. Let us begin by considering in more detail the case of mnemonization.

2. Mnemonizations

Upon closer examination a mnemonization will be discovered to have four determining conditions: (a) a previous enjoyment or enjoyments (which occurred in some preceding trial or trials) of the specific distant object, food or maze-features, now being remembered;[2] (b) a previous enjoyment or enjoyments, also

---

[1] For a definition of memory in the more restricted sense see below, p. 139.

[2] The reader will perhaps need constantly to remind himself that the use of the terms perception, mnemonization and memory implies nothing as to consciousness. We use them here merely for the fact of the "setting" of a present behavior-act with respect to a coming object—a "setting" which in the case of a mnemonization or memory is dependent upon what happened upon some preceding occasion or occasions.

Also it is to be remembered that this use of the word enjoyment implies nothing more than commerce-with. [See Glossary.]

having occurred in those same preceding trials, of certain now perceptually present more immediate objects (maze-features); (c) the enjoyment, during those same preceding trials, of the direction and distance relations between such more immediate objects (maze-features) and such more distant (now-being-remembered) objects or maze-features, and (d) the immediate *re*-presentation, now, in the given trial, of the stimuli corresponding to the more immediate objects (maze-features).

It will be observed that conditions (a), (b) and (c), taken together, constitute a single total complex of commerces-with (enjoyments-of) which occurred in intimate conjunction with one another upon some preceding occasion or occasions. Condition (d) is a *re*-presentation, here and now, of the stimuli which correspond to one feature of that total complex. The functioning of a mnemonization consists, therefore, in the action whereby the repetition of stimuli, corresponding to but one feature of a total commerce-with complex, serves to arouse an expectation for the whole of that complex.

In other words, in the case of a mnemonization, the learning trials function to determine and define a total complex—shall we say *gestalt?*—consisting of immediate discriminanda and manipulanda, and more remote discriminanda and manipulanda, plus the direction-distance relations between these two sets of discriminanda and manipulanda. And when the stimuli corresponding to the one feature of this total gestalt of behavior-supports are *re*-presented, they serve to evoke an expectation of the whole.[3]

3. Signs, Significates, and Signified Means-End-Relations—Sign-Gestalts

For convenience of exposition we shall from now on, designate the remembered food (or distant maze feature) as the signified-objects, or *significates*. Secondly, we shall designate the immediate

---

[3] The doctrine here presented resembles that advanced by Hollingworth which he calls "redintegration"; it is akin also to Semon's law of *Ekphorie* and Woodworth's "law of combination," cf. H. L. Hollingworth, *The Psychology of Thought* (New York: D. Appleton and Company, 1926), p. 181 f., also Richard Semon, *Die Mnemischen Empfindungen* (Leipzig, W. Engelman, 1909), p. 173.

See also C. K. Ogden and I. A. Richards, *The Meaning of Meaning* (New York, Harcourt, Brace and Company, 1923), esp. p. 136 f.

maze-features, the stimuli for which are now *re*-presented, as the sign-objects, or *signs*. And, finally, the direction-distance-relations involved in the manner in which, on the previous occasions, the commerces with the signs led on to the commerce with the significates, we shall designate as the *signified means-end-relations*. The process of learning any specific maze is thus the building-up of, or rather a refinement of and correction in, the expectations of such specific (*sign, significate and signified means-end-relation*)-wholes, or, as we may hereafter call them, *sign-gestalts*.

4. Diagram of Mnemonized Sign-Gestalt

It may perhaps help, here, to draw a diagrammatic representation of the mnemonization of a specific goal-object (e.g., the mnemonization of a specific food). We suggest the following:

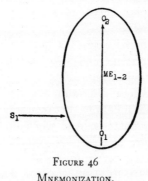

FIGURE 46
MNEMONIZATION.

S_1 represents the stimuli presented by the immediate maze parts, O_1 represents the discriminanda and manipulanda supports corresponding to these immediate maze parts which the animal expects as a result of S_1. The arrow ME_{1-2} represents the previously experienced and now expected means-end-relations (direction-distance correlations) whereby commerce with O_1 leads on to O_2, the more distant food, or maze parts. And O_2 represents these previously experienced and now expected more distant parts. Finally, the oval line inclosing O_1, ME_{1-2} and O_2 represents the fact that these expectations of O_1 and O_2 and the expectation that commerce with O_1 will lead to O_2 have, as a result of the preceding training, been united together in such a fashion that the stimuli for O_1 alone (i.e., S_1) now arouse, expectationally, the entire complex. That is, we have drawn the arrow from S_1 as debouching not into O_1, merely, but rather into the whole complex included in the oval. This is to indicate that all of the support-features included in the oval have now, as a result of learning, become integrated into a single dynamic [4] unit and that this unit is now released by S_2 alone. So much for a mnemonization; let us consider now, in contrast, a perception.

5. Perceptions

The definitive feature of a perception is that, in it, stimuli corresponding to all the parts of the total complex (the remote parts as well as the more immediate) are directly present. Imagine, again, the case of a wire maze. In such a maze there will be, we assume for the purposes of argument, a direct perception of the food. That is, in such a maze, stimuli will come directly to the animal from the goal-object, food, while he is still at the entrance and debating the entering of specific alleys. Further, we assume that here, as in the case of mnemonization, there will also be some degree of fusion between *sign, significate* and *signified means-end-relation*. In this case of the perception, however, the fusion will, by definition, result not from any past experiences; rather, it is to be conceived as prior to any such specific experience of the successive aspects of the whole complex. It will be only the successive sequential separation of the actual commerces with these separate aspects which will make these latter successively prominent and separate from one another. The fusion must be conceived therefore as coming directly, insofar as it does really obtain, from the inter-arrangements of the stimuli themselves. The diagram for the *perception* of a goal-object O_2 we should draw, therefore, as shown in FIGURE 47.

Again we enclose the O_1, ME_{1-2}, and O_2 in a uniting oval to indicate fusion: to indicate that these constitute a fused, dynamic, "gestalted" whole. The releasing stimuli in this case include, however, not only S_1 but also S_2 (as indicating O_2) and S_1S_2 (as indicating the means-end-relation, ME_{1-2} which O_2 has to O_1). This combination of stimuli S_1, S_1S_2 and S_2 we have drawn as

---

[4] For this use of dynamic see W. Köhler, *Gestalt Psychology* (New York, Horace Liveright, 1929), Ch. IX.

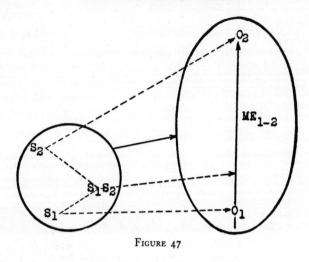

FIGURE 47

interacting among themselves and then tending, as a whole, to evoke the unified sign-gestalt.

6.   Mnemonizations vs. Perceptions—Advantages and Disadvantages

Examine now the two diagrams. In the case of a mnemonization, stimuli corresponding to the first part, i.e., the sign, in the total expected gestalt are alone present. And these stimuli, on a basis of the fusions built up in preceding trials, now function, by themselves, to release expectations for the whole sign-gestalt. In the case of a perception, the stimuli corresponding to *all* the parts (sign, signified means-end-relations, and significates) of the total expected pattern are presented; and, although none of these specific supports, corresponding to the stimuli, need, as such, have been presented before, the stimuli now interact to arouse the expectation for them as a whole.

With reference to probable verisimilitude:—on the one hand, a perception would seem to have priority over a mnemonization, inasmuch as, for a perception, the stimuli corresponding to all the expected support-features and expected means-end correlations are actually presented; but on the other hand, a mnemonization would seem to have priority over a perception, inasmuch as, in a mnemonization, the total pattern of supports has in the past actually been, as such, enjoyed (even though the stimuli for the more distant parts of this pattern are now lacking).

Finally, however, it may be noted that differences between perceptions and mnemonizations are probably, in actuality, always differences in degree only. For it seems that there are probably no actual cases of pure perceptions—i.e., perceptions unaided by any memory—save in new-born organisms. In practically all of the situations met by the least worldly-wise of organisms, some of the stimuli corresponding to certain of the expected support-features are apt to be, then and there, absent; and in probably every case of a so-called perception, as well as in that of a so-called mnemonization, some of the presented stimuli, or rather the corresponding expected supports, will have been met before and function as signs for one another. The honk of an automobile horn will "set" all save a new-born infant, not only for that sound *qua* sound or even merely for the type of horn which produces it, but also for the whole signified complex: automobile plus impatient driver.

7. Mnemonization vs. Memories

It must be indicated now in what way that which we have been calling a mnemonization is more general than and different from a "memory" proper in the usual restricted sense of the latter term. A mnemonization is a more fundamental, *Ur-typ* of, postulation, of which a "memory," in the restricted sense, is a specific sub-variety. Thus, whenever a rat on a basis of past patterns of consecutive enjoyment is now led to expect a total complex interrelation of supports on the basis of stimuli corresponding to only a part of that complex, we designate the case one of mnemonic expectation—a mnemonization. And FIGURE 46 represents that case. It will be our further contention now, however, that for such a "mnemonic" expectation to be further specified as a "memory" there has to be involved, *in addition*, the further feature of an expectation to the effect that the significate lies so and so in the *time* dimension. We have as yet no evidence that any sub-human animal, not even the ape, let alone the rat, can remember in this more restricted temporal sense. We have no evidence, that is, that such animals can choose between alternative objects on a basis of their *degrees* of temporal "pastness," i.e., on the basis of their "dates." [5] Hence we have no evidence as yet of any true "memories" in any animals below man. For an animal to remember, and not merely to mnemonize, he must not only expect a given character in a past significate, but he must also expect a means-end-relation of pastness as obtaining between the present sign and that past significate. No proofs of this ability in any animals below man seem as yet ever to have been presented.

8. Inferences

Finally, it may be well to recall for a moment in passing that in addition to mnemonizations (memories) and perceptions there was, we said (see above, Chapter VI, p. 96 f.), a third "mood" of means-end-expectation, viz.: *inference*. Or, as we should now say, there is a third mood or type of sign-gestalt-expectation. And such inferential sign-gestalt-expectations are to be defined as cases in which the rat, or other animal, releases the given expectation of the to-come significate neither by virtue of actual present stimuli coming then and there from that significate nor by virtue of the past enjoyment of the specific sequence—given sign, given means-end-relation and given significate—but rather by virtue of the action of other correlated sign-gestalt-expectations. A further analysis and experimental demonstration of the possibility of such inferential sign-gestalt-expectations must be postponed for a later chapter (Chapter XI). For the present it must suffice to point out in passing that the diagram for such inferential expectations will have to be the same as for mnemonic expectations. We cannot, that is, easily represent, in any two-dimensional drawing, the difference between the two cases, that where the sequence $O_1 \ ME_{1-2} \ O_2$ has actually been experienced before (i.e., the mnemonization) and that where it has not been experienced before (i.e., the inference).

9. The Three Moods of Sign-Gestalt-Expectation

To recapitulate, means-end-expectations always take the form of sign-gestalt-expectations. And there are what we may call three *moods* of such sign-gestalt-expectations:

[5] Cf. E. W. Atkins and J. F. Dashiell, Reactions of the white rat to multiple stimuli in temporal orders, *J. Comp. Psychol.*, 1921, 1, 433-452.

(i) *Perception.* Stimuli corresponding to all parts of the sign-gestalt, i.e., sign, significate and signified means-end relations, are present.

(ii) *Mnemonization.* Stimuli for the sign only are present, but the stimuli for the significate and the signified means-end-relations are absent. But these latter stimuli, along with the corresponding supports, i.e., the significate and the means-end-relations themselves, have, as such, been specifically experienced in the past. Such mnemonization may in the case of highly developed organisms be a "memory" in the more restricted sense, if the postulated direction and distance of the significate includes, also, a specific degree of pastness in time.

(iii) *Inference.* Stimuli for the sign only are present. Stimuli for the significate and the signified means-end-relations are absent. Furthermore, this particular instance of significate and signified means-end-relation has by hypothesis, never as such been experienced before. The expectation of this particular significate and signified means-end-relation is due to present or past experiences of other related parts of the total means-end field. (See Chapter XI.)

10.   Sign-Gestalts and Direction-Distance Correlations

Finally, the connection should be indicated between this concept of sign-gestalts and that of direction-distance correlations elaborated in the preceding chapters. Obviously the two concepts are closely related. In fact, we shall now assert that what we are here calling sign-gestalts are in fact no more than direction-distance correlations with, however, a further emphasis upon their whole-like or "gestalted" character. In short, that which we formerly designated as the direction of a means-object we are now calling an immediately presented (or a ready-for) "sign-object." And that which we previously designated as the correlated "distance" we are now calling an expected (or ready-for) "shortness" or "longness" of the "signified means-end-relation" between such sign-object and some resulting "significate." The concept sign-gestalt is, however, more inclusive and more useful in two ways: (a) The sign-gestalt concept emphasizes that the distance is always a distance to a significate (possible goal-object) as well as from a sign; and (b) the sign-gestalt concept also emphasizes that the sign-object (i.e., means-object of such and such a "direction") plus signified means-end-relation (i.e., expected "distance") plus signified object (i.e., expected goal-object or possible goal-object) never actually function in behavior as separated or atomized units. They always fuse together into some single, gestalt-like whole.

Such being the situation, the concepts of the sign-gestalt-readiness and sign-gestalt-expectation will very largely replace those of means-end-readiness and means-end-expectation throughout the subsequent discussions.

REFERENCES

Atkins, E. W., and Dashiell, J. F., Reactions of the white rat to multiple stimuli in temporal orders. *J. Comp. Psychol.*, 1921, 1, 433-452.

Hollingworth, H. L., *The Psychology of Thought* (New York, D. Appleton and Company, 1926).

Köhler, W., *Gestalt Psychology* (New York, Horace Liveright, 1929).

Ogden, C. K. and Richards, I. A., *The Meaning of Meaning* (New York, Harcourt, Brace and Company, 1923).

Semon, R. W., *Die Mnemischen Empfindungen* (Leipzig, W. Engelman, 1909).

Chapter X

LEARNING AND DELAYED REACTION

1. Learning and Sign-Gestalts

IT should be clear from the preceding chapter that according to us mnemonizations (or memories) result from the acquisition of immanent sign-gestalt-expectations. In the present chapter we wish to consider such acquisitions in more detail and to note in general all the other phenomena which may be supposed to be involved in such learning. In fact, all the significant changes and phenomena of maze-learning can, we believe, be summarized under the following heads:

(a) Maze-learning involves the mnemonic acquisition of greater precision and differentiation at each point of bifurcation in the maze relative to the sign-gestalt-expectations to be released at that point.

(b) Maze-learning involves an integration of the sign-gestalt-expectations at successive points of bifurcation into one single more extensive sign-gestalt-expectation.

(c) Maze-learning involves the acquisition of temporary goal-characters by what were originally mere sign-objects (means-objects).

(d) Maze-learning involves a reformation, not only of the animal's sign-gestalt-expectations released by the specific maze, but also of the general sign-gestalt-readinesses which he will thereafter tend to carry away with him to other mazes.

(e) Maze-learning may involve the reduction of sign-gestalt-readinesses and sign-gestalt-expectations to the rank of mere "fixations."

(f) "Delayed Reaction" learning involves the holding of aroused sign-gestalt-expectations "in leash" over an interval of time and then having them work themselves out into actual behavior on the basis of "condensed signs" only.

Let us consider these one at a time.

2. Refinement of Sign-Gestalts at Points of Bifurcation

Initially, and before experience, any opening in a maze (or problem-box) must be supposed to arouse a merely relatively vague sign-gestalt-expectation, i.e., a sign-gestalt-expectation that food *may* perhaps be reached by commerce with this kind of opening. Such initial sign-gestalts are really, that is, double-action affairs. The rat which is expecting that a given opening will, or *may*, lead to food or some further explorable object, is, *pari passu,* also expecting a complementary possibility, viz., that it *may* also lead to non-food or to non-further-to-be-explored features, to blind-ends, walls, etc. To be ready to enter any given alley-opening is, that is to say, to be assuming both (a) that such entrance may lead to food or to further explorable features, and (b) that it may lead to non-food, or non-further-to-be-explored features. To expect one thing is, *pari passu,* to expect the "possibility" of the opposite of that thing. Properly to represent this complementary, double-ended, character of sign-gestalt-expectations, we should therefore redraw our diagrams in some such fashion as the following:

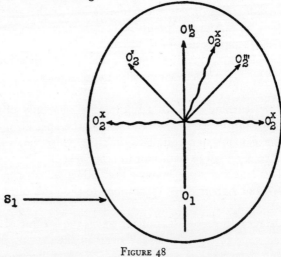

FIGURE 48

In addition to O'_2, O''_2, O'''_2, i.e., the expected or hoped-for food, or further-to-be-explored objects, we have added other

O_2^x's to represent the possible non-foods and non-explorable objects, the expectations of which are also present and which we have depicted by means of wavy arrows. Thus we would suppose that the refinement of sign-gestalts, which comes about with learning, is not merely a selection and rejection as between types of food, or types of to-be-explored object, but also and first a discovery of the routes which actually lead to food or to-be-explored objects, and the differentiation of them from the routes

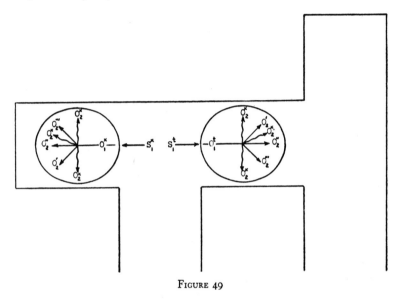

FIGURE 49

which prove rather to lead to non-foods and non-to-be-explored objects. But we may illustrate this more concretely by a concrete maze picture.

Let FIGURE 49 represent the initial sign-gestalt-expectations before learning at some specific point of bifurcation. Before learning, the rat is ready to treat both the alternative alleys as alike. That is, in terms of actual behaviors, he is ready to enter them with equal frequencies, and in terms of immanent expectations he is ready to expect the possibilities of both "good" and "bad" significates and short and long distances as a result of either of them. After learning, on the other hand, the one entrance has become a sign of "good" significates (food or lead-on-ableness), and the other has become a sign of "bad" significates (non-food and non-further-to-be-explored objects). After learning, in other words, the expectation picture will become more like that represented in FIGURE 50. The stimuli at the blind entrance have come to release a sign-gestalt-expectation in which the significate O_2^x is a blind-end, an object, non-explorable; while the stimuli at the true path opening have come to release a sign-gestalt-expectation in which the significate O_2' is either actual food or a further-to-be-explored object.

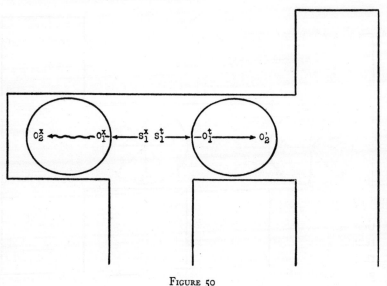

FIGURE 50

In other words, learning as here depicted consists of the development of a differentiation between the characters, i.e., directions, of two sign-objects, O_1^x and O_1', originally responded to as alike, plus a correlative differentiation in the correlated significates and distances. Before learning all the alley-openings were responded to as alike. They were all taken as signs both of possible food, or further-to-be-explored objects, and of possible non-food, or non-further-to-be-explored objects. After learning, on the other hand, they have become differentiated. Some of them have become more specifically signs of food (or leading-on-ness) and short distances and others more specifically signs of something "bad," i.e., non-food and non-further-to-be-explored objects and long distances.

3.   Integration of Sign-Gestalts

We turn now to the second effect of learning listed above. The rat's learning of a maze brings about not only the above refinement and differentiation of the sign-gestalt-expectations at the points of bifurcation, but also it induces a telescoping or integra-

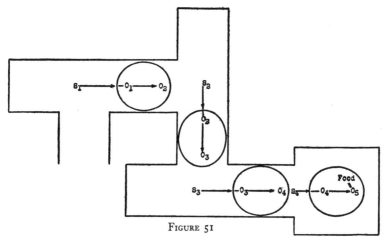

FIGURE 51

tion of successive sign-gestalt-expectations into single more extended ones. That is, the stimuli at any opening of a section of the true path will come to release not only the immediate sign-gestalt-expectation corresponding to that section per se but also a

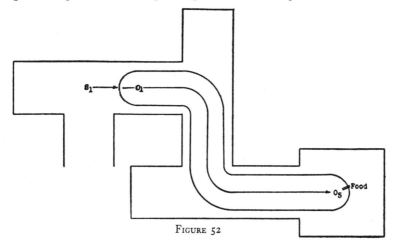

FIGURE 52

more extended, inclusive, sign-gestalt-expectation corresponding to this section plus succeeding sections. Again let us resort to sketches. FIGURE 51 represents the condition before learning and FIGURE 52 that after learning. What happens, as indicated in these sketches, is that the first O comes to absorb all the succeeding ones. That is, the feature of learning here depicted consists in an extension of the O_1 which is released by the initial stimuli.

To sum up: Learning requires first a differentiation between the *this* which leads on, and the *that* which does not lead on; and *then* as here depicted a further integration of the succession of these "thises," into one extensive "this."

4. Sign-Objects Become Goal-Objects

Finally, our third point was that, in so far as in the course of learning certain features become the signs for food rather than non-food, these signs tend to acquire temporary demands in and

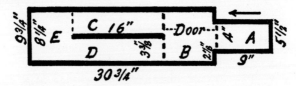

FIGURE 53

"*A* is the starting box from which a door leads into the vestibule *B*. *C* and *D* are choice compartments leading out of this vestibule. *E* is the eating chamber. The whole box is made of redwood but *A* and *B* are unpainted and have green oilcloth on the floor. *C*, *D*, and *E*, on the other hand, are painted white on the inner sides and have white oilcloth on the floor. But in any given trial either *C* or *D* (*C* as shown in the figure) has fitted into it an inner shell in the form of a cardboard box open at one end only and lined with black oilcloth. This cardboard shell can easily be shifted from side to side—then sometimes (as in the figure) *D* is the white open side, and sometimes *C*. The animals thus develop no position-habits but have to learn to take the side which in that trial is white and open. The food dish is always placed around the corner out of sight from the entrance to the white compartment."

of themselves. This is very prettily illustrated in an experiment by Williams.[1]

She used a 14-unit Multiple T-maze (see above, Chapter III,

[1] Katherine Adams Williams, The reward value of a conditioned stimulus, *Calif. Publ. Psychol.*, 1924, **4**, 31-55.

FIGURE 4) and found with this maze that blind entrances and
times will decrease not only, as was indicated by Blodgett's and by
Tolman and Honzik's experiments cited above (pp. 48ff), when
rats previously unfed are suddenly provided with food, but also
when they are provided with features which have become merely
a "sign" for food.

More specifically her procedure was the following. Her rats
were first trained for ten trials a day in a simple white-black discrimination-box, FIGURE 53.

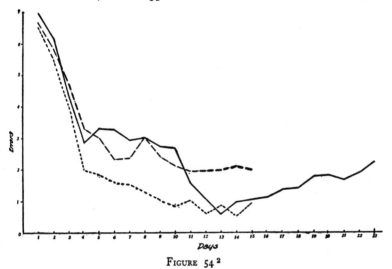

FIGURE 54 [2]

————Group I Experimental
- - - -Group II Non-reward control
......Group III Food control

This discrimination training was continued until each rat made
at least eight correct choices out of ten trials on each of three consecutive days; but, if this criterion was reached before the twelfth
day, the training was continued until that day. All rats thus received at least 120 preliminary training trials in the discrimination
box and some received more.

Next, all the rats were run for one trial a day in the maze. They,
however, continued to have their ten trials in the discrimination
box every afternoon, not less than two hours after the maze running. For the purposes of the maze experiment the rats were

[2] *Op. cit.,* p. 42.

divided into three groups: two control groups and one experimental group. The error and time curves for these three groups
are shown in FIGURE 54 and FIGURE 55.

We may describe Group II first, then Group III, and, finally,
Group I.

Group II, the first control group, never found food at the end
of the maze, merely a new, strange and empty unpainted goal-box
in which they were confined for thirty seconds before being removed to their living cages. They received their daily allowance

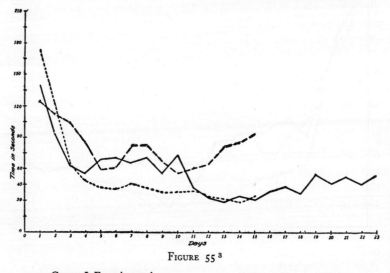

FIGURE 55 [3]

————Group I Experimental
- - - -Group II Non-reward control
......Group III Food control

of food some two hours later in their daily discrimination-box
practice. It is to be observed that this group, while it did to some
extent learn the maze, relatively soon reached a plateau and from
then on made little further improvement.

Group III, the second control group, found throughout their
maze-practice the familiar discrimination-box, now placed at the
end of the maze with food in it. They, like both the other groups,
had ten or more trials in the discrimination-box in the afternoon
in a different part of the room. This group, it will be observed,
showed a normal, rapid learning curve in the maze.

[3] *Op. cit.,* p. 46.

Group I was the experimental group. During the first eight days of their maze running they were treated like Group II. That is, at the end of the maze they found nothing but the new, strange, empty goal-box. From the ninth day on, however, they were suddenly provided with the discrimination-box at the end of the maze, *though now with no food in it.* It is to be observed that after they had thus found the familiar discrimination-box, even with *no food* in it, they began to improve and on the thirteenth day their curves had got down to the level of Group III, who were receiving the discrimination-box *with food in it.* Later, however, they reverted to their previous poor performance, so that by the twenty-third day they were making almost as many errors and taking as much time as they had before the introduction of the discrimination-box as a goal-object for the maze.

What is to be the interpretation of these results? Following Dr. Williams, our interpretation will be that, as a result of the discrimination trials, the discrimination-box had become a sign for food. And when the sign for food was introduced to the animals of Group I as the reward at the end of the maze, it had at first the same to-be-demanded character, or almost the same, as the introduction of actual food would have had. Hence the drop in their maze performance.[4]

After a number of further experiences, however, the animals of the experimental group began to discover that here at the end of the maze the discrimination-box was not a real sign. And, when they had discovered this, they reverted back to their previous poor performance.

5. Changes in Sign-Gestalt-Readinesses

The next feature to be considered with respect to the influence of learning upon the immanent determinants is the fact that after learning has brought about the above sorts of changes in the expected sign-gestalts, such changes are going to react upon and

[4] It is to be noted that the drop in performance curves produced by this introduction of the sign was not so sudden and sharp as it was in the experiments of Blodgett, and Tolman and Honzik (see above, Chapter III, pp. 48 ff.) in which actual food was introduced. This suggests that the sign did not have quite the same to-be-demanded character that the actual food would have had or at any rate that it took longer for all the individual animals to become sensitive to it.

modify the "readinesses" to sign-gestalts which the animal is going to carry with him to subsequent problems. The effect is one of reinforcing the propensities for certain types of means-objects as "probable" ways to given types of goal and weakening it for others.

Thus, for example, the rat who has learned in a given maze that right-turning alleys are more often correct than left-turning ones is going to carry away with him a greater propensity for right-turning alleys to subsequent mazes. He will carry to such subsequent mazes means-end-readinesses different from his original ones. These new readinesses will assert, not merely that explorable objects, such as alleys, are in general good for getting to food, but also that to-the-right-leading alleys are more likely to be thus good than to-the-left-leading ones. Or, again, the rat who has learned in a discrimination-box that a white alley leads to food and a black does not is going to be more predisposed to choose white alleys in subsequent discrimination-boxes and in subsequent mazes than he is black alleys. Whiteness of alleys is going to play a part in his means-end-readinesses which it did not play before. (See above Chapter II.)

Indeed, it will now be obvious that what we are thus designating as the back action of acquired specific means-end-expectations upon the means-end-readinesses is no more than our way of stating the classical phenomenon of "transfer." Wherever an animal exhibits transfer effects from one problem-situation to another, such transfer will be described by us as due: (a) to the fact that learning in the first situation establishes, not merely specific concrete sign-gestalt-expectations, but also more general relatively permanent sign-gestalt-readinesses corresponding to the former; and (b) to the fact that the given animal will then carry such modified readinesses to subsequent situations; and (c) to the fact that, in the given case, this subsequent second situation presents sign-objects similar enough to those presented by the first situation so that these new sign-gestalt-readinesses will tend to operate and facilitate correct performance in this second situation also.

6.   Fixation

Another phenomenon must now be noted as also involved, in some cases at least, of learning. In previous discussions this phenomenon has been largely ignored. It is the phenomenon of fixation.

Such fixation we would conceive as a relatively mechanical sort of attachment to a specific means-activity which sometimes seems to set in on top of, or in place of, a true sign-gestalt-expectation. The animal begins a problem in apparently cognitive, docile sign-gestalt fashion. He seems to embark initially upon a particular means-object route because it fits in with the sign-gestalt-readiness which he brings with him and because it has actually proved good in a considerable number of preceding trials. And then he apparently loses his docility and becomes "fixated" upon this particular means-route. He persists in choosing it, willy nilly, even though in later trials it prove no longer preponderantly good. A familiar example of such fixation, in the case of rats, is the so-called "position-habits" which are prone to appear in discrimination-box experiments and which are such a nuisance to an experimenter.

It will be recalled that in the typical discrimination-box procedure the left alley and the right alley are made correct an equal number of times in the total course of the day's trials. This correctness, and its distinguishing cue of whiteness—or other stimulus —is shifted back and forth from right to left in irregular order. Yet what often happens, and what proves so disturbing to an operator, is that the rat will, on the basis apparently of the first few trials in which a given side, say the right, may have been more often correct, or on the basis, perhaps, of having become in an extraneous fashion frightened on the other side, come to choose that right-hand side persistently and continuously from then on— quite irrespective of the fact that the other side will be, in the long run, just as often correct. In such a case the rat has formed what is called a "position-habit." Or, in our present terms, he has become *fixated* upon the right-hand alley.

Our doctrine is that in such cases the initial sign-gestalt-expectation, on the basis of which he originally chose the right-hand side, has lost its original sign-gestalt character. It has become no longer a true expectation but an almost blind "mechanical" attachment to that particular alley—an attachment which it may take a tremendous lot of "disproving" to break down. Position-habits have been known to persist for many trials in spite of the fact that during this period the operator may have, in order to break them down, forsaken the original fifty-fifty distribution and caused the opposite alley to be the correct one consecutively for many trials.

Fixations must be conceived, then, as both the *antithesis* and the *nemesis* of sign-gestalt-expectations. They overtake the latter with certain animals under certain conditions.[5]

7. The Nature of Delayed Reactions

Last of all, this would seem a good place to raise the question as to what may be involved in that special and relatively unique sort of learning, or memory, known as the delayed reaction. Hunter[6] in his classical experiment on the delayed reaction used an experimental technique devised by Carr which has since come to be known as the "indirect" method of testing delayed reaction, as contrasted with the "direct" method which Hunter himself and also Köhler, Yerkes and Tinkelpaugh have since used.[7]

The essence of the *indirect* method lies in the fact that it involves a preliminary discrimination-training in which the animal is taught to choose by means of some sort of cue, e.g., light, an indicated door in a discrimination-box. After this has been learned the delay procedure proper is introduced. That is, after the animal has been thoroughly trained so that on practically every trial he selects the door which in that trial has the cue (light) turned on over it, the procedure is then begun of removing this cue (light), at shorter or longer intervals, before the animal is released. He is required, in short, to "delay" before making his response relative to the cue which is now no longer present. In Hunter's actual

[5] It must, however, be confessed that the exact nature of these conditions which underlie fixations is probably as yet far from known. For a still further discussion of fixation, see below, Chapter XIX, p. 299 f.

[6] W. S. Hunter, Delayed reaction in animals and children, *Behav. Monog.*, 1913, 2, No. 6.

[7] For discussion and references, see W. S. Hunter, The delayed reaction tested by the direct method: a correction, *Psychol. Bull.*, 1929, 26, 546-548.

W. Köhler, Über eine neue Methode zur psychologischen Untersuchung von Menschenaffen, *Psychol. Forsch.*, 1922, 2, 390-397.

O. L. Tinklepaugh, An experimental study of representative factors in monkeys, *J. Comp. Psychol.*, 1928, 8, 197-236.

R. M. Yerkes and D. N. Yerkes, Concerning memory in the chimpanzee, *J. Comp. Psychol.*, 1928, 8, 237-272.

R. M. Yerkes, The mind of a gorilla: II. Mental development, *Genet. Psychol. Monog.*, 1927, 2, No. 6.

J. A. Bierens de Haan, Über das Suchen nach vestecktem Futter bei Affen und Halbaffen, *Zsch. f. vergl. Physiol.*, 1930, 11, 630-655.

experiment the animal came into the choice chamber and saw the light over one of three doors, but he was restrained by a removable glass partition from actually going to that lighted door until some period after the light had been turned off. The test consisted in determining how long, on the average, a given animal could thus delay after the cue had been removed and still tend to choose correctly when finally released. How long could he hold his sign-gestalt-expectation "in leash"?

Hunter tried the experiment with rats, dogs, raccoons, and children. In the case of the raccoons and the children he found that they could delay successfully, without any maintenance of overt bodily orientation towards the correct door, for periods up to thirty seconds in the case of the raccoons, and for far longer periods in the case of the children. (Fifty seconds in the case of a two and one-half year old child, twenty-five minutes or more in the case of older children.) The dogs and the rats, on the other hand, he found incapable of successful delays unless they took up an *overt bodily orientation* and maintained this throughout the delay interval. With the aid of this gross orientation one rat was capable of a ten seconds delay and the dogs of a five minutes delay.[8]

We shall not further consider those cases in which successful delays occurred only as a result of a gross bodily orientation. Our interest will be rather in the cases of apparently "true delays" (such as were obtained with the raccoons and the children). In these the successes depended upon some internal non-overt state. And, although no such "pure delays" were obtained for rats by Hunter, something closely akin to them (as we shall see in a moment) seems to have been obtained for rats by more recent investigators. In any case, the point we are now interested in is what such "pure delays" amount to, if and when obtained.

Consider, again, the preceding analysis. It is obvious that as far as the preliminary discrimination is concerned the situation is essentially that of ordinary maze-learning. The analysis, given in the just preceding sections, relative to learning at a point of bifurcation can be applied directly. Thus to return to FIGURE 50 we may

---

[8] That dogs are thus capable of successful delay *only* in case they assume a gross bodily orientation was subsequently disproved by Walton. Cf. A. C. Walton. The Influence of diverting stimuli during delayed reaction in dogs, *J. Anim. Behav.*, 1915, **5**, 259-291.

conceive of S_1^t as representing the stimuli from the lighted door on any given trial, and S_1^x as representing those from either of the non-lighted doors. And this preliminary discrimination learning will, then, have consisted in the building up of the two contrasted sign-gestalt-expectations, where the lighted door S_1^t has become a sign for getting on to food O_2', whereas any non-lighted door S_1^x, has become a sign for getting on to non-food O_2^x.

The really new and important question to be considered is, however, what more is implied in the delay tests proper, which are made subsequent to this preliminary discrimination training. Such delay tests involve, it is to be noted, two occasions:—(i) the "presentation" occasion and (ii) the "functioning" occasion. On the presentation-occasion the animal sees the light over one of the doors, but is not allowed to respond to this sign then and there. On the functioning-occasion he is allowed to respond, but the "light" portion of the original sign has disappeared in the interim. Let us analyze the situations involved in these two occasions further.

(i) On the *presentation-occasion* the set-up is the same as in the foregoing discrimination trials. As a result of the discrimination learning, the presentation of the light over one of the doors provides the appropriate stimulus S_1^t, such that the animal has evoked in him the total sign-gestalt-expectation whereby this light-plus-door, O_1^t, is the sign which, if had commerce with, will lead on to the significate, food, O_2'. And any other door plus lack of light is *pari passu* sign that, if had commerce with, will lead on to the significate non-food, O_2^x. But these sign-gestalt-expectations are not allowed then and there to work themselves out into actual behavior. The presentation-occasion presents signs and evokes sign-gestalt-expectations. But these expectations are not allowed to go over into actual behavior then and there. They must be held "in leash."

Furthermore, it is also worth noting that in this typical delayed reaction set-up, as in the simple discrimination experiment, the presentation-occasion involves only one exposure of the sign. The light is exposed but once and the animal has to evoke the appropriate sign-gestalt-expectation as a result of that one exposure. The animal must, in short, in some way retain the last exposure of the light as distinct in its effect upon his nervous system from all the other similar and different exposures which have occurred in preceding trials.[9] He must be able to remember and distinguish the last one out of many light exposures.

Turn now to the functioning-occasion.

(ii) The first point to be noted about the *functioning-occasion* is that on it the total original signs that were involved in the presentation-occasion are no longer all present. The door which was lighted and the doors which were not lighted are, to be sure, still there; but the light which distinguished between them is gone. And yet in the case of the successful delay this distinction between these two sets of doors still operates. The door which had the light is still in some way distinguished for the animal from the doors which did not have the light. So that the former will again call out the proper sign-gestalt-expectation of leading on to food; while the latter will again call out those of leading to non-food. But this means, it would seem, that there is really a further process at work on the presentation-occasion which has not yet been considered.

This further process occurring on the presentation-occasion let us, for want of a better name, designate as the "condensation of the sign." The original presentation operates, that is, not merely to evoke in the animal, then and there, a sign-gestalt-expectation to the effect that the total complex, light plus door leads on to food, but also to establish a condensation of this sign-character from this complex as a whole to the mere door by itself (i.e., the door as characterized by its special spatial position or other still-remaining distinctive feature).

The ability to delay successfully means, that is, that, in the original presentation, the animal not merely achieves the appropriate sign-gestalt-expectation that the given total sign (door plus

---

[9] This fact, that the effect of this last exposure of the light readily keeps itself distinct in the animal from the effects of preceding exposures, is probably to be explained as a phenomenon similar to the finding of Zeigarnik (Cf. K. Lewin, Untersuchungen zur Handlungs- und Affektpsychologie. III. Über das Behalten von erledigten und unerledigten Handlungen. Von Bluma Zeigarnik, *Psychol. Forsch.*, 1927, **9**, 1-85) that an interrupted task is better retained and more readily recalled by human subjects than are completed tasks. As Lewin would say, there is a *Spannung* set up by any projected task and as long as this task remains uncompleted this *Spannung* remains unresolved and active. Completed tasks, on the other hand, lose their *Spannung* and hence do not get confused in the organism with the still uncompleted ones. Sign-gestalt-expectations held "in leash" are more active than ones which have already worked themselves out into actual behavior.

light) will lead on to the desired significate, but also he condenses this sign-character to a mere part or feature of itself, a part or feature which alone will be present on the later functioning-occasion. On the presentation-occasion the animal, who can successfully delay, does not merely make use of his previous learning to evoke in himself the sign-gestalt-expectation that the lighted door leads on to food, but also he establishes in himself the further relation that therefore this door *qua* itself, even though the light be removed, will lead on to food. And then, when on the functioning-occasion, this condensed feature alone is presented, it simply by itself is able to evoke the total sign-gestalt-expectation. And this latter then works itself out in the actual behavior.

To sum up, to delay successfully means three things. It means (a) the ability as a result of a single exposure of a sign to evoke a total sign-gestalt-expectation. It means (b) the ability to hold this sign-gestalt-expectation "in leash" over an interval of imposed delay in which it is not allowed to pass over into actual behavior. And it means (c) after this delay to have this sign-gestalt-expectation able to work itself out into actual behavior on a basis of a mere portion of the original sign, i.e., on the basis of a "condensed sign."

8. Delayed Reaction in Rats

But rats, according to Hunter, were incapable of such delays. At any rate they were incapable of them in the particular sort of set-up which Hunter used. It must be noted, however, that recently somewhat different types of delayed reaction set-up have been tried with rats and in these they have proved successful.

The first of these new experiments we would report is that of Honzik.[10] His method was different from Hunter's in two features. The first of these was probably of minor importance. That is, instead of using a light to indicate the correct door, he used a white curtain as contrasted with two black ones over the two wrong doors. In a preliminary discrimination training, similar to that used by Hunter, his rats were taught to go to the door which in the given trial had the white curtain hanging in front of it and to push through the latter rather than through either one of the black curtains.

---

[10] C. H. Honzik, Delayed reaction in rats, *Univ. Calif. Publ. Psychol.*, 1931, **4**, 307-318.

The second and really important difference between the Honzik and the Hunter techniques appeared in the delay experiment proper. That is, on the presentation-occasion Honzik did not restrain a rat at the entrance, as did Hunter, but allowed the animal actually to choose the white curtain—to make, that is, the overt response of actually coming forward and touching it. The rat was not allowed to pass through the curtain because all curtains now had stiff boards behind them. As soon as this overt choice response had been made, a screen was dropped in front of all three curtains; and the rat ran about in the choice chamber during the desired delay period. The screen was then lifted, all three curtains had in the meantime been changed to black, and the animal, if he were to delay successfully, now had to choose that one of the three doors "where the white curtain had been." With this method Honzik obtained with some animals high percentages of correct choices after delays of from seven to forty-five seconds.

Now the significant feature about this Honzik technique, as we see it, is the fact of the overt choice response which the animal was allowed to make at the time of the original presentation. The function of this overt choice—this overt going to the white curtain— was, we believe, that of aiding and making easy the necessary process of sign-condensation. By virtue of actually going to the given door, the transference of the sign-character from the total complex—white curtain plus door—to the single feature, door, was brought about and made easy. The going to the door on the presentation-occasion emphasized the character of that specific door, i.e., its position and the fact that it was the sign for food. We believe, in short, that the rats delayed more successfully with the Honzik method than with the Hunter method because the former emphasized during the original presentation-occasion certain of the sign-features, which were to remain and continue to be present after the delay. The condensation of the sign to these "continuing" features was thus facilitated.

The second experiment, also seeming to give very positive results as to delayed reaction in rats, which we would report is that of Maier.[11] This experiment, while important and significant in itself, does not, we shall now contend, present a "true case" of delayed reaction in our sense.

[11] N. R. F. Maier, Delayed reaction and memory in rats, *J. Genet. Psychol.*, 1929, **36**, 538-550.

Maier used a set-up that consisted of three ringstands from the top of which elevated paths led to a table and food, but only one ringstand and the path leading from it was correct in any given trial. The rat was first placed at the bottom of the correct ringstand and allowed to run up it and over the path to food three times in succession. He was then delayed on the table or in another room for varying periods of time, from one minute to twenty-four hours, and finally allowed to descend from the table by a fourth ringstand and to choose while on the floor that ringstand and path over which he had run previous to this delay. Maier's results showed that the rats could, in this sense, often "delay" successfully for a number of minutes or even hours.

It is our contention, however, that while this experiment undoubtedly demonstrates a remarkable and unexpected ability on the part of the rat it does not demonstrate a true "delay" ability. For it is to be observed that not just a sign was presented but the whole sign-gestalt was actually "enjoyed"—had commerce-with—before the delay. In fact the situation was really similar to that of maze or discrimination-box. The animal discovered in the three preliminary trials which ringstand was correct. As in the maze, he actually had commerce with the whole sign-gestalt— such-and-such-a-ringstand-running-over-it-getting-to-food. It was not, that is, as in a true delayed reaction performance, a case in which on the presentation-occasion a sign only was exposed.

On the other hand, it of course does indicate a far greater degree of mnemonization- and expectation-ability than that demonstrated by the ordinary maze or discrimination-box. It indicates that the rat can after only three enjoyments of a given total sign-gestalt, differentiate this from two other alternatives, which have themselves been correct on previous occasions, and that he can retain this differentiation over a surprisingly long period of time, and, finally, that he can recognize and approach such a sign-object from a different place from that in which he approached it during the original learning.

9. The Direct Method

Finally, however, in order to complete this analysis of the delayed reaction let us consider what according to us would now seem to be involved in the so-called "direct method," which has been employed with such success with the primates. (See above, footnote 7, p. 154.) A first essential feature of this "direct method" would seem to consist in the fact that on the presentation-occasion the animal "sees" the goal-object actually placed with reference to the sign. He "sees" the food hidden in some specific place or put into some specific container. In other words, instead of having presented the stimuli corresponding to the sign-object only, he has presented stimuli corresponding to the total sign-gestalt. The animal perceives the total sign-gestalt, instead of perceiving merely a sign for that total sign-gestalt and having to mnemonize the rest of the latter.

Further, and this would seem to constitute the second important characteristic feature of the "direct method," the sign which is presented before the delay is, as sign, almost, if not quite, as "condensed" as that which comes after the delay. The animal is not led, as in the "indirect method," to depend upon a color or light and then suddenly made to discover in the delay tests proper that this color or light will be removed. He is led rather to depend upon much the same feature of the sign that he will have to depend upon after the delay. No great degree of "condensation" is required of him.

It is these two features of the "direct-method" which would seem to explain the success of the latter. In the direct method the animal is, it would appear, set an actually easier task. And those who have used the "direct method" seem to assume that because it is thus an easier task that their results are better than they would have been if the "indirect method" had been used.[12] Finally, however, it may be noted that an actual direct experimental comparison between the two methods seems never to have been carried out. The "direct method" can be used only with animals whose vision is sufficiently developed so that they can perceive the initial total sign-gestalt; i.e., the initial placing of the goal-object as well as the position and character and the sign relative to which it is placed. But animals having such vision are usually superior in general to those not having it. In order to test, then, whether the direct method really is superior per se or gives better results

---

[12] See especially Tinklepaugh, O. L., An experimental study of representative factors in monkeys, *J. Comp. Psychol.*, 1928, **8**, 187-236; and

W. Köhler, Über eine neue Methode zur psychologischen Untersuchung von Menschenaffen, *Psychol. Forsch.*, 1922, **2**, 390-397.

simply because it is used with superior animals, the two methods should be compared upon the same animals under comparable conditions. And this, as far as we know, has never yet been done.[13]

10. Summary

In conclusion, we may now summarize the discussions of the present chapter concerning the nature of learning as it is to be found in the rat in the maze—or in other problem-box type of situation.

(1) The rat's learning seems to involve in the first place a change from the mere general sign-gestalt-readinesses, which the animal brings with him as a result of innate endowment and previous experiences, as to where food is likely to be found, to more precise mnemonized sign-gestalt-expectations.

(2) The learning of the ordinary maze also seems to involve the building up of integrated chains or hierarchies among such sign-gestalt-expectations.

(3) Again, it appears that the signs which figure in these sign-gestalts may take on at least temporarily subordinate goal-characters in and of themselves.

(4) There also tends to be a back-action from the new sign-gestalt-expectations upon the sign-gestalt-readinesses which the rat will thereafter carry about with him to new mazes or other similar problems. This carry-over of the modified sign-gestalt-readinesses constitutes, as we see it, the phenomenon of transfer.

(5) The antithesis or nemesis of a sign-gestalt-expectation, or a sign-gestalt-readiness, is a fixation. Fixations seem to appear in some cases of rat learning. They are blind, relatively mechanical, i.e., non-docile, attachments to specific means-objects or types of means-objects.

(6) Delayed reaction learning means three things: (a) an ability as a result of a single exposure of a sign to evoke a total sign-gestalt-expectation; (b) an ability to hold this sign-gestalt-expectation "in leash" over an interval of imposed delay in which it is not allowed to pass over into actual behavior; and (c) an ability, after this delay, to have the sign-gestalt-expectation able to work itself out into actual behavior on a basis of a mere portion

[13] Since the writing of the above such a test has been begun at the University of California.

of the original sign, i.e., on the basis of a condensed sign. The actual experimental results seem to indicate that rats are not capable of all three of these, or at the best they are capable of them, only if before the delay there is some degree of opportunity to let the expected sign-gestalt actually be tried out and directly experienced.

REFERENCES

Bierens de Haan, J. A., Über das Suchen nach verstecktem Futter bei Affen und Halbaffen, 1930, 11, 630-655.
Honzik, C. H., Delayed reaction in rats. *Univ. Calif. Publ. Psychol.*, 1931, 4, 307-318.
Hunter, W. S., Delayed reaction in animals and children. *Behav. Monog.*, 1913, 2, No. 6.
—————, The delayed reaction tested by the direct method: a correction. *Psychol. Bull.*, 1929, 26, 546-548.
Köhler, W., Über eine neue Methode zur psychologichen Untersuchung von Menschenaffen. *Psychol. Forsch.*, 1922, 2, 390-397.
Lewin, K., Untersuchungen zur Handlungs- und Affektpsychologie. III. Über das Behalten von erledigten und unerledigten Handlungen. Von Bluma Zeigarnik, *Psychol. Forsch.*, 1927, 9, 1-85.
Maier, N. R. F., Delayed reaction and memory in rats. *J. Genet. Psychol.*, 1929, 36, 538-550.
Tinklepaugh, O. L., An experimental study of representative factors in monkeys. *J. Comp. Psychol.*, 1928, 8, 197-236.
Walton, A. C., The influence of diverting stimuli during delayed reaction in dogs. *J. Anim. Behav.*, 1915, 5, 259-291.
Williams, K. A., The reward value of a conditioned stimulus. *Univ. Calif. Publ. Psychol.*, 1929, 4, 31-55.
Yerkes, R. M., The mind of a gorilla: II. Mental development. *Genet. Psychol. Monog.*, 1927, 2, No. 6.
Yerkes, R. M. and Yerkes, D. N., Concerning memory in the chimpanzee. *J. Comp. Psychol.*, 1928, 8 237-272.

Chapter XI

INFERENCE—THE MEANS-END-FIELD

1. Inferential Sign-Gestalt-Expectations

IT is to be noted that the facts of learning cited in the preceding chapter were concerned primarily with direct leading-on-nesses. The rats showed themselves capable, upon the presentation of a single sign, of building up, or refining, the appropriate single sign-gestalt-expectation as to the coming means-end-relations and significate. And in these cases of relatively simple and direct sign-gestalt-expectations the only two moods involved were, in general, those of perception and of mnemonization. The rat mnemonizes, or perceives, that such and such a direction (quality) of sign-object will lead by a short, or long, distance to commerce with such and such a given goal-object. Also he can to some extent mnemonize, or perceive, hierarchies of such direct sign-gestalts. We wish to demonstrate now, however, that, in addition, the rat apparently can and does build up to some extent appropriate sign-gestalt-expectations of an "inferential" sort.[1] He reacts to roundabout and alternative routes. And he can infer a given significate before he has actually perceived or mnemonized it. But this will be made clearer by concrete illustrations.

2. Final Common Path

The first experiment we have in mind is that of Hsiao. He used the maze shown in FIGURE 56.[2] It will be observed that there are three paths leading from the entrance, E_2 (E_1 was not used and was kept closed during the part of the experiment here considered), to the FOOD. The beginnings of these three paths are labelled R_1, R_2, and R_3, respectively. Of these, Path $R_1D_1F_c$ is the shortest; Path $R_2D_2F_c$ is the next shortest; and Path $R_3D_3F_3$

---

[1] See above, Chapter IX, p. 140 f.

[2] H. H. Hsiao, An experimental study of the rat's "insight" within a spatial complex, *Univ. Calif. Publ. Psychol.*, 1929, **4**, 57-70.

is the longest. Further, it is to be observed that Paths R_1 and R_2
lead into a final common segment, that between D_1 and D_2, which
segment is not common to Path R_3. The experiment consisted of
two parts: an initial *training* period and a subsequent *test* period.

During the *training* period, the rats were forced in successive
trials through each of the three paths, by closing pairs of doors
such as D_1 and D_2, D_2 and D_3, or D_1 and D_3. And during this
training the animals eventually acquired a very strong propensity

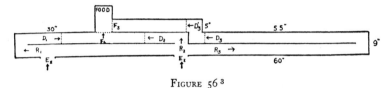

FIGURE 56 [3]

to try R_1, the shortest path, first and then, if they found D_1
locked, to back out and try R_2, the next shortest, second, and only
last, if they found D_2 also locked, then to try R_3.

In the *test* trials, which were introduced only after many days
of preliminary training, not D_1 but the common door, F_c, was
locked. The nature of the resultant behavior (unfortunately Hsiao
was able to use only three rats) is shown in the "Behavior Graph,"
FIGURE 57.

The graph presents the actual paths traversed by each of the
three rats on each of the ten test trials. Consider the first test
trial only. Rat 1, after finding F_c closed, tried to go out D_2 a
couple of times (but, as this was a one-way door, he did not
succeed); he then retraced out of R_1; but entered R_2 only as far
as D_2; he did not actually pass through the latter. Rat 2, upon finding F_c closed, retraced back and forth in the common section
D_1D_2 many times, but then, when he finally retraced out of R_1,
he did not enter R_2 at all. Rat 3 behaved in a manner similar to
Rat 1. No one of the three actually entered through D_2 on his
return from R_1. And the real significance of this is the fact that,
when in the preliminary training these rats had found not F_c but
D_1 closed, they then, on backing out of R_1, almost invariably had
next taken R_2 and gone all the way through it to food (91%
of the time for Rat 1, 89% for Rat 2, and 73% for Rat 3). In
other words, it was something about their experience, in the test

[3] *Op. cit.,* p. 58.

trials of finding F_c closed, which caused these rats on backing out of R_1, not to try R_2 in any whole-hearted fashion, but to go on through R_3.

These results suggest (although with such a small number of animals they certainly do not prove) that the rats had acquired a mnemonically conditioned expectation which grasped the com-

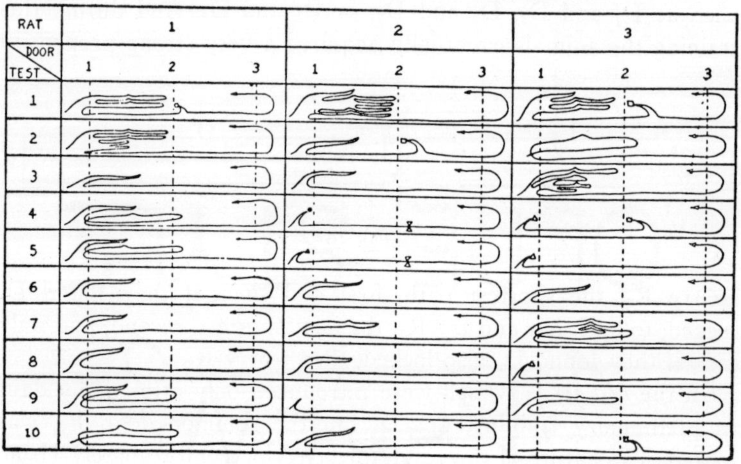

FIGURE 57 [4]

□ = pushing without entering   ○ = turning before reaching the door
△ = peeping   × = hesitating

monness of the final section D_1 and D_2—and that on the basis of this mnemonic expectation of commonness they were able when in the test run they found the common door F_c closed as a result of running down R_1, to infer (inferentially expect) its closedness if they were to approach it from R_2.

3. Inferential Expectation Based on Perception

In order to try to discover further just what was involved in the Hsiao experiment, Tolman and Honzik repeated it under somewhat different conditions.[5] They introduced several variations, especially as to amount of preliminary training and shape of maze. In their first experiment, although their maze was quite

[4] *Op. cit.*, p. 63.
[5] E. C. Tolman and C. H. Honzik, "Insight" in rats, *Univ. Calif. Publ. Psychol.*, 1930, **4**, 215-232.

similar to the Hsiao maze, they did *not* succeed in verifying his findings. They did not, that is, obtain evidence of a grasping of the relation of commonness of the final section as a result of mere mnemonization. This failure, however, may perhaps have been due to the fact that they did not give as great, or as widely distributed, a preliminary training as did Hsiao.

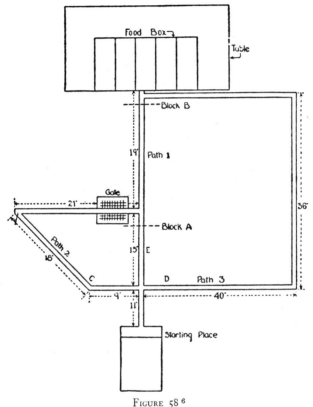

FIGURE 58 [6]

In some later experiments they used a different maze—one which allowed mnemonization to be eked out by direct perception. It was an elevated maze, constructed of one-inch laths, i.e., without sides. This arrangement allowed the rats, if they could, visually to *perceive* something as to the interrelations and common "debouchingnesses" of Paths 1 and 2. A ground plan of the maze is given in FIGURE 58.

[6] *Op. cit.*, p. 223.

It will be observed that the shape is quite different from that of the Hsiao maze. The principle, however, is the same. Again Path 1 is the shortest, Path 2 the next shortest, and Path 3 the longest. And, further, Paths 1 and 2 again have a common final segment which Path 3 does not have.

During the *preliminary training*, Path 1 was blocked at A, and when this was the case the rats soon acquired a propensity, on backing out of Path 1, to take Path 2 next. Only when they found Path 2 also blocked near its entrance (block is not shown in the diagram [7]) did they then, finally, take Path 3.

In the final *test*, the block was placed in the common section of Paths 1 and 2 (Block B). The rats, upon then backing out of Path 1, took not Path 2, as they had when in the training runs they had been blocked at A, but Path 3. Two groups of rats were tested in this fashion. We may consider the results for each group separately. TABLE 1 indicates for each individual of the fifteen rats of the first group the number of times in the *preliminary training* that, upon finding the block at A, he, upon backing out of Path 1, then chose Paths 2 and 3, respectively.

Rat Path	H 58	H 65	W 56	W 53	W 59	H 64	W 74	W 50	W 60	B 51	H 53	W 22	W 29	W 55	W 16	Total
2	84	83	87	78	73	78	84	80	86	81	73	73	88	84	82	1214
3	5	6	10	8	13	8	3	3	3	14	27	15	1	6	6	128

TABLE 1

The results for the seven *test* runs, all given on one day, are shown in TABLE 2.

"Test" run No.	No. of the 15 rats that avoided path 2
1	14
2	13
3	10
4	12
5	11
6	12
7	13

TABLE 2

[7] The placed labeled "gate" was a tunnel with a permanent one-way gate which allowed the rats to pass from Path 2 to the common final section of Path 1, but prevented retracing from Path 1 into Path 2.

It is evident that by far the greater majority of rats, upon finding the block at B in the test runs, then took Path 3 instead of
Path 2, although in the training trials, when they had found the
block at A, they had all preponderantly taken Path 2.[8]

The results for the second group, consisting of ten rats, are
shown in TABLE 3 and TABLE 4.

Rat / Path	H82	W11	H52	W51	H5	H35	W65	W31	W17	H1	Total
2	107	104	106	108	108	109	110	107	111	111	1081
3	8	17	13	5	15	6	1	20	4	8	97

TABLE 3

Test run No.	No. of the 10 rats that avoided path 2
1	7
2	9
3	all
4	8
5	all
6	9
7	9

TABLE 4

Finally, it may perhaps be contended that the reason such positive results were obtained by Tolman and Honzik with this maze
and not with the Hsiao maze may have been due, not, as was
suggested above, to the elevated character and hence perceivable-
ness of the Tolman and Honzik maze, but rather to its peculiarities of shape—the relative positions of Paths 1, 2 and 3—which
are obviously considerably different from those of the Hsiao maze.
Against this latter interpretation, however, is to be reported the
fact that Tolman and Honzik also tried out an alley-maze (i.e., a
maze with sides) of quite similar design to that of their elevated

[8] A possible criticism is to be raised against the results of this group in
that during the course of the training they were each given twelve special runs
of a somewhat similar sort to the test run. In these twelve special runs the
animals were blocked in the common segment at A when they had entered
Path 1. On returning out of Path 1, they could then take either Path 2 or
Path 3. This may perhaps be considered as of the nature of final training
for the test run. And it was in order to obviate this criticism that the next
group was run.

maze but with negative results. It appears probable, therefore, that the positive results they obtained with the elevated maze were, in at least some degree, favored by the fact that in this latter maze *mnemonization* could be eked out by *perception*. Expectation of the commonness of a final segment is easier for perception plus mnemonization than for mnemonization alone.[9] To conclude, it was on the basis of such mnemonization helped out by perception of the commonness of the final path that the animals then "inferred" the block B when they came to Path 2.

4. Multiple Tracks

As a second example of a more complicated type of means-end feature which rats (and simpler organisms as well) can "expect," we may consider the facts concerning "multiple trackness." When an animal is presented with alternative, but equally "short," paths to one and the same goal, it appears that this fact of the mutual equivalence or inter-substitutability, i.e., what we are thus labelling as "multiple tracks," will tend to exhibit itself as immanent in the animal's behavior. He will tend, that is, to alternate among these different paths in a perfectly indiscriminate and seemingly haphazard fashion.

As our first illustration of this point we recall again the findings of Gilhousen for crayfish (see above, Chapter I, p. 18). Gilhousen found that on successive trials a crayfish, who had learned to take the right-hand side of a simple T-maze, tended to indulge in a wide range of varying routes. The animal sometimes followed one side of the stem of the T and sometimes the other. But, in general, it avoided the blind and always turned correctly so as to make the outlet into the aquarium.

Again, we may cite the findings of Muenzinger. The latter found that guinea pigs who had learned to press a button to get into a food cage would continue *indefinitely* to use in ir-

---

[9] It must be noted, however, that several considerations militate against an interpretation that the results were wholly a matter of perception, quite unaided by mnemonization. In the first place (although this was not actually tested) it seemed quite certain that the rats *did* need a considerable amount of preliminary training. Their *initial* perceptual capacities were evidently not enough. In the second place, it is known that rats have relatively *poor* visual powers. And, in the third place, their behavior showed little apparent dependence upon visual cues. They were *never observed* to "stop, look or listen."

regular order any one of the three alternative "tracks": "right paw, left paw, teeth," as the specific route for getting into the food box.[10]

Again, Yoshioka [11] found that a considerable number of rats, when presented with two equally long and practically identical triangular paths to one and the same goal (See Chapter VIII, FIGURE 42:1), would continue indefinitely to choose right-hand and left-hand paths fifty-fifty.

Or, finally, we may again refer to the findings of Dashiell, cited in a preceding chapter (Chapter VIII, p. 118f) that rats when presented with his "open-alley" maze, which allowed a wide variety of equally short routes, would continue to vary among different ones of these routes almost indefinitely.

All these experiments define, in other words, a tendency on the part of the rat to perceive (or to mnemonize) what may be called the *multiple track* character of *different* but equally short alternative means routes to one and the same goal, and to infer the goodness of perhaps altogether new and hitherto untried instances among such multiple tracks. Means-end-relations as expected by an organism are, that is, probably never adequately represented by single lines, but always rather by some degree of *spreading, fanning,* or *networking* of the lines. Means-end-relations are, to put it another way, essentially *field*-relations. The rat mnemonizes and perceives and infers relative to simple succession, and simple direction, but also relative to more complicated affairs such as a final common path, and multiple trackness.

And in the rest of the chapter we shall cite still further evidences to indicate this essentially "field" character in the rat's means-end-expectations.

---

[10] K. F. Muenzinger, Plasticity and mechanization of the problem box habit in guinea pigs, *J. Comp. Psychol.*, 1928, **8**, 45-69.

See also K. F. Muenzinger, L. Koerner, and E. Irey, Variability of an habitual movement in guinea pigs, *J. Comp. Psychol.*, 1929, **9**, 425-436. In this latter experiment the experimenters limited the animals to the use of the right paw only and yet within this limit they still showed a great variability:—thus—"The right paw might be used with a firm and deliberate pressing down of the lever, or a bare touch on the lever, or a quick tap, or a succession of quick taps, or a brushing or sliding over the lever, a circular movement partly around the lever, or a gentle placing of the paw on the lever with pressure after some time, or a crossing of the right paw over the left." *Op. cit.*, p. 427.

[11] J. G. Yoshioka, What is maze learning for the rat? *J. Genet. Psychol.*, 1929, **36**, 51-58.

5. The Mutually Complementary Character of Alternatives

The next experiments, we would cite, demonstrate what, for want of a better name, we shall call the field-principle of the *mutual complementariness of alternative means-objects*. The experiments in question are the classical ones of Hamilton.[12] Hamilton presented his animals (human beings, adults and children,

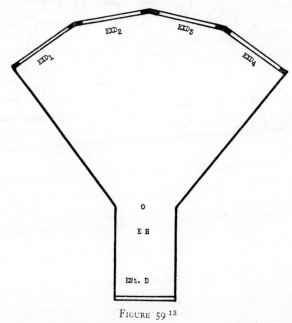

FIGURE 59 [13]

normal and defective; apes; monkeys; dogs, puppies; cats, kittens; a horse; rats, gophers, and a mouse) with a four-door multiple choice box, the essential floor plan of which is shown in FIGURE 59.

[12] G. V. Hamilton, A study of trial and error reactions in mammals, *J. Anim. Behav.* 1911, **1**, 33-66. G. V. Hamilton, A study of perseverance reactions in primates and rodents, *Behav. Monog.*, 1916, **3**, No. 13.

[13] Hamilton, *J. Anim. Behavior*, 1911, **1**, p. 34.

The apparatus used for the rodents was slightly modified from that here shown in the diagram. The essential difference consisted in the substitution of four short alleys for the doors leading from the choice chamber. These alleys ended in goal-boxes, one only of which was open in any given trial. The rodents could not, however, see which alley thus had the open box at the

Each animal was given a total of 100 trials. One door [alley] was correct in each trial (i.e., twenty-five times out of the 100). The order of correctness of the different doors [alleys] was as irregular as possible. The only rule was that the door which had been "unlocked"—"the alley which had had the open box beyond it"—in the trial just preceding should never be the correct one in the given trial. The animals were thus confronted with a series of actually "insoluble" problems. And, when thus confronted, it appeared that their responses could be classified into five types, which Hamilton describes as follows:

Type A: "Response with reference to the experimenter's rule that no alley [door] is the right alley [door] for two successive trials." [14]

Type B: "Response to the rule that it is useless to try any alley [door] more than once during a given trial; all four alleys [doors] tried, and in an irregular order." [15]

Type C: "When No. 4 is the right alley [door] an effort to escape by trying alleys [doors] Nos. 1, 2, 3 and 4 once each, in the order given; or the reverse of this when No. 1 is the right alley [door]." [16]

Type D: "More than one separate effort to escape by a given alley [door] during the same trial, but with an interruption of such efforts by an interval of effort to escape by one or more of the other alleys [doors]." [17]

Type E: (a) "During a given trial the subject enters an alley [door] which does not afford escape, leaves it and reënters it one or more times without having tried any other alley; or, having tried a group of two or three alleys [doors] in a certain order, he reënters all alleys [doors] of the group in the same order one or more times." [18]

Type E (b): "During a given trial the subject persistently

end of it, because they had to climb over partitions, 7½ cm. high, between choice chamber and alleys. One further feature of the rodent apparatus consisted in an electric grid on the floor extending to all portions of the choice chamber and the alleys, by means of which the animals could, if necessary, be given a slight electric shock when they failed to work.

[14] *Behav. Monog.*, 1916, **3,** No. 2, p. 11.
[15] *Op. cit.,* p. 12.
[16] *Op. cit.,* p. 13.
[17] *Op. cit.,* p. 13.
[18] *Op. cit.,* p. 13.

avoids the right alley [door] until he has tried the other alleys [doors] at least six times." [19]

In general, the results of the experiment were that ontogenetically or phylogenetically the higher the individual or species, the greater the percentage of A and B types of response given; whereas the lower the individual or species, the greater the percentages of C, D and E (especially D and E) types of response.

Now it is obvious, from the above descriptions, that the two worst response types, D and E, were ones which are quite oblivious of the fact that if a door [alley] is incorrect once in a given trial, it will remain so throughout that trial. In other words, the D and E types of response were completely blind to the relation of mutual alternativeness, or complementariness, which obtained between the different doors [alleys]. Response types A and B, and to a lesser degree C, were, on the other hand, relatively "wise" to this relationship of mutual complementariness. The results indicate, in other words, that ontogenetically or phylogenetically the higher the animal, the more he is capable of expecting (mnemonizing) this aspect of this particular type of means-end-field, and consequently of "inferring" from having tried one door that some other is likely to be good.

6. Reverse Ends of One and the Same Detour

Still another capacity for means-end-relations, which rats probably possess, we might designate as the ability to "recognize the reverse ends of one and the same detour." Buel [20] is at present examining this phenomenon by means of a maze made up of successive units, in which each unit has the sort of ground plan shown in FIGURE 60. The diagram represents the set-ups for two different groups. For Group I, A and B constitute, it will be observed, separate blinds analogous in general structure to the unchanged blind, C. For Group II, on the other hand, partition X has been removed so that A and B now constitute the reverse ends of one and the same detour. (There are especially constructed transparent wire gates provided which allow the rat to go into A and

---

[19] *Op. cit.*, p. 13.

[20] This is an experiment now in progress in the psychological laboratory of the University of California. We are indebted to Mr. J. Buel for permission to cite it here.

out of it, or into B and out of it; but not into A and out of B, or into B and out of A.)

The results that are being found are that the rats of Group II seem to make relatively fewer entrances into B than those of Group I. In other words, whereas B has to be learned as a separate independent blind for the animals of Group I, for Group II it can be recognized as but the other end of A, already entered. It is

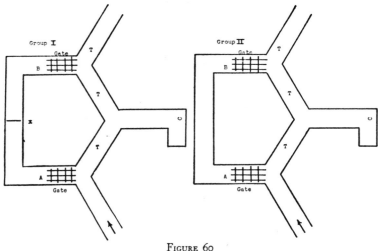

FIGURE 60

therefore eliminated more readily. The rats of Group II perceive or mnemonize this character of the reverse-end of a detour and "infer" from having been in A the unnecessary distance involved in going back into the detour by way of B.

7. Closure Among Partial Paths

Finally, we shall present, as our last example of the capacity of rats to expect total *field* relationships, the extremely suggestive experiments of Maier.[21] Maier performed a variety of different tests, all more or less illustrating the point we would now make, but only one of which we shall here attempt to describe.

First, the rats became thoroughly acquainted with the top of a given table. This had various topographically distinguishing ob-

[21] N. R. F. Maier, Reasoning in white rats, *Comp. Psychol. Monog.*, 1929, **6**, No. 29.

jects placed upon it—such as a low cardboard barrier to be climbed over, and the like. The rats roamed about upon this table for some time at will and without any overt reward.

Second, and quite independently of this free-roaming, table-top experience, the same rats were taught an elevated maze leading from one barred-off corner of the table to another barred-off corner, at which latter spot they obtained food.

Then, third, in the final test part of the experiment, the animals were placed upon the table just outside a small wire enclosure, which separated them from the corner where food was placed and to which they had learned to go by means of the elevated maze. After considerable struggling to get at the food directly through the wire barrier, they turned and made their way with surprising directness to the other corner of the table, from which the maze led, and which was completely screened from them by the intervening cardboard barrier. And they did this, it is to be noted, in spite of the fact that their only previous knowledge of the connection between these two corners of the table was such as had been gathered in their original purely random exploring of the table-top, when there had been no overt reward of any kind involved, and during which they had probably never once taken the direct course, as such, from one corner to the other.

These results indicate, it would seem, very definitely an ability upon the part of the rats to integrate, upon need and without specific further training, the two part-paths (maze learned by itself) and table-top (learned by itself) into one *closed* whole. It indicates, therefore, that the rat has learned each path not simply as an isolated narrow track all by itself, but rather as part of a possible larger field—a field in which each path really implicates the other as well.

8.　Means-End-Field

Summing up the above experiments, the burden of the present chapter has been that rats (and, apparently, to some extent, other still lower organisms as well) expect not only such means-end-relations as distance, simple direction and hierarchicalness but also such more general relations as those of: *common final pathness; multiple tracks; mutual opposition between alternative paths; the identity of the same detour when encountered from opposite ends; the closing or fitting together of the successive parts of one total path*. And, of course, further experiments undoubtedly would discover many other such general *field-relations* to be added to such a list, even in the case of rats.[22]

Means-end-relations are, fundamentally, field-relations. Furthermore, the above enumerated features are probably not to be conceived as wholly separable items but, rather, as mutually coordinate principles, each more or less implicated in all the others. In so far as any organism's behavior involves means-end-read-

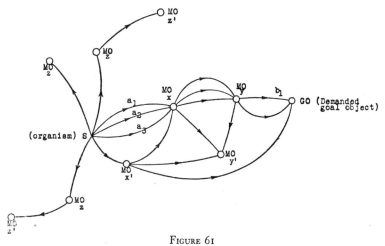

inesses and -expectations, it involves, to some extent, certain of these other complementary aspects, in addition to the simple ones of linear distance, succession and direction. The means-end set-up is not a single linear set-up but a field set-up. The more relationships other than the simple linear ones that we can discover, as immanent in the behavior of a given type of organism, the more rich and complicated we must declare that organism's means-end-field to be.

FIGURE 61 is a schematic diagram to suggest, as far as possible, all the various types of means-end-field relation which a rat or any

[22] What we are here saying seems, in short, to be very similar to what Helson said in 1927 when he argued against the point of view that the white rat "works blindly and mechanically at its problems, needing only time, kinaesthesis, and chance to stamp out the wrong responses and to stamp in the correct" and substitutes a behavior in the rat that is "dominated by the field properties of the situation." Cf. H. Helson, "Insight in the white rat," *J. Exper. Psychol.*, 1927, 10, 378-396, p. 379 f.

other organism might postulate. S indicates the initial position of the organism and GO the position of the final goal-object, which under the given conditions has a final demand value for this organism. The various MO's represent intervening means-objects. And the arrows represent the complications of interconnecting means-end-relations which may be conceived. The diagram represents, in short, the sort of means-end-field which a rat (or some other organism) may be supposed actually to project (means-end-readinesses and -expectations) upon some given environmental set-up.

More specifically, the arrows connecting S to MO_x, those connecting MO_x to MO_y, and those connecting MO_y to GO stand in the simple linear relation of *succession* or *hierarchy*. It is to be noted, on the other hand, that all the various arrows, a_1, a_2, a_3, etc., which connect S to MO_x stand relative to one another in the relation of mutual *substitutability* or *roundaboutness*. Further, it appears that the arrows connecting S to MO_x and S to the various different MO_z's stand, rather, in the relations of *mutual opposition;* and so on.

One defect in the diagram as drawn is, however, to be noted. It exhibits *chain* types of combination only. *Lever* or *tool* combinations (see above, Chapter VI) have not been indicated. This omission is, however, due to pictorial difficulties. And furthermore these lever relations, if they could be actually introduced into the diagram, would bring no fundamentally new sort of arrangement. They would cause funny telescopings of the picture, so that, for example, the having of a given commerce with MO_x, instead of leading on to MO_y, would have to be drawn rather as actually achieving *pari passu* the commerce with MO_y. The picture would be more difficult and more complicated but the general character of a *field* would remain.

9. Means-End-Distances

Finally, it is now to be observed that in such a means-end-field the principle of *relative distance* is fundamental. The lengths of the alternative routes determine all the angles and interrelations of the field. But what, it may be asked now, more specifically, is this principle of relative distance? It is the principle of choice or preference. Those types and kinds of path are "long" which the given organism tends to avoid, and those types and kinds are "short" which he tends to learn or select.

Finally, if, as was suggested in Chapter VII, the three fundamental types of dimension—space, time, force-resistance—can be shown to be ultimately intercommensurable—all to reduce to one single one of physiological "Least Action" (see above, p. 110 f), then means-end-distance will be ultimately synonymous with, and can be equated to, physiological "Least Action." If, however, this does not prove ultimately possible, then spatial shortness, temporal shortness and gravitational shortness, and other dimensional kinds of shortness as well, will remain independent and different determiners of distances and of the general structure of means-end-fields.

10. Lewin's Concept of *"Topologie"*

Before concluding, we must note that this concept of the means-end-field seems to be closely analogous to Lewin's [23] concept of *"Topologie."* Lewin, influenced apparently more or less by the presuppositions of *Gestaltpsychologie,* has arrived at the concept of a (phenomenally created) *dynamic* environmental field, the *Topologie,* in which an organism is to be conceived as immersed. Objects in this field by virtue of their "invitation-characters" or "valencies" (*Aufforderungscharaktere*) exert attracting or repulsing forces. And these forces (*Feldkräfte*) are stresses and strains which finally resolve themselves by causing such and such directions and turnings of behavior. The similarity of this doctrine of *Topologie* and *Feldkräfte* to the present one of the means-end-field, is obvious. The two doctrines really support and reinforce one another. The fact that they have been arrived at from relatively different presuppositions is, it would seem, a hopeful indication of some core of validity in them both.

11. Means-End-Capacity

Finally, we should like to introduce one more term—that of means-end-capacity. This will be the capacity of the given animal

[23] Cf. K. Lewin, *Die Auswirkung von Umweltkräften, Proc. Ninth International Cong. of Psychol.* (Princeton, Psychol. Rev. Co., 1930). Cf. also Untersuchungen zur Handlungs- und Affektpsychologie, especially II, Vorsatz, Wille und Bedürfnis, *Psychol. Forsch.,* 1926, **7,** 330-385. And, finally, cf. his Environmental forces in child behavior and development, *A Handbook of Child Psychology* (Worcester, Mass., Clark Univ. Press, 1931), 94-127.

relative to types and extents of means-end-fields. The more complicated and refined the given animal's success in expecting degrees and types of distance, direction, succession, common final pathness, multiple trackness, alternativeness between paths, reverse ends of one and the same detour, etc., the greater, by definition, will be that animal's means-end-capacity. We coin the term means-end-capacity to designate the underlying capacities which allow successful sign-gestalt-readinesses and sign-gestalt-expectations relative to complicated types of means-end-field.[24]

[24] For a further discussion of means-end-capacities, see the next chapter.

REFERENCES

Hamilton, G. V., A study of trial and error reactions in mammals. *J. Anim. Behav.*, 1911, 1, 33-66.

——————, A study of perseverance reactions in primates and rodents. *Behav. Monog.*, 1916, 3, No. 13.

Helson, H., Insight in the white rat. *J. Exper. Psychol.*, 1927, 10, 378-396.

Hsiao, H. H., An experimental study of the rat's "insight" within a spatial complex. *Univ. Calif. Publ. Psychol.*, 1929, 4, 57-70.

Lewin, K., Die Auswirkung von Umweltkräften. *Proc. Ninth Internat. Cong. Psychol.* (Princeton, Psychol. Rev. Co., 1930), pp. 286-288.

——————, Vorsatz, Wille und Bedürfnis. *Psychol. Forsch.*, 1926, 7, 330-385.

——————, Environmental forces in child behavior and development, *A Handbook of Child Psychology* (Worcester, Mass., Clark Univ. Press, 1931), 94-127.

Maier, N. R. F., Reasoning in white rats. *Comp. Psychol. Monog.*, 1929, 6, No. 29.

Muenzinger, K. F., Plasticity and mechanization of the problem box habit in guinea pigs. *J. Comp. Psychol.*, 1928, 8, 45-69.

——————, Koerner, L., and Irey, E., Variability of an habitual movement in guinea pigs. *J. Comp. Psychol.*, 1929, 9, 425-436.

Tolman, E. C. and Honzik, C. H., "Insight" in rats. *Univ. Calif. Publ. Psychol.*, 1930, 4, 215-232.

Yoshioka, J. G., What is maze learning for the rat? *J. Genet. Psychol.*, 1929, 36, 51-58.

PART III
RATS, CATS, APES, AND MEN

Rats in mazes are very nice. But, after all, they do not constitute the whole universe of behavior. We shall, therefore, in the following section, seek to consider in what ways, if any, the immanent and other behavior-determinants become more complicated as we ascend the animal scale. What, if any, are the new and more "high-faluting" behavior-determinants which appear as we turn to consider the higher animal species?

Chapter XII

MEANS-END-CAPACITIES

1. Means-End-Capacities in Different Species

THE term *means-end-capacity* has been suggested for the organism's abilities relative to means-end-relations. Means-end-relations are essentially field relations. The degree of an animal's capacity to build up correct sign-gestalt-expectations and hence perceptions, mnemonizations and inferences relative to complex means-end-fields defines the degree of his means-end-capacity. Given this definition, it appears that not only different individuals but different species differ greatly in their means-end-capacities. It is meet, therefore, to begin the present section, in which the interest is to be primarily in a comparison of different phylogenetic levels, with a further discussion of this concept.

When representative, i.e., typical, individuals of different species are presented with one and the same complex means-end situation, they will be found to exhibit relatively different adequacies of means-end-readiness and means-end-expectation. These different adequacies may be said to define and result from their differences of means-end-capacity. Let us illustrate by some concrete examples from Köhler.[1]

Köhler presented a chick, a dog, an ape, and a child with practically one and the same problem—that of being barred from food by a three-sided barrier (transparent on the side towards the food). He found that the chick, when put in this situation, will, for the most part, merely run back and forth opposite the food. A chick will not, or will at the most only after much trial and error, learn to go round one of the flanges of the barrier in order to get to the food. A dog in this same situation, on the other hand, will relatively easily go around one of the flanges or sides, though he is

[1] Cf. W. Köhler, *The Mentality of Apes* (New York, Harcourt, Brace and Company, 1925), p. 15 f., p. 17 f.

decidedly less ready to do this, if the food be placed extremely near the center of the barrier, i.e., directly under his nose. Finally, the ape and the child will have no difficulty at all. After only a second or two of trying to get directly at the food, they will turn, see the unblocked flange, and run around it.

The sign-gestalt-readinesses and -expectations requisite for selecting such a roundabout route come very readily to the ape and child, somewhat less readily to the dog, and practically not at all to the chick. The child's and the ape's innate and acquired means-end-capacities provide the possibility of the necessary sign-gestalt-expectations at once; the dog's capacity provides the possibility of these expectations only more slowly and in less complete form; the chick's capacity provides their possibility not at all.

Turn to another illustration. Suppose the barrier be four-sided. Suppose, in short, that the animal be entirely shut up in a cage. And, again, let us imagine the problem presented to a chick, a dog, an ape, and a child. What will these animals severally do? All four will begin by struggling on the side of the cage nearest the food. The chick and the dog will struggle to push their heads through the bars; the ape and the child will struggle to push their "paws" through. That is, all four animals possess a certain modicum of means-end-capacity—viz., a capacity for the expectation of what, considering merely the spatial character of the set-up, should be the most direct route to food. The initial sign-gestalt-expectations of all four accord with the fact of the direct spatial direction of the food and with that of the intervening obstructive cage-bars. It appears, however, that the ape and the child,[2] upon discovering the futility of trying thus to reach the food directly, will be capable of expecting further types of means-end-relationship quite beyond the ken of either chick or dog. If, that is, strings, sticks, or

[2] Cf. A. Alpert, The solving of problem-situations by preschool children, *Teach. Coll. Contrib. Educ.*, 1928, No. 323. P. B. Brainard, The mentality of a child compared with that of apes, *J. Genet. Psychol.*, 1930, **37**, 268-293.

E. L. Lindemann, Untersuchungen über primitive Intelligenzleistungen hochgradig Schwachsinniger und ihr Verhältnis zu den Leistungen von Anthropoiden, *Zsch. f. d. ges Neur. und Psychiat.*, 1926, **104**, 529-570.

O. Lipmann, Über Begriff und Erforschung der "natürlichen" Intelligenz, *Zsch. f. Angew, Psychol.*, 1918, **13**, 192-301.

O. Lipmann, and H. Bogen, *Naive Physik., Theoretiche und Experimentelle Untersuchungen über die Fähigkeit zu Intelligentem Handeln* (Leipzig, Barth, 1923).

rakes be provided, the ape and the child will be capable of using them as ways of pulling in, or raking in, the food,[3]—ways to which the chick or the dog will be quite insensitive. The ape's and the child's means-end-capacities allow of types of field-readiness and field-expectation quite beyond the ken of chick or dog.

2. Formal Capacity; Dimensional-Capacities; Discriminanda- and Manipulanda-Capacities

But we must now refine this notion of means-end-capacities. It has become strikingly evident that differences of such capacity obtain as between different species. The higher the species, the more extensive and complicated and "highbrow" the types of field-relationship to which the individuals are sensitive. The rat is capable of perceptions, mnemonizations and inferences of leading-on-nesses, round-about-nesses, and the like, when these are embodied in simple spatial and gravitational fields. The cat, as has been shown by Adams,[4] can perceive, mnemonize and infer such leading-on-nesses and round-about-nesses in the more recondite situations of levers and strings; while the ape can respond correctly to these leading-on-nesses and round-about-nesses even in such set-ups as those requiring the manufacture of sticks, or the piling of boxes, etc.[5] And, lastly, the human being can respond correctly to these relationships even when involved in such fields as the rhetorical, the social, the numerical, etc.

[3] Cf. R. M. Yerkes and A. W. Yerkes, *The Great Apes* (New Haven, Yale Univ. Press, 1929), for a complete mine of information concerning all the literature on problem-solving (i.e., means-end-capacities) in the apes.

[4] D. K. Adams, Experimental study of adaptive behavior in cats, *Comp. Psychol. Monog.*, 1929, **6**, No. 27.

[5] Cf. H. C. Bingham, Chimpanzee translocation by means of boxes, *Comp. Psychol. Monog.*, 1929, **5**, Serial No. 25.

Also H. C. Bingham, Selective transportation by chimpanzees, *Comp. Psychol. Monog.*, 1929, **5**, No. 26.

For recent work on the means-end-capacities of other species, see also

K. D. McDougall and W. McDougall, Insight and foresight in various animals—monkey, raccoon, rat, and wasp, *J. Comp. Psychol.*, 1931, **11**, 237-274.

J. A. Bierens de Haan, Werkzeuggebrauch und Werkzeugherstellung bei einem niederen Affen (*cebus hypoleucus Humb.*) *Zsch. f. vergl. Physiol.*, 1931, **13**, 639-695.

Also for summaries for the years 1921-1927, see E. C. Tolman, Habit formation and higher mental processes in animals, *Psychol. Bull.*, 1927, **24**, 1-35.

———————— Habit formation and higher mental processes in animals, *Psychol. Bull.*, 1928, **25**, 24-53.

Such facts indicate at once, however, that these differences between the capacities of the different species need not be altogether differences as to the pure means-end-relations, per se. They may be also, in large part, differences in respect to the mere concrete sensory and motor embodiments of such relations. For the character of an environmental field is constituted not only by its purely "formal" means-end-relations but also by the nature of its material or stuff, e.g., space, time, gravitation, etc., in which these formal relations happen to be embodied. Fields differ from one another relative to the complexities of their abstract relations. But they also differ relative to the types of concrete sensory and motor, i.e., discriminative and manipulative, material (i.e., dimensions) in which these abstract relations are embodied. And the superiority of certain species to others would often seem to lie quite as much in their superior grasp of certain types of sensory and motor stuffs, i.e., discriminanda and manipulanda, as in any superiority on their part as to abstract means-end-relations per se. Thus, for example, the reason why the human being and the ape excel the rat and the cat may lie, not so much in the greater means-end-capacities of the former per se, as in their superior sensory and motor equipments—i.e., their greater capacities as regards types of discriminanda and manipulanda. For, as we have seen, when it comes to spatial materials the rat seems almost as good at means-end principles as man. It is when it comes to temporal, rhetorical, gravitational, social, etc., embodiments that the rat's capacities fail.

We shall, therefore, from now on reserve the term *formal* means-end-capacity for the ability for formal means-end-principles, and introduce the more specific term *dimensional* means-end-capacities for the abilities for the special "material" embodiments in space, in time, in gravitation, in the number system, in society, in words, in rhetoric, and the like, of such formal means-end-principles. Such embodiments constitute specific "dimensions." And the capacity for means-end-relations as specifically embodied in the material of some one of these dimensions, we shall call therefore a dimensional capacity.

It must, however, be admitted at once that just what it is which is distinctive of and defines any given dimension is not as yet altogether clear. It seems obvious that the characters of the different dimensions are in some way tied up with the characters of the discriminanda and manipulanda which tend to be found in such dimensions. And, in so far as this is the case, it follows that the possession of a given type of dimensional capacity will be bound up with the possession of certain types of especially good discriminanda- and manipulanda-capacities. (See above Chapter V.) Thus the reason why the rat, for example, has such a surprisingly good dimensional insight *re* space may well be in part by virtue of his having especially keen kinesthetic sense-organs, and that these latter bring with them especially good capacities for the kinds of discriminative and manipulative material primarily involved in space.

The whole problem, however, obviously still needs further analysis. Specific discriminanda- and manipulanda-capacities, dimensional means-end-capacities and formal means-end-capacities are all interrelated. The first and the last are easily distinguished and defined. But to what extent the middle one, dimensional capacities, has any being in and of itself—or to what extent it is merely some sort of a joint product of, or hybrid between, the other two—is not clear. What we have just said is, therefore, intended merely by way of suggestion and for the opening up of new problems and is not intended to constitute any final or complete statement. The question of a distinction between formal capacities and specific dimensional capacities may well prove the starting point for a series of further empirical investigations.

3. List of Formal Principles

Granting now for the sake of argument this distinction between formal capacities and specific dimensional capacities, let us now suggest a list of the formal principles which we may conceive as likely to be found in all types of means-end-fields, irrespective of their specific material.

Tentatively, we propose the following:

Sequence (simple leading-to-, or from-, ness) (i.e., prediction)
Differentiation
Distance
Direction
Similarity (identity in difference)
Reverse Ends of one and the Same Route
Multiple Trackness

Final Common Pathness
Mutual Alternativeness
Closure
Hierarchicalness

Each of these may be further described.

Sequence (Simple leading-to-, or from-, ness) (prediction). By this we would understand the simple, foundation aspect of all means-end-relations. It is the simple fact that commerce with one object leads to, or away from, some other object, or, in the case of tools (see above, Ch. VI, p. 98 f.), that commerce with the one object actually accomplishes, *pari passu,* commerce with such and such another object. The animal must have the capacity for sign-gestalt-readinesses and -expectations relative to this most simple of means-end-relations, if he is to be capable of any "molar" behavior at all.

Differentiation. By the term differentiation we would designate an obvious corollary of the preceding principle. For it would appear that all behavior, in so far as it contains immanent sign-gestalt-readinesses and -expectations relative to specific sequences, i.e., leading-to-or-from-nesses, is necessarily docile relative to the differentiation between such alternatives. Expectations as to sequences necessarily also means *pari passu* differentiations as between alternatives. Maze-learning demonstrates, that is, not only the fact of the rat's capacity, relative to the relationship that this leads on to that, but also *pari passu* his capacity relative to the relationships that "this" this is not "that" this, and "this" that is not "that" that. In building up expectations that given alleys lead on to food, he is simultaneously differentiating these alleys from others and food from non-food. Prediction and differentiation thus, necessarily, go hand in hand.

Distance. Under the caption of *distance,* came the fundamental facts of shortness and differentiations and preferences already discussed in Chapter VII, for the three cases of space-distance, time-distance and force-resistance-distance. The whole concept of the means-end-field involves, that is, the assumption that the organism has capacity for sign-gestalt-expectations relative to the respective distances presented by alternative routes. For his behavior, to be adequate to a means-end-field at all, he must prefer "short" routes to "long" routes and be capable of differentiating in some degree the "shorter" from the "longer."

Direction. Under this head we would designate the other fundamental fact of all means-end-relations discussed in Chapter VIII. It is the fact that sign-gestalt-readinesses and -expectations necessarily involve differentiations of the directions or qualities of their signs. They correlate differences of distance with such differences of direction. In Chapter VIII it was shown (Dashiell, Gengerelli, Yoshioka, Washburn, Tolman and Honzik) that the rat is capable, in the cases of space, of relatively precise direction-distance correlations.

Similarity (or identity in difference). This is probably a relatively "high brow" principle, and very likely is not included in the means-end-readinesses and -expectations of animals below the primates. At any rate, we do not as yet know anything about it for the rat. No experiments seem to have been devised to bring out its presence or absence in any of the lower phyla.

Reverse Ends of One and the Same Route. The discussion of Chapter XI (*vide* Buel's experiment, p. 174 f.) would suggest that, even in the rat, opposite ends of one and the same route (at least when this is a spatial route) are to some extent recognized as such—that the rat's sign-gestalt-expectations express capacity as regards this principle—at least when it is found in space.

Multiple Trackness. The discussions of Chapter XI (see p. 170 f.) indicated that capacity for readiness and expectation involving multiple trackness (see experiments of Gilhousen, Muenzinger, Dashiell, Yoshioka) has been experimentally demonstrated as falling to a very considerable degree within the make-up of the rat or even of the crayfish—again with the proviso that the dimensional embodiment of this principle be that of space.

Final Common Pathness. This principle likewise has been demonstrated as falling within the range of the rat's capacity in the case of space. (See experiments of Hsiao and of Tolman and Honzik, Ch. XI, p. 164 f.)

Mutual Alternativeness. This principle also (see Hamilton's experiment, p. 172 f.) has been indicated as affecting to some degree the rat's readinesses and expectations though to a very much greater degree those of grown cats and dogs and monkeys.

Closure. We have in mind here the principle brought out by Maier's experiment (see above, p. 175 f.). The rat and, to a still greater degree, certain of the higher animals are capable of correct expectations involving this principle. They are capable expectations depending upon the joining together of separately enjoyed divisions of one and the same total path.

Hierarchicalness. By this term we would designate the fact of successions of sequences. Even the rat (see above, p. 128 f.) and to a much larger degree the higher animals, particularly man and the primates,[6] are capable of correct expectations dependent upon this principle.

The above list is not to be conceived as necessarily complete. Furthermore, no attempt has been made to see in how far the separate items in it are really mutually independent—or to what extent they might not, rather, be telescoped one into another. For it is certain that the very notion of a "field" implies that, to some degree, no one of these principles or types of relation is really independent of, or can be talked about separately from, the others. Thus, it might well turn out in the sequel that there is only *one* "capacity" underlying success relative to *all* these principles.

4. Means-End-Relations and Logic

We shall now suggest that these "formal" (field-, means-end-) relations are fundamentally the sort of thing with *which the logician* qua *logician is concerned.* That is, as we see it, the especial task of the logician is to discover just how many such independent means-end-relations have to be assumed—or just in how far they may be reduced one to another. For we are asserting that logic does (or should) concern itself with all the different kinds and complications and correlations of the fundamental means-end-facts of leading-on-ness and direction-distance correlations. It is the task of logic to build up a set of abstract rules with regard to the types and kinds of mutual interdependence of the facts of leading-on-ness and of direction and distance. But we are not logicians and we must not try to usurp their function. We wish merely to suggest that this, as we see it, is the empirical *stuff* of logic. Logic, we assert, does naught but deal with the "forms" to be found in means-end-fields—as these "forms" obtain for man, for apes, for cats, or for rats. For, if the logician be truly open-minded and catholic, he will be as much

6 Cf. Köhler's experiment on using a box to reach a stick hidden in the roof, in order to use the stick to rake in food. Cf. *Mentality of Apes,* 1925, pp. 183 ff.

interested in the logic, i.e., the character of the means-end-relations, which obtain for the cat, or the rat, as he is in those which obtain for the man or the ape.

Finally, we would emphasize that the means-end-capacity of any individual animal, or species of animal, *qua* capacity, is to be defined as the degree of such animal's ability for releasing quickly and adequately the correct means-end-readinesses and -expectations relative to fields involving such "formal" or "logical" interrelations.

5. Dimensional Means-End-Capacities

As has already been said, actual concrete environmental set-ups involve not only these purely formal relationships but also specific types of material embodiment, in the dimensions of space, of time, of gravitation, of social relations, and the rest. Any actual field always involves concrete dimensional stuffs—spatial, temporal, gravitational, social, physiological, verbal, rhetorical or the like. The formal means-end-relationships of differentiation, sequence, direction, similarity, etc., are always embodied in terms of specific dimensional combinations of discriminanda and manipulanda. And an animal, as for example the rat, may be surprisingly good at differentiating, predicting, etc., in spatial set-ups, but poor at differentiating and predicting in mechanics, and *nil* at it in the realms of society and rhetoric, or the like.

This means that any concrete investigation of a given animal's ability to build up the appropriate sign-gestalt-expectations for a given type of problem, must be evaluated not only as regards its showing up of his pure formal capacity, i.e., his ability, or lack of ability, relative to the formal principles of sequence, round-about-ness, etc., but also as regards his more specific dimensional capacities, i.e., his abilities to deal with the specific stuffs in which these relationships are embodied. The reason that the ape is so superior to the rat may not lie so much in his greater formal capacity, i.e., in his greater ability relative to the formal principles of sequence, differentiation, identity, multiple trackness, final common path, etc., but rather in the fact that by virtue of his better eyes and hands the ape can see and grasp types of "material" to which the rat is altogether insensitive. The ape's superiority is, therefore, perhaps quite as much a matter of superior dimensional capacities as of superior formal capacities.

6.   Intelligence vs. Special Abilities

Finally, we would now suggest that this distinction, which we have thus drawn, between formal means-end-capacities and dimensional means-end-capacities is perhaps somewhat parallel to that made by certain mental testers between general intelligence, g, and the special abilities, s_1, s_2, etc. (See below, Chapter XXIV.) Our concept of formal means-end-capacity would seem, in short, closely analogous to a concept of general intelligence while our concepts as to the dimensional means-end-capacities would seem analogous to concepts of special abilities.

Further, if this parallel is to be admitted one other point is suggested. It is a point which seems, thus far, to have escaped in large part the mental testers themselves, and also the animal lovers. It is the fact, namely, that one cannot very successfully compare intelligences (i.e., formal means-end-capacities) save at approximately the same levels of discriminanda- and manipulanda-capacity, save that is, in the same sorts of dimensional embodiment.

One cannot fruitfully compare the intelligences—capacities *re* formal principles—of say, a parrot, a dog and an elephant, although this is just the kind of question which the layman delights in putting to an animal psychologist. Parrots, dogs and elephants have such very different discriminanda and manipulanda capacities (and hence specific dimensional capacities) that one can never really put to them the *same* problem, in order to see which animal is the speediest and most facile at differentiation, prediction, round-aboutness, etc., per se. One is forced to use such very different discriminanda and manipulanda measuring devices that any common units in terms of which to interpret the results *re* the underlying formal principles seem completely lacking.

Similarly, one cannot with much success, or meaningfulness, measure the relative speeds and facilities relative to differentiation, prediction, etc., of a two-year-old baby and a twelve-year-old adolescent. The discriminanda- and manipulanda-capacities of these two types of animal likewise are so diverse that no common task can, as such, really be presented to them. Only by the most complex statistical procedures,[7] if at all, can the scale and measuring instruments appropriate for determining the purely formal means-end-capacities of the one be refined and extended so as to be appropriate also for determining those of the other.

It seems undoubted that the higher up on either the onto-genetic or the phylogenetic scale one goes, the greater the formal capacities, as well as the greater the dimensional capacities. Yet any precise and accurate evaluation of the formal capacities at such radically different discriminanda- and manipulanda-levels seems at present relatively impossible or puerile.

7. Experiments for Comparing Different Phylogenetic Levels

The experiments we have in mind are those of Yerkes and others on the "Multiple Choice" and those of Hunter on the "Temporal Maze."

Multiple Choice. In the Yerkes multiple choice method [8] the animal is presented with a bank of doors, or in the case of man, a bank of reaction keys, in a row side by side. Some experimenters have used twelve such doors, or keys, others only nine. In any given trial not all these doors will usually be open (available)

[7] Such perhaps as that proposed by Thurstone. Cf. L. L. Thurstone, A method of scaling psychological and educational tests, *J. Educ. Psychol.*, 1925, **16**, 433-451.

———————— The unit of measurement in educational scales, *J. Educ. Psychol.*, 1927, **18**, 505-524.

———————— The absolute zero in intelligence measurement, *Psychol. Rev.*, 1928, **35**, 175-197.

[8] Cf. R. M. Yerkes, and C. A. Coburn, A study of the behavior of the crow, *Corvus Americanus* Aud., by the multiple choice method, *J. Anim. Behav.*, 1915, **5**, 75-114.

R. M. Yerkes and C. A. Coburn, A Study of the behavior of the pig *Sus scrofa* by the multiple choice method, *J. Anim. Behav.*, 1915, **5**, 185-225.

R. M. Yerkes, The mental life of monkeys and apes, A study of ideational behavior, *Behav. Monog.*, 1916, **3**, No. 12.

———————— Methods of exhibiting reactive tendencies characteristic of ontogenetic and phylogenetic stages, *J. Anim. Behav.*, 1917, **7**, 11-28.

———————— A new method of studying the ideational behavior of mentally defective and deranged as compared with normal individuals, *J. Comp. Psychol.*, 1921, **1**, 369-394. This reference includes a complete bibliography on the use of the multiple choice method until 1921.

but some variable number such as three, four, five, etc. This array
of open (or perhaps merely unlocked) doors will vary in position
relative to the total bank and in number from trial to trial. The
apparatus as it has been used with rats is shown in FIGURE 62.

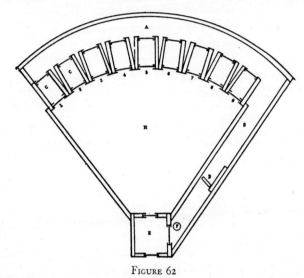

FIGURE 62

"Ground plan of multiple-choice apparatus for rats. . . . E, entrance-box; R,
reaction-chamber; C. reaction-mechanisms; A, back alley; S, side alley; D,
sliding door; F, food-dish. The doors (except D) moved vertically and were
operated by weighted cords through screw-eyes not shown in the figure." [9]

The open doors are always consecutive one to another. The animal is then set by the experimenter a problem of which the
following would be examples: (a) the first open door at the
left; (b) second open door from the right; (c) the middle one
of the open doors. Or in the case of man even such complicated
problems as the following have been used:—(a) alternately second
from the right end and next left of middle; (b) if five are open,
middle; if seven, left end; if nine, right end; (c) two progressions
alternately, beginning at left end toward center, then at right end
toward center, then next on left, next on right, etc.[10]

A problem is solved when the animal chooses the correct door

[9] H. E. Burtt, A Study of the behavior of the white rat by the multiple
choice method, *J. Anim. Behav.*, 1916, **6**, 222-246, p. 224.

[10] Warner Brown and F. Whittell, Yerkes' multiple choice method with human
adults, *J. Comp. Psychol.*, 1923, **3**, 305-326.

in each new set-up at once and without any attempt to enter the incorrect doors, for he has then apparently discovered the "principle" underlying and defining the problem.

It will be observed, from the examples cited above, that this "principle" may vary from a relatively simple spatial affair, such as "the first door at the left of the array" to a principle involving counting, or the like. And the successful solution of a problem demonstrates the capacity of the given animal to differentiate the particular "direction" which defines the correct door by virtue of the given principle. The successful animal is shown to have the capacity for differentiating characters such as "first to the left"; "middle"; "successively first, second, third; etc." Or, in other words, he is found capable (or incapable) of certain spatial, numerical, and temporal "direction-qualities," i.e., discriminanda and manipulanda. And, the higher the animal, the more recondite and subtle are these complex characters which he is capable of differentiating. Increasing complexities in multiple choice problems are quite as much dimensional as formal.[11]

The Temporal Maze. Hunter's temporal maze [12] is essentially a two-way box or track, such for example as that shown in FIGURE 63.

In such a device the animal is forced to make a series of round trips. In each such trip he runs down the center alley first and then turns left or right, as determined by the experimenter by having open (or closed) the doors 1 and 2 or 3 and 4. And the tasks which have been prescribed have been either those of simple alternation, *l r l r l r l r* or of double alternation, *ll rr* and *rr ll*.

---

[11] One point, further. The correct solution of a problem also involves, it would seem, not only the mere ability to differentiate the given defining direction (once it has been, so to speak, "hit upon"), but also to "hit upon it." That is, the getting of the solution seems to involve some sort of an *inventive* or *ideational* process. This latter we shall not, however, attempt to discuss here but leave for a later chapter. See below, Chapter XIV.

[12] Cf. W. S. Hunter, Kinæsthetic sensory process in the white rat, *Psychol. Bull.*, 1918, **15**, 36-37.
——————— The temporal maze and kinæsthetic sensory processes in the white rat, *Psychobiol.*, 1920, **2**, 1-17.
——————— The behavior of raccoons in a double alternation temporal maze, *J. Genet. Psychol.*, 1928, **35**, 374-388.
——————— Sensory control of the maze habit in the white rat, *J. Genet. Psychol.*, 1929, **36**, 505-537.
L. W. Gellermann, The double alternation problem: I. The behavior of monkeys in a double alternation temporal maze, *J. Genet. Psychol.*, 1931, **39**, 50-72.

The general outcome has been that rats could with great difficulty learn a simple alternation, but never a double alternation. Raccoons and monkeys, on the other hand, could learn such a double alternation.

It will be observed, as Hunter has pointed out, that whereas in the single alternation problem the having-just-gone-to-the-left can serve as the cue for then going to the right, and *vice versa* the having-just-gone-to-the-right can serve as the cue for then

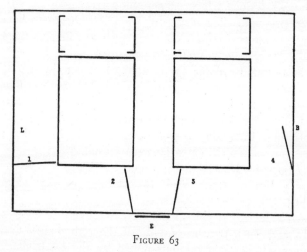

FIGURE 63

"One, 2, 3, and 4 are hinged doors by means of which the pathways are varied. E is the entrance door. The brackets show the location and extent of the electric grills." [13]

going to the left, that in the double alternation problem no such consistent use of the just previous run is possible. In the double alternation problem, such as *l l r r*, the having-just-gone-to-the-left on the first round trip must serve as the cue for the going to the left on the second round trip, while in contrast the having-just-gone-to-the-left on this second trip must then serve as cue for the opposite response of then going to the right. The results indicate, therefore, an ability possessed by the raccoon and the monkey to differentiate and respond to sign-objects distinguished solely by virtue of their position in a temporally spaced order— an ability which is lacking in the rats. The successful raccoons

[13] W. S. Hunter, The behavior of raccoons in a double alternation temporal maze, *J. Genet. Psychol.*, 1928, **35**, p. 379.

and monkeys differentiated between a just-having-been-done *first* left turn and a just-having-been-done *second* left turn. They could take the former as the sign for then going to the left and the latter as the sign for then going to the right. For them the choice point, when approached for the first time, aroused a sign-gestalt-expectation "open route to left." When approached again after having turned to the left once, it aroused again a sign-gestalt-expectation "open route to left." But when approached the third time it aroused the opposite sign-gestalt-expectation "open door to the right." The rats were not capable of this. And Hunter suggests that this means that the higher animals probably possessed some sort of a "symbolic process" (i.e., something functionally equivalent to internal speech) which the rats lacked. By virtue of this "symbolic process" the former were able to distinguish among the successive approaches to the choice point.

But, at any rate, whether or not the necessity for assuming such a symbolic process is involved, it is evident that the positive results with the raccoons and the monkeys, as contrasted with the negative one for the rats, indicate that the former are sensitive to a temporal-order character in their signs of which the rats were incapable. Again the difference appears primarily a dimensional one.

8. Köhler's "Insight" vs. Means-End-Capacity

Finally, before concluding this chapter, it may be well to compare this concept which we have been calling means-end-capacity with a certain other recently much-mooted concept, viz., "insight." The latter has been given especial prominence by Köhler. Both in his analysis of the behavior and problem-solving activities of the apes [14] and in his statement of his general theoretical position [15] he has made frequent use of the term, *insight*.

Let us consider, first, his use of it in connection with his more general theoretical position. In the *Gestalt Psychology* he states that he means by *insight* an "*experienced determination*" between two or more items in one and the same phenomenal field. Insight is present, he says, in situations such as that in which an individual "experiences" that his anger as one item in a phenomenal

[14] Cf. W. Köhler, *The Mentality of Apes* (New York, Harcourt, Brace and Company, 1925).

[15] Cf. W. Köhler, *Gestalt Psychology* (New York, Horace Liveright, 1929).

field points to another individual, i.e., another item in that same field. "Insight," he says, is

"our experience of definite determination in a context, an event or a development of the total field; and in the actual cases there need be nothing like an invention, or a new intelligent achievement, or so forth." [16]

Now it is fairly obvious that this is only indirectly related to our concept of means-end-capacity. Means-end-capacity we have defined as the ability which makes correctly perceived, mnemonized and inferred sign-gestalt-expectations in any given set-up possible. Means-end-capacity is for us the capacity *behind* successful perception, mnemonization and inference in given means-end set-ups and not any mental act of correct expectation per se. Furthermore, the perceptions, mnemonizations and inferences need not, according to us (see next two chapters) be conscious or experienced. Means-end-capacity as we use it, is the capacity *behind* successful expectations, irrespective of whether these expectations are "consciously experienced" or not.

Consider now, however, Köhler's uses of the term *insight* in connection with the apes. He here uses it in two senses—and, while one of them may be absorbed into that just cited, the other, it seems to us is identical with our use of means-end-capacity. In many places in his descriptions Köhler uses "insight" for some sort of a unique "inner happening," e.g., a sudden mental illumination—an illumination, which he finds inferable whenever the animals exhibited a sudden, correct, and relatively indirect solution after a period of hesitation and of more direct, but fruitless, trial and error. And this use is more or less synonymous with that in the *Gestalt Psychology*. In this sense, the animal who gets the new solution does so by virtue of a new "experienced determination" of the relations between items in the phenomenal field (i.e., by virtue of an "insight").[17] The only further point to note as to this use is that in the *Gestalt Psychology* he specifically asserts the further doctrine that insight in this sense is also present in cases where the "experienced determination" involves then and there no new solution—no extension of the field.

[16] *Op. cit.*, p. 371.
[17] Bühler conceives this as an *Aha-Erlebnis*. Cf. K. Bühler, *Die geistige Entwicklung des Kindes*, 3d. ed. (Jena, Gustav Fischer, 1922), p. 21.

Finally, however, as the second use in the *Mentality of Apes*, Köhler seems to us to imply that apes have "insight" in so far as they can actually and successfully solve problems involving such and such differentiations, round-about-nesses, etc., irrespective of whether or not they do so by moments of "experienced determinations." Thus wherever an ape was found to solve a problem involving relatively complicated field principles, Köhler tended to imply, it seems to us, that the animal in so far exhibited *much* insight.[18] And obviously, in so far as we are correct in saying that he used it thus, he used it in the same way in which we have used means-end-capacity. Insight in this sense is no more than the *capacity* behind certain types of action, which makes them successful. It is the capacity behind successful sign-gestalt-expectations. It is means-end-capacities.

9. Insight Learning

Finally, however, we may note a certain other very common use of the term *insight*. Insight has been much used, that is, in discussions of animal learning, ever since the pioneer work of Thorndike,[19] to contrast two ways of learning, viz., (a) supposedly blind "trial and error" learning, on the one hand; and (b) so-called learning with "understanding" or "insight," on the other. Thorndike himself, in the last analysis, seems to have been uncertain as to whether there ever was, or could be, such a thing as any true *insight* or learning with understanding even in human beings.[20] But the contrast, whether or not actually accepted by Thorndike himself, has certainly figured in many subsequent discussions. The assumption has been (and Thorndike himself seems to have been its original father) that an unusually *sudden, sharp drop* in the learning curve would be the objective evidence for "insight." That is, Thorndike denied insight to his cats primarily

---

[18] It is to be noted that his translator found it necessary to use the word "intelligent" as one of her translations for *einsichtig*. And this seems to verify the present assertion that Köhler often meant by insight naught but capacity (intelligence).

[19] E. L. Thorndike, *Animal Intelligence* (New York, The Macmillan Company, 1911).

[20] Cf. For a splendid analysis of Thorndike's conflicting statements on the subject, B. H. Bode, *Conflicting Psychologies of Learning* (Boston, D. C. Heath and Co., 1929), Ch. X.

because he claimed that their curves had no such sudden drops.[21] And Yerkes, upon finding such a sudden drop, in the behavior of a young orang utan, in the Multiple Choice Test, claimed it as obvious evidence that it had learned, i.e., solved the problem, with insight or understanding.[22]

What, now, is the implied definition of this last use of "insight" (disregarding the question as to whether such insight has ever actually been demonstrated or not)? No altogether clear answer seems to be forthcoming. Those writers who have thus used the term in connection with learning seem never to have bothered first to make very clear just what they meant by it. But we may, perhaps, say that, in general, they seem to have conceived of insight as some sort of a "conscious grasping" of the field relationships or field "rules."

At any rate, for the purposes of the present discussion, we shall assume that such is their definition. And, so assuming, we shall now ask what is the relation of such a definition of "insight" to our concept of means-end-capacity? Our answer is that a *capacity* for grasping field-relationships is what *we* mean by means-end-capacity. All learning, therefore, will involve "insight" in this mere capacity sense. And the peculiarity of what has been called *insight learning* would not be the fact that it involved more or even different means-end-capacities, but rather the fact that it was "conscious" and that it usually involves the appearance of *new* relations not previously at the "immediate command" of the organism. So-called "insight learning" would set itself off from

---

[21] Koffka, however, has pointed out that some of Thorndike's curves did show just such sudden drops. Cf. K. Koffka, *The Growth of the Mind, an Introduction to Child-Psychology*, 2nd ed. revised (New York, Harcourt, Brace and Company, 1928), Ch. IV.

[22] R. M. Yerkes, The mental life of monkeys and apes: a study of ideational behavior, *Behav. Monog.*, 1916, **3**, No. 12.

———————— *The Great Apes* (New Haven, Yale Univ. Press, 1929), p. 156.
See also:

W. S. Hunter, *Foundations of Experimental Psychology* (Worcester, Mass., Clark Univ. Press, 1929), pp. 564-628.

G. W. Hartmann, The concept and criteria of insight, *Psychol. Rev.*, 1931, **38**, 242-253.

H. A. Ruger, Psychology of efficiency, *Arch. Psychol.*, 1910, **2**, No. 15.

G. Kreezer and K. M. Dallenbach, Learning the relation of opposition, *Amer. J. Psychol.*, 1929, **41**, 432-441.

C. Spearman, The new psychology of 'shape,' *Brit. J. Psychol.*, General Section, 1925, **15**, 211-225.

trial and error learning only by virtue of (a) its *conscious* or *ideational* character and by virtue of (b) its new or inventive character.

But in order to make this altogether clear we must first decide what we are to understand by consciousness and what by ideation. To these questions we therefore address ourselves in the immediately subsequent chapter.

REFERENCES

Adams, D. K., Experimental studies of adaptive behavior in cats. *Comp. Psychol. Monog.*, 1929, **6**, No. 27.
Alpert, A., The solving of problem-situations by pre-school children. *Teach. Coll. Contrib. Educ.*, 1928, No. 323.
Bierens de Haan, J. A., Die Baukunst eines niederen Affen (*Cebus hypoleucus Humb.*). *Tijdschrift der ned. Dierkunde Vereiniging*, 1930, **2**, 23-27.
——————, Über das Suchen nach verstecktem Futter bei Affen und Halbaffen. *Zsch. f. vergl. Physiol.*, 1930, **11**, 630-655.
——————, Werkzeuggebrauch und Werkzeugherstellung bei einem niederen Affen (*Cebus hypoleucus Humb.*). *Zsch. f. vergl. Physiol.*, 1931, **13**, 639-695.
Bingham, H. C., Chimpanzee translocation by means of boxes. *Comp. Psychol. Monog.*, 1929, **5**, No. 25.
——————, Selective transportation by chimpanzees. *Comp. Psychol. Monog.*, 1929, **5**, No. 26.
Bode, B. H., *Conflicting Psychologies of Learning* (Boston, D. C. Heath & Co., 1929).
Brainerd, P. B., The mentality of a child compared with that of apes. *J. Genet. Psychol.*, 1930, **37**, 268-293.
Brown, W. and Whittell, F., Yerkes' multiple choice method with human adults. *J. Comp. Psychol.*, 1923, **3**, 305-326.
Bühler, K., *Die geistige Entwicklung des Kindes*, 3d ed. (Jena, Gustav Fischer, 1922).
Burtt, H. E., A study of the behavior of the white rat by the multiple choice method. *J. Anim. Behav.*, 1916, **6**, 222-246.
Gellermann, L. W., The double alternation problem: I. The behavior of monkeys in a double alternation temporal maze. *J. Genet. Psychol.*, 1931, **39**, 50-72.
Hartmann, G. W., The concept and criteria of insight. *Psychol. Rev.*, 1931, **38**, 242-253.
Hunter, W. S., Kinæsthetic sensory processes in the white rat. *Psychol. Bull.*, 1918, **15**, 36-37.
——————, The temporal maze and kinæsthetic sensory processes in the white rat. *Psychobiol.*, 1920, **2**, 1-17.

Hunter, W. S., The behavior of raccoons in a double alternation temporal maze. *J. Genet. Psychol.*, 1928, **35**, 374-388.

――――, Sensory control of the maze habit in the white rat. *J. Genet. Psychol.*, 1929, **36**, 505-537.

――――, *Experimental Studies of Learning. Foundations of Experimental Psychology* (Worcester, Mass., Clark Univ. Press, 1929), pp. 564-627.

Koffka, K., *The Growth of the Mind*. 2d ed. rev. (New York, Harcourt, Brace and Company, 1928).

Köhler, W., *The Mentality of Apes* (New York, Harcourt, Brace and Company, 1925).

――――, *Gestalt Psychology* (New York, Horace Liveright, 1929).

Kreezer, G. and Dallenbach, K. M., Learning the relation of opposition. *Amer. J. Psychol.*, 1929, **41**, 432-441.

Lindemann, E. L., Untersuchungen über primitive Intelligenzleistungen hochgradig Schwachsinniger und ihr Verhältnis zu den Leistungen von Anthropoiden. *Zsch. f. d. ges. Neur. und Psychiat.*, 1926, **104**, 529-570.

Lipmann, O., Über Begriff und Erforschung der 'natürlichen' Intelligenz. *Zsch. f. angew. Psychol.*, 1918, **13**, 192-201.

Lipmann, O. and Bogen, H., *Naive Physik., Theoretische und experimentelle Untersuchungen über die Fähigkeit zu Intelligentem Handeln* (Leipzig, Barth, 1923).

McDougall, K. D. and McDougall, W., Insight and foresight in various animals—monkey, raccoon, rat and wasp. *J. Comp. Psychol.*, 1931, **11**, 237-274.

Nellmann, H. and Trendelenburg, W., Ein Beitrag zur Intelligenzprüfung niederer Affen. *Zsch. f. vergl. Physiol.*, 1926, **4**, 142-201.

Ruger, H. A., Psychology of efficiency. *Arch. Psychol.*, 1910, **2**, No. 15.

Spearman, C., The new psychology of 'shape.' *Brit. J. Psychol.*, General Section, 1925, **15**, 211-225.

Thorndike, E. L., *Animal Intelligence* (New York, The Macmillan Company, 1911).

Thurstone, L. L., A method of scaling psychological and educational tests. *J. Educ. Psychol.*, 1925, **16**, 433-451.

――――, The unit of measurement in educational scales. *J. Educ. Psychol.*, 1927, **18**, 505-524.

――――, The absolute zero in intelligence measurement. *Psychol. Rev.*, 1928, **35**, 175-197.

Tolman, E. C., Habit formation and higher mental processes in animals. *Psychol. Bull.*, 1927, **24**, 1-35.

――――, Habit formation and higher mental processes in animals. *Psychol. Bull.*, 1928, **25**, 24-53.

Yerkes, R. M., The mental life of monkeys and apes. A study of ideational behavior. *Behav. Monog.*, 1916, **3**, No. 12.

Yerkes, R. M., Methods of exhibiting reactive tendencies characteristic of ontogenetic and phylogenetic stages. *J. Anim. Behav.*, 1917, 7, 11-28.

——————, A new method of studying the ideational behavior of mentally defective and deranged as compared with normal individuals. *J. Comp. Psychol.*, 1921, 1, 369-394.

Yerkes, R. M. and Coburn, C. A., A study of the behavior of the crow, *Corvus Americanus* Aud., by the multiple choice method. *J. Anim. Behav.*, 1915, 5, 75-114.

—————— and ——————, A study of the behavior of the pig, *Sus scrofa*, by the multiple choice method. *J. Anim. Behav.*, 1915, 5, 185-225.

Yerkes, R. M. and Yerkes, A. W., *The Great Apes* (New Haven, Yale Univ. Press, 1929).

Chapter XIII

CONSCIOUS AWARENESS AND IDEATION [1]

1. Shameful Necessity for Raising Question

UP till now we have avoided any discussion of "consciousness" or "ideas." This was intentional. We desired to emphasize that behavior (*qua* docile) displays purposive and cognitive determinants and that these can, and are, to be discovered and defined quite objectively. A rat's behavior displays docility relative to characters of the environment, and, as thus docile, it is to be said to be purposive and cognitive with respect to those characters. All behavior exhibits immanent means-end-readinesses and means-end-expectations (perceptions, mnemonizations, inferences). And in the analysis and definition of such immanent determinants no statement was found necessary as to whether they do or do not involve conscious awareness or ideas.[2]

And, if psychology could only be content with the lower animals, and preferably with rats, and not try to mess around with human beings, this whole question of consciousness and ideas might well have been omitted. But human beings insist upon being included in any psychological purview. And they insist that they are conscious and do have ideas—however improbable this latter may often appear. The shameful necessity, therefore, devolves upon us of having to invent some sort of an hypothesis as to these matters. Our attempts, however, will be but mere guesses. They will be mere speculations *sub specie temporalitatis*. And, as such, the reader will, we hope, treat them lightly.

---

[1] A slightly different definition of consciousness from that proposed in the present chapter was presented in an earlier article. Cf. E. C. Tolman, A behaviorist's definition of consciousness, *Psychol. Rev.*, 1927, **34**, 433-439.

[2] The terms *consciousness, awareness,* and *conscious awareness* will be used interchangeably. The terms *ideas* and *ideation,* on the other hand, will be used to designate a process which, while involving conscious awareness, is something more than such mere awareness. See below, pp. 210 ff.

Finally because of the penchant of this treatise for rats, we may begin the discussion with them.

2.   The Moment of Conscious Awareness

Its Character. In the first place, we shall declare that the behavior of a rat in the moment when he is conscious is not fundamentally, i.e., metaphysically, other than, and different from, his behavior when he is not conscious. We, as mere behaviorists, are not going to suppose that the rat, in a conscious awareness moment, is in any fundamentally unique sort of metaphysical *situ.* When he is behaving with awareness, he must be supposed to be enjoying the same sort of general relations that he is enjoying when he is behaving without awareness. To behave consciously will be, we must suppose, merely some special "wrinkle"—some elegant, but wholly behavioristically describable, super-structure —imposed upon behaving unconsciously.

Its Locus. We must ask now, however, when does consciousness arise? What are the most probable behavior occasions or *loci* in which, in a rat, conscious awareness may be supposed to occur? Our answer will be that it is primarily in moments of changing behavior, in the moments of learning, that consciousness will appear. Conscious awareness with respect at least to the specific problem in hand, or rather, in "paw," need not be present after a rat has learned a specific maze-item. Neither need it be present before he has learned that item. The awareness process need be present, *if at all,* only during moments of actual learning. Conscious awareness will function, we shall suppose, in some way to aid those changes in the immanent determinants which appear in learning. Consciousness will be pertinent neither to the static conditions which prevail before nor to those which prevail after learning, though human beings often report its continued, i.e., irrelevant persistence afterwards.

Learning a maze involves the building up, or refinement, of appropriate sign-gestalts. That is, in the course of learning, the stimuli presented by a point of bifurcation between two alternative entrances, come to release respectively different sign-gestalt-expectations which were not, as such, released previously. Before learning, the rat tends to enter the alternative entrances fifty-fifty; he releases the same sign-gestalt-expectations for both of them. After learning, on the other hand, he differentiates between them; releases respectively different sign-gestalt-expectations for them. He then enters the one much more frequently than the other. The stimuli from the two entrances thus come, during the course of learning, to release differentiated sets of expectations.

It will, in short, be our hypothesis that conscious awareness, if it appears at all, does so during moments of the acquisition of new, or more refined, sign-gestalt-expectations.

Its Definition. We must now, however, offer our actual definition. *We herewith define conscious awareness as consisting in the performance of a "sampling," or "running-back-and-forth," behavior.* The function and use of such a sampling or running-back-and-forth behavior, i.e., of conscious awareness, will be to enhance, reinforce, throw a spot light upon, some section or area of an environmental field.

Let us illustrate by a concrete case.

3. The White-Black Discrimination-Box

Let us take the case of learning a discrimination-box.[3] Any experienced "rat psychologist" will be willing to testify that in the course of such a learning, there tend to appear, at least in some individual rats, occasions when, upon first coming into the choice chamber, the animal will start to run down the one alley, hesitate, look, or run, back and forth from the one entrance to the other, and only then, finally proceed down one alley or the other.

Our doctrine, now, is that such a running, or looking, back and forth—such a moment of "sampling" defines, or rather *constitutes,* a conscious awareness on the part of the rat—an awareness of the white as contrasted with the black, or of the black as contrasted with the white, or of both together in a "step-up-ness" or "step-down-ness" whole.[4] The running back and forth consti-

---

[3] We propose the case of a discrimination-box rather than of a maze, not because of any fundamental difference between the two, but because the *signs* in the case of the discrimination-box are more easily described by us (the observers) than in the case of a maze.

[4] Cf. W. D. Ellis, *Gestalt Psychology and Meaning* (Berkeley, Sather Gate Book Shop, 1930), p. 144. He says:

"*Stepwise phenomenon.*—Is a term used by some Gestalt psychologists to

tutes, that is, an awareness of this differential aspect in the means-end-field—a differential aspect of the field which, previous to this instant of consciousness, was not determinative or, at the most, only very slightly determinative, of the behavior, and which, after the instant of consciousness, becomes decisively more determinative.

4.   Learning with Consciousness vs. Learning without Consciousness

It must be noted, however, that such running-back-and-forth, or sampling, behaviors do not always occur. The rat, in the course of his "practical" (problem-solving) behavior, may pass from treating the white and black in undifferentiated fashion to treating them in differentiated fashion, quite smoothly, and with no apparent intervention of moments of running-back-and-forth, i.e. consciousness.

This indicates two possibilities. On the one hand, learning may accrue in smooth fashion simply as the result of successive experiences of the two entrances as leading to their respective significates: food, on the one hand, and *cul de sac* end, on the other. Or, learning may involve, in part at least, moments of runnings-back-and-forth, i.e. moments of conscious awareness.[5]

name the type of experience frequently had by subjects in sensory discrimination experiments. The judgment 'heavier' or 'lighter' regarding two weights, for example, is frequently *experienced* as preceding apprehension of the 'actual' weight of either stimulus. It is possible that this temporal priority of judgment may obtain in all such cases even when subjects are not aware of that fact. That 'absolute' judgment or discrimination can be made is doubtful for, even in the case of judgment regarding a single stimulus, it is not unlikely that kinæsthetic or other cues supply a complex matrix which the given stimulus serves merely to upset toward one direction (e.g., the judgment 'heavier') or the other.

The experienced whole can often be revealed by post-analytical discrimination to have been composed of temporally antecedent parts, but such physically temporal priority cannot for that reason alone be postulated as *experienced* priority.

The tension between such post-analytically discernible parts as, e.g., this weight, pause, that weight, contributes to the experience had, a characteristic wholeness designated (in words, however, unclearly) as comparable to a lower-step-and-upper experience."

For a fuller discussion of the "Step-wise phenomenon" see K. Koffka's Perception: An introduction to the *Gestalt-Theorie*, Psychol. Bull., 1922, **19**, 531-585, esp. 537 ff.

[5] The occurrence of such "sampling," "try-first-this-and-then-that" behavior

5. The Functional Significance of Running-Back-and-Forth

But what, we must now ask, is the function or value of such runnings-back-and-forth—such conscious awarenesses, when they do occur? What do they achieve?

The answer would seem to be that such moments of conscious awareness, such runnings-back-and-forth, serve to verify and re-inforce the differentiation between the white and black signs which will, to some extent, have become already established automatically and unconsciously. For it must be noted that the rat will not be impelled to run or look back and forth until, as a result of a certain number of trials, he has already built up in himself some degree of adjustment to the fact that there are two entrances and that there is a difference between them. The appearance of running-back-and-forth requires that the rat, upon being faced with the stimuli from the one entrance, shall have already become adjusted to the fact that there is some sort of another contrasted entrance. The rat must have in some measure learned unconsciously, before consciousness can begin to appear. He cannot be conscious *until* he has already achieved, to some degree, that which being conscious will merely further emphasize. The functional value of being conscious must be said, therefore, to be merely that of emphasizing and re-inforcing field-features, to some extent already become immanent in preceding behaviors. Consciousness can accomplish nothing really *de novo*.

6. Running-Back-and-Forth—a Non-Practical Behavior

In this connection, it should be stressed, further, that to be conscious is thus to hold up a "practical" behavior in order to indulge in a non-practical one. To run back and forth is an interlude. It is, of course, valuable, but it delays and postpones

in monkeys has recently been demonstrated in most striking fashion by Klüver. He has carried out a long series of experiments on form, size, and intensity discriminations. For a brief preliminary report of this work, see:

H. Klüver, The equivalence of stimuli in monkeys, *Proc. Ninth Internat. Cong. Psychol.* (Princeton, Psychol. Rev. Co., 1930), pp. 263-264.

See also H. Klüver, The equivalence of stimuli in the behavior of monkeys, *J. Genet. Psychol.*, 1931, **39**, 3-27.

the ultimately desired practical behavior of actually taking the one side or the other. To be conscious is to hold up and delay in order to enhance, to limn in, some area or aspect of a position-field, an area or aspect which, however, as we have just seen, must have already been in some measure grasped prior to such consciousness.

7. Differentiation Plus Prediction

It is to be noted, next, that a rat, in learning a discrimination-box, may exhibit occasions in which he runs back-and-forth not only from one entrance to another, but also within any one alley itself. And this latter type of running-back-and-forth constitutes a reinforcing and enhancing of the predictive, or sequential, relation obtaining between the entrance and the further "insides" of an alley. The function of the running-back-and-forth, the consciousness, is here to verify and reinforce such a prediction. It is to enhance, as by a spot light, the specific leading-on-ness of the given sign. This fact that we can thus distinguish between two occasions or types of consciousness does not mean, however, that these two are likely ever really to occur in mutual independence. Obviously the rat cannot do both types of running back and forth simultaneously. But he can, and does, do them in close succession. He often runs from one entrance to the other and back and forth within each entrance in close succession. Furthermore, the conditions for doing the one seem to include those for doing the other. That is, the rat probably does not consciously differentiate the one entrance from the other, i.e., run back and forth between them, until he has already acquired, to some extent, an unconscious prediction as to what each entrance leads to. And *vice versa,* he probably does not consciously predict, i.e., run back and forth within either alley, until he has also acquired unconsciously some degree of differentiation as between the two alleys. Differentiation and prediction go hand in hand. Neither seems to be possible without some degree of the other.

Finally, it will now be asserted that prediction, leading-on-ness-to-or-from, and differentiation are probably the two most fundamental of the "formal" means-end principles discussed in the preceding chapter. It appears, in other words, that it is only by virtue of the possession of at least this degree of means-end-capacity that consciousness will be possible. The means-end-capacity for responding at least to differential and predictive relations, will be the necessary pre-condition of a conscious awareness, i.e., of a sampling or running-back-and-forth behavior.

8. Ideation—a Mere "Adjustment" to, a Mere Feint at, Running-Back-and-Forth

But the reader with "mentalistic" proclivities no doubt will have long since (albeit, let us trust, silently) been protesting. "Conscious awareness," he will have been grumbling to himself, "may perhaps be present, whenever there is such an actual running back and forth, but surely it cannot be completely identified with such runnings back and forth. For," he will continue, "I, as a human being, certainly know that I am conscious on frequent occasions when I am not running-back-and-forth. In fact, my conscious awarenesses seldom, if ever, seem to be accompanied by, or to involve, any such runnings."

How are we to answer this charge? We will reply that in such cases where, on other evidence, i.e., "introspection," [6] the experimenter has reason to assume the presence of consciousness in his subject, we may suppose such consciousness to exist not in any actual running-back-and-forth, but rather in what we may designate as a "behavior-adjustment" to, or a mere "behavior-feint" at, running-back-and-forth.

We will suppose that in the higher animals, and perhaps even in rats, there is an ability, upon the holding up of a "practical" behavior, to embark not only upon an actual running-back-and-forth (i.e., consciousness) but also upon mere surrogates for, adjustments to, such "non-practical" runnings-back-and-forth. Such mere adjustments-to, mere behavior-feints, will perform the same function that the actual runnings-back-and-forth would have performed. They will in some way bring the animal into contact with the same stimulus-results with which he would have been brought in contact, if he had actually behaved—that is, if he had actually run back and forth. Actual running-back-and-forth achieves, we supposed, an enhancement of the differentiation and prediction features of the environment, an en-

---

[6] For an evaluation of introspection see below, Chapter XV.

hancement of the immanent sign-gestalt-expectations which are getting ready to function in the animal's behavior. Actual running-back-and-forth enhances, throws a searchlight or spotlight upon, the white-black differentiation and the leading-on-ness of white to food and of black to non-food. And the behavior-feints at running back and forth, these mere surrogates for behavior, achieve, we shall now declare, the same sort of enhancements without, however, the same expenditure of time and energy which are involved in the actual runnings-back-and-forth. To "behavior-adjust" is in some strange way to be brought into contact with the same stimulus-results that one would be in contact with, if one should actually behave.[7]

Now, such behavior-feints at running-back-and-forth, as contrasted with actual runnings-back-and-forth, we shall define as ideations. Simple awareness equals an actual running-back-and-forth. Ideation equals an adjustment to such running-back-and-forth. It is a surrogate or substitute for such an actual running-back-and-forth and accomplishes the same end.

9.   The Doctrine of "Implicit" Behavior

It may now well be asked what is the relation of this doctrine of ours to the Watson[8] and Weiss[9] doctrine of "Implicit Behavior." The latter is a somewhat confused doctrine. But none the less it is a very important and original doctrine, and one to which we owe much. In fact, we shall now assert that it is really the basis for our present concept of behavior-adjustments or behavior-feints. The real meaning of the Watson-and-Weiss "implicit behavior," i.e., sub-vocal speech or sub-gestural gesture, is to be found, we believe, in its character as a surrogate for actual behavior. Implicit behavior, as they describe it, seems to be in essence an activity which, while without going through any actual gross movements, somehow brings the organism into contact with

[7] This is, of course, reminiscent of Bode's doctrine that consciousness is a "bringing of the future into the present." Cf. B. H. Bode, Consciousness and psychology, *Creative Intelligence, Essays in the Pragmatic Attitude,* by John Dewey and others (New York, Henry Holt and Company, 1917).

[8] Cf. J. B. Watson, Is thinking merely the action of language mechanisms? *Brit. J. Psychol.,* 1920, 11, 87-104.

[9] Cf. A. P. Weiss, *A Theoretical Basis of Human Behavior* (Columbus, O., R. G. Adams Co., 1925), esp. pp. 256-266.

the very same types of environmental consequence which the corresponding actual behavior would have achieved for him.

It must be noted, however, that although this is the essence of the doctrine, they actually go somewhat further. In addition, that is, to indicating this essential functional significance of implicit behavior, they go on, in an unnecessary fashion, to suggest the specific neuro-muscular characters of such implicit behavior or such behavior-feints. They assert, in short, that these implicit behaviors are always of the nature of sub-vocal laryngeal contractions, or at least of sub-gestural gestures. But it seems obvious that it is not the precise neuro-muscular characters of the adjustments or feints which are important, but merely their substitute or surrogate character. Implicit behaviors or behavioradjustments are surrogate behaviors, and that is the important point. And the truth of this should not be jeopardized, as Watson and Weiss jeopardize it, by making it dependent upon the further hypothesis that structurally such "implicit behaviors" always involve sub-vocal speech or sub-gestural gestures, or indeed, that they necessarily involve any motor discharges at all.

10. The Relatively Disinterested Character of Both Consciousness and Ideation

We may now emphasize, again, that, either by actually running-back-and-forth or by a surrogate for (i.e., a behavior-adjustment to or behavior-feint at) such an actual running-back-and-forth, the organism enhances some spot or area of the environmental field. He re-inforces or even changes his sign-gestalts relative to this area of the field. He breaks the bonds of immediate necessity in order to "see more clearly" what it is which is really before him. He holds up his "practical" behavior in order to be more certain of the real possibilities with which that practical behavior has to deal. Instead of using his sign-gestalt-expectations, he momentarily holds up and runs over them. He holds them "in leash" [10] while he modifies or enhances them.

---

[10] It will be recalled that the delayed reaction experiment (see above Chapter X, p. 154 f.) was analyzed as indicating an ability on the part of the animal to hold a sign-gestalt-expectation "in leash." It may be suggested now that this holding in leash which is accomplished in a delayed reaction may be closely analogous to what we are now calling ideation—viz., a purely "adjustmental" running-back-and-forth "in front of."

11.   The Causes of Consciousness and of Ideation (Consciousness-Ability and Ideation-Ability)

Finally, however, it may be asked what causes such conscious or ideational moments—such moments of "non-practical" runnings-back-and-forth? Why is it that a rat sometimes stops and runs back and forth in the course of learning and sometimes does not? This is a question to which at present we can suggest tentative answers only. In general, however, we may suppose, first of all, that it is primarily at moments of blockage of the practical behaviors, that the non-practical runnings-back-and-forth, i.e., consciousness and ideation, appear.[11] To state this more concretely, we shall suppose that it is primarily when, and if, in the course of learning the white-black box, the sign-gestalt-expectations for the two sides have become temporarily "jammed," relative to one another, that the animal becomes conscious, i.e., stops to run back and forth between these two sides. Initially, and before any learning, the rat, as we have seen (see above, Chapter X, p. 145), is releasing hopeful sign-gestalt-expectations with respect to both sides. In the course of learning, refinements of these sign-gestalt-expectations set in—such that the one side, "white," becomes the sign of the to-come "good" significate, and the other side, "black," the sign of the to-come "bad" significate. Before this final consummation of learning has been achieved, however, there will tend to appear a halfway stage in which each sign will release expectations of both the "good" and the "bad" simultaneously. The rat will have learned that one is good and one is bad, but he will not yet have become quite sure which

[11] For other more or less related functional theories of consciousness, see:

B. H. Bode, Consciousness and psychology, *Creative Intelligence, Essays in the Pragmatic Attitude*, by John Dewey and others (New York, Henry Holt and Company, 1917).

Geo. H. Mead, A behavioristic account of the significant symbol, *J. Philos.*, 1922, **19**, 157-163.

L. L. Thurstone, *The Nature of Intelligence* (New York, Harcourt, Brace and Company, 1924), esp. Chapters III and VII.

M. F. Washburn, *Movement and Mental Imagery* (Boston, Houghton Mifflin Company, 1916).

H. S. Langfeld, Consciousness and motor response, *Psychol. Rev.*, 1927, **34**, 1-9.

———— A response interpretation of consciousness, *Psychol. Rev.*, 1931, **38**, 87-108.

K. Dunlap, Images and ideas, *Johns Hopkins Circ.*, 1914, No. 3, 25-41.

is which. He will suffer blockages. Whichever side is immediately before him at the moment, he will have a tendency to expect at one and the same time both good and bad significates as going to result from that side. But such conflicting expectations, with their resultant conflicting propensities for actual practical behavior, will cause (or allow?) a breaking out into the "non-practical" behavior of running-back-and-forth. And this running-back-and-forth will enhance the differentiation between the two signs, and it will emphasize the relationship, that it is the white sign which leads to the good significate and the black sign which leads to the bad significate.

Finally, however, it must be noted that there is nothing in the fact of conflicts per se which necessarily need give rise to runnings-back-and-forth. It must be assumed further, therefore, that although it is these conflicts in practical behaviors which provide the occasions for the appearance of consciousness and ideation, it is not they which really cause or create the latter. The ultimate creative causes for consciousness and ideation must then be traced back to some innate trait or aptitude of the organism. To become conscious or to ideate, i.e., to run back and forth or to adjust to such runnings-back-and-forth, upon an occasion of expectational blockage must, in the last analysis, be due to an aptitude possessed by the individual or species. It must be due to the possession, and the working in the individual, in some degree, of a trait which we shall call consciousness-ability and ideation-ability. That is, we would mean by this one phrase: the ability to hold up practical behavior (to hold the immanent sign-gestalt in leash)—in order to run back and forth or adjust to running-back-and-forth; and the ability, on the basis of either such actual runnings-back-and-forth or such adjustments to running-back-and-forth, to suffer enhancements or modifications in the initial immanent sign-gestalts; and the ability finally to act practically on the basis of these enhanced or modified sign-gestalts.

12. The "Raw Feel" of Consciousness

But the "mentalist" will still protest. "The above," he will say, "is all beside the point. Consciousness and ideation may perhaps have as their 'cash value' that which is accomplished by running-back-and-forth or an adjustment to running back and forth. But consciousness per se is not a behavior or the function performed by a behavior. It is a unique 'inner stuff.' It is a unique 'raw feel.' "

"Very good," we reply, "but then, by definition, consciousness is not something with which we, as scientists, need be concerned. 'Raw feels' are by very definition outside the purview of our science. All that can be conveyed about consciousness and ideation from the rat to the scientist or even from one scientist to another is that they perform certain functions. Consciousness and ideation reinforce and bring into the focus of the given organism's behavior, sign-gestalts as determinants which, up to that moment, were acting only weakly. And this is the sole character of such consciousness and such ideation, functionally and scientifically speaking. If consciousness and ideation have unique 'raw feels' these latter are by definition to be left out of our science." [12]

13. Consciousness or Ideation and Drops in the Learning Curve

We have contended that a conscious awareness or an ideation of the differentiation and prediction characters of the two alleys appears only after the immanent sign-gestalts, which control the "practical" behaviors, have already, to some degree, taken on automatically the differentiation of the white from the black, and the prediction that white leads to food and black does not. And the functions of such conscious awareness or ideation, when they do appear, are simply to verify and reinforce these same differentiation and prediction features. This suggests further, however, that, when such runnings back and forth (behavior or adjustments to behavior) do appear, they will tend to evoke larger and more consistent drops in the learning curve than would be likely to appear without them.

If, in short, the above definitions of consciousness and ideation be correct, then, upon the piling up of statistically numerous enough observations, bigger and more empirically certain drops in the learning curve ought to be found on occasions after a running-back-and-forth (a conscious awareness) has appeared

[12] For a further discussion of the problem of "raw feels," see below, Chapters XVI and XXV.

than are found ordinarily at the same point in the learning curve, when no such runnings-back-and-forth have been exhibited. But this opens up the possibility of a concrete investigation which someone should carry out. The fact of sudden drops in the learning curve is of course familiar. (As we saw in the preceding chapter, it has often been taken as the definition of "insight" in the Bühler sense of an *Aha-Erlebnis*.[13]) But what we are seeking, now, is not this mere fact of sudden drops, but rather a correlation between the appearance of such drops and the appearance of just preceding "runnings-back-and-forth." For if this sort of a correlation could be demonstrated, it would be direct evidence for our definition of consciousness. Will someone please try it?

Finally, it should also be noted that if our hypothesis be correct, and if a rat could but introspect, and if we could assume his introspection to be reliable and valid, it should also turn out that the occasions upon which there are relatively big, sudden drops in the learning curve should also be ones with a high percentage of introspective reports of ideation (even though no overt runnings-back-and-forth appeared). We should, in other words, expect a positive correlation between degree of drop in the learning curve and introspective report of ideation as well as between drops and objective appearances of runnings-back-and-forth.

14.   Recapitulation

Our hypotheses are:

(a) Conscious awareness equals an overt running-back-and-forth; and such an overt running-back-and-forth enhances the differentiation and prediction features of the means-end field.

(b) These differentiation and prediction features can, and must, be enhanced without the aid of a conscious awareness moment; but the latter, if it appears, will evoke a special acceleration in this process.

(c) The higher organisms are to be assumed to be capable, not only of actual runnings-back-and-forth, but also of adjustments to such runnings-back-and-forth. Such adjustments will perform

13 See above p. 198, note 17.
For a particularly pretty instance of such a sudden drop in the learning curve in the case of a young orang utan, see again R. M. Yerkes, The mental life of monkeys and apes: a study of ideational behavior, *Behav. Monog.*, 1916, **3**, No. 12.

the same sort of enhancing of differentiation and prediction features which actual running-back-and-forth would achieve. Only they will do so with less expenditure of time and energy. And they constitute our definition of ideation (i.e., thought). (What they may consist in neurologically we do not know.)

(d) Conscious awareness and ideation tend to arise primarily at moments of conflicting sign-gestalts, conflicting practical differentiations and predictions. Such moments provide their occasions. But their ultimate causation must be conceived of as lying in the organism's possession of an aptitude for resorting to them. This aptitude we have designated *consciousness-ability* and *ideation-ability*.

(e) Conscious awareness and ideation, as unique "raw feels," do not concern us. It is only as functioning entities that we are here concerned with them.

(f) And our functional definitions of them would seem capable of being put to an empirical examination and proof.

(g) Finally, however, it is to be confessed that we personally would be loath to put them to such a test. For, as was pointed out at the beginning, they are but the wildest of guesses—mere speculations *sub specie temporalitatis*.

REFERENCES

Bode, B. H., Consciousness and psychology, *Creative Intelligence, Essays in the Pragmatic Attitude,* by John Dewey and others (New York, Henry Holt and Company, 1917).

Dunlap, K., Images and ideas. Johns Hopkins Circ., 1914, No. 3, 25-41.

Ellis, W. D., *Gestalt Psychology and Meaning* (Berkeley, Sather Gate Book Shop, 1930).

Klüver, H., *The Equivalence of Stimuli in Monkeys. Proc. Ninth Internat. Cong. Psychol.* (Princeton, Psychol. Rev. Co., 1930), pp. 263-264.

——————, The equivalence of stimuli in the behavior of monkeys. *J. Genet. Psychol.*, 1931, **39**, 3-27.

Koffka, K., Perception: An introduction to the *Gestalt-Theorie. Psychol. Bull.*, 1922, **19**, 531-585.

Langfeld, H. S., Consciousness and motor response. *Psychol. Rev.*, 1927, **34**, 1-9.

——————, A response interpretation of consciousness. *Psychol. Rev.*, 1931, **38**, 87-108.

Mead, G. H., A behaviorist's account of the significant symbol. *J. Philos.*, 1922, **19**, 157-163.

Thurstone, L. L., *The Nature of Intelligence* (New York, Har-
    court, Brace and Company, 1924).
Tolman, E. C., A behaviorist's definition of consciousness.
    Psychol. Rev., 1927, **34**, 433-439.
Washburn, M. F., *Movement and Mental Imagery* (Boston,
    Houghton Mifflin Company, 1916).
Watson, J. B., Is thinking merely the action of language mechan-
    isms? *Brit. J. Psychol.*, 1920, **11**, 87-104.
Weiss, A. P., *A Theoretical Basis of Human Behavior* (Colum-
    bus, O., R. G. Adams Co., 1925).
Yerkes, R. M., The mental life of monkeys and apes: A study
    of ideational behavior. *Behav. Monog.*, 1916, **3**, No. 12.

Chapter XIV

INVENTIVE IDEATION

1. Inventive Ideation

IN the foregoing chapter it was suggested that relatively sudden drops in the learning curve are probable indicators of conscious awareness and of simple ideation. It will be suggested, now, that when such sudden drops involve the doing of some really new act, not performed at all up until that moment, then such drops are indicators of an especially high type of ideation—a type for which we may coin the new term "inventive ideation." [1]

An inventive ideation is to be conceived as involved in the case where an animal achieves a "behavior-adjustment" to running back and forth over strands of the means-end-field which, as such, he has never actually encountered. He does this, we assume, somewhat as follows. First he "adjusts" to portions of the field which he has actually enjoyed. Next, by some sort of a process of extrapolation, he "adjusts" to new portions of that field. Finally, he actually behaves to these new portions. Whereupon there appears the sudden drop in his learning curve. It is the second step —that of "adjusting" by virtue of some process of extrapolation to the new, not yet actually enjoyed portions of the field which constitutes the inventive ideation, per se.

2. Köhler's Apes

The classical accounts of such inventive ideations are to be found, we believe, in Köhler's descriptions of the behavior of his chimpanzees. The essence of the problems which he set these animals seems to have consisted in the fact that the solutions involved new acts, never, as far as was known, previously done by the given animal. Or, as Köhler himself puts it, the problems he

---

[1] That is, *insight learning*. See above, p. 215 f.

set his animals all involved *Umwege*, i.e., roundabout, and hence *new*, routes for their solutions.[2] A somewhat telescoped list of the problems in which his apes were thus successful is as follows:

(a) Simple spatial detour to food; (b) pulling food into cage by means of attached string; (c) using sticks to rake in food; (d) using boxes, ladders, one another, and even the experimenter to climb upon to reach food hung from above; (e) swinging on ropes to food; (f) removing a box which interfered with directly reaching for food outside the cage; (g) breaking a branch off a dead tree to use as a stick; (h) emptying stones out of a box in order to use this box for climbing on; (i) making a long stick out of two short hollow bamboo tubes by fitting the end of one tube into the slightly larger end of the other; (j) using a short stick to pull in a long stick in order to use the long stick for reaching food; (k) emptying stones out of a box, to use the box to reach a hanging stick needed for reaching food outside the cage; (l) pushing food by means of a stick out of a shallow three-sided drawer lying on the ground outside the cage; (m) pushing food by a stick from one side of box to the other side, where it could be reached by hand between the bars; (n) swinging out on top of a door to reach food hung from ceiling; (o) unwinding two turns in a rope coiled about a bar in order to swing on this rope for food.[3]

It will be observed that in each case, the simple "direct" route to food was blocked or lacking, and the solution consisted in taking a "roundabout" one—e.g., a simple spatial detour; the use, fetching, or perhaps even the manufacturing of a tool; the removal of an obstacle; or the like. Before inquiring further, however, as to the exact methodological significance and import of such roundabout routes, let us quote in some detail the accounts for a few typical cases.

[2] W. Köhler, *The Mentality of Apes* (New York, Harcourt, Brace and Company, 1925). These experiments were similar to types previously carried out by Hobhouse with dogs, cats, elephant, chimpanzees, and insects.
    (Cf. L. T. Hobhouse, *Mind in Evolution* [New York, The Macmillan Company, 1901]; 2d ed. 1915.) But it seems to have been Köhler who first emphasized that exact aspect of their methodological significance, which we are here interested in.
[3] This is not quite a complete list. Some of Köhler's experiments involved changes and modifications of the above which are difficult to epitomize. For an excellent short description and summary of practically all of the experiments, see K. Koffka, *The Growth of the Mind* (New York, Harcourt, Brace and Company, 2d edition, revised, 1928), pp. 198 ff.

We shall cite, first, the account of two cases in which the problem was to use a box to stand on to reach hanging food.

3. The Use of a Box to Stand on

The first case we would quote is that of the young ape, Koko:

"On the third day of his residence at the station (11.7), he [Koko] was given a small wooden box as a toy. (Its dimensions were forty by thirty by thirty centimetres.) He pushed it about and sat on it for a moment. On being left alone, he became very angry, and thrust the box to one side. After an hour had elapsed, Koko was removed and his chain fastened to the wall of a house. On one side, one metre from the ground, the objective was suspended from the wall. The box had been placed between three and four metres from the objective, and two metres from the wall while Koko was being conducted to his new place. The length of his rope allowed him to move freely about the box and by the wall where the objective hung. The observer withdrew to a considerable distance (more than six meters from the box, and the same side), and only approached once in order to make the objective more attractive. Koko took no notice of him throughout the course of the test. He jumped upwards several times to begin with, perpendicularly beneath the objective, then took his rope in his hand and tried to lasso the prize with a loop of it, could not reach so far, and then turned away from the wall, after a variety of such actions, but without noticing the box. He appeared to have given up his efforts, but always returned to them from time to time. After some time, on turning away from the wall, his eye fell on the box: he approached it, *looked straight towards the objective,* and gave the box a slight push, which did not, however, move it; his movements had grown much slower; he left the box standing, took a few paces away from it, but at once returned, and pushed it again and *again with eyes on the objective,* but quite gently, and not as though he really intended to alter its position. He turned away again, turned back at once, and gave the box a third tentative shove, after which he again moved slowly about. The box had now been moved ten centimeters in the direction of the fruit. The objective was rendered more tempting by the addition of a piece of orange (the *non plus ultra* of delight!), and in a few seconds Koko was once more at the box, seized it, and dragged it in one movement almost up to a point directly beneath the objective (that is, for a distance of at least three metres), mounted it, and tore down the fruit. A bare quarter of an hour had elapsed since the beginning of the test. Of course, the observer had not interfered with either the ape or the box, when he 'improved' the objective. The improvement of the objective by the addition of further items is a method which can be employed over and over again with success when the animal is obviously quite near to a solution, but, in the case of a lengthy experiment, there is the risk that fatigue will intervene and spoil the result. It must not be supposed that before the exhibition of the orange, the animal is too lazy to attain its objective; on the contrary, from the beginning, Koko showed a lively interest in the fruit, but none—at first—in the box, and when he began to move the latter, he did not appear *apathetic* but *uncertain;* there is only one (colloquial) expression that really fits his behavior at that juncture: 'It's beginning to dawn on him!' " [4]

A second case described in some detail by Köhler is that of Sultan, the most intelligent of the animals in the colony. We quote:

"The day after Sultan had used the box for the second time, the objective was fastened to the roof of another room which was at a much greater height from the ground. Two boxes were on the ground, standing close together, and about five metres from the fruit. Sultan was alone. At first he took no notice of the boxes, but tried to knock down the objective, first with a short stick and then with one of more appropriate length. The heavy sticks wobbled helplessly in his grasp; he became angry, kicked and drummed against the wall and hurled the sticks from him. Then he sat down on a table, in the neighborhood of the boxes, with an air of fatigue; when he had recovered a little, he gazed about him and scratched his head. He looked at the boxes—stared at them, and in the same moment he was off the table, and had seized the nearer one of them, which he dragged under the objective and climbed on to, having first recaptured his stick, with which he easily secured the prize. The box was not placed vertically, and Sultan was too inexpert at jumping to be able to dispense with his stick." [5]

4.   Removal of Obstructing Box

Next we shall quote the description of a solution which consisted in having to remove a box which was placed at the front of the cage, and which in that position prevented the animal from reaching the food outside the cage.

"A species of reversal of the 'tool-using' experiments consists in placing a movable object across the path of the objective so that

[4] W. Köhler, *The Mentality of Apes* (New York, Harcourt, Brace and Company, 1925), pp. 42-43.
[5] *Op. cit.,* p. 47.

the problem can be solved only by its *removal:* . . . The box was placed in the barred room in immediate contact with the bars and standing on the smaller end so that it could easily be knocked over. Outside the bars, and immediately opposite the center of the box, the bananas lay on the ground; . . . It was the first time that Tschego had carried out any experiment. For a long while her response consisted in useless stretching and groping towards the objective, [banana] . . . Finally, we put down a second objective [banana] outside the bars and nearer to them than the first, a trifle to one side, within Tschego's reach, but still strongly obstructed by the box. Tschego took hold of objective number two, but did not respond to this assistance. She crouched beside the box, facing the bars. For some time nothing happened. Then, however, some of the smaller apes approached from outside the cage —they were permitted to do so as experimental stimulation—and endeavored to approach the prize. Each time, though, Tschego repulsed them with threatening gestures, wagging of her head, stamping with her feet, and pawing the air with her great hands: for she regarded the objective as her property though it was beyond her reach; otherwise she would not have menaced the little creatures, with whom she was generally on the best of terms. The youngsters finally gathered closely around the fruit, but the danger inspired Tschego; she gripped the box, which was like a toy in her arms, jerked it backwards, stepped up to the bars, and took the fruit. In this case we know the *time* is of importance; Tschego began to make efforts towards the fruit at 11 A.M., and succeeded at 1 P.M. If the little ones had not intervened, the test would have taken much longer. . . . The 'obstacle' test was *not* solved either in the case of Tschego or the young apes by a series of imperceptible pushes involuntarily given to the cage [box] in the act of stretching towards the prize. Quite the contrary: *during the lapse of two hours, Tschego did not move the cage one millimetre from its original position,* and when the solution arrived, the cage was not *shouldered* to one side, but *suddenly gripped with both hands, and thrust back."* [6]

[6] W. Köhler, *op. cit.,* 61-65. Also cited by W. S. Hunter in Experimental Studies in Learning. *The Foundations of Experimental Psychology* (Worcester, Mass., Clark Univ. Press, 1929), pp. 576-577, as typical of the so-called *insight* solution. It should be noted that, for us, there is no "insight" solution per se. All solutions represent a progress from less successful sign-gestalts to more successful sign-gestalts. Some of these progressions are relatively slow and gradual and some are relatively sudden. Some occur without much conscious or ideational accompaniment, and some involve a great deal of such accompaniment. In some the new effective means-end-relations are relatively limited and have but a restricted range of applicability; in others the new means-end-expectations are relatively extended and have a relatively far-reaching applicability.

5. Stick and Pushing Food to Further Side of Box

Finally, we shall cite Köhler's description of Sultan's solution
where he had to push the food by a stick from one side of a box
—where the opening was too high for him to reach the food directly with his hand—to the opposite side, in order that he might
then go around to the latter where he could reach it with his hand.

"A big wooden animal cage is closed on one side by bars, between which the animals can pass their hands from outside; but
the cage is so big that the arm of a young chimpanzee standing
outside does not command the whole interior from these bars, but
only about half of it. The side opposite the bars consists of boards
nailed across horizontally; one board is removed, at a place that
enables the young animals to look and put their hand into the
cage, but not touch the floor; the rest of the cage is closed. If
a fruit lies on the floor close to the wall from which a board
has been removed, the chimpanzee will reach after it from the
(opposite) bars with a stick, as the cage (weighed with stones)
cannot be turned over. If one takes care that the stick can be used
only from the side of the gap, the sole solution remaining is to
push the objective from the gap towards the bars, until it can be
reached there with the hand. One therefore removes all possible
sticks and staves except one which can be used quite comfortably
from the gap, but, being fastened near the gap by a rope tied to a
tree, cannot be taken over to the side where the bars are. . . .
[The figure] shows only the ground plan: R is the tree with the

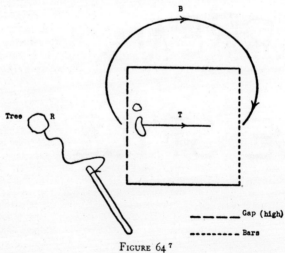

----- Gap (high)

------- Bars

FIGURE 64 [7]

[7] *Op. cit.*, p. 264.

rope and the stick attached to it; the broken line indicates the side with the gap; opposite, the bars are indicated by a dotted line. The lines T and B indicate the two parts of the total procedure running towards each other, one of which is to be covered by the tool, the other afterwards with the animal's body. It is clear that the ape has to work for a later position of its body, which is, as it were, the reverse of the position taken during the use of the tool.

"(27.3.1914) Sultan seizes the stick, pokes with it through the gap, and tries to pull the objective towards him and to lift it up the side to a height where it can be reached. From time to time, he runs off, looking for a blade of straw, or something like it, with which to reach for the objective from the side of the bars—but in vain. After a while—the animal is again using the stick from the gap—the whole direction of the movement suddenly changes; the objective is pushed away from the gap, not to the bars, but to a spot where in one of the sides below, about half way between the gap and the bars, there is a little hole in the wood. Sultan proceeds very carefully, brings the objective in front of the small hole with the stick, then drops the tool, goes round to the place outside the hole, and makes a great effort to squeeze out the fruit with his fingers—but the hole is too small. He soon again approaches the gap, again seizes the stick, and now changes the position of the objective in a way which I could not clearly understand, but probably still counting on that hole, and in any case getting close to it. In doing this the goal comes across the middle of the floor of the cage, a little closer to the side of the bars. All of a sudden, Sultan drops the stick, runs round to the bars, puts his arm through them as far as he can, and actually reaches the objective. The impression upon the observer after this proceeding is *not* that Sultan has immediately before worked in the direction of the bars and now comes round to complete the success thereby rendered possible; it looks rather as if he once again had abandoned the use of the stick in order to try his luck from the bars, as he had done several times before. As the attempted solution with the hole in the wall after all contains the method required, although in a simpler form, and since a human being would probably consider the accidental success just described as a strong help to the animal, all depends now on what he does upon repeating the experiment.

"A new objective is put in the place where the first one was. Sultan seizes the stick and *pushes the food straight towards the bars* without taking any further notice of the hole in the side. On the way, one notices several times indications of the 'changes' into the (biologically evidently very strong) direction of O°, . . . inasmuch as the stick is placed, erroneously, *behind* the objective, for a moment the movement of pulling is made, and if the correction were not made immediately, the objective would return to Sultan. As a matter of fact, the total of the small backward pulls towards himself amounts only to a few centimetres, as the animal itself soon realizes what it is doing. Sultan makes the whole course unnecessarily long, as he does not take into account the length of his arm; with the greatest effort he pushes the objective right up to the bars, that is to say, a distance of about one metre, and finally gives the fruit a push with his stick (which is a little too short for the operation) so that it falls out on the ground between the bars. But in that same moment he is already running round the cage, and gets the objective. The very deviation from his behaviour during the previous chance success (when he reached far into the cage) proves that after this bit of help a genuine solution of the problem has arisen." [8]

6. Theoretical Analyses of Such Round-about Solutions

What, now, are the outstanding characteristics of such *Umweg* solutions. For our present interest, we shall emphasize three: (a) the fact of an initial period of trial-and-error struggling which proves unsuccessful—the fact that the problem is so set that no one of the initially ready trials and errors, i.e., the initially ready simple differentiations and predictions, succeeds in reaching the goal; (b) the fact, appearing frequently though perhaps not always, of a then-subsequent period of no response, filled sometimes at least with external evidences of "cogitation," e.g., surveying the situation with the eyes, scratching the head, etc. (cf. Sultan and the problem of using box to stand on); (c) the fact of the then sudden appearance of the correct response—a response which has not, as such, appeared before, but runs off, when it comes, with relative smoothness and success.

These three descriptive characters we would analyze, however, as involving but the two following significant principles: (1) a relatively sudden, and new, extension or extrapolation of the field-relations at the disposal of the animal's sign-gestalt-expectations; and (2) the bringing about of this extrapolation by virtue of a process to be described as creative or inventive ideation. Let us consider each of these further.

7. New Extrapolations of the Field

In the case of the discrimination-box discussed in the preceding chapter, the moment of consciousness, or of ideation, corresponded

[8] *Op. cit.*, 263-266.

to no more than a sudden reinforcement of the differentiation and prediction features already involved in the trials and errors which had already gone off. In the present sort of situation, the important feature is, rather, that the final successful act is not among the preceding trials and errors. It appears for the first time, after the changes upon those preceding trials and errors have been rung over and over again. It comes then, suddenly, and with more or less of a break; it is an *Umweg*.

And it is an *Umweg*, we would now declare, primarily because it *is* new and *is* a break. The significance of an *Umweg* act lies, that is, so it seems to us, not in its mere physical (geometric or gravitational) indirectness, which may actually be relatively slight, but rather in its outsideness with respect to the previously ready trials and errors. It is because it involves a differentiative and predictive extrapolation, that it is an *Umweg*. An *Umweg* solution is not just a mere reinforcement or enhancement of differentiations and predictions already operative. It brings into play, rather, new strands of the means-end-field, strands which were not, as such, involved in the preceding sign-gestalt-expectations.

8. Creative Ideation

The second point was that such extensions or extrapolations of the field occur as the result of a special type of process, which we are calling creative or inventive ideation. Our assumption is that the apes "ideate" either during the actual trials and errors or during the "blank" or "rest" intervals which occur in the interstices between, or after, such trials; and that this ideation can be divided into: (a) a moment of simple ideation (running-back-and-forth in "adjustment" form) over the differentiations and predictions already at the animal's command and involved in the trials and errors which he has already been taking; and (b) a moment of the appearance of really new ideations—i.e., a moment in which the animal suddenly begins to run back and forth in adjustment form over paths and strands (differentiations and predictions) in the field to which, in the given situation, he has previously been insensitive.

But let us make these two sub-moments clearer, in terms of a concrete example. Let us take the last example quoted—that of the box with two open sides and the food to be poked from the one side to the other.[9]

9. Creative Ideation re the Two-sided Box

Our first assumption is: (a) that Sultan while struggling to get food by means of the stick from the left, was continually ideating (behavior-adjusting to running-back-and-forth-over) the portions of the means-end-field involved in such actions. That is, he was enhancing his differentiations and predictions relative to such facts as: 'the initial position of the banana and its nearer position to be achieved by the stick,' or 'the over-thereness and directly-to-be-reachedness of the banana,'—in the case when he is trying to get at it from the right-hand side. He was "enhancing" and "keeping alive" these sign-gestalt-expectations.

Our second assumption is: (b) that after, or during, these trials and errors, and their accompanying ideations, there occurred suddenly the new ideation or the ideational extrapolation of the field, which was necessary for the solution. We are assuming, that is, that some immediately presented feature of the situation suddenly took on, by virtue of the ape's capacity for field principles such as those of roundaboutness, hierarchicalness, closure, multiple track-ness, etc., at least in this specific type of spatial and gravita-tional set-up, a new sign character (i.e., new differentiative and predictive features) which it did not have before, and that he thereupon extrapolated the necessary new sign-gestalt. But, let us seek to imagine in more detail the specific ways in which this latter might occur.

Consider first the moments when Sultan is at the left of the box. He then sees the fruit as something to be raked in. His initial sign-gestalt-expectation is thus one in which the sign is the stick-in-hand-plus-the-food-at-a-distance, the two together to be had commerce-with in rake-like fashion, and the postulated significate is the resultant fruit-within-reach. But when he responds on the basis of *this* sign-gestalt-expectation, he fails. This initial sign-gestalt-expectation is inadequate and must give way to a better one, if learning is to be achieved. Learning requires the appear-

---

[9] It may be emphasized that this is a very representative sort of problem as in essentials it is practically the same as the tube and pole experiment which Yerkes and others have frequently experimented with. Cf. R. M. and A. W. Yerkes, *The Great Apes* (New Haven, Yale Univ. Press, 1929), p. 508 f.

ance, therefore, of a new, somewhat different, sign-gestalt-expectation. And in this specific instance, we shall assume that this required new sign-gestalt will be one in which the sign, instead of being food-and-stick-used-as-rake, will be one of food-and-stick-used-as-pusher. Further, the expected resultant significate, instead of being food-in-hand-at-the-left, will be food-near-the-hole-or-bars-at-the-right. The old expectation must give way to this new one. Its doing so constitutes the inventiveness of the learning.

But, finally, what is involved in such an occurrence? Our answer is that the invention is brought about in so far as the ape suddenly, by virtue of his capacity for such other field relationships as those of similarity, multiple trackness, roundaboutness, closure, etc., plus the more specific dimensional capacities as regards the spatial and gravitational discriminanda and manipulanda involved, thinks of a related, but different, sort of sign commerce-with from that involved in his initially ready sign-gestalt-expectation. In this specific instance, he must, that is, change from being ready to pull with the stick to being ready to push with the stick. When he does so, the new sign-gestalt-expectation "clicks." In the present case, we shall assume that he breaks out, perhaps by a mere excess of energy, into a new means-end activity, pushing rather than pulling—similar to the initial one. Thereupon the old expectation transmogrifies itself into the needed new one. The new significate of food-near-the-hole-on-the-side appears. The invention or solution comes by "playing" about with similar activities to that involved in the initial sign-gestalt. A new, but similar, means-end-expectation occurs and this happily brings with it the expectation of the wanted new significate.

Finally, perhaps the most interesting point of all is that there thus enters into the ape's behavior-possibilities a new type of "effective" formal means-end-capacity, or at any rate dimensional capacity. In other words, if the learning be truly inventive, then, by definition, pushing objects away to reachable distant points is a new means-end, spatio-mechanical, principle which the ape did not have before among his "immediately ready" trials and errors. This was a "field" principle which before had been merely "potential" in him. It now, however, has become "effective." Or, in terms of our preceding analyses, there has appeared in him a new type of means-end-readiness, which he will thereafter carry away with him, and which will be relatively ready to function in all other similar situations.

10. Inventive Learning—An Acquisition of New Means-End-Readinesses

Finally, it is to be noted that obviously this distinction between merely *potential* and actually *effective* means-end-readinesses becomes fundamental for a description of all the experiments on round-about solutions.

The true essence of the roundabout solution—the real reason, as we see it, why it is properly described as round-about—is that the final act does not lie among the initially ready trials and errors. The solution does not lie within the means-end-readinesses which the animal brought with him to the problem. He has to go *roundabout,* i.e., outside the range, of his initially ready devices. But the final solution, when it appears, must obviously always have been *potentially possible* to him.

In other words, Köhler's experiments (in so far as they really did present instances of types of solution which the animal could not do at first, but then learned to do) were demonstrations both of the limits of the chimpanzee's initial means-end-readinesses and of the wider limits of his final readinesses. They indicated both the sorts of things—using sticks, piling boxes, swinging for food, etc., —which the ape was not ready for at first, and the fact that he was, however, all the time capable of finally becoming ready for these things.

11. New Discriminanda and New Manipulanda

Further, it should now be noted that such inventive ideation may perhaps, on occasion, result from new discriminations and new manipulations rather than from altogether new principles of means-end-readiness. Some of Köhler's new ape solutions may have been due to the popping in of new discriminanda and manipulanda possibilities rather than of new "formal" principles. This would mean that the solution might involve the very same sign-objects and significate-objects as before, only better discrimination and manipulation expectations with respect to them.

12.   Creative-Ability

Also, it must be pointed out that this readiness to *break-out* into new concrete sign-gestalts, spontaneously, seems to be a matter in which individuals with equal potential means-end-readinesses, i.e., with equal final capacities, may differ. Two organisms with one and the same initially effective means-end-readinesses and one and the same final ultimate means-end-capacities may yet differ in the ease with which, when put in such a situation, they achieve the needed new readinesses and expectations. Take two organisms who are, by hypothesis, alike as far as their ultimate abilities for understanding go, and yet one of them will hit upon the new expectations and correlated readinesses much sooner than the other. For the one has more "creative-ability" than the other. He is not so bound down by his initial sign-gestalts. His perceptions, mnemonizations and inferences are more labile, more unstable.

13.   Creative Ideation Works Through Actual or Hypothetical Particulars

Lastly, to return to our analysis of the actual detailed way in which Sultan hit upon the solution—"thinking of pushing rather than pulling"—we would like to suggest, very tentatively, as a concluding word that perhaps this represents the archetype for all creative thinking. Perhaps in all cases of true problem-solving, the growth in means-end-readinesses (i.e., judgments) is an outgrowth of "fooling around with" either actual or hypothetical *particulars*. The thinker would, according to this doctrine, perceive, or mnemonize himself into, the presence of a particular and be led to "infer" new responses which he might make to this particular. Perhaps, in short, there is fundamentally no such thing as "abstract" thought. There are abstractions behind one's thought, and these abstractions grow, but one's thought itself is perhaps always a running-over of presented or imagined particulars or groups of particulars.

Finally, it may be suggested, as a last word, that perhaps all of the experiments cited in Chapter XI (such as the Hsiao, Tolman and Honzik, and Maier experiments) as demonstrating the fact of "inferential" sign-gestalt-expectations were illustrative also of *inventive ideations*. They were cases in which new field-relationships (the badness of route 2, the closure of a total path, etc.) appeared suddenly and before they had actually been tried out. It may be, in short, that all "inferential" sign-gestalt-expectations are always evidence of some degree of consciousness and inventive ideation.[10]

[10] For two very suggestive experiments with respect to the processes of inventive ideation in human subjects and for bibliographies, see E. B. Sullivan, Attitude in relation to learning, *Psychol. Monog.*, 1927, **36**, No. 169, and K. Duncker, A qualitative (experimental and theoretical) study of productive thinking (solving of comprehensible problems), *J. Genet. Psychol.*, 1926, **33**, 642-708.

REFERENCES

Duncker, K., A qualitative (experimental and theoretical) study of productive thinking (solving of comprehensible problems). *J. Genet. Psychol.*, 1926, **33**, 642-708.

Hobhouse, L. T., *Mind in Evolution* (New York, The Macmillan Company, 1901; 2d ed., 1915).

Hunter, W. S., Experimental Studies of Learning. *The Foundations of Experimental Psychology* (Worcester, Mass., Clark Univ. Press, 1929), 564-627.

Koffka, K., *The Growth of the Mind* (New York, Harcourt, Brace and Company, 2d ed. rev., 1928).

Köhler, W., *The Mentality of Apes* (New York, Harcourt, Brace and Company, 1925).

Sullivan, E. B., Attitude in relation to learning. *Psychol. Monog.*, 1927, **36**, No. 169.

Yerkes, R. M. and Yerkes, A. W., *The Great Apes* (New Haven, Yale Univ. Press, 1929).

PART IV
THE PSYCHOLOGIST IN THE LABORATORY

We have been objective and we have refused to introspect. We have assumed that other men likewise were "dumb" and so could not tell us of their conscious experiences. We have sought to build up our psychology as if all the textbooks written up to 1914 (the date of Watson's *Behavior—an Introduction to Comparative Psychology*) had never existed.

But, after all, we cannot really escape the old questions of *sensation* and *image,* of *feeling* and *emotion.* The good old psychologists in their laboratories, who introspected and filled innumerable pages of their *Protokolls* with accounts of these processes, were doing something and doing it ably. What, now, in *our* terms, was this that they were doing?

Chapter XV

SPEECH AND INTROSPECTION

1. Man's Possession of Speech and Introspection

A S yet we have considered only such behaviors and be-
haviors-determinants as seem common to the whole range
of animals. Means-end-capacities, conscious awareness,
ideation, and even inventive ideation are probably found, in some
degree, throughout the whole range of the animal kingdom. But,
now, we must turn to some behavior processes which are apparently the sole prerogative of human beings; viz., "speech" and "introspection."

Speech is a type of response-mechanism which, while approximated by the animal cry, is, in any really developed and characteristic sense, the sole prerogative of the human being. For speech
it is (as has been emphasized by the anthropologists) which, more
than anything else, seems to make of man the unique culture-form-
ing animal that he is. It is speech which first and foremost distinguishes man from the great apes.[1]

Furthermore, it is to be noted that it seems to have been this
possession of speech, by man, which misled the earlier psychologists into the erroneous assumption that "introspection" accomplishes something *sui generis*. It seems to have been the fatal
facility of their "subjects" for talking which seduced the mentalistic psychologists into supposing that in causing "verbalization"
in these subjects they were somehow causing the latter to convey
something about their "insides"—which was not, and could not
be, conveyed by other more gross forms of behavior. Even Watson, the behaviorist *par excellence,* while not making speech the
basis for a mentalism, *in his early writings* did accord to it the

[1] Cf. A. L. Kroeber, Sub-human culture beginnings, *Quart. Rev. Biol.,* 1928,
3, 325-342. Cf. also R. M. Yerkes and B. W. Learned, *Chimpanzee Intelligence and Its Vocal Expressions* (Baltimore, Md., The Williams & Wilkins Company, 1925).

rôle of being the sole mechanism for "thought." The lower animals, he said, do not "think" because they do not speak. And man himself, when he thinks, does so, according to Watson, only by virtue of sub-vocalizing or sub-gesturing.[2]

According to us, on the other hand, speech (though obviously a remarkable phenomenon and as a matter of empirical fact primarily restricted to man) is not in its essence to be considered as anything so very extraordinary, or unique. Speech accomplishes the same sort of result that other behaviors would, only more expeditiously. Speech, in the last analysis, is but a "high-faluting" "tool," not differing in essence from other tools such as "strings," "sticks," "boxes," and the like.

2. The Animal Cry

But to make this doctrine clearer, let us turn first to the forerunners of speech to be found in the lower animals. De Laguna, in her extremely important book,[3] derives speech from the "animal cry"—from, that is, such cries as the "nest-calls" of pigeons, the "warning calls" of a mother hen, and the like. She quotes the following account from Craig.[4]

"When one of the birds has finally hit upon a spot which pleases him, he sits down and utters the characteristic 'nest call.' His mate then joins him and 'both sit together in the chosen spot and call and caress one another for a long period. Then one bird, usually the female, remains in the nest to build and fashion it, while the other bird flies off in search of building material. Each time the male returns with a straw, the female welcomes him with a low, complacent cooing, and an affectionate flutter of the wings; which must serve to confirm still further the union of the birds and the choice of a nesting site.' "[5]

[2] J. B. Watson, *Behavior, an Introduction to Comparative Psychology* (New York, Henry Holt and Company, 1914), No bodily actions (e.g., a shrug, wink, etc.) have anything to do with thought, Watson contends, "until by a process of substitution . . . they come to function as do words," p. 333.

It should be emphasized, however, that later he includes all sorts of other minimal activities as a basis for thought. Cf. J. B. Watson, The place of kinæsthetic visceral and laryngeal organization in thinking, *Psychol. Rev.*, 1924, **31,** 339-348.

[3] Grace A. de Laguna, *Speech, its Function and Development* (New Haven, Yale Univ. Press, 1927), esp. Ch. 13.

[4] Wallace Craig, The voices of pigeons regarded as a means of social control, *Amer. J. Sociol.*, 1908, **18,** 86-100.

[5] De Laguna, *op. cit.*, p. 26.

Or, again, she offers the following account, of her own, of the alarm given by a mother hen when a large bird flies overhead:

"The mother hen that catches sight of a hawk circling over her brood and clucks to them in alarm, *expects* them to come, as evidenced by her uneasy regard of them, the fluffing-out of her feathers to cover them, and her insistent sounding of the call until the last fluttering chick is safe beneath her wings. In short, the animal cry comes—in varying degrees, according to the species— to be given not merely as a simple direct response to the stimulus which excites it, but as an act directed towards the eliciting of a desired response on the part of others. Otherwise, indeed, it could not be *learned*, but would necessarily remain on the level of a purely automatic reaction." [6]

It appears, in short, that the animal cry, like all other behavior, is of the nature of a commerce with a given means-object, or situation, in order to achieve a certain further goal-object, or situation, e.g. the eliciting of a desired response in others of the social group.

3.   Proclamation and Command

Further, de Laguna has pointed out that the animal cry contains within itself the beginning of a differentiation into the subvarieties: *proclamation and command*. She writes:

"The cry, as we have shown, has a certain double character. It is, particularly when called out by external conditions, at once a specific response to a situation [proclamation] and an act directed toward another member of the group [command]. The development of the cry into the complementary proclamation and command depends upon a differentiation of these two characters of the primitive cry. The proclamation is primarily a specific response to a situation, and only secondarily an act directed toward the hearer with the end of influencing his behavior. Or, rather, perhaps, the proclamation is *directly* a response to the situation, and *indirectly* a means of acting on others. The command, on the contrary, is primarily an act directed toward another in order to influence his behavior. Since the command is actually given in view of, and with reference to, the existing situation, it is secondarily and indirectly a response to the situation. Thus, while the proclamation and the command show a differentiation of function, each still retains the double character implicit in the cry." [7]

[6] De Laguna, *op. cit.*, p. 252.
[7] De Laguna, *op. cit.*, p. 262.

4.   Speech as Spoken—Tool Behavior

Next, it is to be emphasized that, both as command and as proclamation, speech, or its forerunner, the animal cry, is a tool-behavior. This is quite obvious for the case of the command. What happens in a command (in so far as it is successful) is that by means of it the speaker causes one of his fellows to do something. Instead of the former having to take the latter by the scruff of the neck and actually push him through the desired act, the speaker, by means of a command, accomplishes the same result, but more easily and with less bodily effort. The command is thus a tool, one end of which the speaking-organism manipulates in such a way that the other end reaches over and pushes the listening-organism. The success of this speech-tool depends, of course, upon the degree of the speaker's means-end-capacities and his discriminanda- and manipulanda-capacities relative to the logical, rhetorical, and social means-end-dimensions involved. A command brings about, or seeks to bring about, a desired rearrangement of the listening organism and some feature or features of the environment—a rearrangement which might also have been brought about by some more lengthy (and more exhausting) non-verbal behavior.

And even for the proclamation, the situation is similar. The only difference is that, whereas for the command, the function of the speech is primarily to induce some specific "practical" behavior in the listener, for the proclamation, the function of the speech is to induce, rather, a certain conscious awareness or ideation in the listener, i.e., a certain specific "non-practical" running-back-and-forth behavior, or behavior-adjustment. (See preceding chapters.)

5.   Speech as Heard—A Set of Signs

Conversely, now, what, it must be asked, is speech to the listener? It is a set of *signs*. Speech, when heard, is a set of immediately presented objects which the hearer thereupon takes as signs for some further environmental situation. The listener, upon hearing a *proclamation*, suffers a release of a specific sign-gestalt-expectation, in which the heard words are the sign-objects and the environmental situation, which is proclaimed, is the significate or signified-object, and the environmental location of the latter, relative to the speaker and his words, the signified means-end-relation. And, similarly, the listener, upon hearing a command, suffers a specific sign-gestalt-expectation in which again the words are the sign-object and the act to be performed is the signified means-end-relation; while the satisfaction of the speaker is the signified goal-object.

To sum up, whereas to the speaker, speech is like an extension of arms and hands and pointing apparatus; to the listener it is like an extension of eyes and ears or other sensory apparatus.

6. Speech as It Functions in Consciousness and in Thought

Much has been made, in late years, of the function which speech plays in thought. Thus, as already noted, Watson at one time made sub-vocal speech the very essence of thinking. Animals, who cannot speak (or gesture), cannot, according to him, think (i.e., have ideas). But this, we contend, is erroneous. Animals, such as the chimpanzee, do most obviously think; they obviously do solve new and quite complicated problems. They do do creative thinking. But they have no speech. The conclusion must be, therefore, that ideation or creative thinking originates ontogenetically and phylogenetically, prior to speech. Ideas (see two preceding chapters) are behavior-adjustments to running-back-and-forth over the differential and predictive paths of a means-end-field. Our notion is, therefore, that an organism cannot speak successfully, i.e., induce the appropriate sign-gestalt-expectations in the listening organism unless he can first hold-up and ideate with respect to his own sign-gestalt-expectations. Speech, as the successful manipulation of a tool, requires, that is, that the capacity for ideation precede it.

The above conclusion does not, however, deny that speech, once acquired, may become, in the *form of talking to one's self,* a great *aid* to thought. Indeed, there seem to be two ways in which speech may thus aid thought.

First, there may be the type of case in which a required ideation has already been achieved in a tentative way and then results in internal speech. Here the resulting internal speech may consist in the naming to oneself of the more distant, or more abstruse, phases of the field-relations. And such a naming will, we may assume, aid in "holding" the difficult thought. It will aid in keeping these distant and abstruse features of the field "before" the organism, so that he can run over them in behavior-adjustment form still further and with more precision.

Second, there may be the type of case where speech, once acquired (and become automatic), can, on occasion, then, lead the organism (in quite automatic fashion) to present new sign stimuli to himself. He talks to himself automatically, and the words which he says act as signs to induce new sign-gestalt-expectations, not present in him before. He speaks to himself automatically as a result of purely rhetorical habits and then is led to adjust, as he would have if some one else had spoken to him. The impetus of his own merely automatic rhetoric carries him over the gaps in his thought.

Normally, behavior-adjustments to running back and forth over features of a sign-gestalt (i.e., understanding) come first and speech follows. Occasionally, however, it may be that speech comes first, and in a purely mechanical fashion, leads to understanding.

Finally, in thus holding that, normally, ideation precedes speech, we are, it is to be noted, taking issue not only with Watson's earlier view but also with Mead.[8] To Mead, even consciousness, let alone higher ideation, depends upon the ability of the animal to take part in a social interchange. An animal cannot be conscious, i.e., cannot think, unless he can view his own act from the point of view of an "organized other" from the various standpoints of the social group as a whole. An animal has to see his own act, as it would appear to others of his social group, in order to haul it up into any independence, in order to make it conscious. And an animal cannot take this attitude of the "organized other" towards his own behavior, save through speech—i.e., through being able to name and describe his act as others would name and describe it. But this doctrine of Mead seems to us a perversion of the true order. According to us, speech (*vide* the animal cry) is an outgrowth of an already achieved social attitude and not *vice versa.*[9]

[8] George H. Mead, A behavioristic account of the significant symbol, *J. Philos.*, 1922, 19, 157-163.

[9] Hunter like Watson and Weiss also makes speech, or more generally what he calls the "symbolic response," the basis of thought and also of mere con-

So much for speech *qua* speech; we may turn, now, to the second half of the problem; viz., the nature and significance of that particular type of speech known as introspection.

7. Introspection

What is the nature and function of introspection? The first point, we would make, is that in introspection the "environmental" objects, about which the introspector is talking, and which his proclamations purport to bring to the listener's attention, are the introspector's own *behavior-adjustments*. Introspection, in so far, therefore, as it claims to be a valid procedure, asserts the possibility of such responses to one's own behavior-adjustments. Introspection requires, if any credence is to be given to it, that an individual can release tool-behavior in which the utterance of the words is the means-commerce and the presence-to-the-listener of the introspector's own behavior-adjustments is the goal-object. In order to be able to introspect, an "observer" must be capable of sign-gestalts in which his own behavior-adjustments, and the words for describing such, are the *sign-objects* (*i.e.*, means-objects) and a presence-of-these-behavior-adjustments-to-the-listener is the desired *signified-object* (i.e., goal-object).

Introspection, if it be a veridical process at all, implies, in short, some sort of an "inner sense." It implies that the introspector can "perceive" not only his actual runnings-back-and-forth, but also his mere behavior-adjustments to such runnings-back-and-forth. It requires that he can report that he is thus adjustmentally running-back-and-forth.

8. *Beschreibung* vs. *Kundgabe*

We note, now, a further feature about introspection. We note, that is, a certain recondite distinction drawn by the high priests between introspection in its "pure" form, and introspection as they

sciousness. See W. S. Hunter, The problem of consciousness, *Psychol. Rev.*, 1924, **31**, 1-31.

———, The symbolic process, *Psychol. Rev.*, 1924, **31**, 478-497.

———, The subject's report, *Psychol. Rev.*, 1925, **32**, 153-170.

———, General anthroponomy and its systematic problems, *Amer. J. Psychol.*, 1925, **32**, 153-170.

———, *Human Behavior* (Chicago, Chicago Univ. Press, rev. ed. 1928), p. 334 f.

say it tends to be misused by the man in the street and even by the unwary in the laboratory. The two terms *Beschreibung* and *Kundgabe* have been suggested to distinguish between these two varieties.[10]

Beschreibung, or "pure" introspection, is said to consist in an immediate *description* of "conscious contents" per se. In pure introspection one is not to state the meanings of one's ideas, but merely to describe their immediate texture or stuff. The Wundtian school and its descendants (i.e., especially the American structuralists headed by Titchener) assumed, that is, that mental processes have a stuff-aspect which was independent of their functional characters as meanings and that this stuff-character could, as such, be described.

Kundgabe, or the ordinary everyday sort of introspection, on the other hand, was said to be simply the naïve report by an inadequately trained individual, psychologist or layman, of what he was thinking about. And such mere *Kundgabe* was, according to the Wundtian and Titchenerian high priests, the forbidden sin. Its ever present ubiquity was indeed such that James called it the *"psychologist's fallacy."*[11] And in the case of psychophysical experiments (i.e., experiments on the discrimination of lifted weights, and the like) it was so frequent that Titchener coined for it the special term *stimulus error*.[12]

Now what, it must be asked, in our terms do these two types of introspection respectively amount to? We may consider *Kundgabe* first; it is the less recondite.

9. *Kundgabe,* Interpreted by Us

Introspection, in the sense of *Kundgabe*, would, according to us, be simply a proclamation by the introspector as to his own signgestalts. In *Kundgabe* the introspector would be proclaiming the features and relations in his means-end-field which were exciting

[10] These terms were first proposed by E. von Aster, Die psychologische Beobachtung und experimentelle Untersuchung von Denkvorgängen, *Zsch. f. Psychol.*, 1908, **49**, 56-160.

[11] W. James, *The Principles of Psychology* (New York, Henry Holt and Company, 1890), I., p. 196.

[12] E. B. Titchener, *Experimental Psychology of the Thought-Processes* (New York, The Macmillan Company, 1909), p. 149. See also E. G. Boring, *A History of Experimental Psychology* (New York, The Century Co., 1929), p. 410.

him at the moment, plus the further fact that he was behavior-adjusting to such features. By means of a commerce with words, he would be attempting to bring these features and relations of his own means-end-field plus the fact that he was behavior-adjusting to them into the means-end-field of his listener. It is a remarkable enough process in all conscience; and it implies that an individual can respond to the fact of his own behavior-adjusting and to another individual as part of one total environmento-social complex. But, essentially, it indicates to his listener nothing that could not be indicated by more gross behavior. That is, instead of thus introspecting, telling what he was thinking about, and that he was thinking about it, an introspector could (theoretically at any rate) let his thoughts out into actual behavior. He could grab his listener by the scruff of the neck and make the latter watch him behave thus and thus.

Consider, again, for example, our friend, the rat and the discrimination box. If the rat could introspect, he might either do so, in *Kundgabe* fashion, or instead he might grab his listener by the neck, haul this listener over to the discrimination box, and then cause the latter to watch him "run back and forth," between the white and the black, or between either alley and its further consequences—thus indicating to the listener that he was being conscious of such and such differentiative and predictive relationships, *re* the discrimination box. To be able to do this, the rat would, of course, require a sensitivity to social relationships, which actually he is incapable of. But the doing of it, if he could, would not convey to his listener anything unique and *sui generis* about his, the rat's, supposed conscious contents *qua* contents.

Turn now to *Beschreibung*.

10. *Beschreibung,* Interpreted by Us

The dyed-in-the-wool mentalist might, conceivably, admit all that we have just said about *Kundgabe*, but insist that in *Beschreibung*, i.e., in "true" introspection, there is none the less conveyed to the listener something *unique* and *sui generis* something not conveyable by, any gross behavior. Our answer will be that *Beschreibung* in this "pure" sense is an abortion. The notion of it is a snare and a delusion. It is something which actually never did or can happen. There is no "stuff" to a·"running-back-and-forth," or to a "behavior-adjustment" to a running-back-and-forth, to be reported.

What actually happens in those situations in which the Wundtian or the Titchenerian would claim that a "subject" is properly *"Beschreibung-*ing" (if we may be permitted this neologism) is that actually he is merely giving information (*"Kundgabe-*ing") with respect to certain rather recondite and artifact sign-objects. He is reporting runnings-back-and-forth with respect to very temporary and personal sign-objects—ones which, normally, are not responded to or perhaps even present as separate items at all. He is responding to momentary, personal objects, located in "funny places,"—"two feet in front of his eyes," "behind his head," "in the pit of his stomach," and which perhaps jump up and down and have holes in them. He is running-back-and-forth with respect, that is, to "sensations,"[13] "images" and "affections," which actually never function as independent objects, save under the peculiar and artificial situations of the introspective laboratory.

He is divorcing these very momentary and personal signs, and, for the most part, the mere discriminanda aspects of these signs, from the larger manipulanda and means-end-relations, i.e., the larger and more enduring sign-gestalt-expectations, in which normally, save when a person has been thus especially "trained" to "introspect," these personal signs alone function.[14]

In short, the dicta of "introspection" present to the listener nothing which, theoretically at least, cannot be conveyed by other more gross forms of behavior.

But let us consider this further and in more detail for the three orthodox findings of the introspectionists:—"sensations," "images" and "feelings." To the first two we turn in the next chapter.

[13] I.e., "sensations" in the artificial technical sense.

[14] A somewhat similar and very trenchant criticism of an introspectionism, which believes in *Beschreibung* only, is to be found in Köhler, Cf. W. Köhler, *Gestalt Psychology* (New York, Horace Liveright, 1929), Chapter III.

REFERENCES

Aster, E. von, Die psychologische Beobachtung und experimentelle Untersuchung von Denkvorgängen. *Zsch. f. Psychol.*, 1908, **49**, 56-160.
Boring, E. G., *A History of Experimental Psychology* (New York, The Century Co., 1929).

Craig, W., The voices of pigeons regarded as a means of social control. *Amer. J. Sociol.*, 1908, **18**, 86-100.

Hunter, W. S., The problem of consciousness. *Psychol. Rev.*, 1924, **31**, 1-31.

——————, The symbolic process. *Psychol. Rev.*, 1924, **31**, 478-497.

——————, The subject's report. *Psychol. Rev.*, 1925, **32**, 153-170.

——————, General anthroponomy and its systematic problems. *Amer. J. Psychol.*, 1925, **36**, 286-302.

——————, Human Behavior (Chicago, Chicago Univ. Press, rev. ed., 1928).

James, W., *The Principles of Psychology* (New York, Henry Holt and Company, 1890), V. I.

Köhler, W., *Gestalt Psychology* (New York, Horace Liveright, 1929).

Kroeber, A. L., Sub-human culture beginnings. *Quart. Rev. Biol.*, 1928, **3**, 325-342.

Laguna, Grace A. de, *Speech, its Function and Development* (New Haven, Yale Univ. Press, 1927).

Mead, G. H., A behavioristic account of the significant symbol. *J. Philos.*, 1922, **19**, 157-163.

Titchener, E. B., *Experimental Psychology of the Thought-Processes* (New York, The Macmillan Company, 1909).

Watson, J. B., *Behavior, an Introduction to Comparative Psychology* (New York, Henry Holt and Company, 1914).

——————, The place of kinæsthetic, visceral and laryngeal organization in thinking. *Psychol. Rev.*, 1924, **31**, 339-347.

Yerkes, R. M., and Learned, B. W., *Chimpanzee Intelligence and Its Vocal Expressions* (Baltimore, The Williams and Wilkins Company, 1925).

Chapter XVI

SENSATION AND IMAGES [1]

1. The Readiness to Discriminate

IMAGINE that we had a "subject" in the laboratory, in whose color "sensations" we were interested. In routine laboratory fashion, we should present him with a bit of color, say the red of a two-cent postage stamp; [2] and we should ask him to "introspect." He would tell us what this red looked like to him. He would describe the "sensation-quality" which he experienced when looking at it. He would "name" it as "red." But what would this describing and naming convey? It would provide merely the same sort of information that we should get if, instead of having him "introspect," we let him discriminate the postage-stamp color in some other, more gross way. We should learn no more than we should if, instead, we were to let him sort differently colored stamps into piles, putting the reds all into one pile; or if we were to let him match and locate this specific postage-stamp color on a chart of all colors, i.e., a chart showing all possible variations in hue, intensity and saturation, or on such a color discriminanda pyramid as was discussed in Chapter V. His introspective naming and "describing" could convey to us no information not conveyed by such gross discriminatory responses.

2. A Man from Mars

But turn to another example. Let us imagine that overworked myth—the Man from Mars. Let us suppose that the Martian descends among us and that we want to study his color sensations; and that, although he is like us in every other way, he is devoid

---

[1] Much of the argument of this chapter has already been presented in a separate article, cf. E. C. Tolman, Concerning the sensation quality—a behavioristic account, *Psychol. Rev.*, 1922, **29**, 140-145.

[2] Of course we would not really use anything as crude as a postage stamp.

of the devices of human language. Let us suppose, in short, that he cannot introspect. We have an urge, none the less, to discover all that there is to discover about his color sensations. Our only recourse, obviously, would be to use methods with him such as we would use with the lower animals. We would run him about in something like a Yerkes-Watson Discrimination-Box.[3]

With such a box [4] built to his dimensions, we should, in a series of experiments, try pairing off the red of the postage stamp as the cue for one alley, with various other colors, in successive experiments, as the cue for the other alley. In this way, we would cause him to indicate, by virtue of learning or not learning always to go toward it, which of these other colors he could and which he could not discriminate from the red. Furthermore, we should also seek to discover, not only which of these other colors he could discriminate from the red, but also to what extent he could discriminate these other colors among themselves.

3. Color Dimensions

Finally, we should take one last step. We should discover, by similar gross discriminatory behaviors, what may be called the ultimate dimensions of hue, saturation, lightness, (see above Ch. V) as these obtained for the Martian.

In order to see, however, how this might really be done, let us

---

[3] R. M. Yerkes and J. B. Watson. Methods of studying vision in animals, *Behav. Monog.*, 1911, I, No. 2.

[4] Actually, in the case of the Martian, we might find it more convenient and *far faster*, as did Köhler in his study of the apes (*vide* W. Köhler, Über eine neue methode zur psychologischen Untersuchung von Menschenaffen, *Psychol. Forsch.*, 1922, I, 390-397), to use a modification of the technique of the Discrimination-Box. Köhler hit upon the device of presenting the reward in one of two boxes placed in front of the ape's cage. These two boxes were mounted with the two stimuli (S_x and S_y) to be discriminated between and the reward was placed in the S_x box. Furthermore, instead of the animal's having to find out (as in the case with the use of the discrimination-box), as a result perhaps of a long series of blind tries, that the reward is always associated with the S_x stimulus, here the animal was allowed actually to "see" the reward being put into the box mounted with S_x. After he had seen the reward placed, a screen was put up and the positions of the two boxes changed about in some way. The screen was then removed and the animal allowed to choose, which he did in the particular case of the apes by pulling in the chosen box with a crooked stick. If the animal could discriminate the given pair of stimuli, S_x and S_y, he indicated it at once on the very first trial. This is the "direct method" in the delayed reaction experiment. See above, Ch. X, p. 154 f.

note, first, a certain feature about sensory discriminations as these tend to occur in the lower animals, viz., the propensity towards relative choices. It is now a well-established point that animals usually choose "relatively" rather than "absolutely." [5] Thus, suppose, for example, that an animal be trained upon two grays: A, a darker gray and B, a lighter, and that in this situation he be taught to choose the lighter, B. And then suppose that he be transferred to a second pair made up of this lighter gray, B, and a still lighter one, C. It will be found that with this new combination, B and C, the animal will select, under ordinary conditions, not B, which he has been trained to select in the combination A and B, but rather the still lighter gray C. In other words, what the animal acquires from the first pair, A and B, is not, in the great majority of cases, a response to the absolute value of B per se, but rather a response to the relative fact of the "lighter-than-ness" of B relative to A. And it is this "lighter-than-ness," "relative" response which carries over to the new situation B and C. In a word, the chicks and the apes, the children, and even the college students, who have been tested, respond unless they are specifically trained otherwise, to the "dimension" of "lighter-than-ness" rather than to the absolute lightness, per se.

But this gives us our cue for the final experiments to be tried with the Martian.[6] For, we wish to discover what the Martian's ultimate color "dimensions" are. And it now appears that to do this, we need merely train him on one pair of colors and see to what other pairs this training does or does not tend to carry over. We shall train him, for example, on such a pair as red and yellowish-red and teach him therein to choose the yellowish-red; and then we may present him with this yellow-red and another still more yellowish-red, and see if he will respond to the still more-yellow-red. And if he does, then our further task will be to discover if, when we have trained him on such a yellow-red *versus* the red and then present him with a green-yellow *versus* a yellow-

[5] For a complete summary of all the experimental literature on this fact of relative choice, see C. J. Warden and J. B. Rowley, The discrimination of absolute versus relative brightness in the ring dove, *J. Comp. Psychol.*, 1929, 9, 317-337. The first empirical demonstration of this fact of relative choice seems to have been made as early as 1902 by Kinnaman, using a monkey (see reference just cited.)

[6] We are indebted to Dr. O. L. Tinklepaugh for suggesting this application of the fact of "relative choice."

red, whether he will or will not carry over the training on the one pair to the other? Or, will he be completely at sea regarding the new pair, just as we should? Will, in short, green-yellow prove to lie in a different "dimension" from yellow-red for him, just as it would for us—so that training on differences in the latter dimension will not carry over and indicate what choices are to be made as regards differences in the former?

And we should proceed in similar fashion regarding the two dimensions of saturation and of brightness. By this same sort of technique of discovering where relative choices would break down, we could discover all there was to know about the Martian's color "dimensions." We could discover whether or not he made the same distinction that we do between "colors" on the one hand, and grays, on the other. We could discover whether lightness and darkness, what the artists call "value," are something that he could respond to, irrespective of "color." And we could discover whether the "hues" themselves range for him, as they do for us, along the four "dimensions" of red-yellow, yellow-green, green-blue, and blue-red. We should discover, that is, without any aid from language or introspection, all that there was to know about the Martian's color-pyramid (see above Ch. V).

But when we had discovered all this—when we had discovered in how far his color "dimensions" are like ours or, if they are not like ours, just wherein they are different—we should have learned all that there was to know about the Martian's original "sense-quality" resulting from the postage-stamp red. We should then know just as much about his color sense-qualities as we now know about those of any fellow man.

· But no, an orthodox introspectionist will protest. There are two ways in which such objective discrimination-box investigations with the Martian will fall short of what a "true introspection" would convey: (a) Such discrimination-box experiments with the Martian can give only the sort of information that *Kundgabe* introspection would give (see previous chapter). Such experiments cannot convey, as would true *Beschreibung*, the real "sensations" by means of which the Martian discriminates the one objective red from such and such other colors. And (b) such discrimination experiments can never convey, as would "true introspection," the "raw feel" of the sensations.

Let us consider each of these criticisms.

4. Discrimination-Box Experiments Correspond to *Kundgabe* but Not to *Beschreibung*

It must be admitted at once that from the usual sort of discrimination-box experiments we should not discover much about the Martian's temporary fleeting "sensations," those very immediate, shifting, moment to moment discriminanda-expectations, whereby as the introspectionist might put it, the Martian is supposed to know the enduring, permanent, "object" color of the postage stamp. For according to the "good introspectionist," a distinction must always be carefully drawn between the momentary, immediate "sensation" as an immediate "sensory" quality, and the independent "object" quality of the stimulus. For the introspecting individual to confuse the two, is to commit the "stimulus-error" (see Ch. XV, p. 242). And we, in assuming that an ordinary discrimination-box experiment could give us information about the former, and not merely about the latter, would likewise be said to be committing something at least very analogous to the stimulus-error.

But, as we shall contend now, this limitation of the discrimination-box technique is a practical rather than a theoretical one. If we could but get at and control the Martian's "moment-to-moment" stimuli, we could so fix it that he would have to compare one of these momentary, fleeting, "perspectively biassed" stimuli, placed on one side of the discrimination-box, with a "standard" stimulus paired with it on the other side. And, in this way, we would eventually get the definition, in discrimanda terms, of the "sensations" corresponding to such a momentary, fleeting, and "perspectively biassed" stimulus.

5. "Raw Feels" Do Not and Cannot Get Across

But, secondly, the dyed-in-the-wool mentalist will again protest. Such discrimination-box experiments may, he will say, "get" the momentary *sensation* defined as discriminanda-expectations "across" but it will not and cannot convey what may be called the "raw feel" of these discriminanda. Only introspection can do this latter.

Sensations, says the orthodox mentalist, are more than discriminanda-expectations, whether indicated by verbal introspection

or by discrimination-box experiments. They are in addition immediate mental givens, "raw feels." They are unique subjective suffusions in the mind. And it is these "raw feels," these suffusions,
which constitute the ultimate entities in which as psychologists we
are, or should be, interested.

Suppose for a moment, for the purposes of argument, that we
admit this, that we admit that the "raw feel" of either a momentary "sensation" or of a more enduring "sense-quality" is that
which psychology should study. But how then we must ask, is
this to be done? The mentalist says: "By introspection." The
"subject" is to be presented with the given stimuli under controlled conditions and asked to "introspect." And, when so asked,
what he tells us is that the given light is "red"—"that it is of
such and such a specific hue, chroma, and intensity," and the rest.

But what does this tell us? Obviously, the very same thing and
no more than do the discrimination-box experiments. Such introspection does not "get the raw feels across" any more than
do the runnings about in the discrimination-box.

I present a colored (or non-colored) light to an introspecting
"observer" and ask him to report his color experience. What does
he do? He "names" this experience. He says it is "red" of such
and such a hue, and saturation, and intensity. But suppose I am
stupid and push him to the limit of his communicatory powers.
What does he finally do to indicate to me what these words
mean? Why, he turns at last to a color chart and points out just
which colors on the chart are for him like his introspected "sensation," and which are not. And he elaborates this by indicating
further just where he sees "dimensional" changes in this chart and
where he does not. He works out a Titchener color-pyramid and
introspects for me in terms of that pyramid. And this is all that he
does. I learn from his "introspection" just what I learned from the
Martian's runnings-about. "Raw feels," if he has any, do not, and
cannot, "get across." Only discriminanda-expectations "get
across."

6. The Case of Color-Blindness

This fact that "raw feels" are quite private is perhaps made
particularly clear if we think of a color-blind individual. Suppose
our "observer" in the introspecting experiment is red-green color-
blind. We ask him to "introspect," or to run about in the dis-

combination-box, or, it may be, to sort Holmgren colored worsteds, or look at a set of Nagel cards, or do whatever else is now the most approved method of testing for color-blindness. It makes no difference which. All that we learn in any case is that certain "red" and "green" and "gray" stimuli will be treated by him as alike. We learn that he cannot respond to one differently from the other two and that sometimes he calls all three of them "red" and sometimes "green" and sometimes "gray." But we do not learn what this "red" or "green" or "gray" "feels" like to him. We never learn whether it "feels" like our "red" or our "green" or our "gray," or whether, indeed, its "feel" is perhaps *sui generis* and unlike any of our own.

But what thus holds as regards a color-blind individual holds *mutatis mutandis* as regards any individual. Whether your "raw feels" are or are not like mine, you and I shall never discover. Your color "feels" may be the exact complementaries of mine but, if so, neither of us will ever find it out, provided only that your discriminations and my discriminations agree.

7. This Doctrine Similar to Lewis's

Finally, it may be noted that this doctrine as to the ultimate privacy of the "raw feel," and hence the fact that the "raw feel" may be ignored in science, is very close to the doctrine of C. I. Lewis. He writes:

"No one can look directly into another's mind. The immediate feeling of red or rough can never be transferred from one mind to another. Suppose it should be a fact that I get the sensation you signalize by saying 'red' whenever I look at what you call 'violet,' and vice versa. Suppose that in the matter of the immediately apprehended qualia of sensation [what we are calling 'raw feels'] my whole spectrum should be exactly the reverse of yours. Suppose even that what are for you sensations of pitch, mediated by the ear, were identical with my feelings of color-quality, mediated by the eye. How should we ever find it out? We could never discover such peculiarities of mine so long as they did not impair my powers to discriminate and relate as others do." [7]

And again:

"You and I mean the same by 'red' if we both define it as the first band of the spectrum, and if we both pronounce the same

[7] C. I. Lewis, The pragmatic element in knowledge, *Univ. Calif. Publ. Philos.*, 1926, **6**, 205-227, p. 213.

presented objects to be red. It does not matter if neither the red rug nor the first band of the spectrum gives to the two of us identical sensations so long as we individually discover that same sense-quality in each thing which we agree in describing as 'red.' " [8]

8. Recapitulation as Regards Sensations

"Sensations," in so far as they have any cash value, are, for the purposes of science, merely readinesses to discriminate in ways relatively enduring, or relatively temporary and perspectively biassed. And no psychology, not even "introspectionism" itself, ever actually succeeded in "getting" anything else "across." If there be "raw feels" correlated with such discriminanda-expectations, these "raw feels" are by very definition "private" and not capable of scientific treatment. And we may leave the question as to whether they exist, and what to do about them, if they do exist, to other disciplines than psychology—e.g., to logic, epistemology, and metaphysics. And whatever the answers of these other disciplines, we, as mere psychologists, need not be concerned.[9]

Furthermore it may be noted in passing that orthodox sensationalism not only mistook discriminanda-expectations for "raw feels," but also left manipulanda-expectations and means-ends-expectations entirely out of account. And this was a bad oversight. For, as we discovered in the section on *The Rat in the Maze,* a rat, in perceiving a maze, must be said to perceive not only sense-qualities (discriminanda) but equally and much more importantly, manipulanda and means-ends-relations—supports for running, turning, rearing on hind legs, and for such and such directional and distance relations among these. But orthodox introspectionism tended to leave all such manipulanda and directional and distance characters out of account as mere "meanings," not to be studied as such by psychologists.[10]

So much for sensations. We turn now to images.

[8] C. I. Lewis, *Mind and the World Order* (New York, Charles Scribner's Sons, 1929), p. 76. Cf. also E. C. Tolman, Concerning the sensation quality—a behavioristic account, *Psychol. Rev.,* 1922, **29,** 140-145; and W. Köhler, *Gestalt Psychology* (New York, Horace Liveright, 1929), p. 14.

[9] See below Ch. XXV, p. 426 f.

[10] This stricture against "meanings" was of course more characteristic of the Wundtian and the Titchenerian structuralists than of other schools. But

9.   Images

If one closes his eyes and obtains in his "mind's eye" a more or less fleeting "visual picture" of this morning's breakfast table, or, if one abstracts himself from surrounding noises and hears again last night's symphony ringing phantom-like in his "mind's ear," these experiences are said to be "images." And they, with their sisters from the other sense modes, of touch, smell, kinesthesis have long figured as *von Grund aus* mental—*i.e.*, floating moments in a stream of "mental stuff." They have been supposed to be essentially private, to have no peripheral source of stimulation, to be *sui generis*, and to be knowable by means of "introspection" only.

10.   Behavior Implications of Images

But it is obvious now, on the analogy of our previous argument *re* sensation, that if images are to have any being in scientific discourse—in a discourse, that is, which involves more than one lone scientist—it must be that they also do, in some way, affect behavior. For, if they did not, nobody but the individual lone scientists could ever know anything about them. They would have remained private to each individual and never have got into psychology.

It appears then that images have got into behavior. It would seem, however, that the only behavior into which they have got with any certainty is introspective (speech) behavior.[11] But in the preceding chapter, we saw that introspection, whatever else it is, is essentially and fundamentally behavior. It is equivalent to a proclamatory pointing to, and classifying of. When I "intro-

even the *Denkpsychologen* of the Würzburg school, who set out to get "meanings" back into consciousness, tended to reduce them, in the end, to but dead contents. See E. G. Boring, *A History of Experimental Psychology* (New York, The Century Co., 1929), p. 400 f.

[11] This is perhaps an over-pessimistic statement. For it may yet some day be discovered that the presence or absence of specific types of images does make some difference for practical action. It may be, in short, that some day the dream of the early "individual" psychologists, that the so-called *imagery types* would prove of importance in determining relative types of success, may yet prove true. A recent step in this direction has been taken by F. C. Davis, Determination of predominant imagery habits in persons of highly specialized training. M. A. Thesis, Univ. Calif., 1922, and Imagery

spect" upon my "image" of this morning's breakfast table, what I do is to indicate the presence of unique momentary discriminanda-expectations and to indicate how they are like and unlike those produced by external stimuli. I declare that my image has such and such "size," such and such "shape," such and such "color" and such and such "spatial distance" in front of my eyes, or perhaps back of my head. That is, I declare it to be like and unlike such and such external stimuli. I make discriminatory responses, which place it with respect to the discriminanda arising from standardized external stimuli. I, figuratively speaking, run about in a discrimination-box for my listener's benefit. I pair the "internal" stimulus, about whose resultant discriminanda-expectations I am introspecting, on the one side of this discrimination-box, with carefully chosen external stimuli, on the other. And I indicate to you from which of these other external stimuli I could discriminate the internal one and from which I could not discriminate it. I reduce my image to a mere discriminanda-expectation no different in essence from those other discriminanda-expectations which I obtain from enduring object-qualities or from momentary "sensations."

11. Images vs. Sensations

But if images, like sensations, are for the purpose of science, nothing but discriminanda-expectations, *only that their stimuli happen to be internal,* it may be asked wherein consist the supposed unique differences between images and sensations. Two points by way of answer suggest themselves.

First, it would appear that we tend to call an individual's momentary, "perspectively biassed," expectations of discriminanda, images when the stimuli which arouse them are obviously not peripherally present then and there. This distinction, however, often breaks down (*vide* hallucinations).

Secondly, it seems to have been supposed that we designate discriminanda-expectations as images when, in addition to their

differences and their functional significance. Ph.D. Thesis, Univ. Calif., 1931. See also:

J. A. Gengerelli, Some quantitative experiments with eidetic imagery. *Amer. J. Psychol.*, 1930, **42**, 399-404.

C. H. Griffitts, Individual differences in imagery, *Psychol. Mon.*, 1927, **37**, No. 172.

other properties, they possess a certain distinctive "texture." This distinction also, however, seems to be of doubtful universality. Perky [12] instructed subjects to project upon a screen an imagined visual image of some common colored object, such as a red tomato, a blue book, a yellow banana, and the like. She then caused to be cast upon this same screen, without the subject's knowledge, a faintly colored, hazily outlined and slightly oscillating actual picture of the required object. And under these conditions she found that almost invariably such "distinctly supraliminal" visual perceptions were mistaken for and incorporated into the images of imagination without the least suspicion on the observer's part that any external stimulus was actually present. It appears in other words, that under appropriate conditions, "images" (of imagination) cannot be distinguished from actual faint sensations or perceptions.[13]

We must conclude, then, that the distinction between images and sensations is primarily one of degree only and not one of kind; that there is no unique texture distinctive of images; and that the distinction, in the last analysis, is merely a physiological one, defined by the degree to which direct peripheral stimuli for the given discriminanda can be determined by the experimenter to be then and there present, or not.

12. Summary

Both images and sensations get into our science as discriminanda-expectations, i.e., as a certain type of immanent determinant only. Their "raw feels" play no rôle. With "images" the behavior in which they function is for the most part introspective speech behavior only. With "sensations," or at any rate, for the more enduring "object-qualities," the behavior may be either introspective or practical. But images, no more than sensations, are, in the last analysis, private or mentalistic. Whatever private and mentalistic characters—whatever "raw feels"—either sensations or images possess, these by definition never get across and

---

[12] C. W. Perky, An experimental study of imagination, *Amer. J. Psychol.*, 1910, **21**, 422-542.

[13] For a survey of the history of the distinction between imagination and images, on the one hand, and perception and sensations, on the other, see E. G. Boring, *A History of Experimental Psychology* (New York, The Century Co., 1929), Ch. 10.

do not enter into our science *qua* science. Sensations and images are for the purposes of science but certain unique, though quite objectively defined, immanent determinants of behaviors.

REFERENCES

Boring, E. G., *A History of Experimental Psychology* (New York, The Century Co., 1929).

Davis, F. C., Determination of predominant imagery habits in persons of highly specialized training. M. A. Thesis, Univ. of Calif., 1922.

——————, Imagery differences and their functional significance. Ph.D. Thesis, Univ. of Calif., 1931.

Gengerelli, J. A., Some quantitative experiments with eidetic imagery. *Amer. J. Psychol.*, 1930, 42, 399-404.

Griffitts, C. H., Individual differences in imagery. *Psychol. Monog.*, 1927, 37, No. 172.

Kinnaman, A. J., Mental life of two *Macacus rhesus* monkeys in captivity. *Amer. J. Psychol.* 1902, 13, 98-148; 171-218.

Köhler, W., Über eine neue Methode zur psychologischen Untersuchung von Menschenaffen. *Psychol. Forsch.*, 1922, 1, 390-397.

——————, *Gestalt Psychology* (New York, Horace Liveright, 1929).

Lewis, C. I., The pragmatic element in knowledge. *Univ. Calif. Publ. Philos.*, 1926, 6, 205-227.

——————, *Mind and the World Order* (New York, Charles Scribner's Sons, 1929).

Perky, C. W., An experimental study of imagination. *Amer. J. Psychol.*, 1910, 21, 422-542.

Tolman, E. C., Concerning the sensation quality—a behavioristic account. *Psychol. Rev.*, 1922, 29, 140-145.

Warden, C. J. and Rowley, J. B., The discrimination of absolute versus relative brightness in the ring-dove. *J. Comp. Psychol.*, 1929, 9, 317-338.

Yerkes, R. M. and Watson, J. B., Methods of Studying vision in animals. *Behav. Monog.*, 1911, 1, No. 2.

Chapter XVII

FEELING AND EMOTION [1]

1. Feeling and Emotion as Objective Immanent Determinants

WE must now show that even feelings and emotions are, likewise, but immanent determinants of behavior. These most "subjective" of experiences also constitute no bogey for our behaviorism. Our first point will be that the so-called simple feelings, pleasantness and unpleasantness, and the so-called emotions, fear, rage, lust, and the like, are fundamentally alike. They both involve, we shall assert, the following three constitutive phases: (a) the release of relatively generalized sign-gestalt-expectations; (b) incipient visceral and skeletal movements going-off appropriately to these sign-gestalt-expectations; and (c) resulting auxiliary sets of organic and kinesthetic sensations, that is, discriminanda-expectations.

(a) Sign-gestalt-expectations we have defined as readinesses of the organism to expect certain types of resulting significates as lying in such and such types of means-end-relation with respect to such and such given, immediately presented, signs. In the case of a feeling or an emotion the given stimulus-situation evokes, we shall suppose, a sign-gestalt-expectation to the effect that the given object, or situation, is a sign for (will lead on to) the coming of some relatively fundamental, desired or undesired, physiological significate. (b) The release of such a sign-gestalt-expectation tends to induce along with itself (through some physiological mechanism) incipient preparatory and consummatory activities, i.e., incipient stages of movements appropriate to the getting to or from the ultimate physiological significate and of reacting, both viscerally and skeletally, to the latter when reached. (c) And, finally, we suppose that these incipient movements give rise to

[1] Cf. E. C. Tolman, A behavioristic account of the emotions. *Psychol. Rev.*, 1923, **30**, 217-227.

kinesthetic and organic stimuli and thus to resulting discriminanda-expectations.

2. This Doctrine—a Derivative of the James-Lange Theory

It will be noted at once that such a doctrine, if not exactly
identical with, is at any rate a close derivative of the James-Lange
Theory.[2] That theory, it will be remembered, defined an emotion as a propensity to behave in a given way (e.g., to run away,
in the case of fear, to strike out, etc., in the case of anger, plus
accompanying activities of the viscera) and then as consisting,
further, in the set of kinesthetic and organic sensations supposed
to result from these responses, overt and visceral. This, as far
as it went, was obviously pretty good behavioristic doctrine, of
which the present theory may be described as merely a further
elaboration. The present theory does, however, involve two additional features. First, it includes in its purview, as fundamentally
the same sort of thing as the emotions, the simple feelings—
i.e., pleasantness and unpleasantness. And, secondly, it substitutes,
for the simpler notion of immediate response, the more analyzed
and, if you will, the more complicated notion of the release, first,
of a sign-gestalt-expectation, and, only then, of resultant incipient
movements and visceral reactions.

Let us indicate this doctrine, first for the case of the simple
feelings.

3. Pleasantness and Unpleasantness as Sign-Gestalt-Expectations

Pleasantness. Our doctrine will be that pleasantness is, first
of all, the release of a sign-gestalt-expectation, i.e., the release
of an expectation to the effect that the presented object or situation is a sign of something "good," i.e., of a final physiological
quiescence. Pleasantness is thus, first of all, an assertion that
staying in the presence of, or having some other type of positive
commerce-with, the given, presented object, or situation, will lead
on to physiological quiescence.

[2] Cf. C. G. Lange and W. James, *The Emotions*, in *Psychology Classics*,
ed. by Knight Dunlap (Baltimore, The Williams & Wilkins Company, 1922).

Two further points about this are, however, to be emphasized. Pleasantness *qua* pleasantness, and nothing more, does not assert just what the ultimate type of this quiescence is going to be— whether, that is, the given commerce-with is going to satisfy food-hunger, sex-hunger, excretion-hunger, esthetic-hunger or what—only that some sort of *good* quiescence is to be reached. And, secondly, it does not assert the precise type of commerce-with which is going to get the organism to the latter. It asserts merely that some sort of a positive engaging with the immediate sign is going to lead on to this good quiescence.

Unpleasantness. Turn, now, to unpleasantness. In it, just the opposite situation obtains. Unpleasantness asserts that the immediately presented object is a sign that something "bad," i.e., a final state of physiological disturbance, will come as a result of having commerce-with such a sign. But, again, there are two subordinate features to be noted.

Unpleasantness *qua* unpleasantness, and nothing more, does not assert the precise character of the ultimate physiological disturbance which is to come: whether it will be injury, balking of other propensities, or what. Nor does it assert the precise character of the commerce with the sign, which threatens this ultimate disturbance—merely that any type of positive commerce with such a sign is likely to lead to such a physiological disturbance.

It is only in the emotions proper, as we shall see shortly, that there are assertions as to the more precise characters of the coming "goods" or "bads," physiological quiescences and disturbances, and also as to the more precise characters of the means-end-relations of these "goods" and "bads" to the immediate sign-situations.

4. Pleasantness and Unpleasantness as Incipient Movements and Visceral Activities

The second main point in the doctrine is that pleasantnesses and unpleasantnesses, as released sign-gestalt-expectations, also involve, in some physiological fashion, not as yet understood, the release of incipient movements and visceral activities. In the case of pleasantnesses, these incipient processes will be primarily slight movements of approach or persisting, plus premonitory forerunners of general visceral quiescence. In the case of unpleasantnesses, such incipient processes will be incipient movements of desisting plus slight premonitory foretastes of general visceral disturbance.

5. Pleasantness and Unpleasantness as Resulting Kinesthetic and Organic Sensations

Finally, the third feature of the doctrine will be the distinctly "James-Lange-ian" one that pleasantness and unpleasantness, as "feelings" or "mental states," are nothing more or less than the resulting organic and kinesthetic discriminanda-expectations. These discriminanda-expectations, these "sensations," become conscious and constitute the "conscious feeling" of pleasantness or unpleasantness, if the organism starts to behavior-adjust to running-back-and-forth with respect to them. Pleasantness and unpleasantness are, that is, as conscious feelings, probably present in an introspective moment only. As conscious entities, they are undoubtedly artifacts of introspection. Furthermore, the very act of introspection introduces new sign-gestalt-expectations which tend to displace those which give rise to the given, to-be-introspected-upon organic and kinesthetic sensations. Hence any accurate introspection on the "sensations" of pleasantness and unpleasantness is very difficult.

6. Relation of Above Doctrine to a Typical Hedonistic Doctrine such as Troland's

It may help here towards the better envisagement and evaluation of the above doctrine if we stop for a moment and compare it with a typical hedonistic doctrine of pleasantness and unpleasantness, such as Troland's.[3] Troland says that, when a response to a situation is such as to cause a resultant "pleasantness" (stimulation of a *"beneceptor"*), this will tend to increase the conductance of the cortical centers for that response; whereas when a response to the given situation is such as to cause a resultant "unpleasantness" (stimulation of a *"nociceptor"*), this will tend to decrease the conductance for that response.

The chief representatives of his beneceptors are (a) certain hypothetical sense organs which he supposes to be stimulated

[3] Cf. L. T. Troland, *The Fundamentals of Human Motivation* (New York, D. Van Nostrand Company, Inc., 1928), Ch. XI, p. 202 f. and Ch. XII.

by a high state of erotic activity; (b) the gustatory receptors stimulated by sweets; (c) some of the olfactory receptors—i.e., those corresponding to certain of the odors; and (d) certain of the skin receptors, especially those activated by moderate warmth. The chief representatives of his nociceptors are the free-nerve endings which induce pain.

It appears now that, whenever beneceptive afferent systems are stimulated, all the neural processes then or just previously conducting, tend to suffer an increase in their conductances; and, whenever the nociceptive afferent systems are stimulated, all the neural processes then or just previously conducting, tend to suffer a decrease in their conductance. He calls this the *retroflex* action of beneception and nociception.

Resultant feelings of pleasantness and unpleasantness (beneceptive and nociceptive sensations, or, if you will, their physiological correlates) then act for him, as they do for all good hedonists, by enhancing and depressing. They predispose the organism to favor those types of activity which have in the past led to pleasantness (i.e., erotic sensations, certain odors, bodily warmth, etc.) and to avoid those types of response which led in the past to unpleasantness (i.e., bodily pains). It is the leading to pleasantness or the having led to pleasantness, or contrariwise, the leading to unpleasantness or the having led to unpleasantness, which thus provide, according to Troland, the fundamental motives for doing and learning. To get to pleasant (i.e., beneceptive) sensations and to avoid unpleasant (i.e., nociceptive) sensations are for him the ultimate *motivations* of behavior.

Contrast, now, such a point of view with our own doctrine as just presented. For us, a "sensation" of pleasantness *results from* an expectation of a good outcome, and the "sensation" of unpleasantness *results from* an expectation of a bad outcome, rather than *vice versa*. To "feel" pleasant is, according to us, already to have released a total sign-gestalt-expectation that the persisting in a positive commerce with the given external situation will lead to a good significate. And, contrariwise, to feel unpleasant is to have already released a total sign-gestalt-expectation that the persisting in a positive commerce with the given external situation will lead to a bad significate. Pleasantness and unpleasantness are thus held by us to be expressions of cognitive expectations *already functioning*.

The organism does not, according to us, do things in order to feel pleasant, and not to feel unpleasant, as Troland supposes. Rather the organism does things in order to get to quiescence and to avoid disturbance. And he feels pleasant when he thinks (i.e., expects) that persisting in the situation before him is going to lead to quiescence. And he feels unpleasant when he thinks (i.e., expects) that persisting in the situation before him is going to lead to disturbance. Pleasantness and unpleasantness are, as we see it, results, not causes. They are indicators of cognitive expectations already made.

It is to be noted, further, that, as such indicators of expectations, they may be either right or wrong. The organism may feel pleasantness when he should not, and *vice versa*. But, if he is docile, he will be able, at least in some measure, to correct these expectations and hence the occurrences of his feelings. He will correct them to coincide with the characters of the actually experienced outcomes which he has had on previous occasions.

Finally, the present account and Troland's may be compared on one further point. According to Troland, pleasantness and unpleasantness are the products of specific end-organs, the beneceptors and the nociceptors. And this is something which would seem to be fixed once and for all by the innate physiological constitution of the organism.[4] According to us, on the other hand, the organism is, to be sure, endowed initially with certain original propensities to expect that certain discriminanda-commerces (for example, the eating of sweets) will lead to good quiescences; but, if these initial expectations prove faulty, he can, within limits, unlearn them. He need no longer feel pleasantnesses relative to these specific types of discriminanda. He does not, according to us (as he would according to Troland), have to go on through life feeling pleasantness in response to specific sweets which actually have resulted in immediate and violent pain time after time.

7. The Emotions

Turn, now, to a consideration of the emotions proper. We use the term emotion to cover such entities as fear, rage, lust, extreme

---

[4] There are, of course, Troland also supposes, a large number of purely neutroceptive sense systems, those of vision, hearing, etc.

food-hunger, extreme fatigue, extreme excretion-hunger. These emotions, like simple pleasantnesses and unpleasantnesses, also consist, we shall claim, in: (a) sign-gestalt-expectations of resulting physiological goods and bads as "promised" or "threatened" by the immediate stimulus-situation; (b) incipient movements and visceral activities resulting, in physiological fashion, from the release of these sign-gestalt-expectations; and (c) resultant organic and kinesthetic stimulations (discriminanda-expectations).

8. The Emotions as Specific Sign-Gestalt-Expectations

An emotion is, first of all, an expectation of a "promised" physiological quiescence, or of a "threatened" physiological disturbance—i.e., an expectation that mere persisting, or desisting, in the given activity will be a proper course to pursue. An emotion is thus, first of all, a pleasantness or an unpleasantness.[5] An emotion is also, however, something more specific. As contrasted with a simple pleasantness or unpleasantness, it is: (i) an assertion as to a relatively specific character in the promised "good" or the threatened "bad"; and also (ii) a more specific assertion as to the sort of means-end-relations which obtain between the immediate sign and this promised or threatened physiological significate.

Fear, for example, is not merely an assertion that the immediately present situation, if persisted in, is a sign for a physiological disturbance. It is not merely an unpleasantness; it is also an assertion that 'this threatened disturbance is going to be of the character of injury, or pain. And, further, it is likewise an assertion that the means-end-relations between such threatened pain or injury and the immediate sign are such that mere staying in the presence of the latter will lead to the pain or injury. Hence, fear tends to evoke the specific avoidance responses of escape or hiding.

Or, again, to take another example, rage likewise is not merely

---

[5] Allport also divides the emotions into the two classes of pleasant and unpleasant and suggests an interesting physiological basis for this distinction. F. H. Allport, A physiological-genetic theory of feeling and emotion, *Psychol. Rev.*, 1922, **29**, 132-139.

an assertion that the immediately present situation is a sign for a physiological disturbance; in addition, and more specifically, rage is: (i) an expectation that this disturbance will have the character of a blocking of, or interference with, other activities; and (ii) it is an expectation that the specific means-end-relations between such threatened blocking and the immediate sign are such that the mere continued existence of this sign (e.g., an enemy) will tend to lead to such blocking or interference. Hence, rage tends to evoke the responses of attacking or destroying the sign-object as the proper sort of avoidance response.

Finally, as a last example, lust is not only an assertion that the given sign-object will lead to some physiological quiescence. It is also an assertion: (i) that this promised quiescence is specifically that kind required by the sexual apparatus; and (ii) that the means-end-relations between the immediate sign and this sexual goal are such that the way to reach the latter is by some sort of intimate bodily contact with the sign.

9. The Emotions as Resulting Incipient Movements and Visceral Activities

Secondly, we assume for the emotions, as for simple pleasantness and unpleasantness, that the excitation in the organism of such a sign-gestalt-expectation causes, by some as yet unknown physiological mechanism, the release, in incipient form, of movements and visceral activities; these incipient activities will correspond to the means-end-relations involved in this sign-gestalt, and also to the final physiological disturbance or quiescence, which figure as the significate of such a sign-gestalt. We assume, for example, for the case of fear, that incipient running away and hiding activities and incipient fore-runners of the final visceral activity appropriate to pain or injury are involved. Similarly, we assume, for the case of rage, that incipient fighting and attack movements, and slight, incipient fore-runners of the visceral disturbance of being blocked or interfered with are released. Or, finally, we assume, for the case of lust, that incipient movements of contact plus incipient foretastes of the final visceral condition of sexual "analepsis" are released.

10. The Emotions as Resultant Kinesthetic and Organic Sensations

Thirdly, our doctrine of emotion is that, as a result of such incipient movements and visceral activities, the organism receives more or less specific types of organic and kinesthetic stimulation. The emotion, as "conscious feeling," is but the complex of resultant organic and kinesthetic "sensations," which enter "conscious awareness." That is, they enter conscious awareness, if the organism proceeds to behavior-adjust to a "running-back-and-forth" with respect to them; if, in short, he introspects with respect to them, though again, as in the case of the simple feelings, the very act of introspection tends mightily to interfere with these particular types of organic and kinesthetic discriminanda which are to be introspected upon. To introspect introduces a new set of sign-gestalt-expectations which tend very much to interfere with those which are involved in producing the emotion itself. Hence the well-known difficulty of introspecting upon the emotions.

11. Distinguishing the Different Emotions

So much by way of general definition; but what, it may be asked next, constitute the real differentiæ of the different emotions. Two answers suggest themselves. On the one hand, it may be said that we differentiate and name the different emotions primarily introspectively, i.e., in terms of the types of organic and kinesthetic and visceral sensations tied to them. Or, on the other hand, it may be said that we name and distinguish them primarily in terms, rather, of (i) the fundamental types of quiescence and disturbance being sought and avoided, plus (ii) the fundamental types of means-end-relations being expected as the ways thus to seek and avoid.

The first answer seems relatively improbable. It has two lacunæ. First, it presumes a very considerable ease and validity in introspection. But it has been pointed out that any adequate introspection of the emotions would seem exceedingly unlikely, because the sign-gestalt-expectations required for introspection tend to interfere with those involved in the emotion itself. And, secondly, the physiologists are now making it doubtful if many of the emotions really do differ very distinctively one from another in their organic make-ups. Thus Cannon, as a result of his investigations of the visceral activities involved in "fear," "rage," "pain," "hunger," has concluded that the differential features in these major emotions cannot be traced to their visceral components. There is too much overlapping among the latter.[6] And Dashiell, collecting together all the evidence including Cannon's, concludes decisively that there is no certain evidence as yet adduced to indicate any "distinctive visceral cores" for the separate emotions.[7]

Consider, now, the second answer. It would assume that the separate emotions are, in the last analysis, distinguished and given separate names by virtue of (i) the differences between the final physiological quiescences and disturbances which they are respectively seeking and avoiding, and by virtue of (ii) the characteristic differences of means-end-relation in which they expect these respective quiescences and disturbances to lie.

Thus fear, on this hypothesis, is distinguished and named, primarily, by virtue of its being (i) an avoidance of the physiological disturbance of pain or injury, plus (ii) an expectation that the way to avoid such pain or injury is by escaping from the sign-object in question. Similarly, rage would be distinguished by virtue of its being (i) an avoidance of the physiological disturbance of blocking or interference, plus (ii) an expectation that the way to avoid such blocking is to destroy the sign-object in question. Or, finally, lust would be distinguished by virtue of its being (i) an approach to the physiological quiescence of sexual analepsis, plus (ii) an expectation that the way to achieve such sexual analepsis is by intimate bodily contacts.

We define the emotion as fear, whether it be in ourselves or in rats, when the organism is observed to run or hide; we define it as rage, when he is observed to fight or attack; and we define it as lust, when he is observed to caress or copulate. And these distinctions we make quite successfully, irrespective of whether or not the visceral components, and hence the introspective feels of these different emotions, are or are not distinctive. And so

---

[6] Cf. W. B. Cannon, The interrelations of emotions as suggested by recent physiological researches, *Amer. J. Psychol.*, 1914, **25**, 256-282.

Also W. B. Cannon, *Bodily Changes in Pain, Hunger, Fear and Rage*, 2nd ed. (New York, D. Appleton and Company, 1929).

[7] J. F. Dashiell, Are there any native emotions? *Psychol. Rev.*, 1928, **35**, 319-327.

it would go in similar fashion for all the other fundamental emotions (whatever the ultimate list of these may eventually turn out to be). In the last analysis each emotion, as a distinctive entity (and this holds also of pleasantness and unpleasantness), is to be defined not in terms of some obvious and certain "introspective givens," but in terms rather of the process's functional character as an immanent determinant of behavior—i.e., in terms of its character as the demand to and from such and such specific quiescences and disturbances plus also its character as an accompanying means-end-expectation as to the "lie" of such quiescences and disturbances. The different emotions, and simple pleasantness and unpleasantness, are important and distinctive, not as different and unique sets of kinesthetic and visceral "sensations," but as distinctive and unique "directions" of behavior.[8]

[8] W. B. Cannon, The James-Lange theory of emotions: a critical examination and an alternative theory, *Amer. J. Psychol.*, 1927, **39**, 106-124.

E. B. Newman, F. T. Perkins and R. H. Wheeler, Cannon's theory of emotion: a critique, *Psychol. Rev.*, 1930, **37**, 305-326.

See for recent discussion of the James-Lange theory W. B. Cannon, Again the James-Lange and the thalamic theories of emotion, *Psychol. Rev.*, 1931, **38**, 281-295.

REFERENCES

Allport, F. H., A physiological-genetic theory of feeling and emotion. *Psychol. Rev.*, 1922, **29**, 132-139.

Cannon, W. B., The interrelations of emotions as suggested by recent physiological researches. *Amer. J. Psychol.*, 1914, **25**, 256-282.

——————, The James-Lange theory of emotions: a critical examination and an alternative theory, *Amer. J. Psychol.*, 1927, **39**, 106-124.

——————, *Bodily Changes in Pain, Hunger, Fear and Rage*, 2d ed. (New York, D. Appleton and Company, 1929).

——————, Again the James-Lange and the thalamic theories of emotion. *Psychol. Rev.*, 1931, **38**, 281-295.

Dashiell, J. F., Are there any native emotions? *Psychol. Rev.*, 1928, **35**, 319-327.

Lange, C. G. and James W., *The Emotions* in *Psychology Classics* (Baltimore, Williams and Wilkins Company, 1922).

Newman, E. B., Perkins, F. T. and Wheeler, R. H., Cannon's theory of emotion: a critique. *Psychol. Rev.*, 1930, **37**, 305-326.

Tolman, E. C., A behavioristic account of the emotions, *Psychol. Rev.*, 1923, **30**, 217-227.

Troland, L. T., *Fundamentals of Human Motivation* (New York, D. Van Nostrand Company, Inc., 1928).

PART V
MOTIVATION AND LEARNING

> " 'The time has come,' the Walrus said,
>   'To talk of many things:
> Of shoes—and ships—and sealing-wax—
>   Of cabbages—and kings—' "

The walrus was an introvert. His interest in his own "be-havior-determinants," more or less ignoring those of the oysters (the "bitter tear" was but sheer introverted emotionalism), and his delight in spinning out such "inventive ideations" as that of the "seven maids with the seven mops sweeping for half a year," prove it.

In short, the walrus was a system-maker. For it is the introverts alone, so they tell us, who make systems. We must suppose, then, that the walrus in his humble Victorian way had developed his own brand of behaviorism and, when he had finished it, that he turned to his friend the carpenter to explain what, summed up in terms of the whole vegetable and animal kingdoms, from the humblest *brassica oleracea* (botanical name for cabbage) to the highest reigning *homo sapiens*, this his behaviorism amounted to.

More specifically the walrus found it time to indicate his stand with respect to the two perhaps most fundamental problems of psychology: the nature of motivation and the nature of learning.

Chapter XVIII

APPETITES AND AVERSIONS [1]

1. The Ultimate Drives

IN the preceding chapter, and indeed implicitly throughout the entire foregoing discussion, it has been assumed that behavior goes off, in the last analysis, by virtue only of certain final physiological quiescences, which are being sought, or of certain final physiological disturbances which are being avoided. Further, it has also been implied, and we wish now definitely to assert, that organisms are provided innately, at least vaguely, with sign-gestalt-readinesses as to how to get thus to and from, and also with the necessary accompanying demands to make them actually try thus to get to and from. Organisms are innately ready, provided they are also suffering at the moment from appropriate initiating organic states or excitements, to demand certain quiescences to-be-reached and certain disturbances to-be-avoided. And they expect that positive or negative commerces with the objects presented by stimuli will, or will not, get them to or from. Organisms are innately ready with certain feelings and emotions, provided they are also in the appropriate initiating states of organic excitement.

Such innate sign-gestalt-readinesses, with the accompanying appropriate demands, we shall designate from now on as the ultimate or fundamental drives. These fundamental drives provide, we shall suppose, the primordial bases for all behavior. All the various specifications and elaborations of motivation, which appear in adult and experienced organisms are to be conceived as

[1] Forerunners of the doctrine presented in this chapter and the next have already appeared in articles.

E. C. Tolman, Instinct and purpose, *Psychol. Rev.*, 1920, **27**, 217-233.

———— Can instincts be given up in psychology? *J. Abnorm. & Soc. Psychol.*, 1922, **17**, 139-152.

———— The nature of instinct, *Psychol. Bull.*, 1923, **20**, 200-216.

———— The nature of the fundamental drives, *J. Abnorm. & Soc. Psychol.*, 1926, **20**, 349-358.

but refinements, modifications, or elaborations built up upon such more ultimate, innate readinesses and demands.

2.   Craig's Doctrine of Appetites and Aversions

This doctrine of certain physiological quiescences and disturbances to be got to or from, given certain initiating physiological states, plus certain innate sign-gestalt-readinesses as to how to get thus to or from has been borrowed almost *in toto* from Craig (although Craig himself might not perhaps be willing to recognize it when thus translated into our language). As a result very largely of observations on the nesting and mating of pigeons,[2] he formulated a theory of what he calls "appetites" and "aversions." He writes:

"An appetite (or appetence, if this term may be used with purely behavioristic meaning), so far as externally observable, is a state of agitation which continues so long as a certain stimulus, which may be called the appeted stimulus, is absent. When the appeted stimulus is at length received it stimulates a consummatory reaction, after which the appetitive behavior ceases and is succeeded by a state of relative rest.

"An aversion . . . is a state of agitation which continues so long as a certain stimulus, referred to as the disturbing stimulus, is present; but which ceases, being replaced by a state of relative rest, when that stimulus has ceased to act on the sense-organs."[3]

Our doctrine makes only certain slight emendations to the above —emendations, furthermore, which are for the most part also implied, although in somewhat different language from ours, in the rest of Craig's own account.

(a) (i) In the case of the appetites, we should hold that, in some of them at least, the ultimate to-be-got-to goal is, not the mere consummatory stimulus-object per se, but rather the final state of physiological quiescence to be reached by commerce with the consummatory object. We hold, that is, that the consummatory responses themselves are usually docile and not wholly blind and reflex—and that, in so far as they are thus docile, the ultimate goal is the final state of physiological quiescence and

---

[2] Cf. W. Craig, Male doves reared in isolation, *J. Anim. Behav.*, 1914, **4**, 121-133.

[3] W. Craig, Appetites and aversions as constituents of instincts, *Biol. Bull.*, 1918, **34**, 91-107, p. 91.

not the mere consummatory object or act itself. (ii) And, similarly, in the case of the aversions, we hold that the ultimately to-be-got-from entity is, not the "disturbing stimulus" per se, but rather, a final state of physiological disturbance (e.g., injury, physiological blocking, or the like), which is "threatened" by that disturbing stimulus. That is, we should hold that the avoidance of the disturbing stimulus is, in most cases, also docile in the sense that, if it be demonstrated to the organism that nothing "bad" will actually result from the specific disturbing stimulus, he will eventually cease to avoid it. The dove will not continue to avoid the loud sudden noise when it is "proved" to him that that specific and particular loud sudden noise threatens no final physiological disturbance.[4]

(b) Our second emendation consists in further characterizations of the "states of agitation" themselves. Such states of agitation are what we are calling "initiating organic states or excitements." And, according to us, such states are both purposive and cognitive. They express (that is, by virtue of their docility relative to the final accomplishment of their ends of getting to and from): (a) demands to get to the quiescences and from the disturbances (with maximum ease); and (b) sign-gestalt-readinesses, however vague, as to how to get thus to or from in "short" fashion.

(c) Finally, the third emendation we should make to Craig's simple statement as quoted would consist in our further dictum that the appetites and aversions do not go off simply by virtue of the external stimuli ("consummatory" or "disturbing") appropriate to them, but that they require also these initiating physiological states. (This is an emendation which Craig himself also develops.) The state of agitation to be called hunger—in our terms the demand for hunger-satiation plus the sign-gestalt-readinesses for exploring and eating as the ways to get to such hunger-satiation—does not arise merely, or primarily, as a result of the presence of food-stimuli or explorable-stimuli, but rather as a result of an internal initiating physiological excitement, viz., physiological *hunger*. Similarly, the state of agitation to be called

---

[4] This is perhaps the only one of our emendations which conflicts definitely with Craig's account. For Craig says pretty specifically and definitely that the consummatory act is reflex. However, he seems to mean by this "reflexishness" more that the consummatory response is given in some form innately, than that it is not capable of any improvement through learning.

fright—in our terms, the demand to get from injury plus the sign-gestalt-readiness to accept certain types of object as to be avoided in order thus to get to safety and to keep from injury— does not arise merely, or primarily, as a result of danger-threatening "disturbing stimuli," but rather as a result of an initiating internal physiological state which, for want of a better name, we may call *timidity*, and which must be present in order to make the animal sensitive to such "disturbing stimuli."

Both appetites and aversions have their initiating physiological excitements or states. And it is only when these states are in force that the demands to get to the given type of quiescence, or from the given type of disturbance, arise. It is only then that the organism seeks consummatory objects and avoids "disturbing" ones. Only the hungry animal seeks and eats foods; and only the at-that-moment timid [5] animal flees from loud noises or the like.

3.   Appetites Are Cyclical; Aversions Are Relatively Continuous

We must note, next, that the appetites and the aversions tend to differ in regard to the periodicities of their initiating states. In the case of appetites, of which hunger and sex are typical examples, the initiating physiological state out of which arises the definitive demand for quiescence plus the accompanying more or less vague sign-gestalt-readinesses, as to how to get to such quiescence, follows a definite metabolic rhythm or cycle. A state of excitation with resulting activity and final quiescence, followed by a state of inertia, which only later gives way to still another state of excitation, is the typical picture.

In the case of the aversions, on the other hand, of which fright and pugnacity are typical examples, the physiological initiating state tends to be a more enduring and constant affair. The organism is in a relatively continuous state of timidity or of belli-

---

[5] It is obvious that we are here using the term "timid" not merely for that extreme form of this condition, which is supposed to deserve opprobrium, but also for its weaker values which, as "cautiousness," are said to be deserving of praise. The term "timidity" designates the possession of the organism, *at the given moment*, by a physiological state or excitement which makes him ready, at that moment, to respond to, and to avoid, injury-threatening stimulus-objects.

cosity. The organism is always relatively ready to be frightened at a danger-threatening stimulus or to get angry at an interference-threatening stimulus; though undoubtedly here also there will be a certain amount of cyclical variation due to changes in metabolic and glandular conditions.

4. Resumé of Doctrine

Let us pause, now, to sum up the discussion. We shall do this by means of a series of propositions:

(a) The fundamental drives or motivations underlying all behavior are to be conceived as certain innately provided, general physiological demands plus certain more or less vague sign-gestalt-readinesses as to how to satisfy these demands. These sign-gestalt-readinesses will be much affected by learning, but their cores are to be conceived as given innately.

(b) These fundamental drives subdivide conveniently into two classes, to be designated the appetites and the aversions.

(c) An appetite has three constitutive phases:

(i) an initiating physiological state, which appears in cycles, metabolically conditioned, and which, when it appears, gives rise to:

(ii) the demand for a given type of physiological quiescence, plus

(iii) a more or less vague sign-gestalt-readiness as to how to achieve this quiescence:—i.e., a more or less vague readiness as to the type of consummatory stimulus-object to be sought and had commerce-with and also as to the type of exploratory objects to be had commerce-with in order to get to this to-be-sought-for type of consummatory object.

(d) An aversion, also, has three similar constitutive phases:

(i) an initiating physiological state, which, however, is relatively enduring and of constant strength for any given organism, and which, whenever thus more or less continuously present, gives rise to:

(ii) the demand against a given type of physiological disturbance, plus

(iii) more or less vague sign-gestalt-readinesses as to the types of "avoidance-object" the presences of which "threaten" such a disturbance and, also, as to the types of means-objects to be had commerce-with in order to get from and to avoid such "avoidance-objects."

So much, by way of general definition; we turn now to a more specific, though hasty, consideration of individual appetites and aversions. We shall limit ourselves to such a "hasty" consideration because, this being one of the most uncertain fields in psychology, we actually know very little about such individual appetites and aversions.

5. The List of Human Appetites

If it be asked what in general is the total list of appetites, the answer will be, of course, that such a list will be different for different species. Birds and insects seem to have more appetites, and perhaps also more aversions, than do human beings. Thus Craig, for example, finds in his pigeons such appetites as: "locating a nesting site," "fetching straws and building them into a nest," "sitting on the eggs," "roosting," etc.[6] And the hymenoptera, to take an example from the insects are, as is well known, provided with very numerous and relatively specific appetites in the way of building and provisioning of nests, caring for and rearing their young, etc.

In the present chapter we shall restrict ourselves, therefore, to a consideration of the appetites and aversions of human beings only. Without any pretense at finality, we shall now suggest as a tentative list of human appetites the following: *Food-hunger, Sex-hunger, Excretion-hungers, Specific Contact-hungers, Rest-hunger, Sensory-motor-hungers (i.e., Esthetic and Play Hungers).*

Such a list is, of course, quite speculative. Many more observations on human beings in both laboratory and "field" than are at present available, will be needed before it can be made final. It is to be taken here, therefore, for its suggestiveness only. It errs undoubtedly on the side of brevity. But it will suffice for purposes of illustration. Let us consider each of the items in it one by one.

Food-hunger. The fact and nature of this appetite is relatively obvious. The initiating physiological state is a characteristic type of disequilibrium which is produced in the nutritive alimentary

[6] W. Craig, Appetites and aversions as constituents of instincts, *Biol. Bull.*, 1918, **34**, pp. 97-100.

system after periods passed without nourishment. When this disequilibrium is in force there is released a demand for the quiescence of hunger satiation together with an accompanying sign-gestalt-readiness to explore and to eat. In a word, food-hunger provides a demand for alimentary satiation plus an innate sign-gestalt-readiness (which can become elaborated and modified by experience) that certain types of food-object (nipple, etc.) are the appropriate ways of getting to satiation, plus the further subordinate sign-gestalt-readiness that exploratory activities are the way to get to such food-objects.

Sex-hunger. The initiating physiological state for this is an internal disequilibrium of glands and sex organs, and it provides a demand for the getting to a complementary physiological state of sexual quiescence—plus some very vague sign-gestalt-readiness, prior to tuition, as to how to achieve the latter, viz., intercourse with a sex-object, normal or perverted. The sexually excited individual demands sexual quiescence, and he releases a sign-gestalt-readiness to the effect that this demanded quiescence lies in the means-end-relation of intercourse with such and such types of sex-object. He also releases a subordinate sign-gestalt-readiness that such a sex-object, if absent, is to be reached by exploring.

Contact-hungers. We have in mind here what Freud [7] designates as the polymorphous perverse expressions of sex in young children, or, indeed, in adults, in so far as these latter have not outgrown their childish ways. We refer to such processes as thumb-sucking, bed-wetting, fæces-holding, and the like, which in certain children and adults seem to provide immediate satisfaction in and of themselves. And our hypothesis is that in such cases, the child or adult is suffering an immediate physiological disequilibrium which requires for its quiescence one of these minor bodily contacts. The child has an appetite for the quiescences, to be obtained by such specific contacts. These general facts do not as such admit of dispute. The only further question is whether or not such minor appetites are, as Freud would hold, in some mysterious way linked up with, and part of, the sex-appetite proper. This, however, is a question for which no really adequate data seem as yet to be at hand.

[7] S. Freud, *Three Contributions to Sexual Theory* (New York, The Journal of Nervous and Mental Disease Publishing Company, 1910).

Excretion-hungers. By the excretion-hungers, we mean the need to micturate and the need to defecate in a suitable place. It must be noted, however, that it is, perhaps, only certain animals in whom these physiological disequilibriums give rise to real "needs," *qua* needs. For in some animals, the lower monkeys and birds, for example, micturation and defecation seem to occur immediately, as mere reflexes. But there are species, cats and dogs, for example, in which the animal does seem to suffer a real need;—namely, the need to perform the act in a "suitable" place. And such animals can be observed hunting for such a "suitable" spot. And here we seem to have a real appetite, the consummatory response of which is that of "voiding" in the appropriate type of environmental spot. The animal expects only "such" a voiding to bring quiescence.

Rest-hunger is our name for that appetite which seems to arise out of the specific physiological disequilibrium of fatigue, and which has as its complementing goal a physiological quiescence of well-being,—"restedness." The final consummatory responses would be those of "lying down on—relaxing in—a quiet place," etc. Such consummatory responses require the presence of, and commerce with, such final environmental objects as ground, couches, or what-not, to lie upon, together with surrounding stillness and absence of environmental disturbances. The rest-hungry animal "rests" with the aid of such consummatory objects, if they already be present, and he explores for such objects, if they be distant. The rest appetite consists, then, in a demand for the final physiological state of well-being plus innate and acquired sign-gestalt-readinesses as to the appropriate sorts of objects for resting on, and in, and as to ways of getting to such final quiescence.

Sensory-motor-hungers (i.e., esthetic and play hungers). We are here on even more debatable ground. But for the purpose of raising an issue, we shall present a definite hypothesis, to wit: that human beings, and perhaps even some of the lower animals, include among their appetites various needs to get to "mild and harmonious" fatigues of their discriminative, manipulative, and means-end "faculties." By "mild and harmonious" we shall understand a fatigue resulting from types of discriminanda-, manipulanda-, and means-end-readinesses and -expectations which come relatively easily to the organism, given his innate structure and his past training. We assume, in short, that when, in the course of general metabolism, one of the higher organisms is in a relatively neutral sort of metabolic condition, i.e., in a condition in which none of his other appetites or aversions is strongly engaged, that such an organism is apt to be in a condition of unspent energy. And such a condition, we shall assume, is in itself a state of physiological disequilibrium which requires a complementary fatigue for neutralization and quiescence. This demanded fatigue will be, to use a word with bad connotations, a fatigue of the "faculty" or "faculties" which happen to be energetic and easily stimulated in the given organism. The organism, when he is in this condition, will set out to find an appropriate environmental object upon which to exercise the given "faculty" or "faculties." He will seek a beautiful picture or a concert for the harmonious (i.e., relatively easy) exercise of eye or ear. He will walk in the hills or go for a swim for the harmonious (relatively easy) exercise of his big muscles. He will "fool" with a mechanical puzzle or play a game of chess for the harmonious exercise of his "ideational" faculty. Such exercises will "gently" tire him and bring him into the demanded state of physiological quiescence.

It is to be noted further, however, that when this demanded exercise is primarily of the sense-organs, society uses the term, "esthetic responses"; but when the demanded exercise is primarily manipulative or a combination of manipulative, discriminative, and means-end-processes, society uses the term, "playing." It seems obvious, however, that no really sharp distinction can be drawn between the two. Every action involves all the processes of discrimination, manipulation, and means-end-activity. The differences between the esthetic responses and playing are differences of emphasis rather than of kind. The important and outstanding feature in both lies in the fact that the final activity, whatever it may be, is done for its own sake, or rather for its own immediate physiological results and not as a means to the satisfaction of some more ultimate appetite or aversion.

Finally, it should also be pointed out, that in actual life it is probable that the esthetic responses and play never occur in pure, isolated form. They are probably always imbedded as minor moments in the going off of other appetites and aversions. Going to the opera or playing golf are, as is but too well known, in large part an expression of social and economic motivations and only in minor degree of play or esthetic demands per se. They satisfy pride and competitiveness quite as much as the need for harmonious fatigue. And as for bridge and chess, they, it is obvious, are often more professional than the professions themselves.

6. The List of Human Aversions

There appear to be in man, and also, it would seem, perhaps in the lower animals as well, only two outstanding aversions, viz., fright and pugnacity. Whether or not more careful consideration would eventually suggest others to be added to this list, we shall not here attempt to decide. For our present, relatively theoretical purposes, it will be sufficient to restrict our examination to these two.

Fright. In fright, the ultimately to-be-avoided physiological disturbance seems to be physiological pain or injury. The frightened individual is one who is seeking by running away or hiding to get away from the fright-evoking object or situation. And, in so doing he is, we declare, both suffering from the demand against a final pain or injury and releasing a sign-gestalt-readiness, partly innate and partly acquired, in the service of this demand to the effect that the given type of fright-evoking (avoidance) object will lead to such pain or injury, if stayed in the presence of.

Pugnacity. In pugnacity the ultimate to-be-avoided physiological disturbance would seem to be an interference with, or blocking of, other activities. The pugnaciously aroused individual is one who is seeking, by striking out or attacking, to get-away from the pugnacity-evoking object or situation. And, in so doing, such an individual is both suffering from the demand against a final blocking of, or interference with, his other activities, and releasing a sign-gestalt-readiness, partly innate and partly acquired, in the service of this demand to the effect that the given type of pugnacity-evoking (i.e., avoidance) object will lead, if allowed to endure, to such blocking or interference.

Pugnacity vs. Fright. Both fright and pugnacity are gettings-away from their respectively evoking disturbing stimulus-situations. But the manner of getting away is characteristically different in the two cases. When the individual is frightened, his ultimate desideratum is prevention of injury. And the best way to do this is to hide or run away. When, on the other hand, the individual is pugnacious, and not frightened, his ultimate desideratum is the prevention of interference—irrespective of possible injury. And the only sure way to prevent a given object or other organism or situation from interfering is to destroy it. In fright, the organism flees or hides; in pugnacity, he strikes and attempts to destroy.

This difference in the characters of fright and pugnacity is particularly obvious and pronounced, when it is one and the same environmental object—something large and obstreperous—which happens in the one individual to arouse fright, and in another pugnacity. Objectively, and from the point of view of a disinterested observer, this large and obstreperous object may actually "threaten" both injury and interference. But the individual who shows fright is, for some reason, innate timidity or past training, sensitive to only one of these threats; whereas the pugnacious individual is sensitive by innate pugnacity or past training only to the other. Given equal or similar past trainings, if the animal be of the "temperament" for which the avoidance of injury is the main desideratum, i.e., if he have a large dose of the initiating physiological state which we have designated timidity, then his fright impulse will be aroused, and the facts of possible and even probable interference will be relatively non-operative. If, on the other hand, he be of the "temperament" for which the avoidance of interference is the main desideratum, i.e., if he have a large dose of the initiating state of pugnaciousness, his pugnacity impulse will be aroused and the facts of possible and even probable injury will be overlooked. In other words, one and the same complex of objective stimuli will "threaten" injury to the one individual and interference to the other, according to their differences of temperament.[8]

[8] Such differences of temperament appear, not only as between human individuals, but also as between individuals in lower species. See, for example, an interesting account as to a social hierarchy (depending principally upon such relative differences in timidity and bellicosity) among the individual inhabitants of a chicken coop.

T. Schjelderup-Elbe, Beiträge zur Sozialpsychologie des Haushuhns, Zsch. f. Psychol., 1921-22, **88**, 225-252.

Cf. also D. Katz, Tierpsychologie und Soziologie des Menschen, Zsch. f. Psychol., 1921-22, **88**, 253-264.

7. Interdependence of Aversions and Appetites

We must note now, however, certain interrelations between the aversions of pugnacity and fright and the appetites. Pugnacity, it is now to be noted, is really a second order sort of affair. It is parasitic upon the other drives. For it is the function of pugnacity to prevent interference with these other drives, that is, with activities motivated by the appetites, or even by fear. If an organism had no other fundamental drives to be satisfied, he would not, presumably, be pugnacious. Pugnacity is ancillary to the satisfaction of such other drives.

Fright also tends at times to combine with the other drives. It tends to fasten on to and wax fat on the appetites. Injury may result from any too long delayed absence of the consummation of an appetite. And this may lead in the fright-sensitive (timid) temperaments, particularly, of course, in the higher organisms where highly developed cognitive elaborations are possible, to activity motivated, not so much by the desire to satisfy an appetite already aroused, as by the impulse to guard against any too pronounced or violent arousal of that appetite. And then we have the spectacle of individuals eating, not as a relief for actual hunger, but for fear they may become hungry; resting for fear they may become tired; and the like.

Finally, it is to be noted, that both fright and pugnacity seem in some individuals to be not merely aversions or activities which go off by virtue of a more or less constantly present initiating physiological state, which operates whenever actual danger or interference is threatened, but also to constitute in themselves real minor appetites. We have in mind, that is, the types of individuals who court danger or invite a "scrap." These individuals seem to have an actual appetite for injury or for interference. Perhaps, however, in such cases the truer explanation would be that after too long periods of safety or of non-interference such individuals have certain excesses of energy that must be worked off. In other words, these appetites for danger or for fright probably belong, rather, under the head of the play or the esthetic appetite. The foolhardy man, and he who goes around with a chip on his shoulder, are, in reality, probably but unique types of esthetic tyro.

8. Evidence for Docility

Finally, in order to substantiate the claim, involved in the above descriptions of the appetites and aversions, that they have as their ultimate goals the final physiological states of quiescence and disturbance, let us briefly review some of the evidence as to the docility of appetites and aversions relative to such physiological goals. We shall consider one or two typical examples, and first we may take the case of food-hunger in human beings.[9]

Docility of Food-Hunger. The human infant is provided innately with a readiness to suck, when hungry. And what little precise evidence (and that of a purely general observational sort) we have suggests that, to begin with, he is ready to suck almost anything—hard rubber, a block of wood, a corner of a blanket, a finger, etc.—which at all conforms in tactual character to a nipple. Later, however, he seems to become to some extent "fixated." That is, he changes from being equally ready to suck at any of these to being ready to suck at nipples only, entities which, in his experience, have actually provided milk; and still later, he changes to being ready to suck only that one specific variety of nipple, whether breast or bottle, from which he has had a great deal of experience of milk. He comes, that is, to be ready to accept only those particular types of object which, in his experience, have led to frequent satiation. His choice of suckable objects is, that is, docile relative to the proved end of satiation. In a word, his manner and choice of sucking can be said to involve a sign-gestalt-readiness to the effect that satiation lies in a direction to be achieved by commerce with that particular type of suckable object. And the breast-fed baby, who raises a rumpus when first put on a bottle, eventually ceases to make that rumpus when finally it has been "proved" to him, by main force, if necessary, that bottle leads to satiation just as truly as does breast.

And what thus holds in regard to infants, could be proved to hold in analogous fashion, we believe, as regards all eating, that of older children and even that of adults. Thus, it is well-known that over-indulgence may often induce a permanent dis-

[9] The account *re* the docility of food-hunger about to be presented has already been offered once before in its main outlines (see above Chapter II, p. 30) but it will do no harm to repeat it here.

taste for a previously favorite food. In other words, this food has now become a sign of resulting discomfort, rather than of resulting satiation. The situation, however, with adults is relatively complicated and obscured by virtue of the fact that foods and manners of eating may become subservient to all sorts of complicated social ends, as well as to food-hunger and to the avoidance of injury pure and simple.

Let us consider next the case for sex.

Docility of Sex-Hunger. In the case of sex, it is as yet unknown, at least for human beings, how much of the character and attachments of the final sex-act are given innately and how much they may have to be learned. But what few facts we have, suggest a great deal of docility. It appears, indeed, that initially there is a wide and variegated range of sexual activities, demands and sign-gestalt-readinesses, all ready to go off, as possibly appropriate routes to satiation. Adult sex-behavior, whether normal or perverted, seems to be a selection from these initial readinesses on a basis of the fruits of early experience. If a given individual has had little or no opportunity for normal experience, he is likely to become "fixated" upon some perverted practice, a practice for which he *has* had the opportunity. The impetus of the original very strong urge is such as to produce a readiness for all the sorts of possible trials and errors, and some one of these is tried out and proves to lead to some degree of sexual quiescence. The whole matter of perversion is, however, complicated. There are probably, in part, actual differences of biological make-up which predetermine some individuals to find more satiation in certain practices than in others. And sex, to a far greater extent than food-hunger, is subject to the control of all sorts of other appetites and aversions, to all sorts of contributing social goals and inhibitions.

Finally, sex-activities get learned, not only on a basis of actual experience, but also on a basis of purely verbal reports. The adolescent human being comes to his sex-life already provided with innumerable *mores*. He has, that is, already made very definite selections as to what the "good" (i.e., satiation producing) sex activities are to be before he has actually tried any of them out.[10]

[10] Cf. W. S. Hunter, The modification of instinct from the standpoint of social psychology, *Psychol. Rev.*, 1920, **27,** 247-269.

Turn now to an aversion, say fright. What are the evidences of docility in it?

The Docility of Fright. Fright we have defined as involving a sign-gestalt-readiness to the effect that the given disturbing object will, if stayed in the presence of, lead to injury, and hence also as involving the further assertion that escape or hiding is the proper sort of means-activity in the presence of such an object. The concrete justification for this definition requires the presence of evidence for docility in the going off of these escapes and hidings.

We must show that any specific stimulus ceases to be a fear-stimulus, i.e., to evoke escape or hiding, when it is "proved" to the organism that this particular instance of that stimulus does not in reality lead to injury. Organisms are provided with innate expectations of injury as a resultant of certain classes of stimuli, such as loud noises, bright lights, etc. But, when any specific instance of such sudden loud noises, bright lights, etc., is proved to them not to lead to injury, they unlearn their fright for that specific type of case.

A first example of such "unconditioning" is to be seen in the facts of simple negative adaptation. A well-known example is that of the spider, who learns not to be "afraid" of a specific sudden loud noise.

"While the spider was on its web, a tuning fork was sounded, and the spider made its regular defensive reaction by dropping to the ground. It climbed back to its web, the fork sounded again, the spider dropped again; but after several repetitions in quick succession, the spider ceased to drop. Next day, to be sure, it responded as at first; but after several days of this, it ceased permanently to respond to the tuning fork." [11]

It appears, in short, that the spider's fear becomes unlearned when nothing "bad" (injurious or painful) actually results. The sound of the tuning fork thereby loses its initial tendency to release the sign-gestalt-expectation of something bad to come. The spider ceases to drop from the web when the fork is sounded.

[11] Cited by R. S. Woodworth, *Psychology*, rev. ed. (New York, Henry Holt and Company, 1929), p. 161. After the experiments of the Peckhams. Cf. G. W. and E. G. Peckham, Some observations on the mental powers of spiders, *J. Morphology*, 1887, 1, 388-419.

To have the complete justification for this interpretation, it would be necessary, however, to state also the reverse, complementary type of experiment. It would be necessary, that is, to try the experiment of giving the spider an injury whenever it *did* stay on the web, and of allowing it to go "scot free" if it dropped off. If, in this other arrangement, it learned *not* to stay on but persisted in dropping off, if, in short, it here did *not* become adapted, then taking the two sets of results together, we should have the complete justification for our own interpretation of the original dropping off as expressing an initial sign-gestalt-expectation—i.e., a sign-gestalt-expectation to the effect that the sudden loud noise of the tuning fork threatened injury.

A second experiment illustrating what we should envisage as this docility of fright is the classical experiment of Jones.[12] Dr. Jones describes the case of a child initially much afraid of a rabbit.[13] She succeeded, however, in gradually overcoming, "unconditioning," this fear by the following procedure. The rabbit was placed in a cage which was first put at such a distance that the child showed no active terror of it. And, while it was at this distance, the child was fed. On the next occasion, while the child was still being fed, the animal was moved slightly nearer. This also caused no disturbance. And throughout a whole series of subsequent occasions, this procedure was repeated, until finally the boy was actually fondling the animal with one hand, and eating with the other.[14]

In suggesting the term *reconditioning* for this procedure, Wat-

[12] M. C. Jones, A laboratory study of fear: the case of Peter, *Ped. Sem.*, 1924, **31**, 308-315.
Cf. also M. C. Jones, Conditioning and unconditioning emotions in infants, *Childhood Educ.*, 1925, **1**, 317-322.

[13] The question as to how Peter originally came by this initial fear need not concern us here. It makes no difference to the present argument whether this fear of an object presenting the somewhat strange appearance and uncertain activities of a rabbit is among those innately feared by children of a certain age or whether it has to be acquired. According to Watson, all such specific fears are acquired through "conditioning" (see below Ch. XXI) by associating with other stimuli which are originally fear-evolving. According to some recent observations of H. E. and M. C. Jones, Fear, *Childhood Educ.*, 1928, **5**, 136-143, on the other hand, there is considerable reason for suspecting that many such fears of particular types of strangeness and wigglingnesses appear "spontaneously" at certain ages.

[14] Dr. Jones reports that some of these especially evident improvements in Peter's "tolerance" of the rabbit occurred on occasions when there were other children present who were unafraid of the rabbit and played with it.

son,[15] referring to this experiment, seems to imply that what happened was a new conditioning of the rabbit stimulus to the eating response. His implication is that by presenting the rabbit simultaneously with the food, Dr. Jones caused the rabbit to get attached, as a conditioned stimulus, to the positive food responses.

We are asserting, however, another interpretation. We are declaring that the function of the food was merely to keep the child quiet and relaxed in the presence of the rabbit *long enough* so that it could *be proved* to him that the rabbit did not lead to injury. The child never wanted or attempted to eat the rabbit (which is what must have happened if the Watson interpretation were correct). He merely learned not to fear it because it moved up on him slowly enough, when he was otherwise relaxed. That is, he was given a *chance* to discover that it did not lead to injury.

So much for the problem of docility.

9. Recapitulation

The ultimate motivators of all behavior—save, of course, the pure reflexes and tropisms, which do not fall under our head of behavior *qua* docile—are, we assume, certain innately provided appetites and aversions. These consist in ultimate demands to get to final physiological quiescences (appetites) or from final physiological disturbances (aversions). Given certain initiating physiological states which occur cyclically in the case of the appetites but are relatively constant and continuous in the case of the aversions, the organism is possessed of the demand to get to given types of physiological quiescence (appetite); and to keep away from given types of physiological disturbance, when these latter "threaten" (aversion). Furthermore, he is provided innately with certain more or less vague sign-gestalt-readinesses as to how to get thus to or from. In the case of an appetite, he is provided innately with some vague final sign-gestalt-readiness as to the type of consummatory object and consummatory response which will lead to the given quiescence—and also, it would seem, with some vague subordinate sign-gestalt-readinesses as to how to explore in order to get to such consummatory objects. That is, when the appropriate

[15] J. B. Watson, Recent experiments on how we lose and change our emotional equipment, *Psychologies of 1925* (Worcester, Mass., Clark Univ. Press, 1926), 59-82. *Ped. Sem.*, 1925, **32**, 349-371.

stimuli are provided he tends to "perceive" the appropriate con-summatory and subordinate objects and to respond more or less correctly to them. In the case of the aversion, he is provided innately with at least some vague final sign-gestalt-readiness which indicates to him that the given type of "threatening" object, would, if stayed in the presence of, lead to the given disturbance. And he is also provided, it would seem, with some vague subordinate sign-gestalt-readinesses as to how to get away from such a "threatening" object.

We suggested as a tentative list of the fundamental appetites and aversions, the following:

Appetites	*Aversions*
Food-hunger	Fright (Injury-avoidance)
Sex-hunger	Pugnacity (Interference-avoid-
Excretion-hungers	ance)
Specific contact-hungers	
Rest-hunger	
Sensory-motor-hungers (i.e., the esthetic and play hunger)	

Lastly, the justification and value of such a formulation is dependent upon an underlying assumption that the goings-off of such appetites and aversions in specific instances will always prove to be docile relative to the proved ultimate appearances or non-appearances of such quiescences and disturbances.[16]

[16] It is obvious that our general theory as thus worked out derives not only from Craig (see above p. 272 f.) but also initially and perhaps most fundamentally from McDougall.

Cf. W. McDougall, *An Introduction to Social Psychology* (London, Methuen, 1908).

——————— *Outline of Psychology* (New York, Charles Scribner's Sons, 1923).

——————— *Outline of Abnormal Psychology* (New York, Charles Scribner's Sons, 1926).

——————— The Hormic Psychology. *Psychologies of 1930* (Worcester, Mass., Clark Univ. Press, 1930), pp. 3-36.

It has also been much influenced by Woodworth and Kempf.

R. S. Woodworth, *Dynamic Psychology* (New York, Columbia Univ. Press, 1918).

——————— *Psychology*, rev. ed. (New York, Henry Holt and Company, 1929).

E. J. Kempf, *The Autonomic Functions of the Personality* (New York, Nervous and Mental Disease Publishing Company, 1918).

REFERENCES

Craig, W., Male doves reared in isolation. *J. Anim. Behav.*, 1914, **14**, 121-133.
——————, Appetites and aversions as constituents of instincts. *Biol. Bull.*, 1918, **34**, 91-107.
Freud, S., *Three Contributions to Sexual Theory* (New York, Nervous and Mental Disease Publishing Co., 1910).
Hunter, W. S., The modification of instinct from the standpoint of social psychology. *Psychol. Rev.*, 1920, **27**, 247-269.
Jones, H. E. and Jones, M. C., Fear. *Childhood Educ.*, 1928, **5**, 136-143.
Jones, M. C., A laboratory study of fear: the case of Peter. *Ped. Sem.*, 1924, **31**, 308-315.
——————, Conditioning and unconditioning emotions in infants. *Childhood Educ.*, 1925, **1**, 317-322.
Katz, D., Tierpsychologie und Soziologie des Menschen. *Zsch. f. Psychol.*, 1921-22, **88**, 253-264.
Kempf, E. J., *The Autonomic Function of the Personality* (New York, Nervous and Mental Disease Publishing Co., 1918).
McDougall, W., *An Introduction to Social Psychology* (London, Methuen, 1908).
——————, *Outline of Psychology* (New York, Charles Scribner's Sons, 1923).
——————, Outline of Abnormal Psychology (New York, Charles Scribner's Sons, 1926).
——————, The Hormic Psychology. *Psychologies of 1930*, (Worcester, Mass., Clark Univ. Press, 1930, 3-36).
Peckham, G. W. and Peckham, E. G., Some observations on the mental powers of spiders. *J. Morphology*, 1887, **1**, 383-419.
Schjelderup-Ebbe, T., Beiträge zur Sozialpsychologie des Haushuhns. *Zsch. f. Psychol.*, 1921-22, **88**, 225-252.
Tolman, E. C., Instinct and purpose. *Psychol. Rev.*, 1920, **27**, 217-233.
——————, Can instincts be given up in psychology? *J. Abn. & Soc. Psychol.*, 1922, **17**, 139-152.
——————, The nature of instinct. *Psychol. Bull.*, 1923, **20**, 200-216.
——————, The nature of the fundamental drives. *J. Abn. & Soc. Psychol.*, 1926, **20**, 349-358.
Watson, J. B., Recent Experiments on How We Lose and Change Our Emotional Equipment. *Psychologies of 1925* (Worcester, Mass., Clark Univ. Press, 1926), pp. 59-82.
Woodworth, R. S., *Dynamic Psychology* (New York, Columbia Univ. Press, 1918).
——————, *Psychology*. rev. ed. (New York, Henry Holt and Company, 1929).

Chapter XIX

SECOND-ORDER DRIVES AND PERSONALITY-MECHANISMS

1. Human and Animal Complexities

IN the preceding chapter, the concept of the fundamental, first-order drives, the appetites and aversions, was developed. These first-order drives underlie all behavior. They provide the organism with his ultimate demands for and against plus his initial, though relatively vague, sign-gestalt-readinesses as to where and how to satisfy such demands.

The total picture as to motivation is, in reality, however, much more complicated. In many of the lower species the list of fundamental appetites and aversions is, it would seem, far more extended and contains items far more specific. For example, birds and insects apparently possess in addition to the more fundamental appetites and aversions, listed in the previous chapter, many other more specific ones, such as: to build a nest, to catch a grasshopper, to sting a caterpillar, to spin a cocoon, and the like. Again, in man and some of the other higher animals, there seem to be in addition to the first-order drives, certain subsidiary, or second-order, drives. These second-order drives are ancillary to the first-order ones. They are such as curiosity, gregariousness, imitativeness and the like. These are, obviously, of a character to be useful, in the long run, to any or all of the more fundamental, first-order drives. Finally, it appears that in human beings (and possibly in the other primates as well) there tend to get developed, on top of both the first-order and the second-order drives, certain still more subsidiary, and acquired, but relatively enduring, mechanisms, which for want of a better name, we may call "personality-mechanisms."

In the remainder of the present chapter we shall consider these two latter classes only: viz., the second-order drives and the personality-mechanisms; while we shall leave for the following chapter a discussion of the more specific appetites and aversions to be found, it would seem, in some of the lower species.

2.   The Second-Order Drives

The second-order drives may be roughly characterized as demands to get to or from certain relatively general environmental situations, plus certain more or less specific sign-gestalt-readinesses as to how to get thus to and from. Further, they are to be characterized by the fact that such demanded, or to-be-avoided, general environmental situations are ones which are likely to prove useful in the long run as means to any or all of the first-order appetites and aversions. Thus, as examples of such second-order drives, we may cite: *curiosity, gregariousness, self-assertion, self-abasement,* and *imitativeness.* Such a list is purely tentative. Other items are probably to be added to it and some of those here included may have to be deleted. It will, however, suffice for the purpose of illustration.

3.   Two Possibilities: (a) the Second-Order Drives Are Docile; (b) They Go Off in Their Own Right

Granting that the second-order drives do thus usually tend to prove ancillary to the first-order drives, there are, nevertheless, two alternative hypotheses as to the true nature of this relationship.

(a) The first of these would be the hypothesis that this usefulness to the first-order drives is, as such, also immanently involved in the going-off of the second-order drive. Whether a given second-order drive went off, in any given instance, would, on this hypothesis, be "docile" relative to the "proved" helpfulness of the goal of this second-order drive with respect to one or more of the first-order drives. If the given second-order drive ceased to prove helpful, it would cease to go off. If this hypothesis be correct, a second-order drive must be said to involve and define a superordinate sign-gestalt-readiness to the effect that the presence of its own end will prove useful for getting on to the more ultimate, physiological ends of quiescence (or prevention of disturbance) demanded by first-order drives. A second-order drive would thus contain both its own immediate sign-gestalt-readiness as to how to get to its own end plus an additional superordinate sign-gestalt-readiness to the effect that its own end will prove a means to the ends of the first-order drives.

(b) The second alternative hypothesis would be that the going-off of the second-order drives is, on the contrary, independent of their specific, immediately proved value or lack of value relative to first-order drives. On this second hypothesis, the second-order drives would be relatively independent phenomena. They would no longer, in any truly cognitive sense, be subsidiary, or subordinate, to the first-order drives. They would have ancillary value relative to the latter. But this value would be outside their own purview and ken. It would result from the happy accidents of evolution, not from any interconnecting cognitive (i.e., sign-gestalt) connections per se.

If, now, it be asked, which of these two hypotheses is the more tenable, the answer is that there is as yet but little empirical evidence for deciding. Our guess, however, is that each hypothesis probably holds in some measure and under some conditions. If, for example, one "ideationally runs back and forth" over the array of one's friends (and even more so perhaps, if one thus "ideationally" reviews one's relatives), one notes a depressingly large number of individuals in whom curiosity, gregariousness, self-assertion, self-abasement, or imitativeness appear surprisingly undocile—individuals in whom it seems impossible to induce any restraint in the exercise of these second-order impulses. Such individuals continue to be curious, gregarious, self-assertive, self-abasive, imitative, wholly irrespective of consequences. For them, the mere contact with, and handling of, strange objects, the mere presence of a crowd, the mere state of being dominant, or conversely of being humble, the mere act of "copy-catting" seem to be ultimate and non-subordinate "goods."

But such observations as to one's friends and relatives is often no doubt biassed. The reverse sort of situation undoubtedly also holds. For there are to be observed other cases in which curiosity, gregariousness, self-abasement, self-assertion, imitativeness, are docile. Certain individuals under some conditions, undoubtedly can be checked and curbed in their excesses of curiosity, gregariousness, self-assertion, etc., by the proved consequences of these relative to the first-order drives.

Our final guess, in default of any really adequate evidence (such evidence might perhaps be obtained more readily by working with some of the higher animals than with man), is that the second-order drives are in some measure due to their own innate initiating physiological states, and that they then have certain final physiological quiescences and disturbances of their own. On the other hand, we shall assume also that in most individuals these demands for and against such second-order quiescences and disturbances are not so strong but that such drives can become in some degree attached, as subordinate, to the more fundamental first-order drives, and come to show docility relative to the latter.

4. Second-Order Quiescences and Disturbances

But another question here immediately arises. What are we to conceive to be the characters of the actual second-order physiological quiescences and disturbances? What physiological quiescences, per se, can we, that is, suppose to be consummated by such very generalized situations as contact with and handling of strange objects, the presence of a crowd, a state of dominance, or one of subservience, the doing of what one sees others doing? Obviously, our present-day physiology is not adequate to an answer. Dunlap, to be sure, has suggested that the demands for dominance and submission are located in some disturbances of the tissues of the circulatory and respiratory systems.[1] And Kempf [2] has evolved a physiological hypothesis of the various drives, basing them upon general disturbances of the viscera and skeletal postures controlled by the autonomic nervous system. But it must be admitted that these are all but arm-chair speculations. The best that can be said about them is that they perhaps do justify the general notion that the second-order drives could have their own physiological initiating states plus their own definitive quiescences and disturbances.

5. The Second-Order Drives Are Aversions

Finally, if we review the above, tentative, list of second-order drives and ask whether these are appetites or aversions, what is

[1] K. Dunlap, *Elements of Scientific Psychology* (St. Louis, C. V. Mosby Co., 1922), p. 324.
[2] E. J. Kempf, *The Autonomic Functions and the Personality* (New York, Nervous and Mental Disease Publishing Company, 1918).

the answer? On the whole it will be that they seem to be aversions. For they appear to be evoked primarily by external situations. They go off when stimuli "threaten" a state of unfamiliarity (and its presumably resulting physiological disturbance), one of lack of company, one of dominance by others, etc. They are like the first-order aversions, continuously ready to go off, whenever such threatening or disturbing stimuli are presented. They are not cyclical and spontaneously aroused, as are appetites. The organism does not, it would seem, wake up in the middle of the night and (out of a clear, moon-lit sky) start to be curious, to be gregarious, to be assertive, to be submissive, or to be imitative; as he may wake up, and be hungry or lustful. He has to be presented first with some "threatening" stimulus.

So much for the second-order drives, let us turn now to what we shall call the personality-mechanisms.

6. Personality-Mechanisms

In the remainder of this chapter we shall discuss, albeit amateurishly, the nature of the "personality-mechanisms" which, it seems to us, get built up on the first-order and second-order drives. It is the operations of such personality-mechanisms which constitute most of the phenomena which are of interest to the psychiatrist and to the psychoanalyst. More specifically we should conceive under this heading such obvious and well-attested affairs as phobias, compulsions and sex-perversions, on the one hand, and the somewhat less certain, psychoanalytically conceived processes of an Œdipus complex, transference, sublimation, compensation, symbols, etc., on the other.

In general, we believe that all these various processes can be profitably conceived from the standpoint of our concepts. They all seem to us to be in the nature of distortions or modifications of the sign-gestalt-readinesses and -expectations released by first-order and second-order drives. But, because what we shall thus have to say is so very speculative, it will suffice, if we here suggest in detail how we would treat only two of the above listed sorts of phenomena, viz., phobias and symbols. Finally it is to be noted that in the consideration of these two we shall discover the operation of three types of sign-gestalt-modification. These we shall designate as *repression, fixation* and *sign-magic*.

Indeed, our final hypothesis will be that all such personality-mechanisms as those listed above, and whatever others there may be, can be reduced to various combinations of, or interactions among, repression, fixation and sign-magic. Phobias illustrate repressions and fixations. They do not illustrate sign-magic. For an illustration of the latter we shall consider symbols.

7. Phobias

A phobia is to be defined as the "fear of some type of object or situation, persistent and without apparent grounds."[3] Agoraphobia ("morbid fear of being in any open space"[4]) and claustrophobia ("pathological fear of closed spaces"[5]) are typical examples. Or phobias may be more individual and unique, as for example, a phobia of being grasped from behind or a phobia of the sound of running water. For purposes of analysis we shall take example of these two latter varieties, which have been reported by Bagby. We quote verbatim:[6]

"Case I"

"A young woman of good heredity developed during her childhood a severe phobia of running water. She was unable to give any explanation of her disorder, which persisted without noticeable improvement from approximately her seventh to her twentieth year. . . .

"Her fear reaction to splashing sounds was especially intense. For instance, it was necessary for her to be in a distant part of the house when the bath tub was being filled for her bath, and during the early years, it often required three members of the family to give the bath. . . .

"During her twentieth year an aunt, Mrs. G., came to visit at her home. This lady had not seen her niece in thirteen years. She was met at the station by the mother of the girl, who told her of

[3] H. B. English, *A Student's Dictionary of Psychological Terms*, 3rd ed. (Yellow Springs, Ohio, The Antioch Press, 1928). In general we shall find it convenient to take our definitions of these different mechanisms from this extremely well-done psychological hand-book.

[4] H. B. English, *op. cit.*

[5] H. B. English, *op. cit.*

[6] E. Bagby, The etiology of phobias, *J. Abnorm. & Soc. Psychol.*, 1922, **17**, 16-18, p. 16 f.

See also in general for what seems to us a conservative and very illuminating discussion of the most of the personality-mechanisms. E. Bagby, *The Psychology of Personality* (New York, Henry Holt and Company, 1928).

the daughter's condition. On arrival at the house, she met the girl and her first words were 'I have never told.' This served to provoke a recall of the following episode.

"The mother, the aunt, and the little girl—she was then seven years old—had gone on a picnic. Late in the afternoon the mother decided to return home but the child insisted that she be permitted to stay longer with her aunt. The mother agreed to this on the child's promise to be obedient to the aunt. The two then went into the woods for a walk and the girl, disobeying her aunt's instructions, ran off alone. The aunt followed, and after a search, found the child lying wedged among the rocks of a small stream with a water-fall pouring down over her head. She was screaming with terror. They proceeded to a farm house where the wet clothes were dried. The child expressed great fear that her mother would learn of her disobedience, but the aunt reassured her with the promise, 'I will never tell.' They returned home and the aunt left the house next morning without seeing her niece. The child was thus left with no one in whom she could confide and had a period of anxiousness. The phobia developed shortly after this.

"After recalling this experience of her childhood, the young woman found it possible to approach running water without discomfort. And gradually the special adjustments, which her phobia had necessitated, disappeared."

"Case II"

"A man suffered from a phobia of being grasped from behind, the disturbance appearing early in childhood and persisting to his fifty-fifth year. When walking on the street he was under a compulsion to look back over his shoulder at intervals to see if he was closely followed. In social gatherings he arranged to have his chair against the wall. It was impossible for him to enter crowded places or to attend the theatre.

"In his fifty-fifth year he returned to the town in which he had spent his childhood. After inspecting his old home, he went to the corner grocery and found that his old boyhood friend was still behind the counter. He introduced himself and they began to reminisce. Finally the grocerman said this, 'I want to tell you something that occurred when you were a boy. You used to go by this store on errands, and when you passed you often took a handful of peanuts from the stand in front. One day I saw you coming and hid behind a barrel. Just as you put your hand in the pile of peanuts, I jumped out and grabbed you from behind. You screamed and fell fainting on the sidewalk.'

"The episode was remembered and the phobia, after a period of readjustment, disappeared." [7]

[7] E. Bagby, The etiology of phobias, *J. Abnorm. & Soc. Psychol.*, 1922, 17, 16-18, p. 17.

Bagby then goes on to point out the following features common to the two cases which seem to him significant:

"1. The disturbance dates from a traumatic episode to which the patient reacted with intense fear.

"2. The episode involves some forbidden action on the part of the patient which prevents discussion of the experience with parents or others who might give reassurance. This element of guilt and the unpleasant character of the experience presumably cause 'protective forgetting,' or repression.

"3. The symptoms disappear when recall is effected. . . ." [8]

8.   The Repression Explanation

In emphasizing the above three points, Bagby seems to point towards what we would term a simple "repression" explanation. But we must be more specific. Our assumption will be that in both these cases the original episode built up a multiple sign-gestalt-field of the sort represented by the following figure:

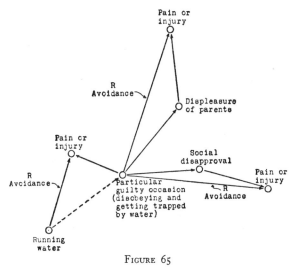

FIGURE 65

(The figure for Case II would be exactly similar—save that in place of "running water" there would be substituted "exposed back," and in place of "disobeying and getting trapped by water" there would be substituted "stealing peanuts.")

[8] E. Bagby, op. cit., p. 17 f.

FIGURE 65 is to be read as follows: The original episode is to be supposed to have established the sign-gestalt whereby the specific sign-object "running water" ("exposed back") became a sign for the particular past guilty occasion as significate. (To stay in the presence of such a sign is to threaten to come again into the presence of that past occasion.) But this past occasion was in its turn, by virtue of its immediately fearful character, a sign for pain or injury. The little girl was probably frightened merely at being trapped under the water per se, and the little boy merely at being jumped out at from behind. Hence the running water, or the unprotected back, was to some extent already a direct sign for injury or pain. And it appears, further, that it also became, as a result of the specific guilty situation, a sign, a threat, for more pain or discomfort to result from the displeasure of the parents. Finally, it seems probable that the moral code was sufficiently developed in the child so that the guilty situation also threatened yet another pain, i.e., one to result from general social disapproval. Running water or exposed back thereafter becomes a sign for all three threats.

But the operation of these threats properly constitutes a phobia, and is not just a mere fear, because the operation of at least two of them is unknown to the patient. They have been repressed. The patient no longer is consciously aware of the original guilty occasion which acts as an intervening term. The reappearance of the original type of stimulus-object, running water or exposed back, still operates as a sign for this guilty occasion and evokes it to the extent that it can then operate as a sign to threaten the further pain. But this intermediate term does not get into consciousness. It operates, but it cannot be consciously attended to— i.e., it cannot be adjustmentally run-back-and-forth in front of.

But what, it may be asked next, is the reason for, and *modus operandi* of, this repression? Our answer would be that the threats of pain, which were released by the original guilty occasion, served to cause at that time an avoidance of the signified resultant displeasures of parents and of society; and that this avoidance of the significates led very properly, in so far as possible, to an avoidance of the sign (i.e., of the guilty occasion itself). This could not, however, be avoided as long as it was actually, perceptually present. But, as soon as it was past, the patient could avoid it in that he could fail "consciously" to remember it. He could avoid any adjustmental running-back-and-forth in front of it. This did not prevent its operating as an intermediate term in the total sign-gestalt sequences, but it did, at least, prevent these sequences from coming to conscious light.

9. The Freudian Unconscious

And here, of course, under this concept of repression we have the basis for the whole psychoanalytical doctrine of the unconscious. Entities which can be repressed from consciousness are not apparently prevented from operating in their original sign-gestalt sequences.[9] But they do seem to be cut off from the effects of new, more recently acquired experiences. It is to be noted that the cure for these phobias came almost at once as soon as the repressed items were brought back into consciousness. For, given the changed make-up, that is, the revised and more extended field of the more mature individual, the particular original occasions no longer threatened pain. The grown girl or man no longer feared parental displeasure as a result of such childhood escapades. Hence the mere bringing of this repressed intervening term into the compass of the consciously get-at-able, caused the whole sign-gestalt sequence in which it was functioning to break down. Repression causes the repressed terms to be insulated. It allows them still to operate in their original sign-gestalt sequences, but it insulates them from the contamination of new circumambient experiences and resultant field-developments.

10. The Given Examples Did Not Involve Fixation

But it appears, further, if we examine other cases in the literature, that there are plenty of instances in which the mere overcoming of the repression, the mere bringing of the repressed items up into the compass of consciousness—up into the realm where adjustmental runnings-back-and-forth relative to them are possible—does not effect a cure. In such cases, our hypothesis must be that *fixation*, as well as repression, has been at work.

We conceive fixation (see above Ch. X, p. 152 f.) as a case where

---

[9] This would seem, in a general sense, to be analogous to the interpretation elaborated by Holt in *The Freudian Wish*. Cf. E. B. Holt, *The Freudian Wish* (New York, Henry Holt and Company, 1922).

what is originally a sign-gestalt-connection becomes reduced to the level of a purely mechanical attachment. Thus, it appears probable, although the necessary evidence seems to us to be by no means as yet altogether at hand, that certain originally preparatory acceptances or rejections of the given objects as signs leading on to such and such to be reached "good" significates (or to be avoided "bad" significates) may through repetition come to lose their original truly cognitive, or *sign* characters and become merely "mechanical," "fixated," "conditioned," "stamped-in."

Thus, to return to our illustrations above, it might have been that the recalling of the original childhood experience of being caught in the water or jumped at from behind by the grocer, even though the latter were the true initial cause of the phobia, would not have caused a cure, or at most only an incomplete one. In such a case we should have to assume that the connection between the water stimulus (or that of the exposed back) and the final resultant fear responses (the R's in the diagram) had become so fixed as to have been reduced practically to the level of a reflex—something going off willy nilly irrespective of consequences. "Fixation" is, in short, our term for such a process of reduction.

11. Symbols and Sign-Magic

English,[10] defining symbol, writes:

"Symbolism plays an important part in psychoanalysis. *Unconscious wishes* are symbolized in consciousness by ideas or action, which (in unexplained fashion) partially satisfy *repressed* cravings, though the goal of the craving is not actually attained. As attempts at satisfaction, Hamilton's term, INDIRECT RESPONSIVENESS, would seem more descriptive. If the fact that the actions reveal the repressed craving is emphasized, symptom rather than symbol is the term. But in addition, the Freudians posit a system of equivalents, certain ideas being the regular representatives of certain cravings, though the patient is unaware of their "deeper" meaning. These are unintentional symbols."

Now our doctrine relative to such symbols (their favorite *loci* seem to be hysterical symptoms and dreams) is that, in them, the patient is operating with the sign as he would with the *repressed significate* of that sign. He is performing a *sign-magic*.

[10] H. B. English, *A Student's Dictionary of Psychological Terms*, 3rd ed. (Yellow Springs, O., Antioch Press, 1928).

In most of the cases discussed by the Freudians the symbols cover or hide an erotic need. The patient draws a picture or dreams a dream which the analyst shows to be of sexual significance—in the sense that the objects of picture or dream are representative, i.e., "signs for" the genitalia or for the sex-act. The patient is for some reason forbidden the actual sexual goal and relieves his tension by having commerce, not with this goal-situation, but with objects, drawings or fantasies, which latter, given the conventions of acts or of speech (see above, Ch. XV, p. 238 f.), are signs for such sexual goal. Furthermore it is often the case that the actual sexual significate itself is "repressed" so that the patient himself is quite unaware of the true relationship between the sign which he thus draws or dreams and its actual significate. He does with the sign as he would like to do with the significate. He performs a sign-magic.

Such sign-magic is not, however, of course always unaccompanied by a knowledge of its significance, especially if the goal be one which is not repressed but merely in some objective way prevented. Burning in effigy is the classical example. The mob does to the sign what it would like to do, but cannot, to the significate of that sign. Or, to turn to more naïve and childish (?) instances, Kempf writes:

"I saw children take angleworms, cook them into a paste and rub this into their backs, arms and legs in order to obtain the angleworm's power of contorting itself. A little girl's mother drank from a glass of water before going on a long journey. The little girl was obsessed with the fear that her mother would die and preserved the glass of water to keep her alive. . . . Some savages sprinkle water on the ground amid religious incantations to stimulate rain. This is a common practice in some present-day religions. We collect mementoes and souvenirs, erect monuments, dedicate books, buildings, charities, etc., all for the purpose of giving ourselves stimuli that, as substitutes, have the capacity of relieving the affective cravings." [11]

Sign-magic is doing to the sign what one would consciously, or unconsciously, like to do to the significate either because one thereby hopes actually to achieve the desired significate-effect or be-

[11] E. J. Kempf, *Psychopathology* (St. Louis, C. V. Mosby Co., 1920), p. 40 f. The book is filled with innumerable instances of such symbolizations, primarily among the insane.

cause, in some strange way,[12] the presence of the sign achieves some degree of the physiological quiescence which, it would seem, could only be achieved by the actual presence of the significate.

So much for our very tentative and meager suggestions as to personality-mechanisms.[13]

[12] The whole situation is, of course, very complicated and needs a lot of strictly physiological analysis and investigation.

[13] For an extraordinarily comprehensive summary and analysis of all the work on personality and related phenomena to date, cf. A. A. Roback, *The Psychology of Character* (New York, Harcourt, Brace and Company 1927).

REFERENCES

Bagby, E., The etiology of phobias. *J. Abnorm. & Soc. Psychol.*, 1922, 17, 16-18.

——————, *The Psychology of Personality* (New York, Henry Holt and Company, 1928).

Dunlap, K., *Elements of Scientific Psychology* (St. Louis, C. V. Mosby Co., 1922).

English, H. B., *A Student's Dictionary of Psychological Terms.* 3d ed. (Yellow Springs, O., Antioch Press, 1928).

Holt, E. B., *The Freudian Wish* (New York, Henry Holt and Company, 1922).

Kempf, E. J., *The autonomic Functions and the Personality* (New York, Nervous and Mental Disease Publishing Co., 1918).

——————, *Psychopathology* (St. Louis, C. V. Mosby Co., 1920).

Roback, A. A., *The Psychology of Character* (New York, Harcourt, Brace and Company, 1927).

Chapter XX

INSTINCT, CHAIN APPETITES AND AVERSIONS, SKILLS

1. The Question Concerning Instincts

IT is obvious that a great deal of the sort of thing which we
have been considering in the two preceding chapters is
closely related to that most moot concept, or at any rate
term, in popular and social psychology, instinct.[1] It may be well,
therefore, to pause for a moment to consider what is to be our
attitude concerning this concept and term. A statement on these
matters is particularly in point here, because the specific phenomena now to be considered are especially of the sort with regard to which the notion of instinct has been in the past most
frequently bandied about.

The recent attack upon the doctrine of instincts seems to have
consisted, in part, in violently asserting that it is inconceivable
that there should be any complete behaviors, or even phases of
behavior, dependent solely upon inheritance.[2] Or else, putting it
in milder terms, it has been pointed out that the character of
any response obviously depends both on a given heredity and
on the character of the environment in which the organism has
matured. Every response, when it first appears, actually has

[1] Cf. L. L. Bernard, *Instinct, a Study in Social Psychology* (New York,
Henry Holt and Company, 1924).
E. C. Wilm, *The Theories of Instinct* (New Haven, Yale Univ. Press, 1925).
[2] Cf. Z. Y. Kuo, Giving up instincts in psychology, *J. Phil.* 1921, **18**, 645-664.
——————— How are our instincts acquired, *Psychol. Rev.*, 1922, **29**, 344-365.
——————— A psychology without heredity, *Psychol. Rev.*, 1924, **31**, 427-448.
——————— The net result of the anti-heredity movement in psychology,
Psychol. Rev., 1929, **36**, 191-199.
J. B. Watson, What the Nursery Has to Say About Instincts, *Psychologies
of 1925* (Worcester, Mass., Clark Univ. Press, 1926), pp. 37-58, *Ped. Sem.*,
1925, **32**, 327-345.
——————— The behaviorist looks at instincts, *Harpers*, **155**, 228-235.

already a past history both of heredity and of the organism's preceding concourse with an environment. An organism and its responses cannot mature without constant aid and stimulation from an environment. Every response when it appears, represents a convergence between the effects of both inherited dispositions and past environmental media.[3] Responses cannot, therefore, it is said, be subdivided into the two neat categories: instinct, or the primarily hereditarily induced, on the one hand; and habit, or the primarily environmentally induced, on the other. There can be no behavior purely dependent upon innate endowment and none purely dependent upon past training.

This latter criticism is certainly, in some very general sense, valid. It is clear (to quote Carmichael) that "in all maturation there is learning; in all learning there is hereditary maturation." [4] Yet this basic situation does not, we must now assert, preclude the possibility of a nonetheless pragmatically useful distinction between such responses, or immanent determinants of a response, as are due primarily to heredity plus mere normal maturation, and such other responses, or aspects, as are due primarily to the effects of learning resulting from special environments.

For, as Marquis has pointed out, a quite workable and useful distinction between the relatively pure effects of heredity and the relatively pure effects of biologically unusual external environments, is still feasible: first, because the individual, while in the embryonic stage, is provided in practically all species with a relatively standardized environment; and, second, also because of the fact that even after birth, an individual's own internal intra-cellular and inter-cellular environments remain relatively standardized. Thus it appears that, whereas it is true that all responses do, absolutely speaking, depend upon both environment and heredity, it is also true that much of this environment remains standardized, e.g., the intra-cellular and inter-cellular environments plus the early hereditarily provided external environments of womb, albumen and shell, cocoon, etc., and can therefore be assumed practically constant for all individuals. And, such being the situation, it seems that there will be varieties, or phases, of

[3] For a recent summary of these arguments and the resultant "convergence" doctrine cf. D. G. Marquis, The criterion of innate behavior, *Psychol. Rev.*, 1930, **37**, 334-349.

[4] L. Carmichael, Heredity and environment: are they antithetical? *J. Abnorm. and Soc. Psychol.*, 1925, **20**, 245-260.

response which may still usefully be called instincts because their maturation depends upon and requires interaction with only such relatively normal and standardized environments. The term instinct can thus be retained for all those types, or determinants, of response, which practically all the individuals of the given species, irrespective of special environmental training, tend to exhibit. Instincts will be varieties, or phases, of response primarily due to innate endowment plus a biologically provided normal, or standard, environment.

2. Lists and Types of Instincts

Granted the above definition, the next question becomes what responses, or phases of response, may be said thus to qualify as instincts. This is a more difficult matter. Particularly in the case of human beings, the development of relatively artificial environments, that is, environments not inevitable, given the mere biological character of the species, is with human beings so much *de rigueur* that the discovery and listing of responses, or phases of response, solely due to heredity, plus a purely biologically provided "normal" environment, seems almost insuperable. We may, however, hazard some guesses.

In the first place, we shall suggest that the appetites and aversions, i.e., the first-order drives, and the second-order drives, discussed in the two preceding chapters, as these are found both in human and subhuman animals, are in their main characters largely innate and will, therefore, qualify as instincts.

Secondly, we shall suggest that, in addition to the above two sorts of general drives, there are also to be found in the lower organisms, and perhaps also in untutored man, certain chains of minor appetites and aversions—that is, such chains of detailed innate [5] demands, and means-end-readinesses as to how to satisfy those demands, as are involved in:—the nest-building and caring-for-young activities of birds, the web-spinning, prey-catching, nest-constructing, egg-laying, young-raising activities of the hymenoptera, the parturition activities of primates, and the like. Such activities consist, we shall say, in chains of relatively detailed in-

---

[5] For convenience we may from now on use the terms "innate" and "hereditary" to cover both that which is truly hereditary plus that which is due also to the effect of biologically normal environments.

nate [6] demands plus innate means-end-readinesses as to the routes for satisfying such demands. The units of such chains will be aroused in some instances by physiologically provided sequences of minor organic excitements. In such cases these units are appetites. In other instances the units seem to arise rather as a result of appropriately provided sequences of environmental stimuli. In this latter case they are aversions. But probably in most cases the chain involves an interlarding of little detailed appetites and little detailed aversions.

Thirdly, we shall suggest that, in addition to the first-order and second-order drives and these chains of specific minor appetites and specific minor aversions, there are also to be found in both human beings and the lower animals certain innate skills or dexterities. These also because appearing to be initially innate, or the product of relatively standardized environments, we shall class under the head of instincts. Such skills are not appetites or aversions in themselves. They do not involve demands or means-end-readinesses. They are, rather, discrimination- and manipulation-dexterities at the service of the latter. They are the skills of eating, fighting, copulating, etc., which seem severally specific to the individual appetites and aversions. Or they are the more neutral skills of flying, swimming, walking, vocalizing, etc., which seem to be at the service of perhaps one and all of the appetites and aversions.

Whereas the first-order and second-order drives and the chains of detailed appetites and aversions are to be defined as demands plus means-end-readinesses as to how to satisfy those demands, the skills are to be defined as discrimination and manipulation capacities. And, further, we are now asserting that such skills often seem to be in large measure innate or the product of purely biologically normal and standardized environments. These skills are innate readinesses for the true discriminanda- and manipulanda-characters of immediately presented objects. They are innate readinesses to "perceive" correctly the innate commerce-with possibilities of the immediately presented stimulus-object—irrespective of whether or not such commerce-with possibilities are at the moment being accepted as "good" by some controlling demand and means-end-readiness or not.

In the two preceding chapters we have already described in

[6] See preceding footnote.

some detail the characters of the first-order and second-order drives. The remainder of the present chapter we shall devote to a further discussion of the chains of minor or detailed appetites and aversions and to a discussion of these seemingly innate skills.

3. Chain Appetites Among the Hymenoptera

Major Hingston, a naturalist who has observed many kinds of insects at length, has, in a recent book, laid emphasis on what he calls the "rhythm of instinct," seeming to indicate thereby this phenomenon of chain appetites and aversions. He writes:

"Instinct frequently reminds us of a chain. It often consists of a series of actions bound together like so many links. All these actions are connected in series. They form an interdependent sequence. Each is caused by the one that precedes it and is the cause of the one that follows." [7]

He then goes on to describe examples from the Mason-wasps:

"The reproductive activities of the Mason-wasps possess a fourfold rhythm. There are four links in their chain of action. *Eumenes conica* shows this clearly. First, she builds a cell; second, she lays an egg inside it; third, she stuffs the cell with caterpillars; fourth, she closes the cell with a lid. Building, egg-laying, provisioning, closing; these are the four links in her instinctive chain." [8]

Each of these four steps would seem to consist, in our terms, in the demand for a certain environmental situation (the presence of a cell, an egg inside it, caterpillars, closed cell, etc.) plus a more or less specific means-end-readiness as to how to achieve such an end.[9]

Hingston goes on to give a more detailed account of one step in this chain.

"*Eumenes conica* has built her cell. She has laid an egg in it and is collecting caterpillars. In other words, she is engaged at the third stage of her fourfold rhythm. While she is absent looking for a caterpillar I cut away the upper margin of her cell. She

[7] Major R. W. G. Hingston, *Problems of Instinct and Intelligence* (New York, The MacMillan Company, 1928), p. 38.
[8] *Op. cit.*, p. 38.
[9] Plus finally, of course, the requisite skills of flying, building, etc., involved in carrying out these means-end-readinesses.

returns. It happens to be only a visit of inspection. For some reason she has failed to find a caterpillar. However, she commences to look to her cell. It is clear that she knows that the cell has been tampered with. She investigates it carefully. Her antennæ play around the cut-away margin. She remains for a long time testing it. One cannot but believe that she knows the nature of the damage that has happened to her cell. Then she goes off. I expect to see her bring a pellet of mud and make good the damage which she has certainly observed. A wrong anticipation. Her burden is a caterpillar, not a pellet. She brings more and more of them, stuffs the cell full of them, finally closes down the cell with its upper margin still cut off.

"Now why did the wasp behave so foolishly? Why did she not re-build the margin which I had cut away? It isn't because she cannot re-build. I have often seen her repair a hole. It is because she must fulfill her rhythm. She happens to be at the provisioning stage when the problem of building is presented to her. Her business is to provision, not to build. She must stick to the business in hand. Instinct impels her to go on with her rhythm. She must keep provisioning just because she is provisioning. She is engaged at number three stage; hence she will not go back to number one." [10]

In other words, she has arrived physiologically at the specific appetite stage, for storing the nest. And this dominates to a surprising extent irrespective of the actual external situation.

Or again, he illustrates a similar situation with an example taken from the Peckhams:

"Those delightful observations recorded by the Peckhams mention a somewhat similar case. *Pompilus quenquenotatus* paralyzes spiders. The Peckhams wished to see the act of stinging. They took advantage of the wasp's habit of placing her victim temporarily on a plant while she runs into the nest to see that all is well. During the absence of the wasp in the nest the Peckhams exchanged her paralysed spider with an unparalysed one of the same species. They expected that the wasp, on her return, would sting it. But the wasp refused. She clearly knew that this was a vigorous spider and not the helpless thing that she had temporarily abandoned. But she absolutely refused to touch it. She went off to hunt for another in the woods. Again we have the same explanation. These victims must be hunted down before the act of stinging can be done. Hunting is link number one in the chain. That link must be completed before link number two can be reached." [11]

[10] *Op. cit.*, p. 39 f.
[11] *Op. cit.*, p. 43.

Again, he cites a similar case which he takes from Fabre:

"It is the habit of many species of Sphex to go through a peculiar ceremony before dragging their crickets into their burrows. They do not just pull them straight in. Their ritual is to leave them close to the entrance, then run inside the burrow, then come out and pull the cricket in. The three stages always take place: the leaving at the entrance, the domiciliary visit, the final dragging in. This little ritual gave Fabre an opportunity to play a trick on *Sphex flavipennis*. He interfered with link one in the chain. The *Sphex* had left her cricket near the entrance and was making her domiciliary visit. Fabre pulled the cricket a few inches from the hole. The *Sphex* came out, her intention being to drag in the cricket. Not finding her cricket where she expected, she had to make a search before she came on it. What did she do then? Not what she came out with the intention of doing. She dragged the cricket back to its place near the entrance and went into the hole alone. Fabre repeated the trick. Again the *Sphex* came out. Again the same manœuvre. The cricket is brought back to the correct place. Fabre repeated it forty times and the wasp always dragged the cricket back. All wasps did not act with the same pertinacity. Yet the incident shows us how strong is rhythm. The leaving of the cricket close to the entrance is the first link in the instinctive chain. This link must be completed for the instinct to follow its normal course." [12]

In all these illustrations the situation seems to be primarily one of a chain of appetites. In all of them the internal condition was more operative than the immediate external stimulus in determining what link of the chain should obtain. The insect suffers a succession of relatively specific demands—to build a cell, to lay an egg, to catch a caterpillar, etc. And she persists in each of these demands until it is satisfied—irrespective of changes in the environment which would make a shift to one of the other stages more appropriate.

4. Chain Appetites in the Nest-Building of Birds

We should cite now as a further example of a chain appetite some general observations of Swindle's on the nest-building of birds:

[12] *Op. cit.*, pp. 44-45.
For other similar observations, see J. H. C. Fabre, *The Hunting Wasps* (New York, Dodd, Mead & Co., tr. 1915), G. W. and E. G. Peckham, *Wasps, Social and solitary* (Boston, Houghton Mifflin Company, 1905).

"In many cases . . . the nests are multiple ones; at first an ordinary simple nest is constructed and then on top of this one another simple one is constructed of another kind of building material, and so on until in cases a complete nest consists of a half dozen or more such simple ones. Owing to the fact that the building material and texture vary in the different cases of the simple nests, the analysis of such a multiple nest is easily made. The first simple nest of a multiple one may consist of large sticks; a second, of smaller sized sticks; a third, of mud; a fourth, of grass or fine roots; a fifth, of hairs or fine fibres of plants; and a sixth, of feathers. I have observed considerable variations in the order of the simple nests which were constructed consecutively by the same birds. I have produced certain pronounced variations in the multiple nest by destroying it as soon as the first, second or third simple nest was constructed. After a few days, in cases after only a few hours, the birds again started building either at the same or at some new place. In many cases, the new multiple nest did not contain any of the elements of the parts which I tore away; that is, the first one or two or three simple nests were omitted in the second attempt at nest construction. In a few cases, the birds continued to collect objects, but upon reaching the tree from which the previous nest had been torn, dropped these one after another until enough material for the characteristic multiple nest of these birds had been brought and dropped. When this happened, the birds generally waited a few days and then began a new nest which, when completed, included all the simple nests as usual." [13]

5. Chain Appetites and Aversions in the Parturition of Monkeys

Finally, we should quote some extremely interesting observations on parturition in monkeys by Tinklepaugh and Hartman.

"In considering the behavior herein described, the question arises as to whether there is, in parturition, a general instinctive pattern, a sort of neural predetermination, as it were, of the succession of behavioral events. Let us point to certain outstanding features we have here presented.

"At each successive stage in the process of birth-giving, the behavior was nearly always appropriate. The swelling and irritation of genital region leads to manual exploration. The presence of mucus, urine, and fecal matter calls forth the posture and straining common to eliminatory processes. Later fetal fluids begin to ap-

[13] P. F. Swindle, Analysis of nesting activities, *Amer. J. Psychol.*, 1919, **30**, 173-186, p. 180 f.

pear. In the course of the manual investigation of the genitals, the animals licked these fluids from their hands, and this act, it seems, may have determined much of their subsequent behavior. Why these fluids are eaten we do not know, but it does appear that to the monkey subjects they are *fluids to be consumed.*

"As labor progresses with its successive contractions, the eliminatory position is taken more often, straining was more intense, and, facilitating the latter, the animals seized hold of the walls or floor of the cage. The fetus advances in the canal, causing the perineum to bulge from the pressure. Then, what have been manual exploratory movements, change to manual eliminatory movements—namely, efforts to remove the source of irritation, and the licking of the fluids from the hands continues.

"The head of the baby eventually appears at the entrance of the canal and then the manual efforts became effective. The wet, newborn baby is drawn forth and around one side to the mother's breast. The fluid is licked from both baby and maternal hands. During the washing process the genitals are again irritated by the frequent tautness of the cord when the baby is shifted from one position to another. The afterbirth is discharged into the vagina. These events result in further exploration and finally in the drawing forth of the afterbirth—a mass of tissue, which like the baby, is covered with fetal fluids. It is licked and then eaten.

"The question, why does the mother consume the afterbirth and only wash the baby, when both are bathed in the same fluids, is a pertinent one. It might be assumed that the mother, even though inexperienced, reacts to the one as a baby and to the other as an inanimate object. But we may suggest that the baby is only covered with the "to-be-consumed" fluids, whereas the afterbirth is *permeated* with them. . . . Such explanations are, naturally, only suggestive and require experimental testing.

"In surveying the very complex series of situations and responses we have summarized above, it might appear that they can be explained on the basis of chain reactions in which the response to one situation is the stimulus for the next. But the process of parturition is made up of behavior at two levels, namely, that involving the skeletal and that involving the visceral musculature, with their respective neural systems. Tabulation of the successive situations and responses would read somewhat as follows:

Situations.	*Responses.*
1. Irritated genital region.	1. Manual exploration followed by olfactory, visual and gustatory examination of hands.
2. Mucus, urine, fecal matter; uterine contractions.	2. Eliminatory posture and straining. No. 1. continued.

Situations.	Responses.
3. Fetal fluids.	3. Fluids discovered through No. 1, then licked from hands.
4. Increased frequency and intensity of uterine contractions.	4. No. 2 facilitated by pulling against walls and floor of cage.
5. Fetus advancing in birth canal; bulging perineum.	5. No. 1 changes to manual eliminatory movements. No. 3 continued.
6. Fetal head at vulva.	6 No. 5 becomes effective. Nos. 2 and 3 continued.
7. Baby's head and shoulders appear.	7. No. 5 effective, baby drawn forth and around front. Nos. 2 and 3 continued.
8. Fluid-covered baby.	8. Olfactory, visual and gustatory examination. Baby washed. No. 3 continued.
9. Tension on cord irritates vulva.	9. No. 5 renewed. No. 3 continued.
10. Afterbirth discharged into vagina.	10. No. 5 effective. No. 3 continued.
11. Fluid-permeated afterbirth.	11. No. 8 repeated. Afterbirth consumed. No. 3 continued.
12. Blood and fetal fluids on hands, feet and floor of cage.	12. Licked off as in Nos. 3, 8 and 11.

"Examination of this list of situations shows that they are for the most part, either directly or indirectly the outcome of smooth muscle functions. Under an anæsthesia affecting only the skeletal or voluntary system parturition would undoubtedly still go on. . . . In the parturitional process we have described, the smooth-muscle situations to which the skeletal behavior served as responses would incur in the given sequence, even though the skeletal behavior were inhibited. The stimuli, then, are in good part at least, the result of functions at the autonomic level, and to each of these there is a relatively appropriate response of the skeletal musculature. In the skeletal responses there is a high degree of variability, as we have shown both in the detailed descriptions and in the later discussions. Most of the mothers did achieve the same general ends, but the results were not due to uniformity of their skeletal behavior." [14]

[14] O. L. Tinklepaugh and C. G. Hartman, Behavioral aspects of parturition in the monkey (*Macacus rhesus*), *J. Comp. Psychol.*, 1931. 11, 63-98, p. 94 f.

In other words, it would appear that the operations of the smooth muscle system automatically bring about in the female, who is in labor, a succession of external or internal disturbances such as irritated genital region, fetal head at vulva, tension on cord, afterbirth, etc., and that each of these releases an innately given demand for a complementary physiological quiescence plus an innately given, more or less precise, sign-gestalt-readiness as to how to achieve this immediate minor quiescence by means of such and such general types of pullings, handlings, lickings, etc.

6. Immanent Sign-Gestalts Within Links and Between Links

Finally, in reviewing all of the above illustrations of chains of specific appetites and specific aversions we must ask to what degree there would seem to be immanent sign-gestalt-relations involved between the steps. To what extent would each little appetite or aversion in the chain seem to go off relative to its position in the whole series? Our answer is that the individual steps seem to be almost wholly blind to this total relationship. For, whenever an experimental variation has been introduced, as in the case of the insects and the birds, it has appeared that the animal had no appreciation of the place of the minor end in relation to the total sequence. The animal could make the appropriate means variations and adaptations to suit each minor end, but it could not drop this minor end itself when it was in the stage of its total "rhythm" which demanded that minor end. The animal almost invariably continued at the particular stage of nest-building, nest-provisioning, etc., which it was in, even though this stage had become useless or positively wrong. Each step in the total chain functioned as a little purposive cognitive unit, but the sequence as a whole was relatively blind and undocile.

7. Innate Skills and Dexterities

We turn, now finally, to the case of innate skills or dexterities. Under this head we understand innate discriminanda- and manipulanda-readinesses—that is, innate propensities, upon the presentation of immediate means-objects, to release appropriate discriminations and manipulations. It is to be noted first that such innate skills and dexterities are provided, in some measure, as has been already suggested, as innate parts of the appetites and aversions. The baby is provided innately, we are now contending, not only with some degree of precision (means-end-readiness) as to "what" to suck but also with a considerable degree of precision as to "how" to suck. And sexually mature male and female rats, as Stone [15] has shown, are provided innately, not only with a considerable precision as to *what* to copulate with, but also with a surprising degree of precision as to *how* to copulate. Or, similarly, the newly hatched chick is provided with not only an innate propensity to peck at small bright objects, when hungry, but also with a very considerable degree of innate skill (i.e., a skill depending mostly upon maturation) as to how to carry out such pecking.[16]

And so it goes. In each of the major, or minor, appetites or aversions, wherever carefully controlled observations have been made, it appears that the animal is in a very considerable degree provided, not only with an innate demand and an innate means-end-readiness as to what to have commerce with, but also with some degree of innate discrimination- and manipulation-skill as to the "how" of such commerces. Of course the degree and precision of such skills varies greatly from organism to organism and from one appetite or aversion to another. But, in general, it would seem to be the dictum of all the carefully controlled observations of recent years that there is at any rate some fair modicum of skill provided innately in the so-called "consummatory" responses of

[15] Cf. C. P. Stone, The congenital sexual behavior of the young male albino rat, *J. Comp. Psychol.*, 1922, **2**, 95-153.

———— The awakening of copulatory ability in the male albino rat, *Amer. J. Physiol.*, 1924, **68**, 407-424.

———— The initial copulatory response of female rats reared in isolation from the age of twenty days to the age of puberty, *J. Comp. Psychol.*, 1926, **6**, 73-83.

[16] Cf. F. S. Breed, Development of certain instincts and habits in chicks, *Behav. Monog.*, 1911, **1**, No. 1.

F. S. Breed and J. F. Shepard, Maturation and use in the development of instinct, *J. Anim. Behav.*, 1913, **3**, 274-285.

C. Bird, The relative importance of maturation and habit in the development of an instinct, *Ped. Sem.*, 1925, **32**, 68-91.

———— The effect of maturation upon the pecking instinct of chicks, *Ped. Sem.*, 1926, **33**, 212-233.

D. Mosley, The accuracy of the pecking response in chicks, *J. Comp. Psychol.*, 1925, **5**, 75-98.

most of the general and specific appetites and aversions—at least in the cases of the lower animals.[17]

Thus far, we have been considering only "consummatory" skills —the skills involved in, and specific to, the final steps of the particular appetites and aversions—i.e., such skills as those involved in the final acts of eating, copulating, laying the straws in nest-construction, and the like. There are, it appears, however, a variety of other, more neutral skills, each of which may tend to subserve many different appetites and aversions. These we are calling the neutral or preparatory skills. They would be, for example, such skills as those involved in the characteristic forms of locomotion specific to a given species, the fundamental units of grasping, and handling or the vocalization of a species.

And our contention would be that controlled laboratory observations suggest that these also are largely innate. They also seem to develop almost wholly as a matter of innate endowment plus a maturation which demands only a biologically provided standard environment.[18] In this connection we would refer merely as examples to the observations of Avery on fœtal and new-born guinea pigs [19] and to those of Carmichael on the development of the swimming movements of frog and salamander embryos.[20]

Avery found that the new-born guinea pig can crawl, stand and walk, and that these responses are possible in fœtuses delivered at least four days prior to term. They do not seem to depend upon special training *in utero*. And when they are ready they require only the appropriate environmental stimuli to call them out.

Carmichael raised frog and salamander embryos from the early

---

[17] For an extraordinarily valuable summary of the experimental literature, see C. P. Stone, Recent contributions to the experimental literature on native or congenital behavior, *Psychol. Bull.*, 1927, **24**, 36-61.

[18] *Vide* again C. P. Stone, Recent contributions to the experimental literature on native or congenital behavior, *Psychol. Bull.*, 1927, **24**, 36-61.

[19] G. T. Avery, Responses of fœtal guinea pigs prematurely delivered, *Genet. Psychol. Monog.*, 1928, **3**, 245-332.

[20] L. Carmichael, The Development of behavior in vertebrates experimentally removed from the influence of external stimulation, *Psychol. Rev.*, 1926, **33**, 51-58.
———————— A further study of the development of behavior in vertebrates experimentally removed from the influence of external stimulation, *Psychol. Rev.*, 1927, **34**, 34-47.
———————— A further experimental study of the development of behavior, *Psychol. Rev.*, 1928, **35**, 253-260.

head and tail bud, non-swimming stage in a chloretone solution of just sufficient concentration to keep them in a state of anesthesia and non-motility, without injuring their developing organs. He then introduced them into tap water, and found that as soon as they became denarcotized (twenty or thirty minutes at the maximum) that they began to swim with the same perfection as a control group of the same age raised in tap water throughout— although the latter had been free swimmers for five days. It appeared, in short, that the development of the skill of swimming was primarily a matter of innate endowment plus a maturation— which required no special external environmental training.[21]

8. Recapitulation

We summarize the contents of the present chapter as follows: (a) Wherever certain behaviors, or determinants of behavior, seem to depend for their development upon a relatively common, standardized and biologically provided environment, it seems appropriate to designate such behaviors or determinants of behavior, as instincts. (b) As the list of such instincts we suggest: (i) the demands and means-end-readinesses of the first-order and second-order drives; (ii) the demands and means-end-readinesses of certain chains of minor appetites and aversions, e.g., in the nest-building and egg-laying, etc., of birds and insects; in the parturition of monkeys, etc.; (iii) a large core in the discriminanda- and manipulanda-skills involved in the final consummatory responses of most of the appetites and aversions; and (iv) a large core in the neutral discriminanda- and manipulanda-skills (such as flying, swimming, walking, handling) which are also required to function in most appetites and aversions in addition to the consummatory skills.

[21] For a critical summary of the earlier work on the development of skill as a result of maturation under conditions where special environmental training was as much as possible prevented, see the second one of Carmichael's articles just cited.

REFERENCES

Avery, G. T., Responses of fœtal guinea pigs prematurely delivered. *Genet., Psychol. Monog.,* 1928, 3, 245-332.

Bernard, L. L., *Instinct, a Study in Social Psychology* (New York, Henry Holt and Company, 1924).

Bird, C., The relative importance of maturation and habit in the development of an instinct. *Ped. Sem.,* 1925, **32**, 68-91.

——————, The effect of maturation upon the pecking instinct of chicks. *Ped. Sem.,* 1926, **33**, 212-233.

Breed, F. S., Development of certain instincts and habits in chicks. *Behav. Monog.,* 1911, **1**, No. 1.

—————— and Shepard, J. F., Maturation and use in the development of instinct. *J. Anim. Behav.,* 1913, **3**, 274-285.

Carmichael, L., Heredity and environment: are they antithetical? *J. Abn. & Soc. Psychol.,* 1925, **20**, 245-260.

——————, The development of behavior in vertebrates experimentally removed from the influence of external stimulation. *Psychol. Rev.,* 1926, **33**, 51-58.

——————, A further study of the development of behavior in vertebrates experimentally removed from the influence of external stimulation. *Psychol. Rev.,* 1927, **34**, 34-47.

——————, A further experimental study of the development of behavior. *Psychol. Rev.,* 1928, **35**, 253-260.

Fabre, J. H. C., *The Hunting Wasps* (New York, Dodd, Mead and Company, 1915).

Hingston, R. W. G., *Problems of Instinct and Intelligence* (London, Arnold, 1928).

Kuo, Z. Y., Giving up instinct in psychology. *J. Philos.,* 1921, **18**, 645-666.

——————, How are our instincts acquired? *Psychol. Rev.,* 1922, **29**, 344-365.

——————, A psychology without heredity. *Psychol. Rev.,* 1924, **31**, 427-448.

——————, The net result of the anti-heredity movement in psychology. *Psychol. Rev.,* 1929, **36**, 191-199.

——————, The genesis of the cat's responses to the rat. *J. Comp. Psychol.,* 1930, **11**, 1-36.

Marquis, D. G., The criterion of innate behavior. *Psychol. Rev.,* 1930, **37**, 334-349.

Mosley, D., The accuracy of the pecking response in chicks. *J. Comp. Psychol.,* 1925, **5**, 75-98.

Peckham, G. W. and Peckham, E. G., *Wasps, Social and Solitary* (Boston, Houghton Mifflin Company, 1905).

Stone, C. P., The congenital sexual behavior of the young male albino rat. *J. Comp. Psychol.,* 1922, **2**, 95-153.

——————, The awakening of copulatory ability in the male albino rat. *Amer. J. Physiol.,* 1924, **68**, 407-424.

——————, The initial copulatory response of female rats reared in isolation from the age of twenty days to the age of puberty. *J. Comp. Psychol.,* 1926, **6**, 73-83.

——————, Recent contributions to the experimental literature on native or congenital behavior. *Psychol. Bull.,* 1927, **24**, 36-61.

Swindle, P. F., Analysis of nesting activities. *Amer. J. Psychol.*, 1919, **30**, 173-186.

Tinklepaugh, O. L. and Hartman, C. G., Behaviorial aspects of parturition in the monkey (*macacus rhesus*). *J. Comp. Psychol.*, 1931, **11**, 63-98.

Watson, J. B., Experimental studies on the growth of the emotions. *Psychologies of 1925* (Worcester, Mass., Clark Univ. Press, 1926), 37-58.

——————, The behaviorist looks at instincts, *Harper's*, 1927, **155**, 228-235.

Wilm, E. C., *The Theories of Instinct* (New Haven, Yale Univ. Press, 1925).

Chapter XXI

THE NATURE AND LAWS OF LEARNING—THE CONDITIONED REFLEX DOCTRINE

1. Theories of Learning

THROUGHOUT the preceding discussion susceptibility to improvement, i.e., docility, has been accepted as the fundamental character of all behavior *qua* molar. It was because, and only because, behavior does thus exhibit docility that the concepts of capacities, immanent determinants and behavior-adjustments were arrived at. Learning was and is the fundamental keystone of the system. Chapters IX, X, XI and XIV presaged a description and theory of such learning. Learning was depicted there as a matter of the refinement, integration and invention of sign-gestalt-readinesses and -expectations. But it is necessary now in order to tie up the ends of our argument to consider again and more explicitly just what this, our doctrine of learning, is and just wherein it differs from (and would criticize) other more generally accepted doctrines.

There are, it seems to us, some three other main theories of learning, to wit: the *Conditioned Reflex Theory,* the *Trial and Error Theory* and the *Gestalt Theory;* though in addition there are various hybrids or sub-varieties of these three. It should have become obvious that the doctrine of learning to be contended for in this book is a subvariety of the Gestalt Doctrine. And we shall not, therefore, attempt any formal presentation of the gestalt doctrine proper. Perhaps indeed the gestalt psychologists themselves would deny that they have a complete or final doctrine. On the other hand, we shall in the present chapter and the next, outline and criticize the Conditioned Reflex Doctrine and the Trial and Error Doctrine. Finally, in Chapter XXIII we shall summarize our own special subvariety of the Gestalt Doctrine.

2. The Conditioned Reflex Experiments

The conditioned reflex theory of learning arose out of the specific "conditioned reflex" experiments. These latter, as is well known, were originally invented and carried out by Pavlov and his co-workers, but are now being widely pursued throughout the entire psychological and physiological worlds.[1] For the benefit of a possible lay reader, it may help to quote the following description of these experiments as given by Woodworth.[2]

"About the year 1900, Pavlov, while actively at work on the physiology of digestion, using dogs as subjects, introduced a minor operation, by which the saliva from one of the glands in the dog's mouth was carried out through the cheek by a little tube, so that it could be easily observed and measured. He then noticed that the saliva flowed rapidly, not only when food was actually in the mouth, but when the dog saw food before him, or when he saw the dish in which the food was usually given him, or when he saw the person approach who usually brought him his food, or even when he heard the footsteps of that person in the next room. Now when the stimulus of food is actually in the mouth, the salivary response is a natural and permanent reflex, but the same response aroused by accessory stimuli, such as the sight of the food or of the dish or the sound of the feeder approaching, depended on the animal's past experience, and was thus artificial or subject to certain conditions. Pavlov therefore called it a conditioned reflex. . . .

"Pavlov wished to discover how these artificial reflexes got started, and so attempted to establish a conditioned salivary response to the ringing of a bell, the flashing of a light, or the brushing of the animal's skin. He soon found the way to establish any such conditioned response. His procedure was as follows.

"A hungry dog—a well-treated animal, quite at home in the laboratory—was placed standing on a table, and loosely secured by slings about the shoulders and hips, suspended from above, so that he could move only a step or two. When the animal was quiet, an electric bell began to ring, and after it had rung for a certain time (often for a minute, but a few seconds were suf-

---

[1] For summaries in English of the work of Pavlov and his students, see I. P. Pavlov, *Conditioned Reflexes. An Investigation of the Physiological Activity of the Cerebral Cortex* (Oxford, University Press, 1927).

———— *Lectures on conditioned reflexes; Twenty-Five Years of Objective Study of the Higher Nervous Activity (Behavior) of Animals* (New York, International Publishers, 1928).

[2] R. S. Woodworth, *Psychology*, rev. ed. (New York, Henry Holt and Company, 1929), pp. 152-153.

ficient), some food was placed in the dog's mouth and his saliva began to flow. After a pause of a few minutes, the bell started up again, and, as before, food was given after the bell had been ringing for a certain time. When this sequence of bell . . . food, bell . . . food had been repeated a number of times, the dog however still remaining hungry, the saliva was observed to flow before the food was supplied. The bell now caused the dog to look and turn towards the source of food, and at the same time his salivary glands became active. There was a complex motor and glandular feeding activity, initiated by the sound of the bell. Pavlov's attention was directed mostly to the glandular part of this total response, because it could be measured by measuring the flow of saliva. At the outset of the experiment, the bell did not excite any flow of saliva, but as the bell-food combination was repeated time after time, the bell began to give a small flow and then a progressively larger amount. Thus the conditioned reflex was established, at least for the moment.

"Next day the same procedure was repeated. No saliva at the first sounding of the bell, but the bell-food combination needed only to be repeated a few times before the conditioned reflex was reëstablished. . . . After a few days of this same procedure, the conditioned response (both motor and salivary) held over from one day to the next, without needing reëstablishment each day."

3. The Conditioned Reflex Theory

It is necessary now, however, for our argument to distinguish clearly between these experimental facts concerning the conditioned reflex and the theory or doctrine, as to the mechanism of all learning, which has grown out of such facts. The conditioned reflex, as a set of facts, cannot, of course, be controverted—(although undoubtedly, even as such facts, it needs considerably more analysis and examination). The conditioned reflex as a theory which has grown out of such facts is, on the other hand, as we shall now attempt to show, decidedly doubtful. For what most theorizers have done is, on the basis of the above facts, to conceive the whole mechanism of learning as reducible to the following simple picture:

Conditioned Reflex Theory

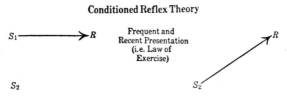

In this diagram, S_1 represents the original unconditioned stimulus which releases the salivary secretion (or other response), R. S_2 represents the conditioned stimulus (color, tone, or what not) which is presented just previously to S_1. And R, originally released only by S_1, comes by many repetitions of the sequence $S_2 - S_1$ to be released by S_2 alone. The main determining law is declared to be that of Exercise. That is, it is the frequent and recent repetition (exercise) of the stimulus-sequence $S_2 - S_1$ which alone is sufficient to establish the connection $S_2 \longrightarrow R$. The conditioned reflex *theory* assumes that *all* learning is ultimately reducible to such simple "conditionings" and that no factors other than frequency and recency are operative in establishing such conditionings.[3]

Dr. Williams [4] has ably summarized and criticized this pure conditioned reflex doctrine and the following discussion is very largely an epitome of hers.

In the first place, it is to be indicated that this simply envisaged conditioned reflex has actually been used by many authorities as constituting the essence of all learning. Thus, for example, Allport has made a very considerable (though not altogether exclusive) use of it in his *Social Psychology*. He says:

"The prepotent reflexes [Allport makes these prepotent reflexes the basis for all social behavior] are subject to synaptic changes in their central portions. The effects of such changes are (1) to extend the range and complexity of the stimuli capable of exciting the response, and (2) to refine and specialize the response itself. The first effect, which may be called an afferent modification, is brought about by the principle of the conditioned response; the second, resulting in an efferent modification, is due to the selection and fixation of successful random movements in the processes of habit formation and thought." [5]

Thus Allport holds the conditioned reflex, as described above, to be the basis for all the afferent changes in social behavior.

Watson seems to have adopted the conditioned reflex as the sole principle of all learning. He writes:

[3] It may of course be contended that the theory has never actually been held in any such "pure form." But such a pure form has been closely enough approximated to make the presentation of it desirable.

[4] K. A. Williams, The Conditioned reflex, and the sign function in learning, *Psychol. Rev.*, 1929, 36, 481-497.

[5] F. H. Allport, *Social Psychology* (New York, Houghton Mifflin Company, 1924), p. 56, cited by Williams.

"The relationship, theoretically, between the simplest cases of the conditioned responses we have studied and the more complicated, integrated, spaced and timed habit responses we are considering seems to me to be quite simple. It is the relationship apparently of part to whole—that is, the *conditioned reflex is the unit out of which the whole habit is formed.*" [6]

And Smith and Guthrie [7] and following them Frank [8] and Wilson [9] have sought to show concretely and in some detail how such a working out of the conditioned reflex principle actually obtains. We cite Williams' summary of their argument as stated for the case of a cat in a puzzle box.

"The question is, how does the cat after repeated trials come to eliminate all the useless reactions and retain only the successful one of pulling the latch which leads to release? The reply of these authors is that this comes about simply through the conditioning of various reflexes. At first the cat is attracted by the sight of the bars, say, and bites at these. But pussy has an innate aversion to the sensation of biting unyielding objects, and so withdraws from the bars. The result of numerous repetitions of this bit of behavior is that the sight of the bars becomes a conditioned stimulus for the withdrawing. The only thing which does not take on such negatively conditioned properties is the latch. The cat, therefore, when placed in the box has nothing left to do but to pull the latch." [10]

It is to be asserted now, however, that all these attempts thus to use the conditioned reflex (conceiving it as a simple matter of frequency and recency of the successive presentations of S_1 and S_2) as the basis of all learning, do so only at the cost of neglecting certain features very pertinent to the conditioned reflex facts themselves. There are indeed certain features about these facts which are quite evident even from the original Pavlov experiments themselves and yet which have been almost completely ignored by the above theories.

[6] J. B. Watson, *Behaviorism*, rev. ed. (New York, W. W. Norton and Company, 1930), p. 207. Italics ours.

[7] S. Smith, and E. R. Guthrie, *General Psychology in Terms of Behavior* (New York, D. Appleton and Company, 1921), pp. 75-133.

[8] L. K. Frank, Suggestion for a theory of learning, *Psychol. Rev.*, 1923, 30, 145-148.

[9] W. R. Wilson, Principles of selection in trial and error learning, *Psychol. Rev.*, 1924, 31, 150-160.

[10] *Op. cit.*, p. 485.

4. The Facts of "Experimental Extinction"

The first such important feature to note is a fact which appeared early in the Leningrad Laboratory, viz., that the conditioned salivary secretion to color or tone dies out rapidly unless the dog is actually given food with a fair degree of regularity, each time after the conditioned secretion has gone off—and has been measured. If, that is, too many occasions are allowed to occur in which food is not given after the conditioned secretion, then this latter tends to die out until again "reinforced" by several occasions in which food does actually follow. This sort of dying out has been designated by Pavlov as "experimental extinction."

We return to Woodworth for a brief description of this process:

"Though the conditioned response can be well established by the procedure just described, we are not to suppose that it has anything like the fixity of the natural reflex. It can be trained out in much the same way as it was trained in. Simply apply the conditioned stimulus (i.e., the artificial stimulus which has come to give the salivary response) time after time *without following it by the natural stimulus.* Here, for example, is the record of one of Pavlov's experiments, in which the conditioned stimulus was the beating of the metronome. The salivary response to this stimulus had been well established. Now on a certain day the metronome was sounded for 30 seconds, without any food, and there was a large flow of saliva. Three minutes later, the same procedure was repeated, with a smaller resulting flow of saliva; and so on, till the flow of saliva was no longer excited by the metronome alone. The gradual decrease and final extinction of the salivary response can be seen in the following table of results:

Time when each thirty-second stimulation by the metronome began	Quantity of saliva produced, in drops
12.07 p.m.	13
12.10 "	7
12.13 "	5
12.16 "	6
12.19 "	3
12.22 "	2.5
12.25 "	0
12.28 "	0

"This extinction, however, is only temporary, for if the dog is now taken away, and brought back the next day, the metronome again gives the salivary response. But if the food is omitted this day also, the extinction is more rapid than on the first day; and repetition of the extinguishing procedure, day after day, finally causes the conditioned response to disappear permanently. After one day's extinction of the conditioned response, it can be readily reëstablished by applying the food along with the metronome, but when the extinction has been very thorough, by repetition on several days, the conditioned response is very difficult to reëstablish." [11]

Now putting this fact of experimental extinction into our terms, its importance, as we see it, is that it suggests that the conditioned reflex goes off only so long as the conditioned stimulus (color, tone, or what not) proves actually, in a majority of cases, to be a "sign" for the coming food. The dog secretes saliva for color, or tone, only so long as, in a fair majority of cases, color or tone does actually precede food; i.e., is actually a sign for coming food. But this means, further, that the conditioned salivary secretion cannot be simply described as a mere reflex connection, stamped in by frequency and recency, between S_2 and R as the theorists have held; but, rather, that it must be envisaged as a response which goes off only when, and insofar as, S_2 has tended in the animal's recent past to be a sign for the coming of S_1. [12]

5. The Conditioned Response May Be Different from the Unconditioned Response

A second feature about the conditioned reflex facts which the theorizers have tended to ignore is the fact that the response "as conditioned" is often an appreciably different entity from the original "unconditioned" response. This appears very prettily in a recent experiment by Wever. In the course of an investigation of the upper limit of hearing in the cat, Wever established a conditioned breathing reflex to a tone. [13] We quote his own account of the course of the experiment:

[11] R. S. Woodworth, *Psychology*, rev. ed. (New York, Henry Holt and Company, 1929), pp. 153-55. Italics ours.
[12] The author wishes to express his indebtedness again to Dr. Williams, *op. cit.*, for this notion of the fundamentally *sign* character of the conditioned-reflex.
[13] E. G. Wever, The upper limit of hearing in the cat, *J. Comp. Psychol.*, 1930, **10**, 221-234.

"It was found that after the animal had been placed in the holder, and had become quiet, the breathing was very regular. The preliminary tests showed it to remain so at the sounding of a tone unaccompanied by shock. But when a shock was introduced, there occurred a considerable respiratory disturbance, which took the form of a sharp inspiration of large amplitude, followed usually by retarded and irregular expiration [see FIGURES 66a, 67a].

"After a number of tone-shock presentations a new feature entered, and a characteristic change in the breathing occurred *on the sounding of the tone.* The response was typically an increase in rate of breathing, with at the same time a marked decrease in amplitude [see FIGURES 66b, 67a, 67b]. This, the 'flutter response' usually occurred in the chest in the inspiratory position. The response appeared in practically the form illustrated in all the animals tested, six in number. . . .

"In the writer's opinion the response here manifested cannot be regarded as a simple, conditioned reflex. The conditioned reflex—at least, that of the text-book-type—is a response originally evoked at the delivery of one (the 'conditioning') stimulus, which by having occurred a sufficient number of times in contiguity with a new stimulus has become elicitable by the latter. The process of conditioning, according to prevalent theory, is simply one of bringing about a new stimulus-response bond; here is no question of the modification of the response, or the emergence of a new pattern of response. On such a theory, the expectation from the setting of the present experiment would be the establishing of a connection between the tonal stimulus and the sharp inspiration originally elicited by the shock. But such is not the case. The response which is finally elicitable by the tone is a *new affair,* the 'flutter,' a response that seems to be a product of the *total situation.* And not even prolonged training, in amount 7 or 8 times that adequate to establish the flutter, sufficed to set up a response to the tone in the form of a sharp inspiration.[14]

"A theory of the nature of the flutter response may be formulated as follows. The tone comes to *signalize* the appearance of a painful stimulus, the shock, and hence the animal gives to the tone the preparatory response that we call the emotion of fear. This emotional reaction probably consists of a diffuse autonomic discharge, involving, in some cases at least, the vagus nerve. That a vagal discharge gives the flutter response is evi-

[14] It appears that Upton (cf. M. Upton, The auditory sensitivity of guinea pigs, *Amer. J. Psychol.,* 1929, **41**, 412-421) also obtained a somewhat similar conditioned breathing response. He called it the "lullaby effect." In his experiments, however, he was able eventually by sufficiently long training to establish in addition to the "lullaby" a conditioned deep inspiration-expiration occurring just subsequent to the lullaby (about the time the shock would normally have appeared).

denced by a comparison of the flutter curves with the curve obtained by Lewandowsky and others by direct stimulation of the vagus." [15]

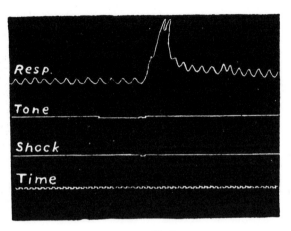

FIGURE 66a [16]

Response to Shock Only. Time in ½ Second. Cat N

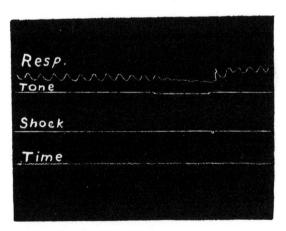

FIGURE 66b [17]

The Flutter Response. Time in 1/5 Second. Cat B

[15] *Op. cit.*, p. 226, p. 229. Italics ours.
"For references, and sample of the curves, see W. H. Howell, *Text-book of Physiology* (Philadelphia, W. B. Saunders Company, 8th ed., 1922), pp. 676 ff."
[16] *Op. cit.*, p. 227.
[17] *Op. cit.*, p. 227.

In other words, it would seem to be Wever's opinion, as it is most certainly ours, that the "conditioned" response, in this case, was a response to the second stimulus, i.e., the tone, not per se, but in its character as a sign for the coming shock. The response

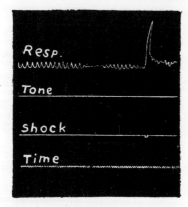

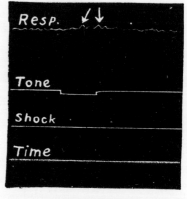

FIGURE 67a [18]

The Flutter Response. Time in 1/5 second. Cat C. The time of incidence of the tone does not show in the record, but may be determined by counting back about 6 seconds from the time of delivery of the shock.

FIGURE 67b [19]

After the establishment of the conditioned reflex
The Flutter Response complicated by vocalization. Time in 1/5 second. Cat A.

made to this sign that is, the flutter response, was appropriate to this, its sign character. It was a different response from that originally made to and appropriate to the original, unconditioned stimulus.[20]

[18] *Op. cit.*, p. 228.
[19] *Op. cit.*, p. 228.
[20] A still more recent experiment suggesting this same conclusion, viz., that the conditioned response is or may be other than the unconditioned response is that of Hilgard on conditioned eyelid reactions. Cf. E. R. Hilgard, Conditioned eyelid reactions to a light stimulus based on the reflex wink to sound, *Psychol. Monog.*, 1931, **41**, No. 184. He concludes:
"The occurrence of response decrement and reinforcement, the appearance of conditioned reactions *as added and altered rather than as substituted responses,* all point to the physiological complexity of the conditioning process.
"The limited experimentation on conditioning as a learning process and the theoretical objections which may be raised against considering the conditioned reaction to be the unit of habit, suggest that for the present it may be better to think of conditioning *as a sample of learning rather than as the foundation for learning theory."* (*Op. cit.*, p. 48. Italics ours.)

6. Molar Behaviors Need External Supports

Finally, we may point out in general that most behaviors, that is all save simple physiological reflexes, such as breathing and salivary secretion and the like, necessarily require (see above, Chapters IV and V) complementing supports from the environment.[21] They require, that is, not merely stimuli to release them, but also appropriate discriminanda and manipulanda to support them. And this means that the "conditionings" of all such behaviors inevitably require more than the simple theory diagrammed above will allow for. The "conditioned" going off of an R requires more than the mere presence of an S_2. It requires also the presence of appropriate "supports": discriminanda and manipulanda. And for these latter the simple S-R connectionism depicted by the theory makes no provision.

In the case of such responses as salivary secretion and breathing, the necessary supports are provided internally by the organism's own structure, so that this need of supports is not evident. It becomes very obvious, however, the moment the attempt is made to apply the conditioned reflex formula to responses of the sort which involve commerces with independent, external environments. For, in such cases, it becomes evident that the R which is made to the conditioned stimulus is a different R, requiring different supports, from that which is made to the unconditioned stimulus. Thus consider, for example, any ordinary discrimination-box experiment. According to simple conditioned reflex theory, the running through of the white side of the discrimination-box is the conditioned response, whereas the final eating of the food is the unconditioned response. Thus, in terms of the diagram, the situation would have to be conceived by the conditioned-reflex doctrinaires somewhat as follows:

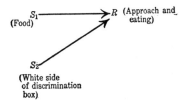

But it appears obvious, to us at any rate, that the conditioned "approach" response made to S_2, the white side of the discrimination-box, involves different supports, i.e., expectations of, and commerces with different discriminanda and manipulanda, from those involved in the original unconditioned response made to S_1, the food. The response which comes to be made to S_2 is, in short, not only, as we pointed out in the preceding sections, appropriate to the sign-character of this immediate object;—it is not only appropriate to the fact that this object (the white side of the box) is a sign for leading-on-ness to the food (the object presented by the unconditioned stimulus S_1)—but it is also appropriate to the immediate discriminanda and manipulanda characters of this immediate S_2-object.

To sum up, we note: (a) that the conditioned response is a response to the sign-relationship $S_2 \longrightarrow S_1$. And this means that it goes off only so long as that sign-relationship is "believed" in by the organism. And we note: (b) that the character of the conditioned response has to be appropriate for an immediate commerce with the object presented by the conditioned stimulus (S_2); whereas the unconditioned response was appropriate to the object presented by the unconditioned stimulus (S_1).

7.   Conditioned Reflex and Sign-Gestalt

In terms of our theory, the above criticisms lead us to say that the acquisition of a conditioned response is in reality the building up of a sign-gestalt-expectation of the form:

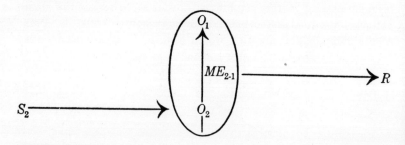

where S_2 is the conditioned stimulus, O_2 is the object indicated as immediately present by that conditioned stimulus, O_1 is the object corresponding to the previously experienced unconditioned stimulus, the arrow ME_{21} is the means-end expectation that O_1 will result from having commerce with O_2 and which has been built up by the conditioned reflex training, and R is the resultant response which results from this sign-gestalt-expectation and which gives evidence of the learning.

Let us now apply this analysis to a number of typical instances of supposed conditioned-reflex or conditioned-response learning. We begin with Pavlov's dogs.

What Pavlov's dogs acquired, according to us, was a sign-gestalt-expectation to the effect that "waiting" in the presence of the sign-object, color or sound, would lead to the significate, food. And in this case, it so happened that the response originally made to the significate was also appropriate to the sign, as a temporal signal of this coming significate. (That is, if it is physiologically good to secrete saliva for actual food, it is also good to secrete it just before the approach of food.) So that the acquisition of the sign-gestalt-expectation in this case demonstrates itself in the carrying over of one and the same response. That is, the response made after learning to the total sign-gestalt-expectation is the same as the response made before learning to the significate-object by itself.

Turn now to Wever's cats. In the case of these animals our doctrine is that what they acquired was a sign-gestalt-expectation to the effect that the sound was a sign which, if waited in the presence of, would lead to the significate, electric shock. But in this case the response appropriate for the sign is not identical with that appropriate for the significate. An electric shock, already received, is to be responded to only by a deep and sudden inspiration-expiration. An electric shock, which is expected, is appropriately responded to, on the other hand, by a sort of "holding of the breath" the "flutter response." Just why this difference we cannot say. It seems conceivable, however, that the holding of the breath (flutter) may serve in some physiological way actually to reduce the physiological injury, or disturbance, to be received from an oncoming shock. In the case of the original shock, on the other hand, no such forewarning was present to the animal, so no expectant holding of the breath was possible—a "startled" deep breath was all that could be achieved. Hence in this example the acquisition of the so-called conditioned reflex evidenced itself, not by a carry over of the original reflex from significate-object to sign-object, but by the appearance of a somewhat modified reflex in response to the sign-object.

Consider, next, the learning of a discrimination box. Our doctrine is that in it the rat achieves a sign-gestalt-expectation to the effect that the white alley, as sign, leads in a certain spatial way to the significate, food. The original "unconditioned response" was that of eating the food. The "conditioned response," on the other hand, is that of "entering" the white alley. In such a case it is obvious that the so-called "conditioned response" is very different from the unconditioned one. The "unconditioned response" was a commerce with one type of object. It was an "eating" of food. The "conditioned response" is, on the other hand, a commerce with quite a different type of object. It is the "entering" of an alley. Here also there is the acquisition of a sign-gestalt-expectation. But, whereas in the case of the simple reflex of Pavlov's dogs the appropriate response to be made to the total sign-gestalt was the same as that previously to be made to the significate-object by itself, here in the case of the discrimination box the appropriate response to the sign-gestalt as a whole is quite different from that to be made to the significate. Whereas the food was to be eaten, the white alley is to be entered and progressed along as the way to food.

Consider still another example—one discussed in a previous chapter, viz., Dr. M. C. Jones' classical experiment on the "unconditioning" of Peter to the rabbit.[22] According to the present analysis the initial fear reaction to the rabbit was the response to an immanent sign-gestalt-expectation, to the effect that the rabbit was a sign for coming injury. And the "reconditioning" or rather "unconditioning" which Mrs. Jones carried out was achieved, as we tried to indicate before, by "proving" to the child that this sign-relationship was incorrect. It consisted in demonstrating to the child that O_2 (rabbit) did not lead to O_1 (injury, or some other ultimate to-be-avoided situation). Therefore the avoidance response appropriate to S_1 was proved not to be any longer appropriate to S_2. For the child had now learned that S_2 was not really a sign of an oncoming S_1.

Finally, as one last example of this application of the sign-gestalt-conception, let us consider a case of so-called sensory-motor

22 See above, Chapter XVIII, p. 286 f.

learning. Gilhousen [23] trained subjects to manipulate a handle in four radial directions corresponding to four types of colored dots presented one at a time in an irregularly repeating stimulus series. The handle had to be moved as rapidly as possible to one or the other of the four "corners" corresponding to each successive dot appearing in the stimulus series. Gilhousen's finding, which is of interest to us here, is that, when the stimulus series was "stacked" so that certain sequences of two colors appeared with relatively great frequency, the subjects developed a strong propensity, when the first color of such a pair had been presented, not only to make the reaction appropriate to it but also to follow that by the reaction to the second color—without waiting for that second color actually to appear. In other words, when a given O_2 was followed by a given O_1 with relatively great frequency the subject built up a sign-gestalt-expectation. And to this he then made the rapid succession of responses R_2—R_1, thus

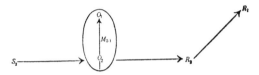

But this, of course, led him to error whenever the actual succedent to O_2 was not O_1 but O_3 or O_4.

8. Conditioned Reflex Learning the Pattern for All Sensory Integration

Finally, we would now point out that the preceding analyses suggest that the conditioned reflex, involving, as we say it does,

the formation of an ⟨gestalt diagram⟩ gestalt typifies all learning

such as that of lists of nonsense syllables, spatial arrangements of drawings, and the like, where the task of the subject is, primarily, that of acquiring means-end-relations—temporal, spatial, or what not—between successive portions of an environmental, i.e., sensory, field. Before learning, the organism is presented with what for him are relatively discrete stimuli. Each of these induces

23 H. C. Gilhousen, An analysis of errors in serial motor action. Univ. Calif. Ph.D. Thesis, 1930.

an expectation of its own immediate supporting-object, and to each of them he makes, or is capable of making, some corresponding appropriate response, thus:

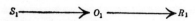

$$S_1 \longrightarrow O_1 \longrightarrow R_1$$

After learning, on the other hand, these become integrated into sign-gestalt wholes such as:

And the responses which are made to these final wholes may or may not (according to the conditions of motivation and according to the task in hand at the moment) be the same as those that were made to any one of the original, discrete items.

9. A Sign-Gestalt Once Acquired May Thereafter Function as a Single Object

One further point should now be made. Whenever a given sensory sequence is actually presented very frequently by the environment, and in such a way that there is practically always the same response to be made to the whole, a sign-gestalt-expectation will be formed. But, further, this sign-gestalt-expectation itself will in time fuse for the organism from a sign-gestalt, in which one object or part is sign for another object or part into a single

"large object." The situation will change from an $\,\bullet\!\!\!\longrightarrow$

sort of affair to an $S \longrightarrow O_{21}$ affair. The two original component O's will be no longer distinguishable, since the organism no longer (except perhaps under very special conditions) will respond to them save in this one specific sequence. What was initially a discrimination-manipulation of O_2, as the means-end-route for getting to and then discriminating and manipulating O_1, fuses into a single discrimination-manipulation of the one single larger object O_{21}.

10. The Laws of Conditioned Reflex Learning— Frequency, Recency, Primacy

Finally, accepting the above analysis of what happens in conditioned-reflex learning, we are ready to ask what are the laws of such conditioned-reflex learning. In Chapter XXIII we shall answer this question in more detail. Here we shall merely point out that frequency, recency, and something like primacy would seem to be important. The strength of the sign-gestalt-expectation that O_2 is going to lead to O_1 is undoubtedly correlated at any given time with the frequency with which this succession has been previously experienced. Similarly its strength is also correlated, it would seem, with the recency with which this sequence has been experienced. Finally, the facts of the "experimental extinction" of conditioned reflexes suggest a law of primacy, or revival after extinction—at the beginning of each new session the animal reverts to his originally previously established (but no longer confirmed) sign-gestalt-expectation. (See above, p. 324 f.)

11. Other Critics of the Pure Conditioned Reflex Doctrine

In conclusion, it must be pointed out that we are not alone in having observed the limitations of the conditioned reflex as a theory. Among those [24] who still hold to the conditioned reflex doctrine, in one form or another, there are many who have nevertheless become aware of the inadequacies of its original formulation. We may mention especially Borovski,[25] Guthrie,[26] Hull,[27] and Winsor.[28]

[24] The present chapter was written before the appearance of Thorndike's recent book, *Human Learning* (New York, The Century Co., 1931). It should be noted that Thorndike also finds "the conditioned reflex principles" *as usually stated* inadequate as an explanation of *all* learning.

[25] W. Borovski, An attempt at building a theory of conditioned reflexes on spinal reflexes, *J. Gen. Psychol.*, 1929, **2**, 3-11.

[26] E. R. Guthrie, Conditioning as a principle of learning, *Psychol. Rev.*, 1930, **37**, 412-428.

[27] C. L. Hull, A functional interpretation of the conditioned reflex, *Psychol. Rev.*, 1929, **36**, 498-511.

———— Simple trial-and-error learning: a study in psychological theory, *Psychol. Rev.*, 1930, **37**, 241-256.

———— Knowledge and purpose as habit mechanism, *Psychol. Rev.*, 1930, **37**, 511-525.

[28] A. L. Winsor, Inhibition and Learning, *Psychol. Rev.*, 1929, **36**, 389-401.

We shall not attempt here, however, to evaluate the relative successes and failures of these different essays at reformulation. They have, variously, been attempting to meet some at least of the difficulties just noted. Our feeling about them, however, is that, in the last analysis they one and all fail, because no one of them seems to have tried to meet the difficulty, that the actual going-off of responses always requires supports, as well as stimuli. Behavior is, that is, always ultimately an $S \longrightarrow O \longrightarrow R$ phenomenon or rather an $s \longrightarrow \oslash \longrightarrow {}_{n}$ phenomenon, and not a simple $S \rightarrow R$ phenomenon.

Finally *one last word*. These strictures of ours against the conditioned reflex theory are strictures against it as an adequate principle at our level of interest, i.e., at the level of behavior *qua* molar. This does not deny, however, its possible validity as a principle for the physiological units underlying behavior. It may still be that the phenomena of sign, of expectation, etc., which we find involved in learning, described at the level of behavior *qua* molar, may be built up upon, or out of, conditioned-reflex sorts of connection among the elementary physiological processes which underlie behavior. But we suspect that even as a principle *re* physiological units the conditioned reflex mechanism may not be as simple as has been supposed. There should be noted in this connection the extremely striking finding of Lang and Olmsted.[29]

They conditioned the flexion reflex in the dog's left hind leg, originally evoked by an electric shock applied to the leg, to the sound of a buzzer. Then they hemisected the cord at the level of the first lumbar vertebra on the side opposite the trained leg. And they found that the conditioned reflex to buzzer thereby disappeared. This hemisection of the cord interfered with the afferent paths from the *original unconditioned* pain stimulus.

As a check experiment they established a conditioned reflex to buzzer, the original stimulus for which was pressure, and found that this was not interfered with after both low and high hemisection of the cord on the opposite side.

They conclude: "It appears that the *whole mechanism must be*

[29] Cf. J. M. Lang and J. M. D. Olmsted, Conditioned reflexes and pathways in the spinal cord, *Amer. J. Physiol.*, 1923, **65**, 603-611.

complete for the conditioned reflex to take place, i.e., the pathways for both sets of stimuli must be intact. This would be the case for the conditioned reflex to pressure after both low and high hemisection of the cord if the fibres did not cross until the cervical region, whereas if the pain fibres cross at once, section of the cord at any level above the segment at which they enter would abolish the reflex." [30]

[30] *Op. cit.,* p. 610 f. Italics ours.

REFERENCES

Allport, F. H., *Social Psychology* (New York, Houghton Mifflin Company, 1924).

Borovski, W., An attempt at building a theory of conditioned reflexes on spinal reflexes. *J. Gen. Psychol.,* 1929, **2**, 3-11.

Cason, H., The conditioned reflex or conditioned response as a common activity of living organisms. *Psychol. Bull.,* 1922, **22**, 445-472.

Frank, L. K., Suggestion for a theory of learning. *Psychol. Rev.,* 1923, **30**, 145-148.

Gilhousen, H. C., An analysis of errors in serial motor action. Univ. Calif. Ph.D. Thesis, 1930.

Guthrie, E. R., Conditioning as a principle of learning. *Psychol. Rev.,* 1930, **37**, 412-428.

Hilgard, E. R., Conditioned eyelid reactions to a light stimulus based on the reflex wink to sound. *Psychol. Monog.,* 1931, **41**, No. 184.

Howell, W. H., *Text-book of Physiology* (Philadelphia, W. B. Saunders Company, 8th ed., 1922).

Hull, C. L., A functional interpretation of the conditioned reflex. *Psychol. Rev.* 1929, **36**, 498-511.

——————, Simple trial-and-error learning: a study in psychological theory. *Psychol. Rev.,* 1930, **37**, 241-256.

——————, Knowledge and purpose as habit mechanisms. *Psychol. Rev.,* 1930, **37**, 511-525.

Lang, J. M., and Olmsted, J. M. D., Conditioned reflexes and pathways in the spinal cord. *Amer. J. Physiol.,* 1923, **65**, 603-611.

Pavlov, I. P., *Conditioned Reflexes. An Investigation of the Physiological Activity of the Cerebral Cortex* (London, Oxford Univ. Press, Humphrey Milford, 1927).

——————, *Lectures on Conditioned Reflexes; Twenty-Five Years of Objective Study of the Higher Nervous Activity (Behavior) of Animals* (New York, International Publishers, 1928).

Smith, S. and Guthrie, E. R., *General Psychology in Terms of Behavior* (New York, D. Appleton and Company, 1921).

Upton, M., The auditory sensitivity of guinea pigs. *Amer. J. Psychol.*, 1929, 41, 412-421.

Watson, J. B., *Behaviorism*, rev. ed. (New York, W. W. Norton and Company, 1930).

Wever, E. G., The upper limit of hearing in the cat. *J. Comp. Psychol.*, 1930, 10, 221-234.

Williams, K. A., The conditioned reflex and the sign function in learning. *Psychol. Rev.*, 1929, 36, 481-497.

Wilson, W. R., Principles of selection in trial and error learning. *Psychol. Rev.*, 1924, 31, 150-160.

Winsor, A. L., Inhibition and learning. *Psychol. Rev.*, 1929, 36, 389-401.

Woodworth, R. S., *Psychology*, rev. ed. (New York, Henry Holt and Company, 1929).

Chapter XXII

THE NATURE OF LEARNING—THE TRIAL AND ERROR DOCTRINE [1]

1. The Trial and Error Experiments

WE turn now to the trial and error doctrine of learning. It, like the conditioned reflex doctrine, has grown out of a special set of the facts. More specifically, it has grown out of the sorts of facts exemplified by the rat in the maze.

The earliest account of such facts—such trial and error learning (although the name trial and error was not applied to it until slightly later)—seems to have been Lloyd Morgan's description of the learning of his fox terrier to open a gate. He writes:

"The way in which my dog learnt to lift the latch of the garden gate, and thus let himself out, affords a good example of intelligent behavior. The iron gate outside my house is held by a latch, but swings open by its own weight if the latch be lifted. Whenever he wanted to go out the fox terrier raised the latch with the back of his head, and thus released the gate, which swung open. Now the question in any such case is: How did he learn the trick? In this particular case the question can be answered, because he was carefully watched. When he was put outside the door, he naturally wanted to get out into the road, where there was much to tempt him—the chance of a run, other dogs to sniff at, possibly cats to be worried. He gazed eagerly out through the railings on the low parapet wall . . . and in due time chanced to gaze out under the latch, lifting it with his head. He withdrew his head and

---

[1] The present chapter and the next were both almost completed before the appearance of Thorndike's *Human Learning* (New York, The Century Co., 1931). The reading of the latter has proved tremendously stimulating and important. And, if it could have been done sooner, would have led us to a somewhat different organization and emphasis in the presentation of our own argument. We should have made greater use than we have here of Thorndike's present attack upon the "Law of Exercise" and of the many interesting experiments which he has presented for substantiating this attack.

Our position, however, would not have been altered as regards his "Law of Effect." And we would have continued to reject the too simple S—R "connectionism" to which even in this last presentation he still seems to cling.

looked out elsewhere; but the gate had swung open. Here was the fortunate occurrence arising out of natural tendencies in a dog. But the association between looking out just there and the open gate with a free passage into the road is somewhat indirect. The coalescence of the presentative and the re-presentative elements into a conscious situation effective for the guidance of behavior was not effected at once. After some ten or twelve experiences, in each of which the exit was more rapidly affected with less gazing out at wrong places, the fox terrier had learnt to go straight and without hesitation to the right spot. In this case, the lifting of the latch was unquestionably hit on by accident, and the trick was only rendered habitual by repeated association in the same situation of the chance act and the happy escape. Once firmly established, however, the behavior remained constant throughout the remainder of the dog's life, some five or six years." [2]

Next, perhaps, in historical significance, comes Thorndike's description of his cat getting out of the puzzle box, which has already been quoted (see above Chapter I, p. 13 f.).

Finally, to emphasize the matter, we may venture a description of our own of the trial and error learning of a rat in a maze.

In the initial trials, the rat runs hither and thither; he sniffs at the walls of the alleys; he stands on his hind legs and seeks to climb out over the sides; he walks upside down on the wire netting which roofs an alley; he falls over backward; he sits and scratches himself; he follows closely along some wall; he comes up against a blind-end; he rears on his hind legs and examines this in some detail; he backs down, turns around and retraces his steps; eventually, i.e., almost it would seem by pure chance, he reaches the entrance to the food-box; but here the door projects in such a way as to attract his attention, and he hesitates; he starts to enter and then backs out again; he repeats this many times until (long after the patience of the experimenter is exhausted) he does finally enter; and the door is dropped behind him; he runs rapidly and curiously about the food-box, sniffing and climbing at all points, often tracking through the food itself; now and then, however, he stops and takes a nibble of food, though with frequent alarums and excursions.

In the later trials, many of these "excessive and ill adaptive movements" [3] have been eliminated; the rat now runs relatively directly and with few hesitations and unnecessary sniffings and rearings into this alley, into that, and so on, until with considerable expedition, he reaches the food-box; and if perchance he goes

---

[2] C. Lloyd Morgan, *Animal Behavior* (London, Arnold, 1900), p. 144.

[3] This phrase is borrowed from Kuo; *vide* Z. Y. Kuo, The nature of unsuccessful acts and their order of elimination, *J. Comp. Psychol.*, 1922, **2**, 1-27.

into a blind, he twirls around and runs out again as rapidly as possible. And when finally he has thus reached the food-box, he goes at once to the food-dish and begins eating; and continues to do so steadily, and with few interruptions, until the time is up and the experimenter takes him out.

2. The Trial and Error Doctrine

Keeping in mind, now, the above illustrations, let us consider the theory of learning which has grown out of these sorts of facts. We may call it the trial and error "theory" (as distinct from these trial and error "facts").[4] It may be readily expounded with the help of the following simple diagram:

TRIAL AND ERROR THEORY

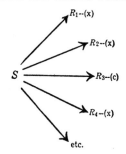

R_1, R_2, R_3, R_4, etc., represent an original array of random responses called out by a stimulus situation S, in which the x's after R_1, R_2, R_4, are to represent the fact that these are incorrect responses, and the c after R_3 is to represent the fact that it is the correct response. The theory assumes that by virtue of many repetitions of the situation, that is, by virtue of the workings of the *Law of Exercise and Effect*, the connection $S \rightarrow R_3$ gets stamped in, the connections $S \rightarrow R_1$, $S \rightarrow R_2$, and $S \rightarrow R_4$, etc., either get actively stamped out or, at the least, drop into innocuous desuetude.

There have been different varieties of this theory according as the relative importances of exercise and effect have been stressed.

[4] This theory, as we shall here present it, derives primarily from Thorndike's earlier statements. (See footnote at beginning of this chapter.) Cf. E. L. Thorndike, *Educational Psychology* (New York, Teachers' College, Columbia Univ., 1913), Vol. II, Chapters II, III and IV. Also *Animal Intelligence* (New York, The Macmillan Company, 1911), p. 244 f.

Thus Watson [5] has contended that the Law of Exercise in the sense of greater frequency and recency on R_3 than on any of the other R's was alone enough to explain learning; while others, notably Hobhouse,[6] Holmes,[7] Thorndike himself,[8] and Carr,[9] while stressing the importance of the Law of Exercise, also resort to the Law of Effect, as a further determiner. That is, all these latter contend that, in addition to differences of exercise, an important reason why $S \rightarrow R_3$ gets stamped in at the expense of R_1, R_2, R_4, etc., is that R_3 is followed by some sort of good effect, while the others are followed by some sort of bad effects. These writers differ from one another, however, in their conceptions of the natures of such goodness and badness and in their conceptions of how these two effects are to be conceived to operate physiologically.[10]

Hobhouse describes the "effects" as confirmation and inhibition. Holmes ascribes them as congruity and incongruity with some total instinctive activity. Thorndike calls them satisfyingness and annoyingness and conceives them as the correlates of such neuronic connections as cause the life-processes of the neurones involved to go on well and ill, respectively. And Carr conceives them as increased and decreased consequences in the way of resultant sensory intensities.

Our own assertion now, however, will be that, whatever the special form of the trial and error theory—whatever its special statement concerning the relative importances of exercise and effect, and whatever its conception as to the character of the

[5] J. B. Watson, *Behavior, An Introduction to Comparative Psychology* (New York, Henry Holt and Company, 1914), Chapter VII. This was prior to his acceptance of the Conditioned Reflex Theory, as referred to in the preceding chapter.

[6] L. T. Hobhouse, *Mind in Evolution*, 2d ed. (London, The Macmillan Company, 1915).

[7] S. J. Holmes, *The Evolution of Animal Intelligence* (New York, Henry Holt and Company, 1911).

———— *Studies in Animal Behavior* (Boston, Richard G. Badger, The Gorham Press, 1916).

[8] E. L. Thorndike, *Animal Intelligence* (New York, The Macmillan Company, 1911).

[9] H. Carr, Principles of selection in animal learning, *Psychol. Rev.*, 1914, 21, 157-165.

———— *Psychology—A Study of Mental Activity* (New York, Longmans, Green & Co., 1925).

[10] For a very able summary of these different variations of the trial and error theory, see F. A. C. Perrin and D. B. Klein, *Psychology, Its Methods and Principles* (New York, Henry Holt and Company, 1926), Ch. V.

"effects"—no trial and error theory is really tenable. We shall assert, indeed, that neither the Law of Effect nor the Law of Exercise, as usually stated, actually holds. First for the Law of Effect.

3. Facts of Latent Learning Which Contradict the Law of Effect

It must, of course, be admitted that in some superficial sense, most cases of ordinary trial and error learning do seem to be consonant with the Law of Effect. Thus, in the usual trial and error set-up, the correct response is usually followed by a good effect, and the incorrect responses are usually followed by bad effects. The animal does, therefore, learn the act which leads to the good effect and unlearn those which lead to the bad effects. But other set-ups are (as we may now recall from the facts presented in earlier chapters) equally capable of resulting in learning—set-ups in which no such differential effects are, during the period of learning, provided. The experiments we have in mind are, of course, the "latent learning" experiments of Blodgett,[11] Williams,[12] Elliott,[13] and Tolman and Honzik,[14] already described.

In all these experiments, the animal is presented initially with alternative response situations, under conditions of no reward or, at the most, of relatively slight reward for the one response as against the others. And as a result he acquires "apparently" only a very slight propensity to take what is later to be a correct route. Yet a very considerable "latent learning" does take place—a learning which manifests itself as having taken place, the moment a real differential reward is introduced. That is, in these experiments, the final amount of learning of a control group which had had strong reward throughout was no greater than that of the experimental group which had received practically no reward throughout most of the learning period. In other words, the excess of reward, experienced by the control groups relative to the experimental groups during the latent period, caused no faster ultimate learning. Differential reward was necessary to make this latent learning appear;

---

[11] H. C. Blodgett, See above Chapter III, p. 48 f.
[12] K. A. Williams, See above Chapter X, p. 148 f.
[13] M. H. Elliott, See above Chapter III, p. 50 f.
[14] E. C. Tolman and C. H. Honzik, See above Chapter III, p. 52 f.

but it was not necessary to establish it. Learning, or at any rate, latent learning, takes place without any aid from the Law of Effect.

It may, of course, be that further experiments will eventually show that differential effects, as between the correct and the incorrect routes, are an additional aid to learning. But, if so, this degree can be but slight. The Law of Effect, if valid at all, is only slightly so, since the amount of improvement acquired without differential effect is practically as great as that acquired with differential effect.[15]

Finally, let us consider also still another type of experiment which is likewise prejudicial to any orthodox formulation of the Law of Effect.

4. Punishment May Stamp in Rather than Stamp Out a Response

The type of experiment we have in mind is one now being tried out in the University of California laboratory by Miss Bretnall and Mr. Hall on the effect of punishing for right responses. The results, as thus far gathered, seem to indicate that, if human subjects are required to learn to choose between successive pairs of responses, and that, if one response of each pair be followed by punishment, the subjects will, under certain conditions at least, learn to perform the punished responses and avoid the not-punished responses more readily than they will learn to do the reverse.

The experimental set-up consists of a large board on an easel, before which the subject sits and which presents to him thirty pairs of holes, distributed in an irregular pattern over its surface. His task consists in running through these pairs of holes with a stylus in a certain prescribed order, and learning, for each pair, that one of the holes is to be punched with the stylus and the other not.

For one group of subjects, the to-be-punched holes gives an

[15] Acknowledgment is to be made to Dr. H. C. Blodgett for first having pointed out to us this fact that the latent learning experiments really disprove the Law of Effect (as well as the Law of Exercise). It is to be noted that we are here, very definitely, taking issue not only with Thorndike's earlier formulations but also with that in his most recent book, *Human Learning*. (See above footnote at beginning of chapter.)

electric shock. For a second group of subjects, the not-to-be-punched holes give the electric shock. And the outcome seems to be that the group of subjects who are required to learn to punch the punishment-giving holes and to avoid the non-punishment-giving do so more rapidly than the group of subjects who are required to learn to punch the non-punishment-giving holes and to avoid the punishment-giving holes,[16] an outcome quite contrary, it would seem, to any ordinary formulation of the Law of Effect.[17]

It appears, in short, that punishment coming after the correct responses, instead of making learning difficult, may actually make it easier. In this particular set-up the "bad" effect of the punishment serves as an "emphasizer" of the difference between the correct holes and the incorrect holes and not as a stamper out.

It will not, of course, be denied that the correct holes, as correct, still present some sort of a "good effect" which the incorrect holes fail to present. It is this "good effect" of their correctness, i.e., the fact that they lead to the satisfactory completion of the task, which causes them "to be taken." But it does not, as such, cause them to be "learned." Indeed learning in such a case is really a differentiating between the correct and incorrect holes, irrespective of which is taken. And to this end a superimposed "badness" on the correct holes seems to be more contributory to learning than a superimposed "badness" upon the incorrect holes. Whatever emphasizes a difference between the correct and the incorrect holes will facilitate the learning. And this will be in part the "correctness" of the correct holes as contrasted with the "incorrectness" of the incorrect holes. But it may be also either punishment applied to the correct holes, as contrasted with no punishment applied to the incorrect holes, or punishment applied to the incorrect, as contrasted with no punishment applied to the correct holes. And the striking thing is that, for some reason, punishment on the correct holes seems to be more "emphasizing" than punishment on the incorrect holes.

[16] Control groups indicate that these differences were not due to any differences in the difficulties of the holes per se.

[17] Since writing the above there has just appeared an abstract of an apparently somewhat similar experiment by Peterson with a similar outcome. Joseph Peterson, Learning when frequency and recency factors are negative and right responses are painful. *Psychol. Bull.*, 1931, **28**, 207-208.

5. Recapitulation *re* the Law of Effect

Let us sum up, now, as regards the Law of Effect. First it appears that "latent learning" takes place perfectly successfully without any very appreciably greater "effect" for what is later to be the correct response than for what is later to be the incorrect response. An animal acquires a capacity to differentiate between the "right" and the "wrong" responses during a period when the one response is only slightly, if any, "righter" than the other. And the amount of this ability to differentiate, thus built up, seems to be quite as great in the end as that accomplished by control animals who, during the same period, are rewarded strongly for taking the one act and not for the other.

Second, it appears, at least in the case of human subjects, that when individuals are punished on the correct responses they may learn to make those correct responses more readily than a control group punished on the incorrect responses, because for some reason a "bad" effect on the correct response seems to be more "emphasizing" than a "bad" effect upon the incorrect response.

Let us turn now to the Law of Exercise.

6. Two Meanings to the Law of Exercise

First, it is to be noted that there are really *two* meanings for the Law of Exercise. In one of these we shall claim that the law holds, and in the other, that it does not. And it is in the latter sense (the one in which it does not hold) that the law has usually been invoked in discussions of trial and error learning. But let us consider each of the two meanings in detail.

(i) *Frequency and Recency of the Problem.* The Law of Exercise, or of "Use" as Thorndike often calls it, holds, we shall assert, when that which is meant by exercise is frequent and recent repetition of the whole stimulus situation, irrespective of whether in the given trial the animal chooses a correct or an incorrect path. Exercise in this sense means the frequency and recency with which the whole problem, as a problem, is met and responded to. When so meant, the law obviously holds. If, for example, with two rats of equal ability, one has had one hundred tries at a given point of bifurcation in a maze, and the other has had only fifty, it is quite obvious that the rat having had the hundred tries will be more likely thereafter to choose correctly than the rat having had only the fifty. And a similar situation would hold regarding recency of the presentation of the stimulus-problem. The rat who has been practised on a given point of bifurcation twenty-four hours previously is going, now, to be more likely to choose correctly at that point, than a rat who has not been practised on this specific bifurcation for sixty days or more. It must be emphasized, however, that in such instances of the frequent, or recent presentation of the stimulus, or problem-situation, the responses will (until learning has already set in) probably include equal numbers of right and wrong choices.

(ii) *Relative Frequencies and Recencies of the Right vs. the Wrong Responses—the Total Frequency and Recency of the Presentation of the Problem, i.e., the Stimulus, Remaining the same.* In the second meaning of the Law of Exercise, and this is the one in which it seems most apt to be used in discussions of trial and error learning, what is meant by frequent and recent exercise seems to be frequent and recent "differential" exercise upon the correct path at the expense of the incorrect paths. Or, to return to our figure, what is asserted, when the law is used in this latter sense, is that greater, i.e., more frequent or more recent, exercise upon R_3 rather than R_1, R_2, R_4, etc., will, as such, stamp R_3 in. But we now claim that this has by no means been shown to hold.[18] In fact, it would appear rather, speaking in terms of the diagram above, that R_1, R_2, R_4, etc., must be taken at least with some frequency and recency if R_3 is ever, as such, to get selected as against them.

Let us turn to the concrete experiments.

7. The Facts Which Lend Little Support to the Doctrine that Learning is Brought About by Greater Exercise on the Correct Path than on the Incorrect Path

Reviewing the literature of recent years, it appears that there have been quite a number of experiments indicating the probable

---

[18] Peterson also seems to have been making this same distinction between the two senses of the Law of Exercise when he distinguished between exercise in the sense of frequency and recency of stimulus, and exercise in the sense of frequency and recency of response.

Joseph Peterson, Learning when frequency and recency factors are negative, *J. Exper. Psychol.*, 1922, **5**, 270-300, p. 271.

invalidity of the law, as so phrased. These may be summarized briefly under the following heads:

(a) Experiments in which the animal starts, normally, with a fifty-fifty choice of right and wrong paths, and yet learns at a natural rate to take the correct path.

(b) Experiments in which the technique of the set-up is such that during the beginning of learning, the subject (human being) tends to take the incorrect path more frequently and more recently, and yet learns.

(c) Experiments in which, in a preliminary training period with two alternative paths equivalent, the animal, for unknown causes, tends to build up a habit of taking one of the two paths more frequently and which yet show no effect of this frequency in a later test period in which the opposite path is made correct.

(d) Experiments in which, in a period of preliminary training with two alternative paths equivalent, the animal is forced to take one path more frequently or more recently than another and which yet show but little effect of such frequency or recency in a later test period when one of the paths is then made correct and the other incorrect.

(e) Experiments in which the animal, during the beginning of training, is prevented from taking what are later to prove the incorrect paths, and is thereby handicapped.

(f) Experiments in which the subjects (human beings) are forced to take the incorrect path with great frequency, with emphasis throughout upon its incorrectness, and are thereby aided.

(g) Experiments in which the subjects (human beings) do not know when they are making correct responses and when incorrect ones, and yet do not learn to do those which they initially perform with the greater frequency and recency.

We may briefly consider each of these types of experiment and their results:

Experiments in Which the Animal Naturally Tends to Start with a Fifty-Fifty Choice of Right and Wrong Paths, and Yet Learns.

We have in mind here the various experiments cited above in Chapter VII (and undoubtedly many other similar experiments with which we just do not happen to be so familiar) in which the rat is presented with two or more alternative routes to the same goal, where one of these routes is in some way preferable, i.e., "shorter" than the others. We refer, that is, to such experiments as those of De Camp on routes of different spatial lengths,[19] of Sams and Tolman on routes of different temporal lengths,[20] etc. In all such experiments the animals start out with equal frequencies and recencies with respect to all the alternatives, but come sooner or later to select (i.e., to have "learned") the "shorter" or "shortest" path only.

Indeed, for purposes of emphasis it may perhaps be well to describe now one other such experiment. Let us consider, for example, the well known experiment by Kuo.[21] Kuo presented his rats with a four-door multiple choice apparatus. One door led by a relatively short route to food, and another by a relatively long route to food. A third led to a confinement box, where the rat was confined for a short time and then had to back out; while the fourth led to an electric shock box from which the rat, as soon as he felt the shock, naturally backed out. To begin with, the rats tended to choose all four doors with exactly similar frequencies and distributions of choices. Soon, however, they relatively suddenly began dropping out the electric shock box; but continued to go with equal frequencies to each of the other three. Next they dropped out, again relatively suddenly, the confinement box, but continued to alternate in a surprisingly regular fashion between the long path and the short path. Finally, they dropped out the long path and went to the short path only. Now the significant feature of these results, from the present point of view, is, of course, that the successive droppings out of the bad routes were in no case due to a preceding greater frequency or recency on the other routes. In each case all the remaining alternative paths were entered with exactly similar frequencies and distributions of repetions *until learning had already set in.* A greater frequency and recency on the still-to-be-accepted paths resulted from learning; but cannot have been said to have preceded, or produced, learning. The order of elimination was determined, not by preceding frequencies and recencies, but by the relative "badnesses" of the different alternatives.

[19] See above, p. 101 f.
[20] See above, p. 106 f.
[21] Z. Y. Kuo, The Nature of unsuccessful acts and their order of elimination, *J. Comp. Psychol.,* 1922, **2,** 1-27.

Finally, it is important to note further, not only that learning occurs, in all such experiments as this of Kuo's and the others cited in which, to begin with, all the alternatives are entered with equal frequencies and recencies, but where certain of these alternatives are "better," i.e., "shorter," than others, but also that it occurs even when during the course of the training, which is in question, no such differential "betternesses" are operative. We here have in mind again the experiment of Blodgett. For it is to be noted now that Blodgett included among his "latent-learning" set-ups one in which he used a simple long-path-short-path maze.[22] During the non-reward period there was no food at the goal-box and hence the short path was not, as such better than the long. And, in fact, the animals continued to take the long path with almost, if not quite, as great a frequency as the short path throughout this period. But they were, in spite of this practically equal frequency and equal goodness of the two paths, none the less "learning"—acquiring information—as to the differences between the two paths. For, once the food was introduced, they on the very next trial began taking the shorter path with almost one hundred per cent frequency. In other words, equal frequencies and recencies cause learning, not only when there is differential effect present, which favors the one path more than the others, but also when there is no such differential effect. Though in this latter case the learning will not, of course, appear until after a differential effect has been introduced. Differential effect is necessary for the "appearance" of trial and error learning, but not for its "acquisition." Or, to put it another way, differential effect is necessary for *performance* but not for *learning*.

Experiments in Which the Technique of the Set-up Is Such that during the Beginning of Learning the Subject (Human Being) Tends to Take the Incorrect Paths More Frequently and More Recently, and Yet Learns.

The experiments we have in mind here are those of Peterson with his Mental Maze.[23] The mental maze was a device invented by Peterson in which letters were presented to the subject in successive pairs. These pairs of letters were analogous

[22] H. C. Blodgett, The effect of the introduction of reward upon the maze performance of rats, *Univ. Calif. Publ. Psychol.*, 1929, **4**, 113-134.

[23] Joseph Peterson, The backward elimination of errors in mental maze learning, *J. Exper. Psychol.*, 1920, **3**, 257-280.—Learning when frequency and recency factors are negative, *J. Exper. Psychol.*, 1922, **5**, 270-300.

to pairs of alternative alleys at successive choice points in a maze. For each pair of letters the subject was required to choose one. If the subject chose correctly, i.e., the one which Peterson had decided was the true path, he was then presented with the next pair; and so on. If, on the other hand, the subject chose wrongly, i.e., that equivalent to taking the blind, he had to choose over again. Furthermore, in the procedure as Peterson carried it out, there was introduced still another feature not present in the usual animal maze. That is, every time the subject made a wrong choice, instead of merely offering him that same immediate choice over again, Peterson began him again with the first pair—i.e., made him go back to the beginning of the maze and start over again. Now this last feature of returning his subjects to the starting point directly after each wrong turn, mechanically brought it about that, until actual learning had set in, the frequency and recency of the wrong responses tended to be greater than those of the right responses. And yet the subjects learned.

Experiment in Which the Animal, from Unknown Causes, Forms the Habit of Taking One of Two Equally Good Paths More Frequently than the Other, but Is Not Thereby Handicapped in thereafter Learning to Take the Opposite Side when the Latter Is Made Correct.

We have in mind here some results obtained by Yoshioka,[24] incidental to an experiment already described (see above, Chapter VIII) using the simple two-path triangular maze (see FIGURE 41:1, p. 125). On this maze he ran 157 male albino and hooded rats, six to eight months old, giving each rat six free choices a day for ten days—a total of sixty free choices. Of these 157 rats he took out the forty-six who came nearest to the theoretical mean of thirty choices of the right path and thirty choices of the left path. The remaining 101 rats then fell into two groups—those that had shown a decided preference for the right path and those that had shown a decided preference for the left path.

He then, experimentally, made what had been thus the preferred path a non-reward path. That is, the originally "right choosers" were now not rewarded when they went to the right and the originally "left choosers" were not rewarded when they went to the left. More specifically the procedure was as follows.

[24] J. G. Yoshioka, Frequency factor in habit formation, *J. Comp. Psychol.*, 1930, **11**, 37-49.

First the rats were given a four-day training period in which they were forced down each side three times, the previously preferred path being now non-rewarded and the previously non-preferred path being rewarded. Then followed a test-period consisting of six free choices a day for ten days. (In these test choices they were also rewarded on the previously non-preferred side and non-rewarded on the previously preferred side.)

TABLE 5 shows the results for the original sixty choices (when both sides were rewarded) and for the subsequent sixty choices when they were rewarded only on the previously non-preferred side. Further, it will be observed that in this table the animals have been divided into the originally "right choosers" and the originally "left choosers," and that they have been further sub-divided into subclasses in terms of the sizes of their original deviations from a mean of thirty right and thirty left choices. Thus Class I includes rats whose original scores deviated two σ's from a mean of thirty and Classes II, III, IV and V includes rats whose score deviations were three, four, five, and six or more σ's from such a mean.

TABLE 5

Class	Original deviation	No. of animals	Original test	Subsequent test Non-preferred rewarded	Improvement
		Originally right choosers			
				Left choices	
I	2σ	15	22.93	22.80	—.07
II	3σ	10	19.60	23.60	4.00
III	4σ	14	15.64	21.29	5.65
IV	5σ	15	11.60	14.80	3.20
V	6σ or more	13	5.38	12.85	7.47
		Originally left choosers			
				Right choices	
I	2σ	7	23.86	24.86	1.00
II	3σ	6	19.33	31.67	12.34
III	4σ	8	15.75	20.88	5.13
IV	5σ	7	11.29	14.43	3.14
V	6σ or more	6	7.00	12.33	5.33

In general it is obvious from this table that the animals who showed the greater preferences for one side or the other in the original learning (Class V) made quite as much improvement in learning to go towards the opposite side as the animals who had shown less strong preferences (Class I). The originally "more frequent taking" of the right side or the left side (Class V) did not, as such, more strongly "stamp in" the taking of that side. These animals broke down the habit, relatively, just as easily as did the animals of Class I who had had less frequency on the given side.

Experiments in Which the Animal Is Forced to Take What Are to Prove Later the Incorrect Paths More Frequently or More Recently than the Correct Paths, and Yet Is Not Handicapped.

We refer here to two sets of unpublished experiments done at the University of California. Both sets of experiments used a simple two-way box of the plan shown in FIGURE 68.

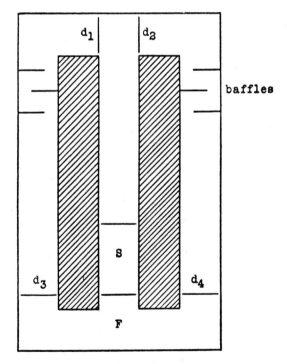

Outside dimensions
40" x 25"
All Alleys 4"-wide

FIGURE 68

S is the starting chamber and F the food chamber; d_1, d_2, d_3 and d_4 are blocks which in any given trial close off the right alley, or the left alley, at the pleasure of the experimenter.

In both sets of experiments the rats were first given 18 preliminary training runs, in each of which only one alley was open. That is, either block d_1 or block d_2 was always closed. It could thus be arranged to have during these 18 "training" runs as much relative frequency or as much recency on the one side, say the right, as desired. This "training" period was then followed by a learning or "test" period, in which both blocks d_1 and d_2 were out, but in which one side, say the left, was now consistently made into a blind-alley by the use of block d_3, while the other side was made consistently into a true path. In this way the effects of different proportions and arrangements of frequency and recency in the 18 training runs upon the later learning or test runs could be determined.

The first of the two experiments to be reported is one devised and carried out by Dr. Nyswander.[25] Her data bear primarily upon the case of recency. All her groups of animals received, during the training period, nine runs to the right and nine to the left, so that the factor of frequency was equalized. But she ran six different training series in which the right and left runs were distributed in different ways as follows:

Series	1	L L L L L L L L L R R R R R R R R R
"	2	L L L L R L R L R L R L R L R R R R
"	3	L R L R L R L R L R L R L R L R L R
"	4	R L R L R L R L R L R L R L R L R L
"	5	R R R R L R L R L R L R L R L L L L
"	6	R R R R R R R R R L L L L L L L L L

Part of the animals trained on each of these series-arrangements were then tested with the true path to the right and part with the true path to the left, and all had to learn until they made four perfect runs out of five. It is obvious that, for the rats subsequently tested to the right, Series-arrangement 1 provided the greatest amount of preceding recency, Series-arrangement 2 provided less, Series-arrangement 6 providing the least; while just the reverse held for the rats subsequently tested to the left.

[25] D. B. Nyswander, Recency, frequency and pattern factors in learning. Ph.D. Thesis, Univ. of Calif., 1926.

Combining the results for both right-tested and left-tested animals with respect to preceding recency scores, she obtained the results shown in TABLE 6.

Training	Test		Number of animals	Mean no. of trials to form habit
LLLLLLLLLRRRRRRRRR	L	*Least*	10	5.10
RRRRRRRRRLLLLLLLLL	R	*recency*		
LLLLRLRLRLRLRLRRRR	L		12	7.08
RRRRLRLRLRLRLRLLLL	R			
LRLRLRLRLRLRLRLRLR	L		15	8.53
RLRLRLRLRLRLRLRLRL	R			
LRLRLRLRLRLRLRLRLR	R		9	9.67
RLRLRLRLRLRLRLRLRL	L			
LLLLRLRLRLRLRLRRRR	R		17	8.06
RRRRLRLRLRLRLRLLLL	L			
LLLLLLLLLRRRRRRRRR	R	*Most*	11	6.63
RRRRRRRRRLLLLLLLLL	L	*recency*		

TABLE 6

A survey of this table reveals, at once, that the recency of having been forced to go to the one side in the preliminary training showed no tendency to favor subsequent learning to take that side as the true path. If anything, the greater the recency, the more difficult thereafter to learn to go to that side.

Further, the thing that appeared most definitely of all was a result depending upon the extent to which, in the preliminary forced training, the right and left runs were given in a "pattern" of relatively solid blocks or the extent to which they were, rather, interlarded. The outcome was very definitely that the greater the interlarding in the original training the more difficult the subsequent learning. Patterns LLLLLLLLLRRRRRRRRR and RRRRRRRRRLLLLLLLLL were the easiest for subsequent learning and Patterns LRLRLRLRLRLRLRLRLR and RLRLRLRLRLRLRLRLRL were the most difficult irrespective of whether the subsequent learning was to the right or to the left.

The other set of experiments of this same sort to be reported were some by Miss D. G. Sherman and Miss E. W. Robinson. In these experiments the same procedure was used save that frequency rather than recency was investigated. The following patterns of training and directions of subsequent tests were used:

	Training	*Test*	
Group I	LLRRRRRRRRRRRRRRR RRRRRRRRRRRRRRRLL LLLLLLLLLLLLLLLLRR RRLLLLLLLLLLLLLLLL	R R L L	Frequency 16
Group II	LLLLLLLLLRRRRRRRRR RRRRRRRRRLLLLLLLLL LLLLLLLLLRRRRRRRRR RRRRRRRRRLLLLLLLLL	R R L L	Frequency 9
Group III	RRLLLLLLLLLLLLLLLL LLLLLLLLLLLLLLLLRR RRLLLLLLLLLLLLLLLL LLLLLLLLLLLLLLLLRR	R R L L	Frequency 2

It will be observed that three degrees of frequency only were used, but all possible combinations of recency and of right and left were used with these different frequencies. The general outcome for their first experiments, in which the apparatus and set-up was exactly like that used by Dr. Nyswander, was that frequency had, *if anything, a slightly deleterious* effect. The rats in Group I learned best and those in Group II next best and those in Group III least well.

This surprising result appeared, however, as due probably to a "curiosity" response. For, when the one side had, in the training series, been the more frequently blocked, it appeared as if the removal of this block then caused a sudden exploratory or curiosity propensity to enter "this place which had previously been closed." Such an interpretation was further borne out by the fact that this tendency to enter the previously blocked path proved greater for those arrangements of training where the blocking of what was later to be the wrong path had come at the end of the series—i.e., just before the test runs. Thus, if the training arrangements were divided into two sets, the set where the path which was later to be the correct one was open at the end of the training series and a set where this path, which was later to be correct, was closed at the end of the training series, the results for the latter set were better than those for the former.

Finally, to examine this curiosity hypothesis further, the experiments were repeated with black cloth curtains in front of both blocks d_1 and d_2 (see FIGURE 68), so that the animal would not see that a given block had been suddenly removed. It then came out that the training arrangements giving greater frequency caused a very slightly better subsequent learning. Furthermore, the two arrangements—blocking of the true path at the end of the training series and blocking of the true path at the beginning of the training series—no longer showed any advantage for the former.

The general conclusion to be drawn from both Dr. Nyswander's experiments and those of Miss Sherman and Miss Robinson would seem to be that, in this general type of set-up, frequency and recency of forced training have little, if any, advantageous effect upon subsequent learning. And, if the set-up is such as to put a premium upon the curiosity factor, then when the "forcing" is removed, a greater frequency and recency may "seem" to have an actually deleterious effect.

Experiments in Which the Animal in Part of the Training Is Prevented from Taking What Are Later to Prove Blind Alleys and Is to Some Extent Handicapped.

We report now a series of experiments, performed in the Chicago laboratory, somewhat similar in implication to those just described.[26] In these experiments ordinary mazes and both human subjects and rats were used. In the case of the human subjects the mazes were stylus mazes. For the rats they were ordinary alley mazes.

The general procedure of all the experiments was to prevent entrances into the blinds for certain numbers of runs (thereby giving excess frequencies and recencies to the true path), i.e., to

[26] H. C. Koch, The Influence of mechanical guidance upon maze learning, *Psychol. Monog.*, 1923, **32**, no. 147.

K. E. Ludgate, The effect of manual guidance upon maze learning, *Psychol. Monog.*, 1923, **33**, no. 148.

T. L. Wang, The influence of tuition in the acquisition of skill, *Psychol. Monog.*, 1925, **33**, no. 154.

A. S. Alonzo, The influence of manual guidance upon maze learning, *J. Comp. Psychol.*, 1926, **6**, 143-157.

L. S. Tsai, Gradual vs. abrupt withdrawal of guidance in maze learning, *J. Comp. Psychol.*, 1930, **10**, 325-332.

See also a more recent experiment performed at the University of Arkansas, R. H. Waters, The influence of large amounts of manual guidance upon human maze learning, *J. Gen. Psychol.*, 1930, **4**, 213-228.

provide "guidance" for a certain number of trials and then, during the remaining trials, to remove this guidance and to discover in how far it has helped (or hindered) learning, by comparing the results with those for control groups who had learned without any such guidance.

In different experiments, different methods of blocking the blinds, i.e., of providing guidance, were tried. In the case of the rat subjects, solid blocks, glass blocks through which the rats could presumably see, and collars with leashes were all tried. In the case of the human subjects, solid blocks not to be distinguished by the stylus from the other alley walls, and verbal commands "not to proceed on a given course" were both tried.

In general, the results were that the guided trials, simply by themselves, were never enough to cause complete learning, although they did usually help to a greater or less extent. When the guidance was removed both types of subject seemed always impelled to do at least some exploring of the newly opened up blinds. Furthermore, it appeared that, the more the form of guidance was such as to allow some discovery of the "fact of the blind" even during the guided trials, as was the case for the glass partitions and the leash for the rats and for the verbal commands for the human beings, the less the apparent need for such exploring of the blinds, and hence the fewer the errors, after the guidance.

Professor Carr sums up the general significance of the experiments, for the case of the human subjects as follows:

"No one learned the maze during these guided trials; in fact, too much guidance was actually detrimental. In other words, a certain number of errors must be made and eliminated before the subject is ever able to run the maze correctly. *Correct modes of response are established in part by learning what not to do.*" [27]

Experiments in Which the Subjects (Human Beings) Are Forced to Take the Incorrect Path with Great Frequency but with Knowledge of Its Incorrectness and Thereby Learn to Avoid It.

We refer here to a doctrine and experiments initiated by Dunlap.[28] After many years of teaching the orthodox law of

[27] H. A. Carr, *Psychology, A Study of Mental Activity* (New York, Longmans, Green & Co., 1925), p. 98. (Italics ours.)

[28] K. Dunlap, A revision of the fundamental law of habit formation, *Science*, 1928, **67**, 360-362.

frequency, Dunlap was led to doubt that the facts actually agree with that law. Specifically he carried out the following experiment upon himself. For a number of years he had been annoyed, when typewriting rapidly, by an occasional tendency to transpose the letters of the word "the," so that it read instead "hte." In the majority of cases he actually wrote "the" correctly, exchanging it for "hte" only in a minority of cases. And this in itself, as he points out, indicated that the mere greater frequency of repetition of the correct response had not, as such, tended to stamp it in. He then proceeded to see if by a frequent repetition of this wrong response with a knowledge and emphasis upon its wrongness he could eliminate it. He typed about half a page, single spaced, of the "hte" combination, with the further thought that this was a "word" that he would *not* write in the future (unless deliberately and voluntarily). Somewhat over a week later, he followed this with a second practice period consisting of less than a third of a page. This was over three months previous to the date at which he is reporting. And in the interim he typed many pages and some of them rapidly, but on reading over found not a single instance of "hte." He says: "This may sound too easy to be true, but as a matter of fact a long standing and troublesome habit has disappeared."

Finally he suggests the applicability of a similar method to the eradication of various undesirable habits in children and adults —to bad habits in gear-shifting, to speech defects, to thumb-sucking, and the like in children, and even to homosexuality in adults. He suggests it, in short, as a method of breaking down "fixations." (See Chapters X and XIX.)

Holsopple and Vanouse, stimulated by the above theory and experiment of Dunlap, performed another minor investigation.[29] In a night class for stenographers, who were just beginning to transcribe on the typewriter from their stenographic notes, they found eleven individuals who tended to misspell four or more common words. They then divided these misspelled words into two groups. For one of these groups of words each student's attention was called to the fact that he had misspelled them consistently in his previous transcriptions, and he was asked to type, spelling as he had misspelled them, eight lines the width of the

[29] J. Q. Holsopple and I. Vanouse, A note on the beta hypothesis of learning, *School & Soc.*, 1929, **29**, 15-16.

page of each word. These instructions were considered "mysterious" or "funny" but were repeated and the practice was supervised to see that it was exactly carried out.

On the other group of words an equal amount of practice in which the word was correctly spelled was carried out.

Dictation was given after practice in such a way that each of the words practiced was used at least four times. The results are shown in the following two tables:

Subject	Words practised as correctly spelled	Errors after practice
A	parcel (parcil)	0
	received (recieved)	2
B	necessary (neccessary)	4
	shipped (shiped)	0
C	their (thier)	0
	occasioned (occassioned)	4
	items (ittems)	0
	transit (transet)	0
D	immediately (emmediately)	2
	instance (instanse)	1
E	source (sourse)	1
	owing (ouing)	1
F	errors (errers)	2
	reduce (reduse)	0
	there (their)	0
	account (acount)	0
G	guarded (gaurded)	2
	belief (beleif)	4
H	account (accuont)	1
	shipped (shiped)	0
I	slight (sleight)	1
	design (desing)	2
J	opportunity (oportunity)	0
	referred (refered)	0
K	through (thruogh)	1
	shown (shoun)	2
	Total	30

TABLE 7

As the authors remark, "the only real difficulty in the interpretation of these data lies in the fact that they 'seem too good to be true.'"

Frequency on the wrong response (with knowledge of its wrongness) seems to be better, in some situations at any rate, than frequency on the right response.[30]

---

[30] Two other minor experiments to test Dunlap's procedure have been carried

Subject	Words practised as misspelled	Errors after practice
A	agreed (agread)	o
	shipments (shippments)	o
B	reduce (reduse)	o
	possibly (posibly)	o
C	fulfill (fullfill)	o
	necessary (neccessary)	o
	owing (oweing)	o
	occasioned (occassioned)	o
D	because (becuase)	o
	receipt (reciept)	o
E	shipped (shiped)	o
	their (thier)	o
F	certainly (certinly)	o
	immediately (imediately)	o
	possibly (posibly)	o
	value (valeu)	o
G	allowance (alowance)	o
	adjusting (ajusting)	o
H	not (mot)	o
	cancel (cansel)	o
I	dropped (droped)	o
	shipped (shiped)	o
J	write (wright)	o
	develop (develope)	o
K	disappoint (dissapoint)	o
	quantity (quanity)	o
	Total	o

TABLE 8

Experiments in Which the Subjects (Human Beings) Make Trial and Error Responses but Are Not Informed Which Are Right and Which Are Wrong, and Show No Piling-up Effect from Frequency.

We refer here to one of the important experiments recently presented by Thorndike.[31] The subjects were instructed, with their eyes closed, to "Draw a four-inch line with one quick movement." They did this for about 200 times at a sitting and

out by Wakeham, with partially, though not completely, successful results. G. Wakeham, Query on "A revision of the fundamental law of habit formation," *Science*, 1928, **68**, 135-136.

————— A quantitative experiment on Dr. K. Dunlap's "Revision of the fundamental law of habit formation," *J. Comp. Psychol.*, 1930, **10**, 235-236.

[31] E. L. Thorndike, *Human Learning* (New York, The Century Co., 1931), p. 8 f. This book of Thorndike's is full of other experiments which might

continued until in all they had done it some 3000 times. The results for the first 12 sittings for one subject are shown in TABLE 9.[32]

There was no improvement. In general, the lines were drawn too long. And they were, on the average, just as much too long on the last sittings as on the first. Furthermore, and this is the significant point that especially concerns the present argument, the lengths of line that were drawn most frequently on any given sitting did not tend, thereby, to get "stamped in" and thus to become still more frequent on subsequent sittings.

Or, to put it in Thorndike's own words, it appeared that "The most frequent response to it [a given stimulus] does not wax at the expense of the less frequent responses." [33]

Or, in a word, the law of exercise—in the sense of differentially greater frequency on one of the responses in a trial and error situation than on the other alternative responses—has been disproved.

8. Summary of Criticisms of the Laws of Exercise and Effect

The above sets of experiments all taken together indicate most certainly and without question that the law of exercise, in the sense of differentially more frequent or recent repetitions of one of the alternative responses as against any of the others as the cause of learning, plays little, if any rôle. But, it will be asked, if it be not thus the greater frequency or recency of the doing of the

also have been included in our argument. See footnote at beginning of chapter.

For other references likewise indicating Thorndike's recent modified attitude towards his original doctrine of learning, see

———— A fundamental theorem in modifiability, *Proc. Nat. Acad. Sci.,* 1927, **13,** 15-18.

———— The Law of effect, *Amer. J. Psychol.,* 1927, **39,** 212-227.

———— The influence of primacy, *J. Exp. Psychol.,* 1927, **10,** 18-29.

———— The refractory period in associative processes, *Psychol. Rev.,* 1927, **34,** 234-236.

———— Fundamental Factors in Learning. *Proc. Ninth Internat. Cong. Psychol.* (Princeton, Psychol. Rev. Co., 1930), p. 429.

———— The Strengthening and Weakening of Mental Connections by Their After-Effects, *Proc. Ninth Internat. Cong. Psychol.* (Princeton, Psychol. Rev. Co., 1930), p. 430.

[32] *Op. cit.,* p. 9.

[33] E. L. Thorndike, Fundamental Factors in Learning, *Proc. Ninth Internat. Congress Psychol.* (Princeton, Psychol. Rev. Co., 1930), p. 429.

Distribution of the Responses at Each Sitting in Drawing Lines to equal 4″ with Eyes Closed: Subject T

Frequencies in Sittings 1 to 12

Response	1	2	3	4	5	6	7	8	9	10	11	12
3.7									1			
3.8								2				
3.9												
4.0			3						3			
4.1			4	1				1	3			2
4.2		4	8			1		3	6	1	2	1
4.3		3	9	1				4	5	3		4
4.4		13	12	6			3	4	12	2	4	3
4.5	3	18	18	14	2	7	3	15	14	8	7	11
4.6		20	23	23	3	7	8	13	14	8	14	11
4.7	6	20	14	22	11	14	16	25	13	9	14	21
4.8	6	22	15	18	14	27	17	16	18	15	19	26
4.9	13	17	24	24	22	28	18	21	16	10	18	30
5.0	25	20	16	24	26	21	29	25	14	24	19	20
5.1	27	10	16	12	25	32	14	15	14	22	31	22
5.2	24	11	8	12	24	21	23	25	16	18	28	16
5.3	30	8	2	11	21	13	17	8	18	18	16	12
5.4	17	4	2	8	10	10	7	8	12	12	7	7
5.5	12	1		4	13	8	7	3	10	13	4	3
5.6	7			2	4	7	4	1	4	5	2	2
5.7	3			1	4	2	5	2	6	4	3	1
5.8					1			1		2		
5.9	1				1					1	2	
6.0									1			
6.1												
6.2	1						1					
Total	175	171	174	183	181	198	172	192	200	175	190	192
Median	5.23	4.83	4.77	4.93	5.15	5.07	5.07	4.96	4.97	5.13	5.09	4.96
Q	.16	.22	.23	.22	.19	.19	.21	.24	.33	.24	.21	.20

TABLE 9

Q is the half of the range required to include the middle 50 percent of the responses.

one response which causes it to be stamped in, what is it which causes learning? The first answer to suggest itself is, of course, the Law of Effect. Thus one immediately starts to answer that the correct response gets learned, because it leads to some good effect and the incorrect responses get unlearned because they lead severally to bad effects.

But, as we saw at the beginning of the chapter, the Law of Effect also does not hold. The latent learning experiments indicated very definitely that just as much learning qua learning goes on without differential effects, or, at the most, with only very minor degrees of such effects, as with strongly differential ones. The latent learning, which thus takes place without any strong differential effects, does not, to be sure, manifest itself until after such effects have been introduced. But, once these latter have been provided, then the sizes of the immediate drops in the performance curves, which appear, indicate that the learning has been just as great as it would have been, if strong effects had been present throughout. Differential effects are, that is, necessary for *selective performance* but they are not necessary, or at the most in only a very minor degree, for the mere learning *qua* learning which underlies such performance.[34]

In other words, the main points to be drawn from the experimental evidence presented in this chapter are, it would seem, two: (a) there is a need for distinguishing between learning and performance; and (b) there is the fact, brought out by all the experiments on the Law of Exercise (in the differential sense), which indicates that the exclusive or excessive taking of the correct path at the expense of the incorrect paths does not as such cause learning. Some, and perhaps considerable, taking of the incorrect path also is necessary.

Combining these points, our final criticism of the trial and error doctrine is that it is its fundamental notion of stimulus-response bonds, which is wrong. Stimuli do not, as such, call out responses willy nilly. Correct stimulus-response connections do not get "stamped in," and incorrect ones do not get "stamped out." Rather learning consists in the organisms' "discovering" or "refining" what all the respective alternative responses lead to. And then, if, under the appetite-aversion conditions of the moment, the consequences of one of these alternatives is more demanded than the others—or if it be "demanded-for" and the others be "demanded-against"—then the organism will tend, after such learning, to select and to perform the response leading to the more "demanded-for" consequences. But, if there be no such difference in demands there will be no such selection and performance of the one response, even though there has been learning.

[34] This need for a distinction between performance and learning was first pointed out to us by Dr. M. H. Elliott. It has also been remarked upon by Lashley. Cf. K. S. Lashley, Learning: I. Nervous-Mechanisms of Learning, *The Foundations of Experimental Psychology* (Worcester, Mass., Clark Univ. Press, 1929), pp. 524-563.

9.   The Sign-Gestalt Theory of Trial and Error Learning

In short, we find ourselves forced back again to the sign-gestalt conception. Trial and error learning consists, we shall again assert, in the refinement, or the building up, of differential sign-gestalts. The stimulus-objects involved in the paths constituting the wrong responses become signs for the sorts of significates to be reached by such wrong responses; and the stimulus-object involved in the path constituting the correct response becomes a sign for the sort of significate to be expected as a result of this correct response. By virtue of trying out both this correct and these incorrect responses, the organism discovers these respective consequences. And he accordingly builds up, or refines, the appropriately differentiated sign-gestalts. And then, finally, he *performs* the one way or the other by virtue of these sign-relationships plus the appetite and aversion conditions of the moment.

10.   The Laws of Trial and Error Learning

Finally, however, the question must still be answered as to what are the laws of trial and error learning. The Law of Effect, as the basis of learning, irrespective of performance, and the Law of Exercise, in the sense of differential exercise on the correct response at the expense of the incorrect response, have been shown not to hold. What remains? Obviously the Law of Exercise in its other more general sense. Learning consists in the building up of appropriate sign-gestalts both as regards the correct responses and as regards the incorrect responses. The formation of any given sign-gestalt will be favored in so far as the sequence of sign-object-means-end-relation-significate involved in the given response has had the advantage of frequency, recency or primacy. In other words, for the development of each individual sign-gestalt-expectation involved in trial and error the favoring conditions are undoubtedly the same as those we discovered in the last chapter for the case of conditioned reflexes. It will be the early, frequent or recent experience of the corresponding (sign-object, means-end-relation, signified object) whole which causes the learning of the respective sign-gestalt-expectations.

11. Laws Dependent Upon the Set-up of the Total Field

A further point now, however, suggests itself. If the notion worked out in the earlier chapters of the essentially field-character of the whole behavior-situation be admitted, then it seems probable that trial and error learning really involves more than just the separate and individual learning of each of the alternative sign-gestalts—each in insulation, by itself. It appears, rather, that the learning of any one of the alternatives will be, to some extent, favored or perhaps hindered, by the simultaneous learning of the other alternatives. For the alternative sign-gestalt-expectations are being built up and learned relative to one another in some larger field whole. And, in so far as this is the case, it should follow that there will be some conditions peculiarly favorable, or the reverse, to such mutual reinforcings. The statement of such favoring and hindering conditions will constitute new additional laws for trial and error learning.

Or, to put it more concretely, what we are suggesting now is that where, say, a rat has to learn to choose between two alternative paths in a maze or two alternative brightnesses in a discrimination box, it may well be that there are certain laws, yet to be discovered, as to especially favorable orders and successions and manners of presentation to the animal of these alternatives.

For example, it was found by Nyswander (see above, p. 353 f.) that, if in the preliminary training rats were alternately forced down one path and then the other, it was harder for them then to learn to go down either path consistently than if they had been forced down each path in relatively solid blocks of trials.

Or, again, to take another example, Tolman and Honzik obtained some indication (see above Chapter III, p. 52 f.) that the condition of "latent learning" may really be more favorable to final performance than is that of constant and continuous reward.[35] Assuming this latter result to be verified, it would mean that the sort of contrasting of the one path with the other, which we are now suggesting as involved in trial and error learning, may perhaps be accomplished more efficiently when the demand to

---

[35] This result is not to be taken too seriously. It may well have been due to slip-up in technique or control. We refer to it here merely by way of illustrating the sort of phenomena we are interested in suggesting.

take either one is reduced than when it is at a maximum throughout.[36]

Learning, even trial and error learning, is the building up of a total, differentiative-predictive field.[37] And there will be, not only laws stating the conditions which favor the connecting together of the individual items in the specific alternative routes of such a field, but also laws, when we shall have discovered them, which will state the conditions which favor the contrasting, the combining, the mutual complementing, the fitting together of such alternative routes in the total field. Trial and error learning is a matter of field-organization.

12. Learning Nonsense Syllables

Finally, it may be desirable to point out how the above analysis of trial and error learning applies to such an affair as the memorizing of nonsense syllables by human beings. In a typical nonsense syllable experiment, the learner is presented a series of nonsense syllables by means of a revolving drum. The drum is hidden behind a screen with a slit on it—the slit just wide enough to allow one syllable to appear at a time. The subject's task is to memorize these syllables so that upon the appearance of the first syllable of the list he can recite the others in proper order without looking at them. This is, of course, the classical procedure—the so-called *Erlernungsmethode*—devised by Ebbinghaus and further investigated by Müller and Schumann.[38]

It will, now, be our contention that in such a situation what

[36] Similarly, it may well be that some of the unusual and unexpected effects of punishment on learning may be due to its hindering or helping in the building up of the total field-relationship between the right and the wrong responses. (See, for example, R. Valentine, The effects of punishment for errors on the maze learning of rats, *J. Comp. Psychol.*, 1930, **10**, 35-54, who found that punishment introduced after a maze was half learned and continued from then until learning was complete was less efficacious than punishment introduced only after the maze was three-quarters learned. Punishment coming near the middle of learning disrupted in a way that punishment coming near the end of learning did not.)

[37] For this general doctrine that there is no true trial and error, but that all learning, even that in the supposedly trial and error situation, is a function of the organism's capacity to respond to a *whole field* we owe a tremendous amount to Koffka's discussion in the *Growth of the Mind*. Cf. K. Koffka, *The Growth of the Mind*, 2d ed. rev. (New York, Harcourt, Brace and Company, 1928).

[38] Cf. H. Ebbinghaus, *Über das Gedächtniss*, Leipzig, 1885 [Eng. Trans. N. Y., Teachers College, Columbia Univ., 1913], G. E. Müller and F. Schumann, Beiträge zur Untersuchung des Gedächtnisses, *Zsch. f. Psychol.*, 1894, **6**, 81-190, 257-339.

the learner really achieves is first the building up of sets of sign-gestalt-expectations in simple conditioned reflex fashion. Each syllable will tend, that is, to become the sign in a lot of alternative sign-gestalts for all the subsequent syllables in the test. Because of the preceding repetitions it has been followed with smaller and larger intervals, by each of these subsequent syllables, and there have been built up according to the laws of conditioned reflex learning various strengths of sign-gestalt-expectations. Thus if Syl represents any syllable and Syl', Syl'', etc., represent later syllables, the first step in learning will consist in the building up of many sign-gestalt-expectations of the form:

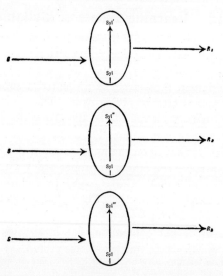

where R_1, R_2, R_3 are the responses of saying these subsequent syllables. Some of these sign-gestalts will, to be sure, be more strongly formed than others—due to the better gestalt-inducing conditions (the nearer togetherness in the series—greater similarity in characters and the like). But still there will, to a very considerable extent, develop all these alternative and conflicting sign-gestalt-expectations. The situation will have become similar to trial and error learning. The individual will then have to learn which one of these alternative propensities to select just as the rat has to learn which one of the alternative alleys to take.

Each syllable when presented (either by perception or by recall) will, in short, finally come to act as a choice point from

Learning—the Trial and Error Doctrine

which the learner then has to select the "correct" subsequent response. The diagram shown above, Chapter X on p. 146 will in short, then hold equally well here.

REFERENCES

Alonzo, A. S., The influence of manual guidance upon maze learning. *J. Comp. Psychol.*, 1926, 6, 143-158.
Carr, H. A., Principles of selection in animal learning. *Psychol. Rev.*, 1914, 21, 157-165.
——————, *Psychology, a Study of Mental Activity* (New York, Longmans, Green & Co., 1925).
Cason, H., Criticisms of the laws of exercise and effect. *Psychol. Rev.*, 1924, 31, 397-417.
Dunlap, K., A revision of the fundamental law of habit formation. *Science*, 1928, 67, 360-362.
Ebbinghaus, H., *Über das Gedächtnis* (Eng. tr., New York, Teachers College, Columbia Univ., 1913).
Hobhouse, L., *Mind in Evolution*. 2d ed. (London, Macmillan, 1915).
Holmes, S. J., *The Evolution of Animal Intelligence* (New York, Henry Holt and Company, 1911).
——————, *Studies in Animal Behavior* (Boston, Richard G. Badger, the Gorham Press, 1916).
Holsopple, J. Q. and Vanouse, I., A note on the beta hypothesis of learning. *School & Soc.*, 1929, 29, 15-16.
Koch, H. C., The influence of mechanical guidance upon maze learning. Psychol. Monog., 1923, 32, No. 147.
Koffka, K., *The Growth of the Mind*, 2d ed. rev. (New York, Harcourt, Brace and Company, 1928).
Kuo, Z. Y., The nature of unsuccessful acts and their order of elimination. *J. Comp. Psychol.*, 1922, 2, 1-27.
Lashley, K. S., *Learning:* I. Nervous Mechanisms in Learning. *The Foundations of Experimental Psychology* (Worcester, Mass., Clark Univ. Press, 1929), 524-563.
Ludgate, K. E., The effect of manual guidance upon maze learning. *Psychol. Monog.*, 1923, 33, No. 148.
Morgan, C. Lloyd, *Animal Behavior* (London, Arnold, 1900).
Müller, G. E. and Schumann, F., Experimentelle Beiträge zur Untersuchung des Gedächtnisses. *Zsch. f. Psychol.*, 1894, 6, 81-190; 257-339.
Nyswander, D. B., Recency, frequency and pattern factors in learning. Ph.D. Thesis, University of California, 1926.
Perrin, F. A. C., and Klein, D. B., *Psychology, its Methods and Principles* (New York, Henry Holt and Company, 1926).
Peterson, Joseph, The backward elimination of errors in mental maze learning. *J. Exper. Psychol.*, 1920, 3, 257-280.

Peterson, Joseph, Learning when frequency and recency factors are negative. *J. Exper. Psychol.*, 1922, **5**, 270-300.

——————, Learning when frequency and recency factors are negative and right responses are painful. *Psychol. Bull.*, 1931, **28**, 207-208.

Thorndike, E. L., *Animal Intelligence* (New York, Macmillan Co., 1911).

——————, *Educational Psychology* (New York, Teachers College, Columbia Univ., 1913), Vol. II.

——————, A fundamental theorem in modifiability. *Proc. Nat. Acad. Sci.*, 1927, **13**, 15-18.

——————, The law of effect. *Amer. J. Psychol.*, 1927, **39**, 212-222.

——————, The influence of primacy. *J. Exper. Psychol.*, 1927, **10**, 18-29.

——————, The refractory period in associative processes. *Psychol. Rev.*, 1927, **34**, 234-236.

——————, Fundamental Factors in Learning. *Proc. Ninth Internat. Cong. Psychol.* (Princeton, Psychol. Rev. Co., 1930), 429.

——————, The strengthening and weakening of mental connections by their after-effects. *Proc. Ninth Internat. Cong. Psychol.* (Princeton, Psychol. Rev. Co., 1930), 430.

——————, *Human Learning* (New York, The Century Co., 1931).

Tsai, L. S., Gradual vs. abrupt withdrawal of guidance in maze learning. *J. Comp. Psychol.*, 1930, **10**, 325-332.

Valentine, R., The effects of punishment for errors on the maze learning of rats. *J. Comp. Psychol.*, 1930, **10**, 35-54.

Wakeham, G., Query on "A revision of the fundamental law of habit formation." *Science*, 1928, **68**, 135-136.

——————, A quantitative experiment on Dr. K. Dunlap's "Revision of the fundamental law of habit formation." *J. Comp. Psychol.*, 1930, **10**, 235-236.

Wang, T. L., The influence of tuition in the acquisition of skill. *Psychol. Monog.*, 1925, **33**, No. 154.

Waters, R. H., The influence of large amounts of manual guidance upon human maze learning. *J. Gen. Psychol.*, 1930, **4**, 213-228.

Watson, J. B., *Behavior, an Introduction to Comparative Psychology* (New York, Henry Holt and Company, 1914).

Yoshioka, J. G., Frequency factor in habit formation. *J. Comp. Psychol.*, 1930, **11**, 37-49.

Chapter XXIII

THE NATURE OF LEARNING—THE DOCTRINE OF PURPOSIVE BEHAVIORISM

1. Recapitulation: Conditioned Reflexes, Trial and Error, and Inventive Learning

IN Chapter XXI it was found that the "conditioning of reflexes" is not just the simple "stamping in" of a new $S \rightarrow R$ connection that it has been supposed to be. Rather, it is the building up of a sign-gestalt-expectation. It is not an $S \rightarrow R$, but

an $s \longrightarrow \bigcirc \longrightarrow_R$, affair.

In Chapter XXII, it was seen that trial and error learning reduces to the establishing of an array of alternative sign-gestalt-expectations. The final "performance" in trial and error learning is a "selection" based upon such alternatives.

In Chapter XIV the concept of learning by means of inventive ideation was examined. Such inventive ideation was our name for that which has often been called *insight learning*.[1] The essence of such inventive learning was found to lie in the organism's "hitting upon" some wholly new aspect of the field—in his bringing into play some new manner of differentiation and prediction, in a manner never applied by him before to that particular type of situation. Such invention will, or may, result from an "adjustmental" (ideational) running-back-and-forth over those portions and aspects of the field, given to him initially. By virtue of his initially active means-end-readinesses and discriminanda- and manipulanda-readinesses he can behavior-adjust, initially, to certain por-

[1] We, however, reject the latter term, because when this term *insight learning* has been used in the past it has tended to have a double sense. On the one hand, it has been used to mean at least something similar to what we have thus called inventive, ideational learning. But, on the other hand, it also seems to have been used to mean what we would call mere means-end-capacities—quite irrespective of whether the functioning of such capacities involve any ideational inventiveness or not.

tions of the field and then, if he is fortunate, the requisite new discriminanda-, manipulanda-, or means-end-readinesses (i.e., sign-gestalt-readinesses and -expectations) will "click."

Learning is an affair of sign-gestalt formation, refinement, selection or invention. Such is our doctrine, and it is obvious that we cannot be satisfied with the ordinary list of laws. We require a reformulation of these and the addition of new ones. To such reformulations and additions we now turn.

2. The Laws of Learning, Envisaged by Purposive Behaviorism

We present a list of our modified and new laws:

Conditioned Reflex Learning

I. *Capacity Laws.*
  (a) Formal means-end-capacities. (Differentiation and prediction.)
  (b) Dimensional means-end-capacities and discriminanda- and manipulanda-capacities.
  (c) Retentivity.

II. *"Stimulus" Laws, i.e., Laws relative to interrelations in the material and in the manner of presentation.*
  (1) Interrelations in the material (Gestalt-inducing conditions).
  (m) "Togetherness" of sign, significate and means-end-relation.
  (n) Fusibility of sign, significate and means-end-relation.
  (o) Other gestalt-like laws.
  (2) Presentation Conditions.
  (u) Frequency, recency.
  (v) Revival after extinction, primacy, distributed repetitions, etc.
  (w) Motivation.
  (x) Not "effect" but "emphasis."

Trial and Error Learning

I, *Capacity Laws.*
  (a) —— as in conditioned reflex learning.
  (b) —— as in conditioned reflex learning.

(c) —— as in conditioned reflex learning.
(d) Additional formal means-end-capacities—i.e., alternativeness, roundaboutness, etc., etc.
(e) Consciousness-ability and ideation-ability.

II. *"Stimulus" Laws, i.e., Laws relative to interrelations in the material and in the manner of presentation.*
  (1) Interrelations in the material (Gestalt-inducing conditions).
    (m) —— as in conditioned reflex learning.
    (n) —— as in conditioned reflex learning.
    (o) —— as in conditioned reflex learning.
    (p) Interrelations among the spatial, temporal and other characters of the alternatives.
  (2) Presentation Conditions.
    (u) —— as in conditioned reflex learning.
    (v) —— as in conditioned reflex learning.
    (w) —— as in conditioned reflex learning.
    (x) —— as in conditioned reflex learning.
    (y) Temporal orders and sequences in the presentations of the alternatives.

Inventive Learning

I. *Capacity Laws.*
    (a) —— as in conditioned reflex learning.
    (b) —— as in conditioned reflex learning.
    (c) —— as in conditioned reflex learning.
    (d) —— as in trial and error learning.
    (e) —— as in trial and error learning.
    (f) Greativity (creative instability).

II. *"Stimulus" Laws, i.e., Laws relative to interrelations in the material and in the manner of presentation.*
  (1) Interrelations in the material (Gestalt-inducing conditions).
    (m) —— as in conditioned reflex learning.
    (n) —— as in conditioned reflex learning.
    (o) —— as in conditioned reflex learning.
    (p) —— as in trial and error learning.
    (q) Characters in the material favoring new closures and expansions of the field.

(2) Presentation conditions.
    (u) —— as in conditioned reflex learning.
    (v) —— as in conditioned reflex learning.
    (w) —— as in conditioned reflex learning.
    (x) —— as in conditioned reflex learning.
    (y) —— as in trial and error learning.
    (z) Temporal relations between the presentation of certain of the already given alternatives and the true solution.

This list distributes our laws under the three kinds of learning. All the laws involved in conditioned reflex learning are repeated under trial and error learning, and certain new ones are added. And all these are repeated under inventive learning and still other new ones added. It is to be remarked, however, that such a classification is probably not absolute. All the new laws, which seem to come in, when one passes from conditioned reflex learning to trial and error learning or from the latter to inventive learning—are probably really operative to some slight degree throughout. It is merely that they begin to play a more outstanding and appreciable rôle as one passes to the higher situations.

It will be observed, further, that the laws all fall under the two main heads: (I) Capacity Laws; and (II) "Stimulus" Laws. Again, the latter have been further subdivided into: (1) Laws relative to interrelations in the material; and (2) Laws relative to the manner of presentation.

Let us examine the table in more detail. Let us begin with the *capacity laws,* and carry them through all three kinds of learning.

3. Capacity Laws (Conditioned Reflex Learning)

The *capacity laws* are to be conceived in general as listing certain fundamental traits, capacities, aptitudes, the possession of which in the given individual or species will favor learning.

(a) *Formal means-end-capacities (i.e., capacities for simple differentiation and prediction)* are obviously essential even to such simple sign-gestalt formation as is involved in conditioned reflex learning. An animal must, then and there, be capable of differentiating the given sign, significate, and means-end-relation from others and of forming the connecting predictive relations. And the quicker and more facile he is at such differentiation and such prediction, the better he will be at such conditioned reflex learning.

(b) *Dimensional means-end-capacities and discriminanda- and manipulanda-capacities.* The animal must be capable also of achieving correct expectations with respect to the specific sorts of dimensional material—space, time, gravitation, social relations, or what not—constituting the stuffs of the given sign, the given significate and the given means-end-relations. And the greater his capacities for such materials, again the better he will be at the given conditioned reflex learning.

(c) *Retentivity.* Finally, the animal must be capable of "retaining" these differentiations and predictions from trial to trial. And the better he is at retaining, the sooner he will thus learn.

4. Capacity Laws (Trial and Error Learning)

Consider now the new capacities which come to the fore in trial and error learning. They are two: (d) more complicated means-end-capacities, such as those of alternativeness, roundaboutness, final common-pathness, etc., and (e) the capacities for consciousness and for ideation (consciousness-ability and ideation-ability).

(d) *Formal means-end-capacities, alternativeness, roundaboutness, final common pathness, etc.* It seems quite obvious that, since trial and error learning is, as we have seen, not merely a discovery of what the individual paths lead to, but also an eventual selection among those paths, trial and error learning will be especially favored by the capacity for the more general field-relationships of alternativeness, roundaboutness, final common pathness, etc., (See above, Chapter XII.)

(e) *Consciousness-ability plus ideation-ability.* We are assuming that consciousness-ability, i.e., the capacity to run back and forth in a disinterested fashion over the elements of the field (see above Chapter XIII, p. 213 f.), and also ideation-ability, the capacity to "adjust" to such runnings-back-and-forth, are not involved to any appreciable extent in simple conditioned reflex learning. The animals that are conscious probably do not acquire conditioned reflexes any more rapidly than the animals that are not thus conscious. (An interesting experiment to try in this connection would be to see whether simple conditioned reflexes could be acquired in sleeping conditions as readily as in waking ones.) We shall assume, however, that, when it comes to trial and error learning, this being conscious or this ideating are of very considerable advantage. The more the given animal, or species of animal, can "hold up" his practical behavior in order to reinforce by "actual" or "adjustmental" runnings-back-and-forth relative to the predictive and differentiative relations in the total field, the more rapidly, we must suppose, he will be able to build up a total field and the relations among the alternatives within such a field.

5. Capacity Laws (Inventive Learning)

Consider now, inventive learning. All the capacities listed under trial and error learning will again play a part, and in addition we note the rôle of one new capacity, viz., creativity.

(f) *Creativity* (*creative instability*). It seems obvious that a capacity to break out into new lines of behavior, ideationally or actually, will be fundamental for inventive learning. Two individuals of one and the same species may be exactly equal in formal and dimensional means-end-capacities, in consciousness-ability, ideation-ability, retentivity, etc., and yet the one is more inventive than the other. The less inventive will "understand" the matter, once it has been shown to him, with facility equal to that of the other. But he will be less likely to "hit upon" this matter initially and for himself. The more inventive will be better at inventive learning solely by virtue of being endowed with a larger dose of something to be called creativity, or perhaps even *creative instability*. This more inventive individual will be one who, for some reason, is especially prone to break out into new differentiations and predictions. He will break out, into responses which, as far as the given type of situation is concerned, have never occurred with him before. This inventive individual will be one who is labile and "unstable." He will by virtue of some sort of internal breakdown, tend to do something "queer" and "foreign" in any given situation. He will have a large dose of creativity.

6. Summary for Capacity Laws

To sum up, the total list of capacity laws is:

(a) Formal means-end-capacities (differentiation and prediction).

(b) Dimensional means-end-capacities and discriminanda- and manipulanda-capacities.

(c) Retentivity.

(d) Additional formal means-end-capacities:—alternativeness, roundaboutness, etc.

(e) Consciousness-ability and ideation-ability.

(f) Creativity (creative instability).

Of these, only (a), (b) and (c) would seem to play any considerable rôle in simple conditioned reflex learning (i.e., single sign-gestalt formation). It is probable, however that (d) and (e) also enter into trial and error learning; while, lastly, (f) most certain enters into inventive learning.

These laws state, severally, certain types of ability or capacity the possession of which will aid a given individual to achieve the learning. And, the greater the amounts of any one of the capacities, the easier, other things being equal, the given learning will be. Such capacity laws state the conditions whereby certain individuals or species will learn better than others—stimulus conditions remaining the same.

7. "Stimulus" Laws

We turn, now, to the second group of laws—those concerning the interrelations in the material and in the manner of its presentation. The capacity laws, as we saw, stated the conditions whereby certain individuals or species of individual will, as such, other things being equal, tend to learn better than others. The second group of laws states, in contrast, the conditions whereby certain types of material, or types of presentation of that material will, as such, be more easily learned than others, when the individuals or species in question all have equal, or approximately equal, capacities. Whereas the capacity laws stated the conditions within the individual which make for easy learning, this second group of laws state the conditions in the "stimulus" [2]—i.e., in the material and in the manner of its presentation—which make for easy learning. The capacity laws are the ones which are of prime interest to the students of "individual psychology" (see next chapter), whereas the "stimulus" laws are the ones which have in the past been of

[2] It is obvious that we here use the term *stimulus* in a loose sense, as a convenient single word to cover both the nature of the total complex of material to be learned and the details in its temporal manner of presentation.

prime interest to students of what we may call the "normative psychologies." (See next chapter.)

Further, as regards the two subdivisions under this group of "stimulus" laws, (1) laws relative to the interrelations in the material, and (2) laws relative to the interrelations in the manner of the presentation of the material, we note, further, that the laws coming under the first of these subheads we owe primarily to the *Gestalt* psychologists, whereas those coming under the second, we owe primarily to what we may call the pre-*Gestalt* psychologists. That is, the importance of the presentation factors, e.g., those of frequency and recency, in making the learning easy, have long been investigated and given much emphasis by both human and animal psychologists.[3] But the fact that the products of learning are always organizations—*Gestalts*—and not just "tied-together" elements, and hence that there are laws as to the kinds and characters and interrelations in the material itself, which favor learning, seems never to have been sufficiently emphasized prior to the gestalt psychologists. And hence it is due primarily (though, of course, not exclusively) to the impetus of *Gestalt Psychology* that we owe the discovery of these conditions in the stimulus material.

We turn now to a review of all these laws—one at a time.

8. Laws Relative to the Nature of the Material (Conditioned Reflex Learning)

Given the necessary formal dimensional means-end capacities and discriminanda- and manipulanda-capacities and the necessary retentivity, then simple conditioned reflex learning consists, as we have declared, in the acquisition of single sign-gestalt-expectations and -readinesses). What now are the conditions in the "stimulus" material itself which will affect the formation and retention of such sign-gestalts? We seem to find three such conditions which we shall summarize under the heads of the *Law of Togetherness* and the *Law of Fusibility* and *Other Gestalt-like Laws*.

(m) *The Law of Togetherness* (i.e., of sign, significate, and means-end-relation) would state that in order that a specific sign-gestalt-expectation may be acquired readily, the parts of that

---

[3] From Ebbinghaus down in the former case, and from Thorndike down in the latter.

gestalt, i.e., the specific sign, means-end-relation and significate, must be presented by the environment in some sort of a "togetherness" fashion which sets them off as a unit or "figure" from the total background of surrounding experience. Or, in other words, the given sign, means-end-relation and significate must vary together concomitantly, whatever the changes or lack of changes in the other surroundings. The dog will not learn to secrete saliva for the given color unless this color, together with the subsequent fact of its leading on to food, are actually placed by the experimental conditions into a single temporal "togetherness," which makes them stand out from all the million and one other concurrently bombarding stimuli. And the rat that learns to take the white side of the discrimination box as the sign for coming food, will not learn to do so unless again these parts—whiteness, entering, getting food—are, as such, placed "together" spatially, temporally and sequentially, or whatever it may be. This fact of the need of a "togetherness" for learning has indeed been prettily illustrated by Thorndike. He has called it the principle of "belongingness." We cite but one of his experiments for illustrating it.

"We announced to the subjects, 'I shall read you a long list of pairs of words and numbers like bread 29, wall 16, Texas 78. You will listen as I read them. Pay about as close attention as you would in an average class. Be sure that you hear each pair as I read it.' The series of 1,304 pairs contained, among other pairs, four pairs (dregs 91, charade 17, swing 62, and antelope 35) each occurring twenty-four times and so placed that

dregs always came just after 42,
charade always came just after 86,
swing always came just after 94, and
antelope always came just after 97.

"After the series had been read, the subjects were asked to write which numbers came just after certain words and also which words came just after certain numbers, namely, 42, 86, 94, 97.
"The average percentage of correct response for the numbers following words in pairs occurring eighteen or twenty-one times each scattered throughout the series was 37.5 (median 38). The average percentage of correct responses for the words following the numbers twenty-four times each was 0.5 per cent, which is no more than mere chance guessing would give.
"The nature of the instructions, the way in which the pairs were read, and the habits of life in general, led the subjects to consider each word as belonging to the number that followed it, and each

number as belonging to the word that preceded it. In this experiment, the temporal contiguity of a number with the word following it, the mere sequence without belonging, does nothing to the connection." [4]

Or, in our own terms, it appeared that quite without any motivation on their part, the subjects did tend to connect the pairs into sign-gestalt wholes whereby the presentation of the first member of a pair did lead the subject then to expect the second member of that pair. Some sort of a "togetherness" of the members of a pair against the rest of the numbers and words as background caused them to form sign-gestalt wholes in which the first-coming word of each pair became the sign for the later-coming number of the same pair.

But indeed this fact of some sort of a "togetherness" as the essential condition for the formation of "organizations" (gestalts) is perhaps the main burden of the contributions of Gestalt Psychology to the problems of learning and memory. Köhler in particular seems to have emphasized this point. [5]

(n) *The Law of Fusibility.*—The second gestalt law which seems to us to be involved even in Conditioned Reflex Learning—i.e., single sign-gestalt formation—we have designated as the law of the *Fusibility of sign, significate and signified means-end-relation.* And what we mean by this law is that certain characters of signs, means-end-relations and significates will undoubtedly fuse together into single sign-gestalt wholes more readily than will others. It appears, in short, that there will be stronger dispositions toward gestalt-formation when the characters of the parts have certain relations to each other than when they have other relations. Some characters will organize themselves into gestalt wholes more readily than will others.

In the case of the conditioning of simple physiological reflexes, this would mean, say, that certain types of to-be-conditioned stimuli, perhaps odors, should come to evoke salivary secretions, i.e., become a sign for coming food, more readily than will others. Whereas other types of stimuli—say, perhaps, noises—will more readily come to evoke avoidance responses. And, in the case of

---

[4] E. L. Thorndike, *Human Learning* (New York, The Century Co., 1931), p. 23 f. Also see above, footnote at beginning of Chap. XXII.

[5] Cf. W. Köhler, *Gestalt Psychology* (New York, Horace Liveright, 1929), esp. Chapters VIII and IX.

rats learning mazes, it would mean, perhaps, that it should take fewer trials to establish the running-on response to food than, say, to acquire the response of merely waiting in a detention-chamber for food or the like.

Again, however, it is to be noted that this law of the greater fusibility of some characters than others into single sign-gestalts is in a sense merely a further extension of the preceding law of "togetherness." The Law of Togetherness as worded above stated that some sort of temporal and spatial, or other, "togetherness" was essential to easy "gestalting," whereas this *Law of Fusibility* adds the further point that certain types of "qualitative togetherness" will also make for easier gestalting than will others.[6]

(o) *Other Gestalt-like Laws.* Finally, it may be pointed out that probably certain still other gestalt-like laws ought to be included by us somewhere about here,—viz., laws concerning the career of the sign-gestalt-expectations in the course of forgetting. For the *Gestalt* psychologists have brought it now to the attention of us all that the process of forgetting is not a simple one of mere weakening or dimming but is, rather, one tending to involve also actual changes and rearrangements in the qualities of the material which has been learned. Their doctrine is that, with the passage of time, the remembered material tends to be modified always in the direction of greater *Prägnanz*—that is, in the direction of "better," "clearer," "more stable," (more "pregnant") gestalts.[7] And the first experiments indicating this fact of increasing *Prägnanz* in remembered material with the passage of time were done in Koffka's laboratory by Wulf.[8] Wulf presented nonsense drawings to his subjects and he found that with the passage of time these drawings, when the subjects later tried to reproduce them, tended to take on either a more and more simplified or a more and more articulated form—i.e., the Law of *Prägnanz* operated, and the retained patterns tended to become ever "better" gestalts

[6] For a gestalt discussion of learning, of which our two laws of "togetherness" and "fusibility" are very reminiscent, see Chapter VIII in Köhler's *Gestalt Psychology*. Cf. W. Köhler, *Gestalt Psychology* (New York, Horace Liveright, 1929).

[7] This term *Prägnanz* seems to have been first suggested by Wertheimer. (Cf. M. Wertheimer, Untersuchungen zur Lehre von der Gestalt II., *Psychol. Forsch.*, 1923, **4**, 301-350.)

[8] Cf. F. Wulf, Über die Veränderung von Vorstellungen (Gedächtnis und Gestalt); Nr. VI der Beiträge zur Psychologie der Gestalt, herausgegeben von K. Koffka, *Psychol. Forsch.*, 1922, **1**, 333-373.

in some one way or another. Later Gibson repeated a somewhat similar experiment [9] with a somewhat similar outcome. But, according to Gibson, these changes which appeared were in reality always conditioned by the manner of the original apprehension. The drawings were always originally apprehended, he found, *as like such and such actual concrete objects,* or as like such and such nameable *geometric figures* or combinations of such figures, or as so and so like or different from such and such *other drawings* in the same series. And he found that in the later attempts at reproduction the reproduced figures tended to approach these other entities to which they had thus been likened in the original apprehension. Gibson tends to conclude, therefore, (though he is careful not to commit himself completely) that a similar explanation probably also holds for all of Wulf's results.

At any rate, we, on our part, shall now adopt this interpretation made by Gibson. Our doctrine will, in short, be that in the original apprehension what really happens is the establishing of complete sign-gestalts in which the presented drawings function as signs and in which such and such common-sense objects, or such and such nameable geometric figures, or such and such of the other patterns in the series function as the significates of those signs. That is, we shall hold that the original apprehensions always arouse complete sign-gestalts and not just signs without significates. The presented drawings function as signs and the things they are likened to as the significates of those signs. And the resulting law of forgetting we will describe, therefore, not so much as a law of *Prägnanz,* as a law to the effect that:—with the passage of time the sign-object in an acquired sign-gestalt tends (unless the re-presentation of the original stimulus conditions prevents) always to approach more and more to the character of its own original significate.

9. Laws Relative to the Nature of the Material (Trial and Error Learning)

Under this head there has been listed only one new law—

(p) *Interrelations among the spatial, temporal and other characters of the alternatives.* We present this as an additional law

[9] Cf. J. J. Gibson, The reproduction of visually perceived forms, *J. Exper. Psychol.,* 1929, **12**, 1-39.

because, although this law has not yet, as far as we know, been demonstrated, it seems to us indubitable that the future must discover such a law. The field as a whole is a gestalt which grows out of the minor gestalts corresponding to the individual trials and errors. It seems probable, therefore, that there will be some especially gestalt-favoring relationships whereby such bigger wholes will most readily appear. Certain temporal, spatial, or qualitative interrelations between the alternatives will undoubtedly be more favorable to the building up of such total field-wholes, than will others.

Indeed, as a bit of empirical evidence for such a law, in the case at least of the rat, we should cite an experiment now in progress at the University of California. Miss E. P. Bretnall is carrying out a comparison of two arrangements in a simple white-black discrimination experiment. The rat enters a choice chamber and is confronted with two alley entrances leading from the opposite wall, each of which has a curtain hanging down in front of it, one white curtain and one black curtain. The animal has to learn always to take the white curtain, which is sometimes on the left and sometimes on the right. Miss Bretnall is discovering that, if the box is so made that the two alleys to be chosen between lie closely contiguous one to another in the opposite wall of the choice chamber, the rats learn the discrimination sooner than if it be constructed so that these two alleys are spread farther apart—all other dimensions remaining the same. If her result be substantiated, it would provide an example of our law. It would demonstrate that, at least as regards space, certain interrelationships between two alternatives make the building up of the total trial and error field easier than do other such interrelationships.

And indeed another point should also be noted in this connection. For Köhler [10] has suggested that not only will certain interrelations among alternative choice-objects or choice-routes be especially favorable to the original acquisition of the requisite organizations (i.e., sign-gestalts), but also that these more favorable interrelations would probably likewise lead to more permanent retention—(e.g., to longer possibilities of delay in a delayed reaction experiment). Thus, for example, if Miss Bretnall's result that doors near together can be learned more readily than doors

[10] W. Köhler, *Gestalt Psychology* (New York, Horace Liveright, 1929), Ch. IX, pp. 305 ff.

farther apart be confirmed, it should also be found that in a delayed reaction set-up similar to that used by Honzik [11] two doors near together should give longer and more stable delays than would a similar set-up with the two doors farther apart.

Evidence for very much this sort of thing has in fact already been obtained by Yarborough [12] in that he found that with three doors he could get a delay with cats of only about four seconds whereas with only two doors he could get delays of four times that amount. And Hertz,[13] whom Köhler likewise cites in this connection, found in somewhat similar fashion that birds could perceive and *remember* under which container a nut had been hidden much better when the given container had some sort of a visually "accented" position with reference to the other containers.

10. Laws Relative to the Nature of the Material (Inventive Learning)

Passing on, now, to the case of Inventive Learning, again we have only one new law of the gestalt variety to suggest.

(q) We have designated it rather vaguely as the *Law of presentations and characters favoring new closures and expansions of the field*. Inventive learning differs from trial and error learning in that, whereas trial and error learning involves merely the building up of a total means-end-field out of alternative parts, all of which are actually experienced, inventive learning requires the extrapolation of such a field to parts never actually enjoyed. Such inventive learning will, therefore, be favored by whatever conditions, of content and the like, the gestalt psychology discovers as favorable to such extrapolations. There will, that is, no doubt be conditions in the placement—and order—and character-interrelations of the parts of the field, already given, which will be especially favorable to the invention of the required new parts. An instance of this would be the discovery by Köhler [14] that in the

---

[11] Cf. C. H. Honzik, Delayed reaction in rats, *Univ. Calif. Publ. Psychol.*, 1931, **4**, 307-318. (See also above Chapter X, p. 158 f.)

[12] Cf. Yarborough, The delayed reaction with sound and light in cats. *J. Anim. Behav.*, 1917, **7**, 87-110.

[13] M. Hertz, Wahrnehmungspsychologische Untersuchungen am Eichelhäher, I. & II. *Zsch. f. vergl. Physiol.*, 1928, **7**, 144-194; 617-656.

[14] W. Köhler, *The Mentality of Apes* (New York, Harcourt, Brace and Company, 1925), p. 37 f.

case of the apes' learning to use a stick to rake in food, the solution came sooner when the stick lay on the ground in the front of the cage near the food, so that it and the food could be grasped in a single *coup d'oeil*.[15]

11. Laws Relative to the Manner of Presentation

We are ready, now, to turn to the second group of *"stimulus"* laws—those which concern not so much the nature of the material itself as the nature of the formal, temporal or other conditions of its presentation. These, as we have said, have long been subject-matter for the study of the "pre-gestalt" students of "normative psychology." Attempts at formulations concerning these general "formal" conditions of presentation have led to the laws of learning which have flourished in the past. Indeed, it is primarily these "pre-gestalt" and "pre-individual-difference" laws which have already been considered in the two just preceding chapters, with reference to the Conditioned Reflex and the Trial and Error Doctrines of Learning.

The nature of these favorable formal conditions of presentation do, of course, constitute an important consideration for any doctrine of learning. They have to be revaluated, however, in the light of recent experiments and in the light of our present sign-gestalt notion.[16]

We turn to their detailed consideration under each of the three types of learning.

12. Laws Relative to the Manner of Presentation (Conditioned Reflex Learning)

Conditioned reflex learning is simple sign-gestalt formation. Given the requisite capacities in the individual and given the requi-

---

[15] This fact of the importance of the set-up for the necessary expansions or contractions of the field requisite in inventive learning is one which seems to have been particularly clearly emphasized by Koffka. Cf. K. Koffka, *The Growth of the Mind,* 2d ed. rev. (New York, Harcourt, Brace and Company, 1928), Chapter IV.

[16] The distinction we have been drawing between these formal laws of presentation, on the one hand, and the laws involved in the nature of the material itself, on the other, seems to be much the same as that Koffka (*Growth of the Mind*) emphasizes between the "problem of memory" and the "problem of achievement." What he calls the problem of memory concerns the formal conditions of presentation; while what he calls the problem of achievement seems to concern, rather, the conditions in the material itself.

site togetherness and fusibility in the material to be learned, it is obvious that the degree to which any required conditioned reflex will be established will be a function of the manner and conditions of presentation. Let us consider these manners and conditions one at a time.

(u) *Frequency, Recency.* This of course corresponds to what in the preceding chapter we designated as the correct use of the "law of exercise." For it is obvious that the more frequently and more recently the actual sequence of sign, means-end-relation and significate has been presented, the stronger, other things being equal, this resulting sign-gestalt will tend to be.

(v) *Revival after Extinction, Primacy, Distributed Repetitions.* Under this single, rather omnibus, heading, we have sought to gather together a variety of further conditions which, no doubt, still need more investigation but all of which have to do with the temporal relations of the presentation. It has been seen (see Chapter XXI, p. 324 f.) that the simple conditioned reflex, after it has been made to wane on a given day because of lack of confirmation, will nevertheless tend to revive on a subsequent day. And this, it seems, is closely related to the old doctrine of primacy, viz., the doctrine that those connections which are established early have an undue tendency to persist and revive. And again there is also the well-established orthodox finding that temporally spaced repetitions are better than temporally concentrated ones. We are concerned here, that is, with the various temporal conditions of presentation, and with the laws whereby some such temporal conditions are more favorable than others.

(w) *Motivation* (?). Next, as a third law under the head of conditioned reflex learning, we should suggest (with a question mark), the law of motivation. We should suggest, that is, that in so far as the significate is either a strongly to-be-got-to or a strongly to-be-got-from object, by virtue of a given appetite or aversion or by virtue of some established subordinate drive, that the formation of the given sign-gestalt-readiness and -expectation will tend to be facilitated. The evidence on this point is, however, by no means clear.

When we recall the latent learning experiments, we remember that they indicated that latent learning conditions (in which the food box was not strongly to-be-got-to) seemed, as far as pure learning was concerned, to lead to the requisite sign-gestalt-formations just as rapidly as and perhaps more rapidly than did the control condition in which the rewards were always present.

It appears possible, therefore, that learning without any very obvious motivation can occur. But, on the other hand, it might also be contended that in such cases the learning would not have occurred, if it had not been for some "general" motivation of curiosity, or the like, which made all paths to some degree interesting.

Obviously further experiments and further analysis are needed.

(x) *Not "Effect" but "Emphasis."* Finally, it now appears that, irrespective of whether or not the Law of Motivation holds, there is a Law of Emphasis which does hold. Any strongly inciting situation, good or bad, accompanying either the sign or the significate, or both, does tend to facilitate learning. Pleasant or repulsive odors, electric shocks and the like seem always to aid learning. And, further, it is to be noted that this seems to be all that we have left of the old, orthodox Law of Effect. The *significate* or the *sign* must, probably, have some "interest," positive or negative, to the animal (though perhaps not too much) if he is to respond to it and its relations at all. But it makes no difference whether this "interest" is due to its "goodness" or its "badness." In fact, if there be any differential effect at all, it may well be that the "bad," "unpleasant" consequences will "stamp in" the sign-gestalts leading to them more rapidly than "good" or "pleasant" consequences will stamp in the contrasted sign-gestalts. (See experiment by Bretnall and Hall, Chapter XXII, p. 344 f.) It may well be, in other words, that on a basis of further experimentation, it will turn out that avoidance associations (sign-gestalts) are generally, other things being equal, "conditioned" more readily than approach associations (sign-gestalts). And, if such be the case, the Law of Effect in any differential sense is flatly denied and contradicted.

Again, however, it is evident that this situation also is in need of further investigation.

13. Laws Relative to the Manner of Presentation (Trial and Error Learning)

There is only one new law relative to the conditions of presentation which seems to appear when we pass from conditioned reflex learning to trial and error learning.

(y) It may be labeled the *Law of Temporal orders and se-quences in the presentations of the alternatives*. There is perhaps as yet no very good experimental evidence as to this law. But it seems more than probable that, since, in trial and error learning, the animal has to build up a grasp of the interrelations in a total field, certain orders and successions in trying out these alterna-tives should be more helpful than others. If, for example, there are only two paths to be distinguished between, it may well be that alternate trying of the one and then the other may be less helpful in building up the total relationships than a concentrated bunch of takings of first the one path, followed by a concen-trated bunch of takings of the second path. (Or it may be that just the reverse holds.[17]) But in any case, it seems indubitable that there will be some law of this general sort, if we can but discover it.

14. Laws Relative to the Manner of Presentation (Inventive Learning)

Finally, turning to inventive learning, we find but one more law. We have designated it:

(z) *Temporal relations between the presentation of certain of the already given alternatives and the true solution.* We have in mind here the undoubted fact that a final solution (i.e., the new sign-gestalt-readiness and -expectation) will be hit upon more successfully as a result of a recent dwelling upon certain of the other already given sign-gestalts than as a result of a recent dwelling upon others of them. We recall again in this connection the experiments of Brown and Whittell.[18] It must be noted that these investigators found that the difficulty of any given multiple choice problem depended very much upon what problems had just preceded it. Certain just preceding types of solution (types of field-principle) rendered the hitting upon the new type of solu-tion (field-principle with resultant sign-gestalt-formations) rela-tively difficult, whereas others facilitated it.

Indeed, it appears that the classical "transfer" experiments

[17] Dr. Nyswander's results (see above, Chapter XXII, p. 353 f.) suggest the first conclusion.
[18] W. Brown and F. Whittell, Yerkes' multiple choice method with human adults, *J. Comp. Psychol.*, 1924, 7, 469-475. See above Chapter XII, p. 194.

really bear upon this point. Transfer experiments are of course usually considered under the head of trial and error learning. They are experiments in which one trial and error problem is followed by another; and the positive or negative effect of the first upon the second is measured. In many cases, however, the effect of the first problem upon the second is, it seems to us, really analogous to the effect of a first problem upon a second inventive problem. If, in the transfer experiment, the effect is positive, it means that the first solution was such as to make the "hitting upon the solution of the second problem" in the sense of recognizing it, easy. Whereas, if the effect is negative, it means that the solution of the first problem was contrary to a ready "hitting upon" (i.e., a ready recognition of) the solution of the second problem.

The difference between trial and error learning and inventive learning is here merely one of degree. In both cases some type of early problem will favor the recognition of, or invention of, the solution of a given second problem, whereas other types of early problem will hinder the recognition of, or invention of, the solution of this second problem.

15. Summary of Doctrine

We may now briefly sum up the above doctrine of learning as expressed in all of the above laws. Two features with regard to it are to be emphasized, viz., (i) its relations to pre-gestalt psychology and (ii) its relations to pre-individual or "normative psychology."

(i) The orthodox, pre-gestalt, laws of learning are to be classed under the head of "stimulus" laws, inasmuch as they, in general, tend to concern merely the conditions of presentation. But gestalt psychology has emphasized that learning is essentially the formation, or modification, of gestalts. Hence there will also be certain laws relative to the fundamental types of relationship in the material itself. And this gives rise to a second set of "stimulus" laws, viz., the "gestalt-inducing" laws.

(ii) Again, it appears that both pre-gestalt psychology and gestalt psychology proper have tended to overlook the facts of individual differences. They have neglected the facts of the individual capacities involved in learning. Purposive behaviorism, on the other hand, has tried to emphasize these latter facts. It adds a list of capacity laws to the merely "stimulus" laws of pre-gestalt and gestalt psychology.

16. The Probable Interdependence of Stimulus Laws and Capacity Laws

Finally, it may now be suggested that when, in the future, the investigation and control of individual differences shall have progressed much farther than at present, it may turn out that the various actions, or at any rate weightings, of the different "stimulus" laws will prove to be modified, accordingly as different degrees of capacity are present. It may turn out, for example, that "bright" animals (i.e., animals with strong amounts of means-end-capacity, discriminanda- and manipulanda-capacities, retentivity, consciousness-ability, ideation-ability, creativity) will prove to be quite differently affected by frequency, recency, spaced repetitions, and the like, than will "dull" animals—and similarly for "togetherness," "fusibility," and the like.

Indeed, a hopeful empirical program for the immediate future would seem to lie in an experimental reëxamination of the "stimulus" laws for individuals of different capacities. In other words, all our regulation, classical, learning experiments should be tried over again, separately, for "bright" animals and "dull" animals and "medium" animals.[19] And, when this is done, it may well turn out that these "stimulus laws" will prove to be different, or at least to have different weightings, for different capacity-levels. It may well be, in short, that eventually (in the psychology of the future) there will have to be a much closer give and take, than there is at present, between a doctrine and description of capacities and a doctrine and description of the "normal" stimulus-response processes.[20]

---

[19] This will soon be possible in the case of rats by using the strains that are being bred by Prof. R. C. Tryon. Cf. R. C. Tyron, The genetics of learning ability in rats, *Univ. Calif. Publ. Psychol.*, 1929, **4**, 71-89.

[20] Throughout this chapter we have entirely neglected any discussion of "fixation" although in Chapters X and XIX such fixation was pointed to as one of the frequent fates attending learning. The reason for our omission is, however, obvious. Nothing is as yet known as to the *laws* of such fixation. Nothing is known as to the special conditions which favor "fixations," occurring

REFERENCES

Brown, W. and Whittell, F., Yerkes' multiple choice method with
human adults. *J. Comp. Psychol.*, 1924, **7**, 469-475.

Gibson, J. J., The reproduction of visually perceived forms. *J.
Exper. Psychol.*, 1929, **12**, 1-39.

Gilhousen, H. C., An investigation of insight in rats. *Science*,
1931, **73**, 711-712.

Hertz, M., Wahrnemungspsychologische Untersuchungen am
Eichelhäher, I. & II. *Zsch. f. vergl. Physiol.*, 1928, **7**, 144-194;
617-656.

Koffka, K., *The Growth of the Mind*, 2d ed. rev. (New York,
Harcourt, Brace and Company, 1928).

Köhler, W., *The Mentality of Apes* (New York, Harcourt, Brace
and Company, 1925.

——————, *Gestalt Psychology* (New York, Horace Liveright,
1929).

Thorndike, E. L., *Human Learning* (New York, The Century
Co., 1931).

Tryon, R. C., The genetics of learning ability in rats. *Univ. Calif.
Publ. Psychol.*, 1929, **4**, 71-89.

Warden, C. J. and Aylesworth, M., The relative effects of reward
and punishment in the formation of a visual discrimination
habit in the white rat. *J. Comp. Psychol.*, 1927, **7**, 117-127.

Wertheimer, M., Untersuchungen zur Lehre von der Gestalt, II.
Psychol. Forsch., 1923, **4**, 301-350.

Wulf, F., Über die Veränderung von Vorstellungen (Gedächtnis
und Gestalt); Nr. VI der Beiträge zur Psychologie der Gestalt,
herausgegeben von K. Koffka. *Psychol. Forsch.*, 1922, **1**, 333-
373.

superimposed upon—or, perhaps, at the expense of—true sign-gestalt-formations.

It may be noted, however, that very recently a program for attacking this
problem of "fixation" as something detachable from learning, as such, has been
outlined by Gilhousen. He has discovered that rats who have learned a jumping
path to food seem to become surprisingly "fixated" to such "jumping" at
the expense of taking a smooth and much easier running path. And he pro-
poses various ways of discovering how soon such fixation occurs and what sort
of conditions favor it. (Cf. H. C. Gilhousen, An investigation of insight in rats,
Science, 1931, **73**, 711-712.)

PART VI
THIS SYSTEM *QUA* SYSTEM

It is obvious that the preceding pages have attempted to offer a new "system" of psychology. But system-making is very properly open to suspicion. It is the resort of arm-chair hiders from reality. And, once set up, a system probably does as much harm as good. It serves as a sort of sacred grating behind which each novice is commanded to kneel in order that he may never see the real world, save through its interstices. And each system is so obviously bound to be wrong. It is twisted out of plumb by the special cultural lack of building materials inherent in the time and place of its origin, as well as by the lack of skill of its individual architect or architects.

An apology, therefore, is in order. We can, in short, merely hope that the propositions summarized in the succeeding pages, when set up in front of you as a pattern of mullions through which to observe the psychological landscape, will serve (but only temporarily) to limn into prominence for you new areas for the gathering of data.

But may neither you nor we ever seek to hold up these propositions, save in a somewhat amused, a somewhat skeptical, and a wholly adventure-seeking and pragmatic behavior-attitude.

Chapter XXIV

THE FINAL VARIABLES OF PURPOSIVE BEHAVIORISM [1]

1. The Variables Assumed by the Present System to be Compared with Those Assumed by Other Systems

WE wish now to summarize all the variables and inter-relationships which have been assumed. We want to indicate, that is, the complete doctrine of Purposive Behaviorism relative to: (a) the dependencies of behavior upon what have been designated as the behavior-determinants—i.e., capacities, immanent determinants and behavior-adjustments; (b) the interrelations of these latter among themselves; and (c) the final dependencies of the behavior-determinants themselves upon external stimuli, initiating physiological states, heredity and past training.

But first, by way of introduction, it will be helpful to review the sorts of variables and their interrelations which have been assumed by other psychologies. Other academic psychologies can, we believe, be usefully grouped into three main varieties to be designated as—"Individual Psychologies," "Normative Psychologies" and "Complete Psychologies." Let us begin, then, by considering the sort of variables assumed by typical instances of each of these three.

2. "Individual Psychologies"; "Normative Psychologies"; "Complete Psychologies"

The psychologies of individual differences ("individual psychologies") are, of course, now most rampant. Taking as their subject-matter arrays of different individuals and concerning

[1] Grateful acknowledgment is to be made to Dr. R. C. Tryon for stimulating much of the present chapter, for a number of the ideas incorporated in it and for much helpful criticism with respect to it.

themselves primarily with the differences between such individuals, these individual or "capacity" psychologies have evolved special sets of variables of their own—intelligence, mental age, achievement, general factor, specific factors, aptitudes, and the like. Thus, according to these psychologies, a concrete behavior-performance, upon any given occasion, is to be conceived primarily as a function of: (a) the nature of the particular stimulus-situation, and (b) the allotments in the given individual of certain measurable capacities or traits.

Contrasted with such "individual psychologies" [2] stand the interests and techniques of what we may now call the "experimental," [3] "stimulus" or "normative" psychologies. These latter types of psychology, in the sense in which we are meaning them here, are to be distinguished from the individual psychologies in that they are interested primarily, not in the differences between individuals, but rather in the "normal mental processes" or "events" which are supposed to go on in every "normal" or "average" individual, of the given species, in response to such and such stimuli. The normative psychologies have evolved their concepts of intervening "mental processes" or "events" to explain why the various different stimuli produce the different responses, or tendencies to response, that they do, in one and the same normal, or average, individual.

Finally, the "complete psychologies," of which it seems to us there have as yet been all too few, attempt to combine the techniques and results of both the individual psychologies and the normative psychologies. A complete psychology is concerned both with what specific standard stimuli do to many different individuals (individual psychology) and with what any given

[2] It is obvious that we here use the term "individual psychology" not in the restricted sense of Adler (cf. A. Adler, *The Practice and Theory of Individual Psychology* [New York, Harcourt, Brace and Company, 1924]), to apply primarily to differences of the emotional and motivational lives, but rather in the more general sense, such as that which was developed by Stern (cf. W. Stern, *Über Psychologie der Individuellen Differenzen* [Leipzig, Barth, 1900]) to apply to all types of differences between individuals.

[3] That the term *experimental psychology* does, historically, set itself off as applying to something other than a "psychology of individual differences," (such as has grown up out of the mental test movement) is testified to by Boring when in his History of Experimental Psychology (cf. E. G. Boring, *A History of Experimental Psychology* [New York, The Century Co., 1929], esp. pp. 545-549) he finds that a consideration of the mental test movement, as such, can be appropriately left out of the main body of his account.

stimulus does to the average or standard individual (normative psychology). And, it may be noted, as is but meet, that Purposive Behaviorism purports to be such a complete psychology.

Let us now, however, seek to indicate more specifically the sorts of variables and determinants of behavior which are arrived at by each of the three kinds of system. Let us begin with some typical instances of normative psychology.

3. The Variables of a Normative Psychology

Normative psychologies, as we have said, tend to take an average (normal) individual or an average (normal) sample of individuals, of some given group or species, and then to apply all sorts of different stimuli or combinations of stimuli, such as S_1, S_2, $S_1 + S_2$, etc., to such an individual (or sample of individuals) and to note the final responses, such as R_x, R_y, R_z, etc., which result. These responses may be either gross behaviors or introspections. The normative psychologies then seek to explain the connecting causal interrelationships between these stimuli, or combinations of stimuli, and these final responses. And their explanations consist in hypostasizing certain intervening "mental processes" or "events" as aroused by the given stimuli in the typical individual. A description of these typical mental processes or events serves for them as an explanation of why the given stimuli pass over into the given final responses.

To illustrate, let us briefly describe two typical instances of normative psychology, viz., American Structuralism and *Gestalt* Psychology.

4. American Structuralism

In general, we may symbolize "intervening mental events" as M variables. And in the case of American Structuralism it seems to us that these M variables may be divided into two subclasses which can be appropriately distinguished as the M_s variables and the M_c variables, respectively. Let us consider the former.

American Structuralism assumes first certain mental process relatively immediately dependent upon stimuli—i.e., "sensations," "images" and "affections." These are its M_s variables. Furthermore, the especial forte of Structuralism lay in the discovery and description of these immediate M_s's. For each S presented to the normal individual there was supposed to be evoked a corresponding specific M_s. Each stimulus produced its own "sensation," "image" or "affection."

Further, Structuralism also proceeded to try to work out, relatively completely, the exact laws of this immediate dependence of these M_s variables upon the stimuli. These were its laws as to sense-polygons, psycho-physics, imagery types, and the like.

But sensations, images and affections do not, as such, constitute the whole universe of mind. Even the structuralists were also led to talk, though rather half-heartedly, about "perceptions," "meanings," "purposes." And it is our contention that such perceptions, purposes and meanings, etc., in so far as Structuralism admitted them, really constituted a further set of mental variables ("central processes") which can be appropriately designated as the M_c variables. These M_c variables were conceived as arising out of the M_s variables and to be a step on towards the determination of the final responses, R. Furthermore, Structuralism suggested that the functional operations, whereby the M_s's were thus turned into M_c's, were, primarily, merely a matter of an algebraic cementing together by means of simple association bonds.

Finally, however, it is to be noted that, when it came to the final question as to how the M_c's then went over into behavior, Structuralism was largely silent. Probably because Structuralism per se was very little interested in behavior.

In conclusion, we would suggest the following as a symbolic representation of the variables and laws as thus assumed by Structuralism:

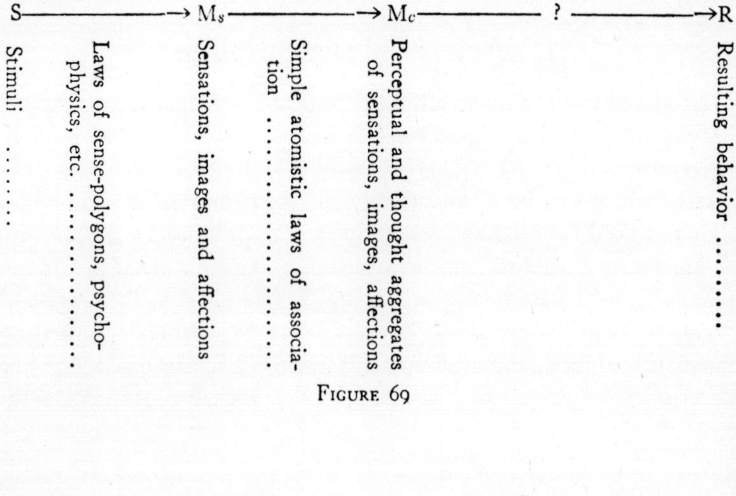

S—————→ M_s —————→ M_c ————— ? —————→R

Stimuli ....

Laws of sense-polygons, psycho-physics, etc. ....

Sensations, images and affections

Simple atomistic laws of association ....

Perceptual and thought aggregates of sensations, images, affections

Resulting behavior ....

FIGURE 69

5. Gestalt Psychology

It appears to us that much this same symbolic diagram may be used again for Gestalt Psychology. Thus, the distinctive concepts of the gestalt school, i.e., the gestalts, belong, we would say, in the class of the M_c variables. Furthermore, it also seems to us that a great deal of what Gestalt Psychology is concerned with doing is the discovery of the laws, such for example as those of "closure," "grouping," "figure-round," etc., whereby the M_s variables are transmuted into gestalts. We must, however, hasten to justify this last assertion, for Gestalt Psychology itself seems, in its formal pronouncements at any rate, to deny the M_s variables. It seems to deny that there are any such things as pure "sensations," "images" or "affections." But this denial, when properly understood, is rather, we shall contend, a denial that these latter ever exist separately and in their own right—uncaught up into gestalts. Gestalt Psychology cannot, we believe, ever completely and in all senses ignore sensations, images and affections. It can and does turn them into purely "functional" variables which have no independent existences. The gestalt psychologists do, that is, assume M_s variables in the sense of the ultimate possibilities of sensory discrimination and of motor manipulation. These ultimate possibilities are, functionally, the data upon which their laws of closure, grouping, figure-ground, etc., operate. But these possibilities have no existential being either prior to or independent of the full-blown gestalts which they mediate. There are not temporally *first* sensations, images, etc., and *then* gestalts. There are, however, as two separate logical items, first, the ultimate possibilities of discrimination manipulation, etc., and then, second, gestalts which derive by virtue of the laws of figure-ground closure, grouping, etc., from these ultimate possibilities.

Gestalt Psychology differs from, and is, an improvement over, Structuralism in that (a) it has a better and more detailed description of the M_c variables than has Structuralism; and in that (b) it has better laws than the old too simple laws of association as to how the M_c variables arise out of the M_s variables; and in that (c) it brings out the fact that the M_s variables are really only functionally defined entities and never have actually an independent existence in and by themselves.

Finally, it must be noted that Gestalt Psychology, like Structuralism, seems to be relatively weak and silent on the question as to how the M_c variables (the gestalts) finally go over into and cause behavior. No more than Structuralism does it seem to have gathered any of the laws relative to this last, and very important, step in the whole process.

To sum up symbolically, we would suggest the following figure for Gestalt Psychology:

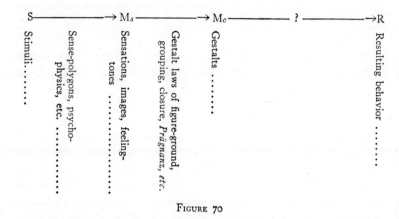

FIGURE 70

So much for an indication of the variables and the laws assumed by two typical normative psychologies. Let us consider, next, the sorts of variables and laws assumed by an individual psychology.

6. The Variables of an Individual Psychology

The first point to remember about individual psychologies is that they are primarily interested in the differences between individuals. This means that they always try out their experiments on many different persons or animals. Whereas the normative psychologies try many different stimulus-situations with one and the same, or a very small number of, individuals, the individual psychologies tend to try out a smaller number of stimulus situations, but many different individuals. More specifically, their procedure is to present a controlled stimulus-situation, S, and then measure the variation among individuals in response, R. But the fact that this S leads to this type of R at all (which is the point that the normative psychologists would be primarily interested in) they tend to leave unexplained or to accept without much question. Finally, they develop, as is well known, their concepts of the aptitudes or "factors" as the primary intervening variables between stimulus and response. These "aptitude-factors" explain why some individuals are relatively good and other individuals relatively poor in one and the same $S \rightarrow R$ sequence. As regards these "factors," they have arrived at a number of principles as follows:

First Principle. Any given aptitude-factor will tend to be possessed by different individuals in different degrees. Some individuals will tend to possess a large amount of the given factor; other individuals will tend to possess very little. In fact, the amounts of a given factor possessed by the individuals, of any large enough sample of individuals, will probably tend to distribute according to a normal Gaussian distribution curve.

Second Principle. Success in any specific performance will be the result of the possession of certain requisite factors. The greater the allotments of these factors in any given individual, the greater will tend to be his success in this given type of performance.

Third Principle. A given performance which depends upon a number of different factors will, however, usually tend to depend more upon certain ones of these factors than upon others. Each type of performance can be evaluated in terms of the degrees to which the possession of any given factor is important for it.

Fourth Principle. The amounts of the specific allotments in given individuals of each of the fundamental factors will be the fruit of heredity, on the one hand, and of past environmental training, on the other.

Let us consider now a typical instance of such an individual psychology. For convenience, and because it is perhaps the best known, we may take Spearman's individual psychology.

7. Spearman's Individual Psychology

As is well known, the aptitude-factors are divided by Spearman into two sorts: a small number of general factors, these he symbolizes by g, c, o, and w (g = "mental energy," c = "retentivity or mental inertia," o = "oscillations of efficiency, fatiguability," w = "self control") which are supposed to be involved in various degrees in all performances; and a great number of specific factors, symbolized as s's, each of which is supposed to be specific to some given relatively narrow range or type of performance.[4]

Thus, the reason according to Spearman, why a particular stimulus-response situation leads, with a particular individual, to the degree of success in the final performance that it does is:

(a) because this specific performance, say $S_1 \rightarrow R_1$, involves all (though in various degrees) of the different general factors, g, c, w, and o;

(b) because it also involves its own special factor s_1; and

(c) because the individual in question possesses such and such allotments of g, c, w, and o and s_1.

Finally, the individual's allotments of the special and general factors will, in the last analysis, be due to his specific heredity and his past training, though Spearman does not as a matter of fact hazard much as to the manner of operation of these latter.

8. Spearman's Complete Psychology

It must be noted now further, however, that Spearman, when we consider his system as a whole, also advances, in addition to the above individual psychology, a normative psychology.[5] He assumes, that is, in addition to the above listed capacity-factors certain "qualitative" principles which we would assert to be his assumptions concerning the typical or normative "mental events" which, as he sees it, intervene between stimuli and responses. He presents, that is, an individual "plus" a normative psychology, or as we would designate it, a "complete" psychology.

The "qualitative" or the "normative" principles which he adds are "sentience," "apprehension of experience," "eduction of relations" and "eduction of correlates." Spearman designates the last three as cognitive. The first is a pre-condition of the latter three.

Sentience results directly from the physical stimuli and the

---

[4] Cf. C. Spearman, *The Abilities of Man—Their Nature and Measurement* (New York, The Macmillan Company, 1927).

[5] C. Spearman, *The Nature of 'Intelligence' and the Principles of Cognition* (London, The Macmillan Company, 1st ed., 1923, 2nd ed., 1927).

intervening chemical activities in the afferent nerves and sensorium. But the result of sentience, i.e., mere lived experience, is not, as such, conscious or cognized.

To be conscious, these "lived experiences" must be apprehended. Sentience plus apprehension (the latter comes temporally after mere sentience), together produce something analogous to what in our previous diagram we have represented by M_s's.[6]

The "eduction of the relations" between the separate items or "fundaments" occurs and is apprehended. The nature of this eduction of relations may be represented by the following

diagram. 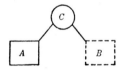 A and B are two fundaments

given directly in apprehension and C is the relation which subsequently is educed as between them.

Finally, as his last cognitive principle or activity there appears the eduction of correlates. When a character and a relation are already given, then the correlative character will tend to be educed. This may be represented by the following figure.

A and the relation C are already given but the correlative character B has to be educed. "For example, if the idea of 'good' [the character A] and that of 'opposite to' [the relation C] are presented, there can out of these be obtained the correlative idea of 'bad.'"[7]

In terms, now, of the sorts of diagrams which we drew for Structuralism and Gestalt Psychology, we should say that the eduction of relations and the eduction of correlates take place between the M_s's, thereby producing M_c's or between the M_c's, thereby producing new M_c's.

[6] It should be also noted that, according to Spearman, apprehension may cover other material besides that presented in simple sentience. Other affections (e.g., pleasure, unpleasure, excitement, tranquillity, etc.) cognition, conation, appetites and aversions, impulses, desires, wills, consent, satisfaction, the "I" and the products of eduction are also apprehended.

[7] *Op. cit.*, p. 343.

In fact, we should now represent Spearman's "complete psychology" by a diagram as follows:

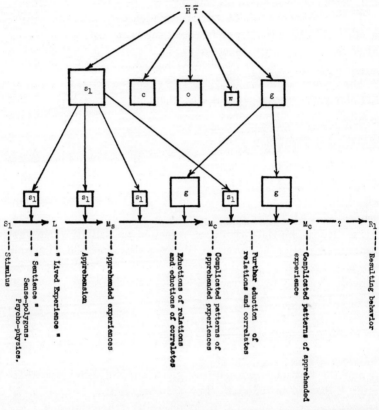

FIGURE 71

Spearman's Complete Psychology

This diagram indicates pretty well the main outlines of Spearman's total doctrine. The lower part is analogous to the diagrams already drawn above for Structuralism and for Gestalt Psychology. It presents Spearman's "Formative psychology." The upper half indicates Spearman's "individual psychology." It symbolizes the manner in which the factors of s, c, o, w and g, deriving, as they do, from hereditary endowment (H) and previous training (T) contribute to the sequence of mental events depicted by the normative psychology. Let us consider each of these parts of the diagram in more detail.

Comparing the lower part of the diagram with those that we drew for Structuralism and Gestalt Psychology, it will be observed that there has been introduced a new mental event, L, to correspond to what Spearman calls merely "lived experiences." Also there has been introduced a second M_c to allow for the complications which must be supposed to arise out of the applications and reapplications of the processes of "eduction." Further, it is to be observed that Spearmanism, no more than Structuralism or Gestalt-ism, seems to present any account of when or how the mental contents go over into final responses. Finally, one last point as to the normative feature is to be noted. We have drawn the diagram to represent one single and specific S — R situation, viz., $S_1 \rightarrow R_1$ only. That is, we have not attempted to draw a sufficiently generalized diagram to allow for all possible $S \rightarrow R$ connections.

Consider now the upper half of the diagram, which is to represent the individual-difference features of this system. H and T indicate the two independent variables, hereditary endowment and previous training. The fact that they have bars over them thus, $\overline{H}$, $\overline{T}$, is to indicate that we here wish to represent the specific values which these variables have for some particular individual. Further it is to be noted that we have indicated this particular $\overline{H}$ and $\overline{T}$ as producing (see upper sets of arrows), in this individual, specific amounts of the special factor s_1 and of the general factors, g, c, o and w. That is, these specific amounts which are thus supposed to be in the given individual by virtue of his heredity and training are represented by the sizes of the upper row of small rectangles. The size of each of these upper rectangles indicates the amount of the factor in question which the given individual is supposed to possess as a result of his $\overline{H}$ and his $\overline{T}$. Thus, in the diagram as drawn, we have assumed that the individual in question had a relatively large dose of s_1 and somewhat smaller doses of all the general factors, and especially that he had quite a small dose of g. (We have not bothered to represent the other specific factors s_2, s_3, s_4, etc., since, by hypothesis, these will not enter into the particular performance here in question, i.e., $S_1 \rightarrow R_1$.)

Next, it will be observed that lower down in the diagram we have represented by a second row of rectangles: the amounts and places where s_1 and g may be supposed to enter into the actual

$S_1 \rightarrow R_1$ performance. (For the sake of simplicity in drawing we have left out the indication of where the c, o and w may also be supposed to enter in and affect the actual performance.) As we have represented it, this performance $S_1 \rightarrow R_1$ is to be conceived as requiring relatively small amounts of the specific factor, s_1, and relatively large amounts of the general factor, g. The upper rectangles represent the funds from which the lower rectangles must be filled. And in this case we have represented the given individual as possessing a large fund of s_1 but only a small fund of g, whereas the actual performance, $S_1 \rightarrow R_1$, we have represented as requiring only a little of s_1 and a great deal of g. Hence his performance is going to be relatively poor. He hasn't a big enough fund of g to provide the large amounts of g required by this particular $S_1 \rightarrow R_1$ performance.

Finally, although Spearman himself has not been perhaps altogether clear on the point, we have suggested in the diagram that the s_1 is involved all along the line of the performance, whereas the g (and presumably also the c, o and w) are involved primarily in the higher, more central, or eductive steps only.

So much for Spearman's complete psychology. If the truth be told, we have presented it and the precedingly considered systems of American Structuralism and Gestalt Psychology at length, partly because of their own intrinsic merits, but largely and much more because they would serve us well as a way of introducing the final summary of our own system.

9.   Purposive Behaviorism—a Complete Psychology

In FIGURE 72 we have drawn a diagram for Purposive Behaviorism, which is analogous to that for Spearmanism, and should now, therefore, be fairly easily understood. There are, however, several new features in it, which need elucidation.

First, it will be observed that in the upper right-hand side of the diagram we have introduced a new independent variable P (initiating physiological state). And, descending from this through a succession of innate or acquired means-end-readinesses, we have indicated a succession of D's (demanded types of goal-object). In Purposive Behaviorism there is, in short, a fourth type of independent cause of behavior. According to it the final behavior is a function, not only of S and of H and T, but also of the initiating physiological state, P, which may happen to be active at the moment. The organism responds to the given stimuli only, by virtue of an initiating physiological state which, given his innate or acquired means-end-readinesses, gives rise to demands, D (superordinate or subordinate)—one or more of which leads him to respond to the given S as presenting an appropriate means-object. These depending demands control the whole line of the S → R process.

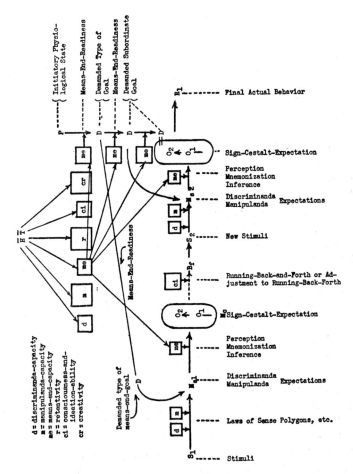

FIGURE 72

It appears, in short, that whereas Structuralism and Gestalt Psychology seemed to assume but one final type of cause underlying behavior, viz., S; and Spearmanism added but two more, viz., H and T; Purposive Behaviorism finds, in all, four such ultimately independent causes of behavior, viz., S. H. T and P.

Consider, next, the nature of the stimulus-response sequence as shown in the diagram. From what has gone before in the preceding chapter this $S_1 \rightarrow R_1$ sequence, as here drawn, should be readily understood. The principal point to note is that for the purposes of this illustration we have taken a case in which the first sign-gestalt-expectation arrived at is relatively uncertain. The uncertainty leads the organism to break out into either an actual running-back-and-forth or a "behavior-adjustment" to such a running-back-and-forth. And these actual or adjustmental "back-and-forths" we have symbolized by B_f. As a result of this B_f the organism reinforces its stimuli. In the place of the original S_1 he achieves an improved S_2. And he thereby arrives at a new sign-gestalt-expectation. And it appears then, finally, that the O_2 of this latter is such as to be accepted as goal-object by one of the superordinately, or subordinately, released demands. The final actual behavior thereupon results. Purposive Behaviorism thus explains, in terms of such demands, the final going off of the R—a matter that was left largely unconsidered by either Structuralism, Gestalt Psychology or Spearmanism.

Next, consider the matter of capacities. It will be observed that, to avoid confusion, we have not attempted for the most part to draw the interconnecting arrows from the innate or acquired "funds" represented at the top of the diagram and the actual operations of such factors indicated below in connection with the actual $S - R$ performance. The one exception is in the case of *me* (means-end-capacity). It will be observed, further, that this drawing for the capacity-features of Purposive Behaviorism is somewhat analogous to that for Spearmanism. That is, he and we both seem to accept about the same number of factors. And a discriminating reader will observe a certain likeness between our *d* (discriminanda-capacity) and *m* (manipulanda-capacity) and Spearman's *s*'s (specific factors). Further our *me* (means-end-capacity), *r* (retentivity), *ci* (consciousness-ability and ideation-ability) and *cr* (creativity) seem somewhat analogous to his *g* and other general factors (*c, o* and *w*). At any rate, our *me, r, ci* and *cr* are, like his *g* (*c, o,* and *w*), relatively general and operative in some degree in all types of performance. Accepting this similarity it must next be pointed out, however, that we would now wish to raise a criticism against both the Spearman doctrine of capacities and our own, as thus far outlined.

10. Criticism of the Capacity Doctrines of Both Spearmanism and Purposive Behaviorism

The criticism now to be presented is twofold. In the first place, it is to be noted that both Spearmanism and our own Purposive Behaviorism, as thus far presented, have left out any real statement, or indication, of the laws whereby the "funds" of the capacity-factors in the various individuals actually derive from their respective heredities and past trainings. This, of course, is not surprising, considering how little controlled evidence we have as yet as regards the independent effects of heredity and training.[8] But still it is none the less quite evident that any acceptable theory of capacities should agree with the probabilities of genetics and training, and this, we now believe, the above proposed sets of factors do not do.

We turn to our second criticism. It is to the effect that it now seems highly improbable from what we at present know of the laws of genetics and training, that the ultimate "funded" capacities would turn out to be any such small number of independent affairs as are to be found in the lists which have been suggested both by Spearman and by Purposive Behaviorism. This is a criticism which we owe directly to Dr. Tryon.[9] According to him, a "highly multiple factor" theory is alone probable both in regard to the effects of heredity and the effects of training. Only, if in the traits, as we actually measure them, there were a *great number* of mutually independent and relatively minor units acting jointly, should we expect to get the smooth distribution curves for such traits that we do. What seems probable is, there-

[8] Again, we should call attention to Dr. Tryon's experiments on the "inheritance of maze-ability in rats" as the one hope for the immediate future in such a direction. See above, Chapter XXIII, footnote 19.

[9] Cf. R. C. Tryon, Multiple factors vs. two factors as determiners of ability. (Mss. to be published shortly.) R. C. Tryon, so-called group factors as determiners of ability. (Mss. to be published shortly.)

fore, that, genetically, the organism's behavior is due perhaps to some thousand or more independently segregating genetic factors, and further that the result of training is to overlay these genetic factors with innumerable further likewise minor units of habit in the way of specific detailed associations (sign-gestalt-readinesses and -expectations). This would then mean that the animal approaches any new problem not with just a few, neatly insulated, capacities such as discriminanda-capacity, manipulanda-capacity, means-end-capacity, retentivity, consciousness- and idea-tion-ability, and creativity, but rather with a multiplicity of very minor capacities which may add together in all sorts of compli-cated, varying, and overlapping ways to produce the actual dis-crimination, manipulation, means-end-successes.

Or, to revamp our theory in line with such a criticism, our final assumption as to the nature of capacities would be such that a finally acceptable picture for Purposive Behaviorism would take on more the form of FIGURE 73.

In place of the original d, m, me, r, ci, and cr as the immedi-ately provided genetic and training "funds" or endowments we would now substitute a tremendously numerous array of more unitary genetic and training factors. These very many genetic and training factors would contribute in various overlapping ways to d, m, me, r, ci and cr, considered now solely as the immediate and specific "response-requirements." Furthermore, it would now appear that each of these five types of "response requirements" may well be, after all, only approximately identical with itself in different responses or even in different aspects of one and the same response. The terms *discriminanda, manipulanda, means-end-capacity,* etc., would thus, in the last analysis, be conceived as designating only roughly identical affairs. Each response would involve its own relatively specific discrimination, manipulation, means-end processes. These processes would be only roughly iden-tical on successive occasions or in successive parts of one and the same total response. On each occasion, and in each place, they might well tap slightly different arrays of the innumerable under-lying genetic and training units.[10]

So much for what is really a suggestion for the future.

[10] And in so far as they did tap slightly different arrays the correlation be-tween two measurements for one of these capacities on two successive occasions would prove something less than unity.

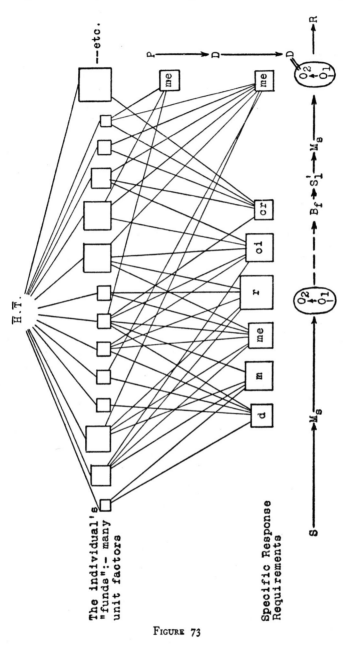

FIGURE 73

11. Conclusion

Finally, we can now, on a basis of all the above, summarize the causal and explanatory variables and their interrelations as assumed by Purposive Behaviorism in the following statements:

(1) The ultimately independent causes of behavior are four, viz., stimuli, heredity, past training, and momentary initiating physiological states (S, H, T, and P).

(2) Intervening between these "ultimate causes" of behavior and behavior itself there are a set of intermediate variables which, for convenience, may be called the behavior-determinants.

(3) These behavior-determinants are to be subdivided into four sub-groups:

(a) Capacities considered as ultimate genetic and training factors in the individual. These are of the nature of innate and acquired "funds" and are, it would seem, "very many" in number, and each relatively minor in character.

(b) Capacities considered as the "immediate response requirements," or needs, of actual S → R sequences. These, it would seem, probably vary from occasion to occasion, and hence can be only roughly identified and sorted out under such general headings as such-and-such discriminanda-capacity, such-and-such manipulanda-capacity, such-and-such a means-end-capacity, such-and-such retentivity, such-and-such consciousness- and ideation-ability, such-and-such creativity.

(c) The immanent purposive and cognitive determinants, which lie in the very warp and woof of the S → R sequence, viz., demands, means-end-readinesses, discriminanda- and manipulanda-expectations, means-end-expectations, (sign-gestalt-expectations).

(d) A unique sort of substitute for, or rather interregnum, in ordinary "practical" behaviors, viz., the back-and-forth behaviors, and the back-and-forth-behavior-adjustments.

REFERENCES

Adler, A., *The Practice and Theory of Individual Psychology* (New York, Harcourt, Brace and Company, 1924).

Boring, E. G., *A History of Experimental Psychology* (New York, The Century Co., 1929).

Spearman, C., *The Nature of 'Intelligence' and the Principles of Cognition* (London, The Macmillan Company, 1st ed., 1923; 2d ed., 1927).

——————, *The Abilities of Man—Their Nature and Measurement* (New York, The Macmillan Company, 1927).

Stern, W., *Über Psychologie der Individuellen Differenzen* (Leipzig, Barth, 1900).

Tryon, R. C., Multiple factors vs. two factors as determiners of ability. (Mss. to be published shortly.)

——————, So-called group factors as determiners of ability. (Mss. to be published shortly.)

Chapter XXV

SUMMARY AND CONCLUSIONS FOR PSYCHOLOGISTS AND PHILOSOPHERS

1. The Variables

OUR system has been presented. It conceives mental processes as functional variables intervening between stimuli, initiating physiological states, and the general heredity and past training of the organism, on the one hand, and final resulting responses, on the other. These intervening variables it defines as behavior-determinants. And these behavior-determinants it subdivides further into (1) immanent purposive and cognitive determinants, (2) capacities and (3) behavior-adjustments. All three of these types of determinant are to be discovered, in the last analysis, by behavior experiments. They have to be inferred "back" from behavior. They are precipitated out from the empirical correlations which can be observed between specific stimuli and initiating physiological states, on the one hand, and specific resultant acts, on the other. They are to behavior as electrons, waves, or whatever it may be, are to the happenings in inorganic matter. There is nothing private or "mentalistic" about them. They are pragmatically conceived, objective variables the concepts of which can be altered and changed as proves most useful. They are not the dictates of any incontrovertible moments of immediacy.

We must finally bring out, however, certain general characteristics of the system which, though implied in all the foregoing, have not, perhaps, been sufficiently stressed.

2. Purposive Behaviorism Concerns Itself with Docile Behavior Only

The first of these general characteristics to be emphasized is the fact that this system concerns itself with, and is valid for,

414

docile behavior only. This point is implicit in all the preceding, and needs only a little reiteration. It has been implied throughout that, only in so far as behavior is docile, can it be said to be purposive and cognitive. It is only docile behavior which can be examined for immanent sign-gestalts and hierarchies of demands. In so far as behavior is not docile, but goes off willy nilly by virtue of invariable reflex stimulus-response connections, a description of it in terms of immanent sign-gestalt-readinesses and -expectations and hierarchies of demands, and the like, would be both silly and meaningless.

The empirical question, therefore, arises with regard to each species as to in what degree its acts are docile or in what degree they are reflex. And the answer to this empirical question is, of course, as yet far from completely known. The lower the organism, or the more internal and physiological the response, the more likely, it would seem, that a given act is non-docile, i.e., of a purely reflex or tropistic variety. But many more observations need to be made. There is some evidence of learning, or at any rate of modifiability, the exact nature of which needs further analysis, even in protozoa,[1] not to mention earthworms [2] and the lower insects.[3]

3. The Rôles of Physiology and Neurology

The other general characteristic of the present system which needs perhaps to be further emphasized concerns the relation of purposive behaviorism to physiology and neurology. In how far are we, as mere psychologists—i.e., mere purposive behaviorists —interested in, and dependent upon a knowledge of the underlying neurology and physiology of behavior? Inasmuch as the ultimate ends of all behavior are, we assume, the physiological states of disturbance and quiescence, we are necessarily interested in discovering and listing, if we can, these ultimate types of physiological disturbance and quiescence. And in so far as the immanent determinants, the capacities and the behavior-adjustments,

[1] Cf. H. S. Jennings, *Behavior of the Lower Organisms* (New York, The Columbia Univ. Press, 1906), 170-179.

[2] Cf. R. M. Yerkes, The intelligence of earthworms, *J. Anim. Behav.*, 1912, **2**, 332-352.

[3] Cf. J. E. Wodsedalek, Formation of associations in the may-fly nymphs, *Heptagenia Interpunctata* (Say), *J. Anim. Behav.*, 1912, **2**, 1-19.

are ultimately dependent upon matters of neurology, we are like-wise interested in all that the most advanced work can tell us about such neurology.

But, first and foremost, and this is a point which it is im-portant to stress, our task, *as psychologists,* is the collecting and ordering of the *molar behavior* facts per se. And this task can, in large part, be performed in relative ignorance of both physiology and neurology. Our task is to find out the behavior facts and the appetite and the aversion facts which are to be explained, before attempting too much explanation. Let us not, in short, be misled, as we believe many of the simple stimulus-response psychologists of the immediate past have been, into substituting inadequate and, if Lashley [4] and Franz [5] and Coghill [6] be cor-rect, arrantly erroneous, neurological explanations in place of a direct and adequate account and systematization of the immediate behavior data themselves. Behavior is a stimulus response affair. But it is not for that reason a simple aggregation of mere reflexes

[4] Cf. K. S. Lashley, *Brain Mechanisms and Intelligence* (Chicago, Chicago Univ. Press, 1929), 186.

———— Basic neural mechanisms in behavior, *Psychol. Rev.,* 1930, **37,** 1-24.

[5] S. I. Franz, On the function of the cerebrum: the frontal lobes in relation to the production and retention of simple sensory motor habits, *Amer. J. Physiol.,* 1902, **8,** 1-22.

———————— On the functions of the cerebrum: the frontal lobes, *Arch. Psychol.,* 1907, **1,** No. 2.

———————— On the functions of the cerebrum: concerning the lateral por-tions of the occipital lobes, *Amer. J. Physiol.,* 1911, **28,** 308-317.

———— With G. R. Lafora. On the functions of the cerebrum: the occipital lobes, *Psychol. Monog.,* 1911, **13,** No. 56.

———————— On some functions of the occipital lobes, *Govt. Hosp. Insane Bull.,* 1912, **4,** 5-20.

———————— With J. D. Stout. Variations in distributions of the motor cen-ters, *Psychol. Monog.,* 1915, **19,** 80-162.

———————— The retention of habits by the rat, after destruction of the frontal portion of the cerebrum, *Psychobiol.,* 1917, **1,** 3-18.

———————— With R. Ogden, On cerebral motor control: the recovery from experimentally produced hemiplegia, *Psychobiol.,* 1917, **1,** 33-49.

———————— With K. S. Lashley. The effects of cerebral destructions upon habit-formation and retention in the albino rat, *Psychobiol.,* 1917, **1,** 71-139.

[6] G. E. Coghill, The early development of behavior in amblystoma and in man, *Arch. Neur. & Psychiat.,* 1929, **21,** 989-1009.

———— *Anatomy and the Problem of Behavior* (Cambridge, University Press, 1929).

———— The genetic interrelation of instinctive behavior and reflexes, *Psychol. Rev.,* 1930, **37,** 264-266.

as a premature neurologizing misled the early behaviorists into supposing. Furthermore, these early behaviorists were distracted from honestly and open-mindedly continuing to observe the behavior facts at their own truly behavioristic (i.e., molar) level. They were misled when, for example, they were observing the behavior of a rat in a maze, into seeing it as simply, and as possessing as few hesitations and hitches, as though it were the action of a simple billiard ball caroming on a pool table.

4. Relation to Other Systems

As our next question, let us consider the affinities of the present system to other psychological systems. Ours we have called a Purposive Behaviorism. And this name summarizes at once two of its affinities; viz., that with purposivism and that with behaviorism. But it has, of course, a third affinity which we were unable to include in the title; viz., that with Gestalt Psychology. Let us briefly summarize each of these three relationships. We begin with the relation to behaviorism.

5. Wherein the Present System Is a Behaviorism

By way of introduction to the question of the relations of the present system to behaviorism, we may recall McDougall's entertaining division of all behaviorists into *Strict Behaviorists, Near Behaviorists,* and *Purposive Behaviorists.*[7] As has been remarked the present system owes its title to McDougall and falls into the last category; and our question becomes: Wherein does a purposive behaviorism differ from a strict behaviorism? A Purposive Behaviorism agrees with a strict behaviorism in asserting that organisms, their behavior and the environmental and organic conditions which induce the latter, are all that there is to be studied. It differs from a strict behaviorism such as that of Watson,[8]

[7] W. McDougall, Men or Robots? I and II, *Psychologies of 1925* (Worcester, Mass., Clark Univ. Press, 1926).

[8] Examine especially:

J. B. Watson, *Behavior—An Introduction to Comparative Psychology* (New York, Henry Holt and Company, 1914).

———— An attempted formulation of the scope of behavior psychology, *Psychol. Rev.,* 1917, **24,** 329-352.

Weiss,[9] or of Meyer[10]—in that for a purposive behaviorism behavior *qua* molar has characteristic descriptive properties all its own. For us, behavior has emergent patterns and meanings which are other than the patterns and meanings of the gland secretions and muscle contractions which underlie it, though no doubt they are completely dependent upon the latter. For a Purposive Behaviorism, behavior, as we have seen, is purposive, cognitive, and molar, i.e., "gestalted." Purposive Behaviorism is a molar, not a molecular, behaviorism, but it is none the less a behaviorism. Stimuli and responses and the behavior-determinants of responses are all that it finds to study.

J. B. Watson, *Psychology from the Standpoint of a Behaviorist* (Philadelphia, J. B. Lippincott Company, 1924), 2d ed. 1930.

————— Is thinking merely the action of language mechanisms? *Brit. J. Psychol.*, 1920, **11**, 87-104.

————— Behaviorism—a psychology based on reflexes, *Arch. Neur. and Psychiat.*, 1926, **15**, 185-204.

————— *Behaviorism* (New York, People's Instit. Publ. Co., W. W. Norton and Company, 1930).

[9] Examine especially:

A. P. Weiss, Relation between structural and behavior psychology, *Psychol. Rev.*, 1917, **24**, 301-317.

————— Relation between functional and behavior psychology, *Psychol. Rev.*, 1917, **24**, 353-368.

————— Conscious behavior, *J. Phil. Psychol., etc.*, 1918, **15**, 631-641.

————— The mind and the man within, *Psychol. Rev.*, 1919, **26**, 327-334.

————— The relation between physiological psychology and behavior psychology, *J. Phil., Psychol., etc.*, 1919, **16**, 626-634.

————— Behavior and the central nervous system, *Psychol. Rev.*, 1922, **29**, 329-342.

————— Behaviorism and behavior, *Psychol. Rev.*, 1924, **31**, 32-50.

————— One set of postulates for a behavioristic psychology, *Psychol. Rev.*, 1925, **32**, 83-87.

————— *A Theoretical Basis of Human Behavior* (Columbus, O., R. G. Adams Co., 1925, rev. ed. 1929).

[10] Examine especially:

M. F. Meyer, *The Fundamental Laws of Human Behavior* (Boston, Richard G. Badger, The Gorham Press, 1911).

————— The present status of the problem of the relation between mind and body, *J. Phil., Psychol., etc.*, 1912, **9**, 365-371.

————— *Psychology of the Other-One* (Columbia, Mo., The Missouri Book Company, 1921).

————— *Abnormal Psychology—When the Other One Astonishes Us* (Columbia, Mo., Lucas Bros., 1927).

6. Wherein the Present System Is a Gestalt-ism

Next, it may be asked in how far the present system, asserting as it does that behavior has meaning, is molar, and does not break up into atomistically defined reflex units, is a Gestalt Psychology. Undoubtedly, the final answer to this second question must be stated by the Gestalt Psychologists themselves. What is to be admitted as a brand of Gestalt Psychology, the Gestaltists themselves, in the last analysis, alone can say. We, however, it should be noted, would be proud to be admitted to their fold. There are certain features of our system, however, which in all honesty and fairness should be brought to the Gestalt-ists' attention as possible blemishes, which may unfit us, in their eyes, for being enclosed in their exclusive corral.

A first such blemish will consist, perhaps, in our emphasis upon inference back from behavior and stimuli as the way to get at mind, rather than by introspection. But this difference from what would seem their point of view may well be more a matter of terminology and historical accident than anything fundamental and logical. The Gestalt Psychologists began life as orthodox mentalists and introspectionists. They started, that is, with the notion of mental phenomena as immediate introspective givens (Köhler's "direct experience" [11]). And, although they have thrown an atomistic description of this immediately mental overboard, they often seem to have retained mentalistically conceived gestalts, and along with the latter a psychophysical parallelism between these introspectively given "mental" gestalts, on the one hand, and physical, neurological gestalts, on the other. It is possible, however, that such an inference accords more with their words than their sense. We, on the other hand, starting life as crass stimulus-response behaviorists, who saw, to begin with, nothing between stimulus and response but neurology, have come only gradually, and perforce by much travail, to the concept of objectively defined capacities, immanent determinants and behavior-adjustments. But it may well be that our emphasis on all these determinants rather than upon "direct experiences" is but a hangover from our initial crassness. It may be that our

[11] Cf. W. Köhler, *Gestalt Psychology* (New York, Horace Liveright, 1929). Esp. Chapter I.

capacities, immanent determinants and behavior-adjustments and their directly experienced gestalts will, in the end, turn out to have one and the same final, methodological and metaphysical status.

The second feature of our system which may, perhaps, be abhorrent to true Gestalt-ists is that we have included among these determining variables not only the immanent sign-gestalts and the behavior-adjustments but also: (a) a variety of preceding determinants; viz., capacities and (b) a series of *analyzed* variables within the sign-gestalts; viz., means-end-readinesses and means-end-expectations, and discriminanda- and manipulanda-readinesses and -expectations.

That is, we have found it necessary, for purposes of discourse and prediction, to look *behind* and *within* the gestalts to independently distinguishable variables to be treated as the determiners and components of such gestalts. These "behind-variables" and "within-variables" do not, of course, ever occur and operate in insulation one from another, i.e., outside of the sign-gestalt wholes. But they can and must, none the less, be torn and analyzed out for the purposes of discourse and of predictive science.[12] Now, such tearing apart and out often appears abhorrent to the Gestalt Psychologists. However, here again, the difference is probably one more of words than of meaning. The Gestalt-ists themselves really have their own part-variables—their figures vs. grounds, their contours, their accents, etc., etc. What the Gestalt Psychologists have, in fact, really been contending against seems not so much analysis per se, but what they conceive to have been the incorrect and erroneous analyses of their predecessors.[13] So that the final question becomes rather in how far the "behind-vari-

[12] Cf. J. Loewenberg, Are relations effable? *J. Philos.*, 1930, **27**, 309-319, also Pre-analytical and post-analytical data, *J. Philos.*, 1927, **24**, 5-14. Loewenberg has strikingly pointed out the lineaments and the difficulties of this situation; viz., that data and relations as they actually function in behavior (i.e., as pre-analytical) have an interfusing, interpenetrating character which is necessarily falsified as soon as for the purposes of discourse and of science (i.e., as "post-analytical") they are torn out and analyzed. But this situation does not thereby condemn all such tearing apart as illegitimate and to be eschewed. However falsifying analysis may be, it has to be done and inevitably *is* done for the purposes of all description and prediction.

[13] See in this connection, W. Köhler, An Aspect of Gestalt Psychology, *Psychologies of 1925* (Worcester, Mass., Clark Univ. Press, 1926), 163-195. Cf. also W. Köhler, *Gestalt Psychology* (New York, Horace Liveright, 1929), 182-183.

ables" and the "within-variables," which we find, are or are not translatable into the contours, accents, groupings, etc., of Gestalt Psychology. Here again we must leave the issue for the future to decide.

Finally, the third possible blemish, from the Gestalt point of view, which may leave us as mere maverick outsiders, is our emphasis on the purposive structure of all gestalts—though in the light of Lewin's construance of purposive concepts to gestalt ends,[14] this should hardly prove a final difficulty. For it is again to be emphasized that all *gestalts* are for us sign-gestalts—and all relations, in the last analysis, means-end-relations. Types of organization [15] of the environmental field are for us always held together by, threaded upon, means-end-strands. Up and down, right and left, good and bad, near and far, figure and ground, are for us ultimately but *means-end* affairs.

7. Wherein the Present System Is a Purposivism

We turn now to a consideration of the third affinity of the present system; viz., its relationship to a thorough-going pur-posivism, such, for example, as McDougall's.[16] McDougall's psy-

[14] See above Chapter XI, p. 179.
Cf. K. Lewin (Hrg), Untersuchungen zur Handlungs und Affektpsychologie.
I. Vorbemerkungen über die seelischen Kräfte und Energien und über die Struktur des Seelischen, *Psychol. Forsch*, 1926, **7**, 294-329.
II. Vorsatz, Wille and Bedürfnis, *Psychol. Forsch.*, 1926, **7**, 330-385.
III. Über das Behalten von erledigten und unerledigten Handlungen. Von B. Zeigarnik, *Psychol. Forsch*, 1927, **9**, 1-85.
IV. Über Rückfälligkeit bei Umgewöhnung, I. Teil, Rückfalltendenz and Verwechslungsgefahr. Von C. Schwarz, *Psychol. Forsch.*, 1927, **9**, 86-158.
V. Psychische Sättigung, Von A. Karsten, *Psychol. Forsch.*, 1928, **10**, 142-254.
VI. Die Wiederaufnahme unterbrochener Handlungen, Von M. Ovsiankina, *Psychol. Forsch.* 1928, **11**, 302-373.
VII. Psychische Sättigung in Menstruum und Intermenstruum. Von A. Freund, *Psychol. Forsch.*, 1930, **13**, 198-217.
VIII. Das Vergessen einer Vornahme. Isolierte seelische Systeme und dynamische Gesamtbereiche. Von J. Birenbaum, *Psychol. Forsch.*, 1930, **13**, 218-284.
IX. Erfolg und Misserfolg. Von F. Hoppe, *Psychol. Forsch.*, 1930, **14**, 1-62.
[15] For a discussion of organization from the *Gestalt* point of view, see Köhler, *Gestalt Psychology* (New York, Horace Liveright, 1929), Chapters V and VI.
[16] Cf. W. McDougall, *Outline of Psychology* (New York, Charles Scribner's Sons, 1923). *Outline of Abnormal Psychology* (New York, Charles Scribner's Sons, 1926). Men or robots? I and II, *Psychologies of 1925* (Worcester, Mass.. Clark Univ. Press, 1926). The hormic psychology, *Psychologies of 1930* (Worcester, Mass., Clark Univ. Press, 1930).

chology, called by him a "hormic" psychology,[17] bases all behavior and all mental activity of whatever sort upon the functioning of certain fundamental "instincts." Now it is obvious that McDougall's "instincts" are in many ways similar to what we have called the appetites and aversions. It must be emphasized, however, that whereas, for McDougall, the hormic drives, and their dependent purposes and cognitions, which are resident in the instincts, seem to be in the last analysis, mentalistic, introspectively defined affairs for us, they are, as has been emphasized perhaps *ad nauseam,* but functionally defined entities—quite objective variables invented to be inserted into the objectively definable equations which exist between stimuli on the one side and responses on the other. Thus, whereas for McDougall the objective behavior facts of purpose and cognition are a mere external testimony—a testimony to a probably ultimate dualism [18] in nature—a testimony to the fact that mind is somehow, in some degree, metaphysically other than body—for us, these same facts of purpose and cognition are but an expression of certain very complex activities in organic bodies.

Our purposivism is, in short, not a fundamental or metaphysical purposivism. The purposes we have been talking about were purely objectively determined entities. In discovering purposes (and cognitions) in organisms, we have been asserting nothing about the ultimate texture of the universe. We have been neither asserting nor denying that there is some fundamental purpose (or mind) running through all nature.

And, even should it finally turn out, on a basis of further experiments, that there is for the behavior of organisms, just as for the behavior of electrons, some principle of ultimate indeterminateness (i.e., a kind of Heisenberg's uncertainty principle), this need not lead us to assume or suppose any metaphysically "other" as "butting in" to the course of organic nature. The finding of such an uncertainty principle would, to be sure, mean important and exciting things. It would mean that we must talk in terms of probabilities, of statistical averages, rather than in terms of unique in

[17] It appears that the first use of *horme* (ὁρμή meaning impulse) and *hormic* in this sense is to be credited to Sir P. T. Nunn, *Education, its Data and First Principles* (London, Arnold, 1920), p. 224.

[18] In his latest statement of his position (*Psychologies of 1930,* pp. 34-35) he seems to weaken a bit and to suggest that no such animistic dualism really is involved in his hormic psychology.

dividual cases. It would not mean, or at any rate would not need to mean, however, any metaphysical bifurcation or dualism—any breakdown in the possibility of final deterministic, descriptions per se.

In a word, the fact of purpose, as we conceive it, is an objective fact. It is the fact that behavior is docile relative to objectively determinable ends. Our psychology is a purposivism; but it is an objective, behavioristic purposivism, not a mentalistic one.[19]

8. Apologia to Philosophers and a List of Questions

The above considered questions of purpose, and of the degree to which our system does or does not imply a final teleology, obviously begin to trespass upon the interests of the philosophers. So that for having raised these questions and for proceeding to raise now certain even more distinctly philosophical questions, we herewith offer an apology. Indeed, what we are now about to say will have a double temerity. For, on the one hand, it will suppose that the account of mind given in the preceding pages has sufficient verisimilitude, or at least novelty, to be of interest to the true philosopher. And, on the other hand, it will suppose that we, mere purposive behaviorists, mere psychologists that we are, are sufficiently conversant with the problems of philosophy to be able to point out to the truly philosophically-minded the significant implications of our account. Both suppositions are temerarious.

It must be emphasized, however, that nothing bumptious is intended. We are presenting here no dogmatic assertions, either that the system propounded in the foregoing pages is true or, even if it were, that we are herewith correctly deducing its wider implica-

[19] It is a sibling of the systems of Perry and Woodworth, and only a first cousin of that of McDougall.

Cf. R. B. Perry, *General Theory of Value* (New York, Longmans, Green & Co., 1926).

R. S. Woodworth, *Psychology, A Study of Mental Life* (New York, Henry Holt and Company, 1921).

——————, *Dynamic Psychology* (New York, Columbia Univ. Press, 1918).

——————, Dynamic psychology, *Psychologies of 1930* (Worcester, Mass., Clark Univ. Press, 1930), 327-336.

We must, of course, acknowledge, however, a very great debt to McDougall. The original impetus to a purposivism of some sort probably came from his instinct psychology. Cf. W. McDougall, *An Introduction to Social Psychology* (London, Methuen, 1908).

tions. Rather, all we are attempting is to direct a series of questions toward some friendly philosopher. We are asking him: "Is not this the sort of thing we have been implying? And, if it is, do not this and these farther things follow from it?"

Indeed it appears to us that there are probably some four fundamental philosophical issues raised by the preceding account. Putting these into question form, they would read: (a) What is the doctrine as to the ultimate methodology and status of science which we have been adopting? (b) What have we done with "raw feels?" (c) What is the relation between the immanent cognitive determinants and behavior-adjustments, as we have assumed them, and "outside" reality—i.e., what is the epistemological status and function of such immanent determinants and behavior adjustments? (d) What finally follows in our system as to the metaphysical status of "outside" reality?

9. Methodology and Status of Science

In the building up of the present system we have attempted to do for psychological phenomena what the other sciences have done for physical phenomena. We have attempted to reduce the former to a series of functional relationships by virtue of which it is possible to predict and control. In place of the concrete, but ineffable, richness of real experience, as it comes, i.e., of our hopes, our feelings, our images, our thoughts—we have substituted a barren and "unfelt" array of functionally defined immanent determinants and behavior-adjustments. As scientists, we started with real, rich, immediate experience but, in the interests of prediction and control, we have ended up with demands, means-end-readinesses, sign-gestalt-expectations and the rest.

But this distortion and emasculation of the realities of immediate experience is, we should suppose, no more violent and repulsive than that which is pursued by the physicist or the chemist. These thinkers likewise start with rich, concrete realities—chairs, tables, clocks, dye-stuffs. But, in the interests of prediction and control, they end with electrons and protons, or is it waves? All science necessarily presents, it seems to us, but a map and picture of reality. If it were to present reality in its whole concreteness, science would be not a map but a complete replica of reality. And then it would lose its usefulness. For it would have to cover as many pages as does life itself; it would no longer serve as a brief and a handbook. One of the first requisites of a science is, in short, that it be a map, i.e., a short-hand for finding one's way about from one moment of reality to the next—that it be a symbolic compendium by means of which to predict and control.

But to what does this lead in the way of an ultimate doctrine concerning the metaphysical status of science? Our account of mind is, we hold, a map-account. And so also is the physicist's account of matter. Furthermore, our map is one which relatively easily fits on to and complements the physicist's. Both maps abandon *qualia*, raw feels, or whatever else one wishes to call them, and are left only with functionally defined quantities—electrons, waves, or whatever it may be on the one hand, and capacities, immanent determinants, and behavior-adjustments, on the other. Now such a procedure, such an abandonment of the qualities of experience per se, for functionally defined quantities seems to imply the type of metaphysics which is known as naturalism.

Ours does, however, perhaps differ from a true naturalism in that we admit and stress the fact that naturalism is truncated— that it does present a map-account only. If ours is a naturalism, it is a naturalism plus. For it includes the frank acknowledgment that naturalism leaves something out. We are here, it would seem, adopting a position similar to that proposed by Pepper.[20] For, according to Pepper, every type of metaphysics—realism, naturalism, idealism, or mysticism—is essentially an attempt to expand some single projection or attitude—some single way of mapping, or projecting reality, some root-metaphor—into a single all-inclusive system—and then to believe in that system as God's last word. And, as he points out, each such attempt, while successful within certain limits, is necessarily doomed to final incompleteness. Each system will have, however, a certain usefulness and success within the narrow direction of interests which leads to its original formulation.

Naturalism is the type of metaphysics which takes the features of prediction and control as all-important. And we are adopting the naturalistic position, but we are going further and admitting with Pepper that it is only a map. We tend, however, it may be noted, to differ from Pepper in that we believe the naturalistic

[20] S. C. Pepper, Categories. ————— Studies in the problem of relations, *Univ. Calif. Publ. Philos.*, 1930, **13**, 73-98.

map to be the only map. The other maps, i.e., mysticism, idealism, etc., seem to us to be not maps but poems.[21] They are momentary attitudes, not expandable into complete maps. Prediction and control are of the very essence of "mappishness."

10.   The Status of Raw Feels

We turn now to the second question—that of the status of the "raw feels." The answer has been implied in what has just been said. "Raw feels" are our naturalistic "map-name" for a side of mind which our map then ignores, or reduces to impotency. But, it may be asked, having thus reduced the richness of immediate reality to mere "raw feels," what more specifically (to mix our figures) is the precise scrap-heap into which our map then chucks such "raw feels"? This question, given our presuppositions, is really inconsequential, and so also will be any answer to it. We may, however, amuse ourselves by suggesting what some of the various alternative scrap-heaps might be.

Scrap-Heap #1. First, it may be contended that 'raw feels' just have to be ignored. They are mere scientific will-of-the-wisps. They are subject matter for poetry and esthetics and religion, not for science. And hence the only thing that a scientist can say in answer to one who insists on raising a final question concerning them, is to retort in the language of the street, "Aw, forget it." This, though not so vulgarly put, seems to be the answer of Lewis.[22] He says:

"In the end, the supposition of a difference in immediate experience [i.e., our raw feels] which is *not* to be detected through divergence in discrimination and relation, is a notion very difficult to handle. Because such difference would, *ex hypothesi,* be ineffable. We can have no language for discussing what no language or behavior could discriminate. And a difference which no language or behavior could convey is, for purposes of communication, as good as non-existent. But this consideration only serves to enforce the fact that the assumption of qualitatively identical immediate experience is unnecessary for community of knowledge

[21] In this matter Pepper would be in some degree like Münsterberg, who asserts that two sorts of maps are possible, the purposive and the causal. (Münsterberg, *Psychology, General and Applied* [New York, D. Appleton and Company, 1914]). Our own opinion would be that anything like a complete purposive map (in Münsterberg's sense) is really a self-contradiction.

[22] Cf. C. I. Lewis, *Mind and the World-Order* (New York, Charles Scribner's Sons, 1929). Especially Chapter IV.

—that it is germane at all only so far as it affects that pattern of relationships here called the concept.

"The only reason that the possibility of such ineffable individual difference of immediacy is not altogether meaningless, is that we have interests which pass beyond those of cognition. Interests such as those of appreciation, sympathy, love, concern the absolute identity and quality as immediate of other experience than our own. Esthetics, ethics, and religion are concerned with such interests, which transcend those of action and of knowledge, as that term has here been used." [23]

Scrap-Heap #2. *Second,* it may be answered that a more reasonable assumption is to assume some sort of consistent correlation between raw feels and correlated immanent determinants —so that, in so far as the determinants operating in one individual seem to approximate those in another individual, the raw feels of the first may be said at least to *approximate* those of the second. When, that is, two individuals agree, in their immanent demands, means-end-readinesses, discriminanda- and manipulanda-expectations, etc., their corresponding raw feels are to be assumed also to agree. It is to be noted, however, that for all the cases of non-agreement, and these far outweigh in number those of agreement, no absolute inference from the one individual's raw feels to those of the other can be made. The best that can be done is to guess or approximate. But as our own raw feels have by hypothesis been reduced in our map to impotency, this perhaps makes no difference.[24]

Scrap-Heap #3. *Finally,* however, still a third answer has been suggested. Raw feels may be the way physical realities are intrinsically, i.e., in and for themselves. Bertrand Russell believes that experienced qualities are the intrinsic nature of a nervous process. E. B. Holt, on the other hand, argues that qualities are the intrinsic nature of those environmental objects to which the organism responds. The former position is near to that which is traditionally called "pan-psychism"; the latter is the claim of neo-realism.[25]

[23] *Op. cit.* footnote, p. 112.
[24] Such a relationship between the intrinsic orders (our immanent determinants) and the immediate *qualia* themselves (our raw feels) seems to be the one suggested by D. W. Prall, *Æsthetic Judgment* (New York, Thomas Y. Crowell Company, 1929).
[25] We are indebted to D. C. Williams for this description of the neo-realist's scrap-heap.

11. The Relation between the Cognitive Determinants and Outside Reality

We turn now to the third question, the traditional epistemological issue as to the relation between idea and thing. It is the issue as to duality or oneness in the knowing situation. Are idea and object-known numerically one or two? And, if the former, how are they ever distinguished between? And if the latter, how is veridical knowledge ever possible?[26]

Our first answer will be to declare that obviously, in terms of our system, idea and object-known are two. It is clear that discriminanda-, manipulanda-, and means-end-readinesses and -expectations are logically, and usually also temporally, prior to the realities which would verify them or, in cases of error, fail to verify them. Discriminanda-, manipulanda-, and means-end-readinesses and -expectations assert moments and successions of hypothetically, or actually, possible discriminanda-, manipulanda-, and means-end-enjoyments. Discriminanda-enjoyments, manipulanda-enjoyments, and means-end-enjoyments are the objects asserted, i.e., known—correctly or incorrectly—by these corresponding immanent readinesses and expectations. Our doctrine is, therefore, in this degree, an epistemological dualism.

It must be stressed, however, that even though it be a dualism, it is a dualism which still allows for an actual verification of the idea, or, so to speak, a direct comparing of the idea and the thing. For the thing, i.e., the enjoyment, at the moment of its occurrence, also comes inside the compass or periphery of the organism. It, no more than the idea, is fundamentally external. Our doctrine is not, in short, a transcendentalism or a metaphysical dualism, even though it be an epistemological dualism.

But perhaps it will clarify this last statement to be more specific. Our doctrine really supposes two sorts of "knowing"-moment or "knowing"-situation—(1) a judgmental (readiness) or an expectational moment; and (2) a verification moment. In the former, idea and thing are obviously two—an expectation (or judgment), on the one hand, and a possibility or non-possibility

---

[26] It may be noted, in passing, that much of the traditional discussion of the relation of ideas and reality seems to have been really concerned with the disposal of raw feels. We are disregarding this issue here, however, as already dealt with.

of a support for that expectation (or judgment) on the other. In the latter, idea fuses into and is either actually supported, or not supported, by thing. In this latter moment, the expectation (or judgment), if correct, fits on to and fuses with its support. And here, when the knowledge is correct, idea and thing become one.

This seems to be the situation which Professor G. P. Adams, from a point of view predominantly introspective, describes as the claim-making character of an idea.[27] A claim must "trade on credit," until "direct possession replaces the mere idea." We turn to the last question.

12. What Is the Metaphysical Status of Outside Reality?

Objects, it now appears from the above discussion, are known, in the last analysis, only in their guise as possible *behavior-supports* for the given organism. The lower animals and men know the world only for the purposes of behaving to it. If the universe has characters other than discriminanda- manipulanda- and means-end-relations, relative to human beings or sub-human beings, these other characters will never be known. Physics and our own purposive behaviorism are but the most generalized sets of behavior-support-characters which we, men, have ascribed to the external world.

Physics has been created by us men when we have tried to abstract from as many as possible of the immediacies of specific concrete behavioral situations. The stimulus-object, as physics describes it, is made of those most abstract discriminanda- manipulanda- and means-end-characters which men have attributed to it, when they have tried to conceive it as the support for all possible behaviors, independent of the particular, specific sensory and motor and appetitional conditions of the moment. Physics seeks to describe the external object with relation not only to immediate momentary adjustments and needs but also with relation to all possible adjustments and needs. The physical object is described in terms of those very abstracted support-characters left in the external world when men have sought to describe it irrespectively of whether they were blind or seeing, whether

[27] G. P. Adams, Ideas in knowing and willing, *Univ. Calif. Publ. Philos.,* 1926, **8,** 25-48.

they had hands or wings or claws, whether they were in reality men or merely pelicans or rats, whether they were hungry or thirsty or lustful.

Psychology, on the other hand, gives an account of the external world which has been created by men when at a higher, i.e., less analyzed, level they have sought to describe the external object in terms of the ways in which it evokes specific, particular, concrete, sensory motor adjustments in them and in the lower animals. For the purposes of a behavioral psychology the stimulus-object, as physics describes it, becomes thus the "source" of the discriminanda- manipulanda- and the means-end-supports, which the given organism in some concrete sensory motor situation or set of situations expects and finds—or perhaps fails to find.

Finally, however, it is to be emphasized that in the case of physics human knowledge of the external object is still limited and conditioned by a sort of distillation from all human behavioral needs and capacities. Even physics' account of the external world is, in the last analysis, an ultimately, though very abstracted, behavioral account. For all knowledge of the universe is always strained through the behavior-needs and the behavior-possibilities of the particular organisms who are gathering that knowledge. That "map" knowledge is "true" which "works," given the particular behavior-needs and the particular behavior-capacities of the type of organism gathering such knowledge. Physics and purposive behaviorism are both, therefore, but humanly conditioned, "behavioral" maps.

In conclusion, it seems—we ask the philosopher—that we are asserting, are we not, a pragmatism? For we are asserting that all human knowledge, including physics, purposive behaviorism and our own present remarks, are but a resultant of, and limited by, human behavioral needs and human behavioral capacities. Outside reality is for us human beings that which our limited biological needs and our limited behavioral capacities find it to be. Such outside reality has for us, to be sure, one set of characters, i.e., gross, concrete, macroscopic discriminanda- manipulanda- and means-end-relations, when we are simply and immediately behaving and another set of characters, i.e., minute microscopic discriminanda- manipulanda- and means-end-relations—those of electrons, protons (or is it waves)—when we are trying to behave very abstractly and very disinterestedly.

But what outside reality may be, in and for itself, abstracted from all human behavioral needs and all human behavioral capacities, we do not, cannot, and need not know.

REFERENCES

Adams, G. P., Ideas in knowing and willing. *Univ. Calif. Publ. Philos.*, 1926, **8**, 25-48.

Coghill, G. E., The early development of behavior in amblystoma and in man. *Arch. Neur. & Psychiat.*, 1929, **21**, 989-1009.

——————, *Anatomy and the Problem of Behavior* (Cambridge, University Press, 1929).

——————, The genetic interrelation of instinctive behavior and reflexes. *Psychol. Rev.*, 1930, **37**, 264-266.

Franz, S. I., On the functions of the cerebrum: the frontal lobes in relation to the production and retention of simple sensory motor habits. *Amer. J. Physiol.*, 1902, **8**, 1-22.

——————, On the functions of the cerebrum: the frontal lobes. *Arch. Psychol.*, 1907, **1**, No. 2.

——————, On the functions of the cerebrum: concerning the lateral portions of the occipital lobes. *Amer. J. Physiol.*, 1911, **28**, 308-317.

——————, On some functions of the occipital lobes. *Govt. Hosp. Insane Bull.*, 1912, No. 4, 5-20.

——————, The retention of habits by the rat, after destruction of the frontal portion of the cerebrum. *Psychobiol.*, 1917, **1**, 3-18.

——————, and Lafora, G. R., On the functions of the cerebrum: the occipital lobes. *Psychol. Monog.*, 1911, **13**, No. 56.

——————, and Lashley, K. S., The effects of cerebral destructions upon habit-formation and retention in the albino rat. *Psychobiol.*, 1917, **1**, 71-139.

——————, and Ogden, R., On cerebral motor control: the recovery from experimentally produced hemiplegia. *Psychobiol.*, 1917, **1**, 33-49.

——————, and Stout, J. D., Variations in distributions of the motor centers. *Psychol. Monog.*, 1915, **19**, 80-162.

Jennings, H. S., *Behavior of the Lower Organisms* (New York, Columbia Univ. Press, 1906).

Köhler, W., An aspect of Gestalt psychology. *Psychologies of 1925* (Worcester, Mass., Clark Univ. Press, 1926), 163-195.

——————, *Gestalt Psychology* (New York, Horace Liveright, 1929).

Lashley, K. S., *Brain Mechanisms and Intelligence* (Chicago, Chicago Univ. Press, 1929).

——————, Basic neural mechanisms in behavior. *Psychol. Rev.*, 1930, **37**, 1-24.

432 This System *qua* System

Lewin, K., [Hrg.] Untersuchungen zur Handlungs- und Affect-psychologie. I. Vorbemerkungen über die seelischen Kräfte und Energien und über die Struktur des Seelischen. *Psychol. Forsch.*, 1926, 7, 294-329. II. Vorsatz, Wille und Bedürfnis. *Psychol. Forsch.*, 1926, 7, 330-385. III. Über das Behalten von erledigten und unerledigten Handlungen. Von Zeigarnik, B. *Psychol. Forsch.*, 1927, 9, 1-85. IV. Über Rückfälligkeit bei Umgewöhnung, 1. Teil, Rückfalltendenz und Verweckslungsgefahr. Von Schwarz, C. *Psychol. Forsch.*, 1927, 9, 86-158. V. Psychische Sättigung. Von Karsten, A. *Psychol. Forsch.*, 1928, 10, 142-254. VI. Wideraufnahme unterbrochener Handlungen. Von Ovsiankina, M. *Psychol. Forsch.*, 1928, 11, 302-373. VII. Psychische Sättigung im Menstruum und Intermenstruum. Von Freund, A. *Psychol. Forsch.*, 1930, 13, 198-217. VIII. Das Vergessen einer Vornahme. Isolierte seelische Systeme und dynamische Gesamthbereiche. Von Birenbaum, J. *Psychol. Forsch.*, 1930, 13, 218-284. IX. Erfolg und Misserfolg. Von Hoppe, F. *Psychol. Forsch.*, 1930, 14, 1-62.

Lewis, C. I., *Mind and the World-Order* (New York, Charles Scribner's Sons, 1929).

Loewenberg, J., Pre-analytical and post-analytical data. *J. Philos.*, 1927, 24, 5-14.

——————, Are relations effable? *J. Philos.*, 1930, 27, 309-319.

McDougall, W., *An Introduction to Social Psychology* (London, Methuen, 1908).

——————, *Outline of Psychology* (New York, Charles Scribner's Sons, 1923).

——————, *Outline of Abnormal Psychology* (New York, Charles Scribner's Sons, 1926).

——————, Men or robots? I and II, *Psychologies of 1925* (Worcester, Mass., Clark Univ. Press, 1926), 273-305.

——————, The hormic psychology. *Psychologies of 1930* (Worcester, Mass., Clark Univ. Press, 1930), 3-36.

Meyer, M. F., *The Fundamental Laws of Human Behavior* (Boston, Richard G. Badger, The Gorham Press, 1911).

——————, The present status of the problem of the relation between mind and body. *J. Philos., Psychol., etc.*, 1912, 9, 365-371.

——————, *Psychology of the Other One* (Columbia, Mo., The Missouri Book Company, 1921).

——————, *Abnormal Psychology—When the Other One Astonishes Us* (Columbia, Mo., Lucas Bros., 1927).

Münsterberg, H., *Psychology, General and Applied* (New York, D. Appleton and Company, 1914).

Nunn, Sir P. T., *Education, its Data and First Principles* (London, Arnold, 1920).

Pepper, S. C., Categories.—Studies in the problem of relations. *Univ. Calif. Publ. Philos.*, 1930, 13, 73-98.

Perry, R. B., *General Theory of Value* (New York, Longmans, Green & Co., 1926).

Prall, D. W., *Æsthetic Judgment* (New York, Thomas Y. Crowell and Company, 1929).

Watson, J. B., *Behavior—an Introduction to Comparative Psychology* (New York, Henry Holt and Company, 1914).

—————, An attempted formulation of the scope of behavior psychology. *Psychol. Rev.*, 1917, 24, 329-352.

—————, *Psychology from the Standpoint of a Behaviorist* (Philadelphia, J. B. Lippincott Company, 1929, also 1930 ed.).

—————, Is thinking merely the action of language mechanisms? *Brit. J. Psychol.*, 1920, 11, 87-104.

—————, Behaviorism—a psychology based on reflexes. *Arch. Neur. & Psychiat.*, 1926, 15, 185-204.

—————, *Behaviorism*, rev. ed. (New York, W. W. Norton & Company, 1930).

Weiss, A. P., Relation between structural and behavior psychology. *Psychol. Rev.* 1917, 24, 301-317.

—————, Relation between functional and behavior psychology. *Psychol. Rev.*, 1917, 24, 353-368.

—————, Conscious behavior. *J. Philos., Psychol., etc.*, 1918, 15, 631-641.

—————, The mind and the man within. *Psychol. Rev.*, 1919, 26, 327-334.

—————, The relation between physiological psychology and behavior psychology. *J. Philos., Psychol., etc.*, 1919, 16, 626-634.

—————, Behavior and the central nervous system. *Psychol. Rev.*, 1922, 29, 329-342.

—————, Behaviorism and behavior. *Psychol. Rev.*, 1924, 31, 32-50.

—————, One set of postulates for a behavioristic psychology. *Psychol. Rev.*, 1925, 32, 83-87.

—————, *A Theoretical Basis of Human Behavior* (Columbus, O., R. G. Adams Company, 1925).

Wodsedalek, J. E., Formation of associations in the may-fly nymphs, *Heptagenia Interpunctata* (Say), *J. Anim. Behav.*, 1912, 2, 1-19.

Woodworth, R. S., *Psychology, a Study of Mental Life* (New York, Henry Holt and Company, 1921).

—————, *Dynamic Psychology* (New York, Columbia Univ. Press, 1918).

—————, Dynamic psychology. *Psychologies of 1930* (Worcester, Mass., Clark Univ. Press, 1930), 327-336.

Yerkes, R. M., The intelligence of earthworms. *J. Anim. Behav.*, 1912, 2, 332-352.

GLOSSARY

GLOSSARY

Affection. The term *affection* may be applied to those organic or other sensations which according to the doctrine of this treatise constitute one of the three constitutive features of the simple feelings (*q.v.*) of pleasantness and unpleasantness.

Appetites. The appetites and the aversions (*q.v.*) constitute the two classes of fundamental drives underlying all behavior.

An appetite arises out of a cyclically appearing, metabolically conditioned, initiating physiological state, or excitement (*q.v.*). And it consists in a resultant demand for a certain complementary type of physiological quiescence (*q.v.*) plus a set of partly innate, partly acquired, more or less definite, means-end-readinesses (*q.v.*) as to the types of means-objects and goal-objects to be had commerce-with (*q.v.*) in order to reach this demanded quiescence. Typical appetites are hunger and sex.

For a suggested list of the other human appetites see Chapter XVIII, p. 288.

Aversions. The aversions and the appetites (*q.v.*) constitute the two classes of fundamental drives underlying all behavior.

An aversion is to be conceived as arising out of an initiating physiological state or excitement (*q.v.*) caused by a certain actual or "threatened" physiological disturbance (*q.v.*). It expresses itself as a demand to get from, or to avoid, this actual or threatened disturbance plus a set of means-end-readinesses (*q.v.*) (more or less definite, partly innate and partly acquired) as to the types of means-objects to be had commerce-with (*q.v.*) and the types of subordinate goal-object to be avoided in order to get from and to avoid the given finally defining physiological disturbance.

Typical aversions are fright and pugnacity. In the case of fright the ultimately being-avoided physiological disturbance is injury, in the case of pugnacity it is blockage.

Avoidance-object. A goal-object (*q.v.*) which is to be got from.

Awareness, conscious. The process of "sampling" by "running-back-and-forth" in front of environmental objects, placed as alternatives or as succedents. This running-back-and-forth may be overt and with respect to environmental objects then and there actually sensorially present. In this case it is to be designated simple awareness (*q.v.*). Or it may be in the form of mere behavior-adjustments (*q.v.*) and be relative to environmental objects not then and there sensorially present. In this latter case it is to be designated ideation (*q.v.*)

Awareness, simple. In contrast to ideation (*q.v.*) simple awareness is conscious awareness (*q.v.*) in which the "running-back-and-forth" is overt and relative to environmental features then and there present.

Behavior-adjustment. The non-overtly observable surrogate for an actual running-back-and-forth. It usually occurs when the environmental features to be "sampled" (to be run-back-and-forth in front of) are not actually sensorially present. It constitutes ideation (*q.v.*) in contrast to simple awareness (*q.v.*).

The neurological or other physiological constitution of such behavior-adjustments are unknown. The important feature about them is, however, not their physiological make-up, whatever the latter may be, but rather their functional character as surrogates for actual runnings-back-and-forth. The important thing about them is that, whatever they are, sub-vocal speech, minimal gestures or what not, they achieve the same "sampling" of alternatives or succedents which actual runnings-back-and-forth in front of such alternatives or succedents would have achieved.

Behavior-aspect. The same as immanent determinant (*q.v.*).

Behavior-determinants. *Behavior-determinants* is the general term used in this treatise for the intervening variables to be conceived as functioning between the initiating (independent) causes of behavior (*q.v.*) on the one side of the equation, and the final resulting behavior on the other side of the equation.

Under this general head of behavior-determinants three subclasses are distinguishable, viz.: (a) capacities (*q.v.*), (b) immanent determinants (*q.v.*) and (c) behavior-adjustments (*q.v.*).

Behavior-feints. The same as behavior-adjustments (*q.v.*).

Behavior as such. Same as behavior *qua* molar (*q.v.*).

Behavior qua *molar.* Behavior, that is behavior *qua* molar in the sense used in this book, is any organic activity the occurrence of which can be characterized as *docile* (*q.v.*) relative to its consequences. Behavior in this sense is to be distinguished from such other organic activities as are neither a result of past learning nor capable of future learning. Behavior *qua* molar possesses characteristic *molar* properties which a mere detailed, *molecular* (see behavior *qua* molecular) description of its underlying physics and physiology completely leaves out. The terms *a behavior* or *a behavior-act* are used to designate any gob of such behavior *qua* molar delimited in terms of some *one* goal-object (*q.v.*) and some *one* means-object (*q.v.*).

Behavior qua *molecular.* A conception of behavior which stresses its underlying physical and physiological character. This is one of two conflicting notions of behavior. And it is the one most frequently espoused by Watson, Weiss and Meyer. Opposed to such a molecular conception stands the *molar* conception adopted in this treatise. (See Behavior *qua* molar.)

Behaviorism. Any type of psychology which, in contrast to mentalism, holds that "mental events" in animals and human beings can, for the purposes of science, be characterized most successfully in terms wholly of the ways in which they function to produce actual or probable behavior.

Purposive Behaviorism, the specific brand of behaviorism defended in this treatise, asserts that these "mental events" are to be described further as a set of intermediating variables, "immanent determinants" (*q.v.*) and behavior-adjustments (*q.v.*), which intermediate in the behavior-equation between environmental stimuli and initiating physiological states on the one hand and the finally resulting behavior or behavior-adjustments, on the other.

Behavior-supports. Characters in the environment required by behavior-acts in order that they may go off without disruption (*q.v.*). More specifically behavior-supports divide into discriminanda (*q.v.*), manipulanda (*q.v.*), and means-end-relations (*q.v.*).

Behavior-supports are the discriminable, manipulable, and direction-distance (*q.v.*) characters of the environment which permit such and such acts to complete themselves.

The going off of a given behavior-act requires in addition to stimuli to release it, actual appropriate environmental contacts to support it. Behavior cannot go off *in vacuo,* it rests upon actual sensory, motor and direction-distance features in the environment. For such sensory, motor and direction-distance (means-end) features we have coined the general term, behavior-supports, or, often just "supports."

Capacities. The term *capacities* is used to designate one of the three sub-varieties of behavior-determinant (*q.v.*). Capacities are the endowments of the individual or the species which result from two of the initiating independent causes (*q.v.*) of behavior, viz., innate endowment and past training. An individual, or a species, responds to given stimuli (*q.v.*) and to given initiating physiological states (*q.v.*), as it does, by virtue of the capacities which it possesses.

Such capacities are to be subdivided, for the purposes of an initial analysis, into: discriminanda-capacities (*q.v.*); manipulanda-capacities (*q.v.*); means-end-capacities (*q.v.*); retentivity (*q.v.*); consciousness-ability and ideation-ability (*q.v.*); and creativity (*q.v.*). This short list of capacities is to be conceived as having, however, but an initial tentative validity. It is to be supposed that ultimately, when the laws of heredity and of environmental effect are better known, the immediately given hereditary and training factors must be counted (at least in the case of man) as legion. The above list of capacities will then be considered not as the ultimate division of hereditary and training endowments but as a rough list of "immediate response requirements" which must be satisfied by the hereditary and training factors if such and such responses are to be successful. (*See* Chapter XXIV, p. 409 f.).

Chain-appetites, chain-aversions. See Instinct.

Chain successions. See Means-end-field.

Cognition (*cognitive*). A generic term for one of the two classes of immanent determinants (*q.v.*) of behavior. A cognition (a means-end-readiness [*q.v.*] or an expectation [*q.v.*]) is present in a behavior in so far as the continued going-off of that behavior is contingent upon environmental entities (i.e., types of discriminanda, manipulanda, or means-end-relations) proving to be "so and so." And such a contingency will be testified to whenever, if these environmental entities do not prove to be so and so, the given behavior will exhibit disruption (*q.v.*) and be followed by learning.

Commerce-with. Any behavior-act in going off involves an intimate interchange with (support from, enjoyment of, intercourse with) environmental features (discriminanda, manipulanda, and means-end-relations). For such interchanges or enjoyments with behavior-supports (*q.v.*) we have coined the term *commerce-with.*

Condensed sign. In delayed reaction experiments the animals have to react after the delay to only a part of the sign-object with which they are presented before the delay. For example, in the original Hunter "indirect method" the animals are presented before the delay with a light plus a specifically placed door, but after the delay they have to react upon the basis of the specifically placed door only (i.e., without the light). This last we have designated a reaction to a condensed sign.

    The ability to react to such condensed signs is thus one of the requisites for successful delayed reaction.

Conditioned reflex learning. That change in behavior which involves, and results from, the mnemonic formation of a *single* sign-gestalt-expectation (*q.v.*). (See also *trial and error learning* and *inventive learning.*)

Consciousness-ability and ideation-ability. Certain individual organisms and species of organisms possess a greater capacity for "holding up" their ordinary "practical behaviors" than do others in order to run-back-and-forth or to behavior-adjust to running-back-and-forth. In other words, certain individuals and species possess a greater capacity for simple awareness (*q.v.*) and for ideation (*q.v.*) than do others. These capacities have been lumped together under the one phrase *consciousness-ability and ideation-ability.*

Consummatory objects. See Goal-objects.

Creativity. Creativity or creative instability is to be conceived as that capacity, due to heredity (nature) or past environmental training (nurture) or both, the possession of which is conducive to inventive learning (*q.v.*) on the part of the given organism.

Demand. An innate or acquired urge to get to or from some given instance or type of environmental presence or of physiological quiescence (*q.v.*) or disturbance (*q.v.*).

Demands (i.e., purposes [*q.v.*]) and cognitions (*q.v.*) together constitute the two fundamental types of immanent determinant (*q.v.*).

A demand, or purpose, is objectively defined, and testified to, whenever an organism persists through trial and error to or from a given type or instance of goal-object (*q.v.*) or situation and shows a capacity for docility (*q.v.*) in thus persisting to or from.

Determinants. See Behavior-determinants.

Dimension. Means-end-fields (*q.v.*) may often be roughly characterized by certain general characters in the discriminanda and manipulanda of the component superordinate and subordinate means-objects. These means-objects may be primarily spatial, temporal, gravitational, numerical, social, verbal, rhetorical, physiological, etc. Such general characters are called dimensions. It appears, further, that individuals and more especially species of organisms will differ widely from one another in their capacities relative to such types of dimensions. See Means-end-capacity.

Dimensional means-end-capacity. See Means-end-capacity.

Direction. Direction and distance (*q.v.*) are the two fundamental types of means-end-relation (*q.v.*).

Direction is any character in a means-object (sign-object) which distinguishes it for the given organism, in the given situation from other alternative means-objects. Spatial direction is thus but one sub-variety of direction in this its more general sense. Color, shape, gravitational properties, may also function as distinguishing directions.

Further, it appears that the direction of the given means-object (sign-object) (*q.v.*) comes to carry (either innately or as a result of previous training) the implication, for the given organism, that this type of means-object (sign-object) will lead either by a relatively short or by a relatively long distance to such and such a given goal-object.

Means-end-fields (*q.v.*) are thus hierarchies of direction-distance correlations.

Direction-distance features and correlations. See Distance and see Direction.

Discriminanda. Discriminanda are the characters of objects which support (see Behavior-supports) sensory differentiations. They are to be conceived as the relatively enduring sensory characters of objects strained through the sense organ capacities of the given organism.

The Titchener color pyramid tabulates the "normal" human discriminanda in the realm of vision. In similar fashion the Titchener tone-pencil tabulates them for tones, and the Henning smell polygon for odors. (No tabulations seem as yet to have been made, in any systematic fashion, for the other sense modes or for the sub-human organisms.)

The statement and definition of discriminanda is purely objective. No question of "raw feels" (*q.v.*) is involved. The discriminanda of a rat or of a cat are as completely definable as are those of a man.

Discriminanda-capacity. The term is used in this treatise to designate the innate (and acquired) capacities of an organism relative to having commerce-with (*q.v.*) and expecting (see Expectation) discriminanda (*q.v.*).

The data of the sense-polygons and of psychophysics indicate the character and extent of discriminanda-capacity in human beings.

Discriminanda-expectation. See Expectation.

Disruption. The term *disruption* designates a breakdown and upset in behavior produced when some change, not previously met, is introduced into a given environment. This change may be one in discriminanda, in manipulanda, or in means-end-relations. It will be followed by learning, and it can be used as an indicator to discover and define the characters of the expectations (*q.v.*), as to discriminanda, manipulanda and means-end-relations; which were immanent in the behavior which preceded the disruption.

Distance. Distance and direction (*q.v.*) are the two fundamental types of means-end-relation (*q.v.*).

Distance is that property of a means-object whereby it will be selected (or rejected) in competition with other alternative means-objects as a route to or from one and the same goal-object. In so far as a given direction of means-object tends to be selected in contrast to other competing directions of means-objects, it is because such direction is accepted by the given organism as correlated with a relatively "short" distance to the given goal. In so far, on the other hand, as a given direction of means-object tends to be rejected in favor of some one or more of the other alternative directions of means-objects, it is because such former direction is accepted by the given organism as correlated with a relatively "long" distance to the given goal.

Means-end-fields (*q.v.*) are thus successive and radiating hierarchies of distance-direction correlations.

Docility (docile). *Docility* is the term used to designate that character of behavior *qua* molar (*q.v.*) which consists in the fact that, if a given behavior-act in a given environment proves relatively unsuccessful, i.e., does not get to the demanded type of goal-object at all or gets there only by a relatively long distance (*q.v.*), it will, on subsequent occasions, tend to give way to an act or acts which *will* tend to get the organism to this demanded type of goal-object and will tend to get him to it by a relatively short route.

All behavior *qua* molar exhibits docility, is docile.

When a behavior-act *A* is docile, it will give way (following disruption [*q.v.*]) to a subsequent act *B* as a result of any major change in the environmental situation. The new act *B* will conform to the new environmental situation (get to the demanded type of goal-object) in a way that *A* did not.

Drive. The general term used to designate a motivation, superordinate or subordinate, i.e., a demand (*q.v.*) for or against a given type of goal-object or situation plus an attached more or less vague sign-gestalt-readiness (*q.v.*) as to the appropriate sorts of means-object to be selected for commerce-with in order to get thus to or from.

Drives (*first-order*). The term *first-order drives* is used synonymously with *appetites* and *aversions* (*q.v.*).

Drives (*second-order*). The term *second-order drives* is used to designate certain secondary demands and sign-gestalt-readinesses (e.g., gregariousness, curiosity, imitation, self-assertion, self-abasement, etc.). Such second-order drives tend to be ancillary in their effects to the ends of the first-order drives (*q.v.*).

A second-order drive, in so far as it is innate, is to be designated as an aversion going off innately in response to a relatively general type of environmental situation such as: separation from one's fellows (gregariousness); unexplored unfamiliar objects (curiosity); dominance by one's fellows (self-assertion); being isolated and thrown on one's own responsibilities (self-abasement); etc. Each such environmental situation must be supposed, merely on the basis of the organism's innate endowment, to "threaten" to the organism a specific type of physiological disturbance.

This assumption of innate, and characterizing, second-order physiological disturbances is perhaps a somewhat doubtful hypothesis. Furthermore, in so far as there appears docility (*q.v.*) on the part of the organism relative to the value of the end situation of the second-order drive with respect to the ends of the first-order drives, a second-order drive would seem to be lacking in any specific and finally defining physiological disturbance of its own. Only if the given second-order drive persists in going off in its own right, irrespective of the first-order consequences, can it be conceived to have an innate and defining type of physiological disturbance of its own.

Emotion. An emotion is defined as made up of three constitutive phases: (a) the release of a relatively general sign-gestalt-expectation (*q.v.*); (b) resultant incipient visceral and skeletal activities; and (c) resulting sets of organic and kinesthetic sensations (discriminanda-expectations). As far as (b) and (c) are concerned, this doctrine is a derivative of the James-Lange theory.

Applying this definition to a specific case, the emotion of "fear" would be defined as consisting of: (a) the release of a relatively generalized sign-gestalt-expectation to the effect that the immediately presented object (fear stimulus) will lead on (just as a result of mere staying in its presence) to physiological pain or injury; (b) certain accompanying incipient visceral and skeletal movements; and (c) certain resultant visceral and kinesthetic sensations (see sensation).

Encounter. See Commerce-with.

End. See Goal-object.

Engage-with. See Commerce-with.

Enjoyment. See Commerce-with.

Environmental presence. A present behavior-support (*q.v.*).

Expectation. An expectation is an immanent cognitive determinant aroused by actually presented stimuli. An expectation probably always actually occurs as the expectation of a total sign-gestalt (*q.v.*). But for purposes of analytical discourse there may be abstracted out for separate consideration, within such a total sign-gestalt-expectation, discriminanda-expectations, manipulanda-expectations—as to the sign-object (*q.v.*), i.e., means-object (*q.v.*); as to the signified-object (*q.v.*), i.e., goal-object (*q.v.*); and as to the means-end-relations (*q.v.*), i.e., direction-distance correlations (*q.v.*) between the former and the latter.

There are three fundamental moods of expectation, viz., perception (*q.v.*), mnemonization (*q.v.*), and inference (*q.v.*).

Feeling. There are two fundamental types of feeling: pleasantness and unpleasantness. These may be conceived as very generalized emotions (*q.v.*).

Like the more specific emotions, they are defined as involving three constitutive phases: (a) the release of a relatively general sign-gestalt-expectation; (b) accompanying incipient visceral and skeletal activities; and (c) resulting organic and kinesthetic sensations.

For mere pleasantness the defining sign-gestalt-expectation is to the effect that the given presented sign-object will, if had commerce-with, lead on to "some" (unspecified) sort of a final physiological quiescence; whereas for unpleasantness this defining sign-gestalt-expectation is, rather, to the effect that the given presented sign-object will, if had commerce-with, lead on to "some" (unspecified) sort of a final physiological disturbance.

Field. See Means-end-field.

Field-principle. See Means-end-relations and Means-end-field.

Fixation. In so far as the acceptance by an organism of a given type of superordinate or subordinate means-object as the means for getting on to or from a given environmental goal-object or to or from some final type of physiological quiescence or disturbance, proves to be relatively non-docile to the actual facts of success or failure, the given organism may be said to have become fixated on that type of means-object.

Fixations may thus be said to be due to sign-gestalt-readinesses and -expectations "gone bad." They are a result of sign-gestalt-readinesses and -expectations which have lost their initial docility and have become not sign-gestalt-entities at all, but something for which the terms reflexes and tropisms would be more appropriate. Thus, if all behavior were due to fixations, it is obvious that a purposive behaviorism, such as ours, which talks in terms of immanent purposes (demands) and cognitions (means-end-readinesses and -expectations, etc.) could not survive.

Further, it appears that there seem to be two levels of behavior at which such fixations are most likely to occur. On the one hand, they seem prone to appear as regards the final stages of the first-order and second-order drives. At such levels they give rise to such phenomena as the sex-perversions and the phobias. And, on the other hand, they appear to rise at relatively superficial levels in the form of the dominance of some particular type of environmental object as means. An example of the latter is probably to be found in the so-called "position habits" which often prove so troublesome in discrimination experiments with rats.

Finally, it must be emphasized that as yet almost nothing seems to have been done in the way of an experimental attack upon the nature of the conditions which relatively favor or hinder the establishment of such fixations either at the fundamental drive levels or at the more superficial means-object levels.

Formal means-end-capacity. See Means-end-capacity.

Goal-object, goal-situation, goal. A demanded (see demand) to-be-got-to (or to-be-got-from) internal physiological condition or external environmental object.

Examples:

The to-be-got-to goal-object of the series of acts to be called hunger is the physiological quiescence of hunger-satiation.

The to-be-got-from goal-object of the series of acts to be called fright is the physiological disturbance of pain or injury.

The immediately to-be-got-to goal-object of a simple act, such as entering an alley in a maze, is the environmental presence of the insides of that alley.

The immediately to-be-got-from goal-object of a simple behavior-act such as balancing on a narrow elevated track maze is the avoidance of the environmental presence of all-lack-of-support.

In a complicated series or hierarchy of behavior-acts, goal-objects concatenate into superordinate and subordinate. Subordinate goal-objects are, from the point of view of the superordinate goal-objects, to be designated as means-objects.

Hierarchies. See Means-end-field.

Ideation. The more recondite form of conscious awareness (*q.v.*), in which the sampling of alternative or succedent means-end possibilities occurs by virtue of mere behavior-adjustments (*q.v.*) to runnings-back-and-forth.

Images. Discriminanda-expectations, the stimuli of which are relatively fleeting and central (rather than peripheral).

Immanent. See Immanent determinant.

Immanent behavior-aspects. See Immanent determinants.

Immanent determinant. A functionally defined variable (purposive or cognitive) which is inferred as immanent or "lying" in a behavior-act. One of the three sub-classes of behavior-determinant (*q.v.*). Such immanent determinants can be inferred only. They are inferred from the docile variations which appear in the character of a behavior as the result of experimentally controlled conditions.

Immanent determinants subdivide into two fundamental kinds: (a) purposes (demands) and (b) cognitions. The cognitions, in their turn, still further subdivide into (i) means-end-readinesses (*q.v.*); and (ii) expectations (*q.v.*).

Inference. One of the three moods of sign-gestalt-expectation (see expectation). The other two moods are perception (*q.v.*) and mnemonization (*q.v.*). In inference commerce with the sign-object only has ever occurred before. Nevertheless (perhaps because of past experience with "relatively similar" situations, or because of pure creativity) the organism is led to invent the sort of signified object and sort of direction-distance relations to this signified object which will result from commerce with the given sign-object.

The action of such inferential sign-gestalt-expectations is probably the fundamental feature in inventive learning (*q.v.*).

Inventive ideation (*q.v.*) is to be conceived as a special, sophisticated, and recondite form of inference as just defined.

Inferential expectation. The same as inference.

Initiating (independent) causes of behavior. The ultimately independent variables determinative of behavior are to be conceived as four: (a) the given organism's heredity, (b) his past environmental training, (c) the stimuli which are presented then and there or have been presented more or less recently, and (d) the initiating physiological states then and there active in him.

Intervening between these ultimately independent variables and the finally resultant behavior and determining the form of

the equation by which the latter results from the former there
have been hypostasized a set of intervening variables, viz., the
behavior-determinants (*q.v.*).

Initiating physiological state. The releasing physiological cause of
an appetite or of an aversion.

In an appetite (*q.v.*) this initiating state is a metabolically
aroused condition which, while present, evokes the demand
(*q.v.*) for a certain specific type of complementing physiological
quiescence (*q.v.*).

In an aversion (*q.v.*) this initiating state results from: (a)
a specific environmental presence plus (b) an innate, or acquired, means-end-readiness (sign-gestalt-readiness) (*q.v.*), to
the effect that such a type of environmental presence "threatens"
some ultimately to-be-avoided physiological disturbance (*q.v.*).
And, while present, such an initiating state evokes, and keeps
going, a demand to avoid the given physiological disturbance,
and in subordinate fashion to avoid the environmental presence
which "threatens" such final disturbance.

Insight. The term *insight learning* has often been used to designate that process which we have called *inventive ideation*
(*q.v.*).

Instinct. This term, if it is to be retained at all, is to be used for
all those demands and sign-gestalt-readinesses which practically
all the individuals ·of a given species, irrespective of "special"
environmental training, tend to exhibit. The term in this sense
will cover all such varieties or phases of response as are primarily due to innate endowment plus a biologically provided relatively "normal" or "standard" environment.

In the case of man, or at any rate in the case of many of the
lower species, there seem to be three main types of activity
which qualify as instincts as thus defined, viz., (a) first-order
and second-order drives (*q.v.*), (b) certain chains of minor appetites (*q.v.*) and minor aversions (*q.v.*), which are to be
found in especially developed form in birds and insects; and
(c) certain innate discrimination and manipulation dexterities
or skills. These latter are to be conceived as of the nature of
capacities for successful discriminanda and manipulanda commerces-with.

Introspection. In introspection an organism behaves both to his
own behavior-adjustments (*q.v.*) and to a listener. Introspective behavior expresses a sign-gestalt-expectation (*q.v.*) in
which the goal-object (or significate) will be the immediate conjunction between the introspector's own behavior-adjustments
and the listener, and in which the sign-object is the very complex one consisting of the behavior-adjustments which are thus
to be presented to the listener plus the listener, and in which
the means-end-relations are a very complicated set involving
social, verbal, rhetorical, etc., dimensions (*q.v.*).

    We should claim that in introspection, in the technical laboratory sense of *Beschreibung,* the behavior-adjustments which the introspector is thus reporting to his listener are runnings-back-and-forth relative to certain more or less artifactual immediate sign-objects, to wit, kinesthetic and organic sensations (*q.v.*) or images (*q.v.*).

Inventive ideation. The type of ideation (*q.v.*) called "inventive" is that in which the ideational "runnings-back-and-forth" involve, in addition to the alternative and succedent routes of a given means-end-field which the organism has already actually overtly been over, new routes or features, never as such actually experienced by the organism. In inventive ideation these new routes are ideationally extrapolated. Such extrapolation is to be conceived as brought about by behavior-adjustments (*q.v.*) to those portions of the field which are already grasped perceptually or mnemonically plus the presence in the organism of a certain amount of creative instability.

Inventive learning. That change in behavior which involves, and results from, the inferential (see inference) extrapolation of a new sign-gestalt. Inventive learning involves inventive ideation (*q.v.*). (See also, Conditioned reflex learning and Trial and error learning.)

Judgment. See Means-end-readiness.

Least effort, the principle of. This principle, which is found in numerous sciences under a variety of names, when applied to the study of behavior would assert that the final choices between alternative means-routes will always tend to occur in the direction of a minimum expenditure of physical energy.

    The doctrine of the present treatise is that whereas this may ultimately be true for behavior, it has not yet been proved. At present all that can be done is to list, in each type of dimensional situation, the kind and degrees of preference that have been experimentally shown.

Lever successions. See Means-end-field.

Manipulanda. Manipulanda are the characters of objects which support (see Behavior supports) motor activity (manipulations). They derive in character from the independent physical character of the environmental object and from the response-organ make-up of the given organism. They are such properties of environmental objects as lengths, widths, weights, resistances, solidities, fluidities, etc. But they are these properties defined not as such, and in themselves, but in terms of the range and refinements of manipulations which they will support in the given organism. They are stand-on-able-nesses, pick-up-able-nesses, sit-in-able-nesses, etc., etc.

Manipulanda-capacity. The term is used in this treatise to designate the innate (and acquired) capacities whereby a given organism or species is capable of having commerce-with and

expecting (see Expectations) types and kinds. of manipulanda
(*q.v.*).

No adequate study and analysis of the relative extents and
compasses of such manipulanda-capacities in different individuals and different species seem ever yet to have been made.

Manipulanda-expectation. See Expectation.

Means-end-capacity (formal, dimensional). The term is used to
designate the innate (and acquired) capacities whereby a given
organism or species is capable of having commerce-with and
expecting means-end-relations (*q.v.*).

Any means-end-field (*q.v.*) involves a manifold of the formal
relations of direction and distance and their derivatives—sequence, differentiation, similarity, reverse ends of one and the
same route, multiple trackness, final common pathness, mutual
alternativeness, closure, hierarchicalness, and the like. And, in
so far as the capacity in question involves the ability to have
commerce-with, to be ready for and to expect these purely
formal relations it is to be designated as *formal means-end-
capacity.*

Any means-end-field is characterized, however, not only by
such purely formal relations between its component means-
objects and goal-objects but also by the characters of the
specific dimensional media (e.g., space, time, gravitation, words,
rhetoric, number system, society, physiology, etc.), in which
these formal relations happen to be embodied. And in so far
as the capacity in question concerns an ability to have commerce with, to be ready for and to expect such specific types
of dimensional embodiment of the formal relations, it is to be
designated as *dimensional means-end-capacity.*

Finally, it is obvious that these capacities to have commerce-
with, to be ready for, and to expect such specific dimensional
embodiments of means-end relations will be closely related to,
or dependent upon, discriminanda- and manipulanda-capacities for the types of means-object characteristic of such types
of dimension. Dimensional means-end-capacities are perhaps
properly to be considered as a fusion or combined product of
formal means-end-capacity, on the one hand, and of discriminanda-capacities and manipulanda-capacities, on the other.
Much further analysis, however, is needed.

Means-end-expectation. The specific and particular embodiment
of a means-end-readiness (*q.v.*) which results from the presentation of particular, immediate, means-object stimuli. Given
that the organism is provided with the corresponding means-
end-readiness, then when stimuli appropriate to an instance
of the type of immediate means-object, which figures in such
a means-end-readiness are presented, the organism is immediately ready to have commerce with this particular instance
as the *way to get to* (*or from*) an instance of the given type

of goal-object. He expects that this means-object will *lead on* to or from an instance of the type of wanted goal-object.

A second term used practically synonymously with *means-end-expectation* is *sign-gestalt-expectation* (*q.v.*). But in the use of this latter term there is an emphasis not only upon the expectation of the means-end-relation but also upon the expectation of the two *termini* of that relation, viz., the sign-object (*q.v.*) and the signified-object (*q.v.*).

Means-end-field. Any sequence of behavior-acts involves a sequence of commerces with selected pairs of means-objects and subordinate goal-objects in order to get to, or from, some relatively final goal-object. The total complex of successively selected (and rejected) means-objects (hierarchy of superordinate and subordinate goal-objects and means-objects) plus the ultimate goal-object itself, together with all the various means-end-relations of direction, distance, similarity, reverse ends, multiple trackness, final common pathness, mutual alternativeness, closure hierarchicalness, etc., holding between such means-objects and goal-objects, in so far as this total complex can be shown to determine the given sequence of behavior-acts, is to be called a *means-end-manifold, means-end-field* or *means-end-hierarchy.*

Further, the means-object—goal-object successions, which are thus constitutive of such manifolds, fields, hierarchies, may appear in either one of two relatively distinguishable varieties. They may have the form either of chain successions or of lever (or tool) successions.

In the case of chain successions the superordinate-subordinate means-object pair under consideration are related to each other as the successive links in a chain. Commerce with No. 1 brings about the presence of No. 2, with which latter commerce must then be had.

In the case of lever or tool successions a pair of successive means-objects range themselves, rather, as the two ends of one and the same tool or lever. Commerce with the one means-object in such a case achieves *pari passu* commerce with the next subsequent means-object, just as the movement of the one end of the tool or lever operates simultaneously the other end of the same lever or tool.

Finally, it is to be observed that the extent or complexity of any such means-end-field which can determine a given behavior in a given organism will depend not only upon the objective environmental situation but also upon the degree of the organism's means-end-capacities (*q.v.*)—both formal and dimensional.

Means-end-manifold. See Means-end-field.

Means-end-readiness. A means-end-readiness (sign-gestalt-readiness) is one of the most important kinds of immanent determinant (*q.v.*). It is a selective condition which an organism, due to innate endowment or past training, brings with him to specific concrete stimulus situations. It is set in action by virtue of a demand (*q.v.*) to get to or from some given type of goal-object. It is equivalent to a "judgment" that commerce-with such and such a "type" of means-object should lead on by such and such direction-distance relations to some instance of the given demanded type of goal-object. It causes the organism to be responsive to stimuli (see Responsiveness to stimuli) and to perceive, to mnemonize or to infer particular instances of such "ready-for" means-objects. That is, it is means-end-readi-nesses (sign-gestalt-readinesses) which determine the selective responsiveness of organisms to stimuli.

It is the carrying over of such means-end-readinesses from one situation to another which constitute the so-called phenomenon of "transfer" of training.

A second term used practically synonymously with *means-end-readiness* is *sign-gestalt-readiness* (*q.v.*).

Means-end-relations. Direction (*q.v.*) and distance (*q.v.*) are the two fundamental means-end-relations. Means-objects, combined together into direction-distance manifolds, possess as further derivative properties the means-end-relations of similarity, reverse ends, multiple trackness, final common pathness, closure, hierarchicalness, and the like.

Means-end-relations, signified. One of the three parts of a sign-gestalt (*q.v.*). The other two parts are the sign-object and the signified object.

Means-end-succession. See Means-end-field.

Means-end-pathways. The same as routes (*q.v.*).

Means-object (*means-situation*). Is any object or situation defined by virtue of the fact that it is had commerce-with in order to get to or from some further object, i.e., goal-object (*q.v.*).

A means-object is the same as a sign-object (*q.v.*) save that a sign-object may be considered as divorced, for the purposes of analytical discussion, from any accompanying demand to get to or from the given goal-object (significate [*q.v.*]).

Memorial expectations. See Mnemonization.

Memory. Used in this treatise to designate a special case of mnemonization (*q.v.*) in which the expected and absent signified object is expected, not only as distant in space, etc., but also as distant and past in time.

Mentalist, mentalism. These terms designate a certain type of psychological approach explicitly avoided in the present essay. They are used here in reference to the orthodox or classical psychologists who assumed that "minds" are essentially inner happenings primarily available to introspection only.

Mnemonic expectation. The same as mnemonization.

Mnemonization. One of the three moods of sign-gestalt-expectation (see Expectation). (The other two are perception (*q.v.*), and inference [*q.v.*].) In mnemonization, stimuli for the sign-object only are present, but the stimuli for the signified-object, or the signified means-end-relation, the mnemonization for which is under consideration, have as such been specifically present one or more times in the past.

Memory (*q.v.*) is the name for that special limited variety of mnemonization in which the signified means-end-relation contains a dating of the signified object as temporally past.

Molar. See Behavior *qua* molar.

Moods. The three "moods" of sign-gestalt-expectation (*q.v.*) are perception (*q.v.*), mnemonization (*q.v.*), and inference (*q.v.*).

Molecular. See Behavior *qua* molecular.

Perception. One of the three moods of sign-gestalt-expectation. (The other two are mnemonization [*q.v.*] and inference [*q.v.*].) A perception is any expectation (*q.v.*) of the component of a sign-gestalt (*q.v.*) when this expectation results primarily from *present* stimuli coming then and there.

Perceptual expectation. The same as perception.

Personality-mechanism. Is a general term for acquired and relatively permanent modifications or distortions in the sign-gestalt-readinesses and -expectations released by the first-order and second-order drives (see Drives). The term is, thus, a general one to cover such phenomena as phobias, compulsions, sex-perversions, Œdipus complex, transference, sublimation, compensation, symbols, and the like.

As to the manner in which these modifications appear, three specific types of operation have been suggested, viz., repression (*q.v.*), fixation (*q.v.*), and sign-magic (*q.v.*). There are undoubtedly other kinds of operations which a more thoroughgoing analysis than any which has been attempted in this treatise might show up.

Physiological disturbances. See Initiating physiological states.

Physiological quiescences. See Initiating physiological states.

Pleasantness. See Feeling.

Purpose (purposive). Is a generic term for one of the two classes of immanent determinants (*q.v.*) of behavior. A purpose is a demand (*q.v.*) to get to or from a given type of goal-object. Such a purpose is testified to objectively by the fact that behavior tends to persist to or from and to show docility (*q.v.*) relative to getting to or from specific types of goal-object (*q.v.*) or goal-situation.

Raw feel. A name for the peculiar *quale* of experience—assuming experience to have a *quale*.

It is the doctrine of this book that such raw feels do not need to enter into or affect any merely psychological account of mind.

Repression. As used in this treatise repression is an operation whereby certain features of an expected sign-gestalt become no longer capable of being consciously "run-back-and-forth-in-front-of" (see Consciousness). This "banishment" of features of expected sign-gestalts do not prevent those features from affecting actual behavior. It merely insulates these features from being modified and affected in their turn by other more recently acquired sign-gestalt-features.

A repression is equivalent to an avoidance response made relative to certain features of some total sign-gestalt (*q.v.*).

Responsiveness to stimuli. By virtue of any means-end-readiness (*q.v.*) (sign-gestalt-readiness) which an organism brings with him to a concrete situation he will be especially responsive to some stimuli and not to others. He will be responsive to those stimuli which, given his discriminanda- manipulanda- and means-end-capacities, seem to indicate the presence of a concrete instance of the type of sign-gestalt for which he is, by hypothesis, in readiness.

Retentivity. The capacity which favors correct mnemonizations,

Route. Any succession of superordinate and subordinate goal-objects and means-objects in a means-end-field (*q.v.*).

Sensation. Sensation, if the term is to be retained at all, may be used to designate those very fleeting moment-to-moment discriminanda-expectations which the organism consciously (*q.v.*) experiences when he runs back-and-forth relative to certain very immediate and momentary stimuli.

Sign. The same as Sign-object (*q.v.*).

Sign-gestalt. Is a complex behavior-support (*q.v.*), consisting of a sign-object (*q.v.*) (i.e., means-object [*q.v.*]), a signified object (*q.v.*) (i.e., goal-object [*q.v.*]), and a signified means-end-relation (*q.v.*) (direction-distance correlation [*q.v.*]) between such sign-object and signified object.

Properly the term *sign-gestalt* should be reserved for the external environmental object or situation. Occasionally, however, it has been used as a convenient single term to cover at one and the same time the two types of immanent determinant, more specifically to be designated as (a) sign-gestalt-readinesses (*q.v.*) and (b) sign-gestalt expectations (*q.v.*).

Sign-gestalt-expectation. In the case of a sign-gestalt-expectation the organism is ready either as a result of perception (*q.v.*), mnemonization (*q.v.*), or inference (*q.v.*) to have some sort of positive or negative commerce with an immediately presented object (i.e., the sign-object) as the means-end-route (i.e., the signified means-end-relation) to get to or from such and such a further object (i.e., the signified-object).

Sign-gestalt formation. Equals the formation of a sign-gestalt-readiness (*q.v.*).

Sign-gestalt-readiness. The same as means-end-readiness (*q.v.*). In the case of a sign-gestalt-readiness (a means-end-readiness) the organism is possessed of a generalized "universal" propensity whereby, in order to get to or from a given demanded type of goal-object, he is ready to have such and such positive or negative commerce with such and such means-objects (sign-objects) whenever particular instances of (i.e., the appropriate stimuli for) the latter are presented.

Sign-magic. Sign-magic is doing to the sign (*q.v.*) what the organism is predisposed to do to the significate (*q.v.*) of that sign, but is prevented from doing to the latter by virtue of its too great distance away.

Sign-object. One of the three parts of a sign-gestalt (*q.v.*). The other two parts are the signified means-end-relation and the signified-object (or significate).

Significate. The same as signified object (*q.v.*).

Signified-object. One of the three parts of a sign-gestalt (*q.v.*). The other two parts are the sign-object (or sign) and the signified means-end-relation between sign and signified object.

Skills (innate). See Instinct.

Speech (relative to the speaker). Is a special sort of tool in which the words in the speaker's mouth are the one end of the tool and the listener himself the other end of the tool. The speaker by having a certain commerce with the words in his mouth causes his listener (the other end of his tool) to have a certain commerce with the environment.

Speech (relative to the listener). Is a special set of sign-objects (*q.v.*), a commerce-with-which (i.e., the listening-to-which) brings the listener into the presence of certain specific goal-objects (i.e., the environmental entities "meant" by the speech).

Stimuli. Are environmental entities which evoke expectations: i.e., sign-gestalt-perceptions -mnemonizations or -inferences. Stimuli are environmental entities which "set" the organism to expect certain complexes of behavior-support.

Support. See Behavior-support.

Tool successions. See Means-end-field.

Transfer of training. See Means-end-readiness.

Trial and error learning. That change in behavior which involves, and results from, the mnemonic formation, and selection from, a number of alternative sign-gestalt-expectations radiating from the same initial point in a means-end-field (*q.v.*). (See also Conditioned reflex learning and Inventive learning.)

Unpleasantness. See Feeling.

INDEX OF SUBJECTS

INDEX OF NAMES

(Page numbers in bold-faced type refer to the lists of references at the ends of chapters.)